f

For Human Rights

Publication of the Department
for Justice, Peace and the Integrity of Creation
of the United Evangelical Mission

Edited by
Jochen Motte

Volume 20

KAIROS
FOR CREATION

Confessing Hope for the Earth

The "Wuppertal Call" – Contributions and Recommendations from an
International Conference on Eco-Theology and Ethics of Sustainability

Wuppertal, Germany, 16 – 19 June 2019

Edited by
Louk Andrianos, Michael Biehl, Ruth Gütter, Jochen Motte, Andar Parlindungan,
Thomas Sandner, Juliane Stork and Dietrich Werner

Cover illustration: MediaCompany – Agentur für Kommunikation GmbH
www.mediacompany.com

Printed on Recycling-Offset paper. CO_2 compensated.

Edited by
Louk Andrianos, Michael Biehl, Ruth Gütter, Jochen Motte, Andar Parlindungan,
Thomas Sandner, Juliane Stork and Dietrich Werner

ISBN 978-3-938180-69-3

TABLE OF CONTENTS

The Wuppertal Call: Kairos for Creation – Confessing Hope for the Earth 9

Kairos for Creation – Editorial
Ruth Gütter and Jochen Motte 13

Introduction
Dietrich Werner 15

ECUMENICAL LEARNING JOURNEYS

Freedom for Limitation. Protestant Theological Insights for a Culture of Sustainability
Ruth Gütter 23

What is God really up to in a Time like this?
Discerning the Spirit's Movements as Core Task of Christian Eco-Theology
Ernst Conradie 31

Eco-Theology – Elements of the Learning Journey in the Ecumenical Movement
Dietrich Werner 45

Integral Ecology in the Witness of the Orthodox Church.
The CEMES Ecological Project
Petros Vassiliadis 59

Eco-Theology and Human Responsibility –
A Catholic Perspective to the Ecological and Climate Crises
Ingeborg Gabriel, Guillermo Kerber 71

The Theological Confession of Barmen – Its Significance 1934 and Today
Jochen Motte 79

Eco-Theology and Perspectives from the Tradition of Barmen
Markus Mühling 83

REGIONAL PERSPECTIVES

Justice by Faith and Eco-Justice
Daniel Beros 91

Inter-religious Cooperation in Eco-ethics. A Latin-American Perspective
Neddy Astudillo 99

Environmental Sustainability and Eco-Justice:
Reflections from an African Pentecostal
Emmanuel Anim 107

Eco-Theology in an African Perspective:
Why the Delay to Embody Eco-Theology in African Christianity?
Kambale Kahongya Bwiruka 121

Mapping Recent Major Eco-Theological Initiatives from Scandinavian Perspectives
Henrik Grape 133

The role of Interreligious Dialogue in Preserving the Ecological Environment:
Indonesia as an Example
Andar Parlindungan, Daniel Sinaga 137

Alternative Concepts of Growth and the Ecology of Life in China Today
Theresa Carino 141

Regional Approaches to Eco-Theology in Korea: Different Focuses and Emphases
Meehyun Chung 151

Christian Identity Approaching Climate Change in a Dialogue with Secularity
Peter Pavlovic 155

Islam as God's Mercy for the Universe (Rahmatan lil Alamin). A Crucial Need for
Trustworthy Dialogue among Religious Communities on Global Climate Change
Syafiq Hasyim 157

Shortcomings in Teaching Eco-Theological Awareness
in the History and Life of the Batak Church (HKBP)
Victor Tinambunan 161

THEMATIC CONTRIBUTIONS

Worship as Place-Based Ecological Formation
Chad Rimmer 171

Economy of Life Index and Greed Line as Alternative Concepts of Sustainability
Louk Andrianos 181

The Third Party in the Covenant: a Theology of Animals
Bernd Kappes 203

Noken - An Eco-Ethic Metaphor for a Creation-Based Mission Model:
From "Soul Evangelism" to "Life-Flourishing Evangelism"
Maraike Bangun 213

The Created Lived and Vulnerable Body Resonating with the World. Perspectives for
a Non-Anthropocentric Anthropology and a Body-Sensitive Eco-Theology
Claudia Jahnel 223

Eco-Feminism and Eco-Feminist Theology. Reclaiming Earth-Based Spirituality
Muriel Orevillo-Montenegro   235

Towards Ecological Sensitization and Ecological Justice – A Call for A Joint (Women's)
Inter-religious Peace-Building
Nadja Furlan Štante   243

PRACTICAL CASE STUDIES

Changes in Eco-Theological Attitudes in Germany
Anja Vollendorf   255

Recent Eco-Theological Initiatives as Promoted by the Lutheran World Federation
Chad Rimmer   259

Eco-Theology and Climate Justice in Rwanda
Gloriose Umuziranenge   263

Recent Latin-American and Caribbean Ecumenical Initiatives – A Reading Guide
Guillermo Kerber   271

Pastoral Action Program for the Care of Creation of the Evangelical Church
of the River Plate
Daniel Beros   275

Priorities for Ecumenical Eco-Ethics in the 21st Century. Thoughts and Lessons
from SAFCEI, a Multi-Faith Eco-Justice Organization in Southern Africa
Geoff and Kate Davies   281

Eco-Friendly Activities Implemented by Syunik-Development NGO, Armenia
Hayarpi Aghankanyan   291

Eco-Theology as a Practical Dimension.
A View from the Armenia Inter-Church Round Table
Karen Nazaryan   295

Regional Approaches to Eco-theology in the Context of Ethiopia
Misgana Mathewos Detago   299

Christian Conference of Asia's Initiatives in Developing Eco-Consciousness
and Eco-Theology
George Matthews Chunakara   305

APPENDIX

The Wuppertal Call in Different Languages   317

    The Wuppertal Call in German: Kairos für die Schöpfung –
    Hoffnungsbekenntnis für die Erde. Die Wuppertaler Erklärung   317

The Wuppertal Call in French: Kairos pour la création –
une confession de l'espérance pour la Terre. L'appel de Wuppertal   322

The Wuppertal Call in Spanish: Kairós para la Creación –
Confesión de esperanza para la tierra. La Declaración de Wuppertal   326

The Wuppertal Call in Greek: ΚΑΙΡΟΣ για τη Δημιουργία –
Ομολογώντας την Ελπίδα για τη Γη: Η έκκληση του Βούπερταλ   331

The Wuppertal Call in Indonesian: Kairos for Creation –
Confessing Hope for the Earth. The Wuppertal Call   335

The Wuppertal Call in Chinese   339

The Barmen Declaration   343

"Lent to us is the Star, on which we Live"
Ruth Gütter   347

Faith for Earth: It is Time for a Behavioral Revolution Towards Earth
Iyad Abumoghli   351

List of Contributers   357

Table of Contents

KAIROS FOR CREATION –
CONFESSING HOPE FOR THE EARTH
THE WUPPERTAL CALL

"If my people who are called by my name humble themselves, pray, seek my face, and turn from their wicked ways, then I will hear from heaven, and will forgive their sin and heal their land" – 2 Chron. 7:14.

"If anyone is in Christ, the new creation has come: The old has gone, the new is here! All this is from God, who reconciled us to himself through Christ and gave us the ministry of reconciliation" – 2 Cor. 5:17-18

Preamble

From 16 to 19 June 2019, 52 participants from 22 countries and from different confessional and faith traditions gathered in Wuppertal, Germany for a conference entitled "Together towards eco-theologies, ethics of sustainability and eco-friendly churches".[1] In Wuppertal we were reminded of the courageous confession of faith articulated in the Barmen Declaration (1934) against the totalitarian, inhuman and racist ideology of the time. Barmen continues to encourage us today for "a joyful liberation from the godless ties of this world for free grateful service to his creatures" (Barmen 2).

We shared stories from Africa, Asia, Europe, Latin America, North America, and Oceania. We heard the cries of the earth, the cries of people vulnerable to the effects of climate change, especially children and the elderly, the cries of youth demanding intergenerational justice and the concerns of experts over current trends.

We recognize the urgency of the years that lie ahead, nevertheless express the courage to hope and are compelled to call the global ecumenical movement towards a comprehensive ecological transformation of society.

Kairos: A decisive turn in the pilgrimage of justice and peace

The ecumenical movement has long committed itself to a pilgrimage towards justice, peace and the integrity of creation. These goals will require urgent steps on the road ahead. The urgency of the crisis calls us to read the signs of the time, to hear God's call, to follow the way of Christ, to discern the movement of the Spirit and, in response, to recognize the positive initiatives of churches all around the world.

---

1 The conference was planned and organized together by Protestant Association of Churches and Mission (EMW), Evangelical Church in Germany (EKD), United Evangelical Mission (UEM), Bread for the World, World Council of Churches.

The symptoms of the crisis touch on all the building blocks of life and are there for all to see:
- Fresh water is contaminated; glaciers are melting; oceans are polluted with plastics and are becoming acidic so that corals reefs are bleached (water).
- Land is degraded through unsustainable agriculture and unhealthy eating habits, extractive economies ruled by global financial powers, deforestation, desertification and soil erosion; animals are groaning and creatures are being genetically modified; fish populations are depleted; habitat loss leads to the unprecedented loss of biodiversity (earth). Both the land and the health of people are being poisoned by industrial, agricultural, municipal and nuclear forms of waste and by pesticides and chemicals. An increasing number of people is forced to migrate and to become climate refugees.
- Global carbon emissions are still increasing, greenhouse gases are accumulating in the atmosphere and climates are disrupted (air).
- It is the still increasing use of energy from fossil fuels that is driving such changes (fire).

The delicate systems of balances in creation has been disturbed to an unprecedented extent in the Anthropocene. We have transgressed planetary boundaries. The earth seems no longer able to heal itself. Creatures are groaning in travail (Rom. 8:22). We have been unable to hold together ecumenical concerns over justice amid poverty, unemployment and inequality, over a participatory society amid various forms of violent conflict and over sustainability amid ecological destruction.

Although humans have not contributed equally to the root causes of this crisis, as Christians we come together to confess our complicity and bondage to sin:
- We have been arrogant in assuming that the whole earth centres around us humans and our needs (pride).
- We have become trapped in an abysmal desire for unlimited material growth, driven by a pervasive culture of consumerism (greed).
- We have exploited God's gifts, resorted to violence against God's creatures and violated human dignity (violence).
- We have become alienated from ancestral land and indigenous wisdom, from animals as our co-creatures and from Earth as our God-given home (the privation of the good).
- We have been overcome by folly, injustice, denial and greed (vice).
- We have been slow in coming to terms with our responsibility to address the defining crisis of our age (sloth).

To make matters worse, the authenticity of ecumenical witness is being undermined by a range of distortions of the gospel, toxic narratives and theologies that legitimize a totalitarian logic of death and destruction. These include theologies of dominion in the name of differences of race, gender, class and species, the theological legitimation of patriarchal domination; dualist and reductionist ways of relating heaven and earth, soul and body, spirit and matter; the denial and ridicule of cientific expertise and insights in order to maintain the current order, the prolonging of myths of unlimited progress, putting trust only in technological solutions to ecological problems instead of realizing their cultural, moral and spiritual nature; the pseudo-gospel of emphasizing the accumulation of wealth and prosperity, self-serving ways of always blaming problems on others; and escapist ways of addressing the victims of ecological injustice.

Hope: Courage in an age of anxiety and despair

Amidst the unprecedented despair associated with an overwhelming ecological crisis, we proclaim a hope in the Triune God in the midst of a groaning creation, "for in this hope we were saved" (Rom. 8:24). God has not abandoned the earth. We hold onto God's promises symbolized in the covenant that is made "with every living creature, for all future generations" (Gen. 9:12). We believe in God's presence as revealed in Jesus the Christ amidst the mess around us. We are comforted by the power of the Spirit to "renew the face of the earth" (Ps. 104:30).

In the face of economic and political narratives that distort our understanding of proper relationships between humans, creation and Creator, such hope may seem counter-intuitive. The hope that we proclaim not only critiques oppressive and patriarchal systems of dominion but inspires us to participate in the healing of creation (2 Chron. 7:14). Hope is not the same as blind optimism that trusts in the mere extension of current trends. Such hope is not cheap; it is costly. It springs forth despite overwhelming evidence to the contrary because it rests in the Triune God. It is such hope that encourages us and compels us towards a comprehensive ecological transformation of society.

A call to the global ecumenical movement

At the heart of the required transformation is a need for ecological conversion (metanoia), a change of heart, mind, attitudes, daily habits and forms of praxis (Rom. 12:1-2). This has implications for all aspects of Christian life: for liturgy and worship, reading the Bible, proclamation, the sacraments, congregational fellowship and practices, prayer, fasting, spirituality, doctrine, ethos, education, art, music, ministries and missions. This ecological reformation of all of Christianity has been encouraged by our fathers and mothers in the Christian tradition, by the examples of our sisters and brothers around the world and by ecumenical leaders such as Ecumenical Patriarch Bartholomew, Pope Francis, Archbishop emeritus Desmond Tutu and many other voices.

We call upon the global ecumenical movement, Christian world communions and all other churches to plan for a decade of ecological learning, confessing and comprehensive action to reorient the priorities of churches to the following commitments:

1. To renew the full range of liturgical and spiritual practices and ancient church traditions on creation in the light of the current kairos;
2. To reread the biblical texts and study them with ecological sensitivities;
3. To create frameworks for nurturing eco-congregations, providing them with the necessary staff and financial resources and supporting existing grassroots initiatives;
4. To promote gender justice in church and society given its multiple connections with ecological concerns;
5. To encourage youth to exercise leadership in church and society for the sake of a future that is theirs;
6. To mainstream eco-theological reflection across all levels of education;
7. To cultivate ecological virtues and nurture sustainable lifestyles in households and communities;
8. To equip the laity for their vocations in order to exercise ecological responsibility wherever they live, work and worship.

9. To engage in multi-disciplinary dialogue that can hold together and do justice to insights from the sciences, indigenous wisdom traditions and diverse theologies;

10. To advocate inter-disciplinary alliances, networks and partnerships with all levels of government, with business and industry, with civil society, with multifaith ecological networks, with other living faiths, and with all people who share a commitment to find sustainable alternatives to dominant forms of production and consumption.

In view of the forthcoming 11th assembly of the World Council of Churches in 2021 we recommend to the WCC, in particular, that it declares a "Decade for the Healing of Creation" with the following goals:

–   To mobilize member churches to re-orient their priorities to the commitments as indicated in the Wuppertal Call;

–   To engage with the UN's agenda of Sustainable Development Goals (SDGs) through various alliances, networks and partnerships and to go beyond the SDG-agenda in order to redefine notions of growth, wealth and well-being which are not sufficiently clarified yet with regard to the existing planetary boundaries.

–   To advocate to global decision makers that the increase in global greenhouse emissions should be halted and drastically reduced as soon as possible in order to reach net-zero carbon emissions and to keep global warming below 1.5 degrees Celsius.

–   To promote UN processes to create a legal framework for a binding "Universal Charter of the Rights of Mother Earth" (Cochabamba 2010), an Earth international jurisprudence system, and explore the possibilities of a UN Council for the Rights of Nature and to explore recognition of ecocide as a criminal offence in the International Court of Justice.

These commitments follow from an understanding of the Kairos moment in history in which we find ourselves. The task ahead is immense and will require decades of dedication. The urgency of the situation implies that a comprehensive response cannot be delayed. The next decade will be decisive to allow the Earth a time of rest. The biblical motifs of Sabbath and Jubilee provide a unique source of hope and inspiration, an interruption in the cycle of exploitation and violence, expressed in the vision that there shall be "a year of complete rest for the land" (Lev. 25:5).

Come Holy Spirit, renew your whole creation!

"KAIROS FOR CREATION" – EDITORIAL

The international and ecumenical conference about "*eco-theology, ethics of sustainability and eco-friendly churches*" took place from 16th-19th of June 2019 in Wuppertal/Germany and was organized jointly by Bread for the World, the Protestant Association of Churches and Mission (EMW), the Protestant Church in Germany (EKD), United Evangelical Mission (UEM) and the World Council of Churches (WCC). It was a conference with lasting impressions, enriching and encouraging experiences of sharing and a remarkable outcome in content:

51 participants from 22 different countries and nearly all continents, men and women from different cultural, denominational and religious backgrounds, theologians, eco-activists, scientists and representatives of Faith Based Organizations (FBOs) gathered to share their insights, their experiences, their convictions, their doubts, their joy and their sorrows about fundamental eco-theological questions which are becoming more and more important and crucial for the continuation of life in our world, which is God's creation.

For three days participants worked together in plenary discussions, intensive cross-cultural dialogue and in thematic workshops. Almost everybody contributed significantly about his or her specific insights and experiences. People joined in beautiful, spiritually moving and encouraging occasions of worship and prayer. During an excursion to a major historical place, the local church of Barmen-Gemarke participants were reminded about the history and struggle of the confessing church in Germany during the Nazi regime.

At the end of the conference the participants adopted the "Wuppertal Call: Kairos for creation – Confessing Hope for the Earth" which recommend to the World Council of Churches (WCC) to declare a "Decade for the Healing of Creation" at the 11th assembly of the World Council of Churches envisaged to take place in 2021 in Karlsruhe in Germany. The Ten Years Decade for the Healing of Creation should have the following goals:

"– To mobilize member churches to re-orient their priorities to the commitments as indicated in the Wuppertal Call;
– To engage with the UN's agenda of Sustainable Development Goals (SDGs) through various alliances, networks and partnerships and to go beyond the SDG-agenda in order to redefine notions of growth, wealth and well-being which are not sufficiently clarified yet with regard to the existing planetary boundaries.
– To advocate to global decision makers that the increase in global greenhouse emissions should be halted and drastically reduced as soon as possible in order to reach net-zero carbon emissions and to keep global warming below 1.5 degrees Celsius.
– To promote UN processes to create a legal framework for a binding "Universal Charter of the Rights of Mother Earth" (Cochabamba 2010), an Earth international jurisprudence system, and explore the possibilities of a UN Council for the Rights of Nature and to explore recognition of ecocide as a criminal offence in the International Court of Justice."

In the subsequent weeks and months, the Wuppertal Call found a remarkable international attention and ecumenical reception which still continues until today. It was translated into seven languages. Many churches, theological institutions and Christian networks worldwide discussed and welcomed the message and intention of this call.

The conference in Wuppertal continued and deepened an important process of intercultural and theological learning in the international ecumenical movement about central end essentials questions on climate justice and eco-theology which are currently raised mainly by young people worldwide. Many participants told us how important the conference was for their work and that they want to support this important learning process which was started in Wuppertal. The conference and the Wuppertal Call also for the EKD and the German protestant churches provided a very important stimulus and encouragement in their ongoing discussions about ethics of sustainability and climate change. We also received encouraging messages that the recommendation to the WCC about a Decade for the Healing of Creation will be discussed in the preparing committees for the next WCC assembly as well. Thus, we are confident that ways will be developed to allow issues of eco-theology and ethics of sustainability (and the role of the churches to promote them) also to be substantially discussed in Karlsruhe in 2021.

At this occasion, we want to express our gratitude to many people who made the conference in Wuppertal and the following process so successful and fruitful:

Firstly: We are grateful that so many participants from different countries and churches did follow our invitation and were willing to contribute. This provided rich input and the main value for this conference which is documented in this volume.

Secondly: Without good preparation, a conference like this cannot work. We therefore want to thank all those who contributed – together with both of us who represented the EKD and UEM - significantly for preparing this conference: Dr. Louk Andrianos from WCC, Dr. Michael Biehl from EMW, Dr. Andar Parlindungan from UEM and Dr. Dietrich Werner from Bread for the World. These organizations, churches and international church- associations also financed both the implementation of the Wuppertal conference and the documentation of its major contributions. The cooperation between Bread for the World, EMW, UEM, WCC and EKD was exceptional and it will continue, particularly in the area of ethics of sustainability and eco-theology.

We add our word of thanks also to those who worked behind the scenes on many organizational and administrative issues involved with such a complex project, particularly Mrs Roziewski (EKD) and Mrs Bähr (UEM). We include in our gratitude also all the stewards who helped us significantly during this conference. We want to add a special word of heartfelt thanks also to the international drafting group which - during demanding intensive day and night sessions - prepared and worked out diligently the draft of the final document, the Wuppertal Call Kairos for Creation.

Thirdly and finally: We complete our words of gratitude in expressing deep appreciation to the team of Rev. Dr. Dietrich Werner and Thomas Sandner from Bread for the World and Juliane Stork who took great efforts for collecting and editing the contributions of the Wuppertal conference and worked out this impressive documentation, which will help to deepen and to continue our learning process started in Wuppertal towards Karlsruhe and enrich many regional consultative processes in other regions of the world.

We hope that this documentation will find many attentive and interested readers and will create another momentum contributing new insights and practical examples of care, responsibility and proper lobbying work for issues of environment, climate justice and protection of diversity from inside as well as outside the worldwide ecumenical fellowship of churches as the present stage of the global ecological crisis desperately cries for the "land to have a year of rest"(Lev 25,5).

Dr. Ruth Gütter, Protestant Church in Germany (EKD), Executive Secretary for Sustainability
Dr. Jochen Motte, United Evangelical Mission (UEM), Executive Secretary for Justice, Peace and the Integrity of Creation

INTRODUCTION

Dietrich Werner

In a global report released on 5th November 2019 some 11.000 Climate Scientists have articulated a detailed and serious warning related to an emerging Climate Emergency for the whole of inhabited earth: Never since the prophets of doom in Old Testament traditions (see Hosea 4,1-6; Micha 6,1-16), who predicted national catastrophes with drastic ecological implications over against the people of God as a result of their inability to listen to the word of God in time, have voices of contemporary prophets, the natural scientists of today, become so drastic and deeply concerned about the future prospects for human civilization on this precious planet:

> "Despite 40 years of global climate negotiations, with few exceptions, we have generally conducted business as usual and have largely failed to address this predicament. The climate crisis has arrived and is accelerating faster than most scientists expected. It is more severe than anticipated, threatening natural ecosystems and the fate of humanity. Especially worrisome are potential irreversible climate tipping points and nature's reinforcing feedbacks (atmospheric, marine, and terrestrial) that could lead to a catastrophic "hothouse Earth," well beyond the control of humans. These climate chain reactions could cause significant disruptions to ecosystems, society, and economies, potentially making large areas of Earth uninhabitable."[1]

We are facing a Kairos for God's Creation and we need "a decisive turn in the pilgrimage of justice and peace" – this was argued by the *Wuppertal Call "Kairos for Creation"* which was formulated as a key message of the Wuppertal conference "Together on eco-theologies, ethics of sustainability and eco-friendly churches" which was held from 16-19 June 2019 with more than fifty international participants from 22 countries. The suggestion to plan for a Decade for the Healing of Creation, a *"decade of ecological learning, confessing and comprehensive action to re-orient the priorities of churches"* according to a number of crucial commitments was accompanied by an overwhelming range of contributions, perspectives and concrete action examples by churches from North and South, East and West representing different ecumenical learning journeys which are documented in this volume and which point to the need to continue and deepen the learning process in the area of eco-theologies and ethics of sustainability in World Christianity.

Ruth Gütter from Germany in her contribution analyses the modern trend to gravely exceed the limits of the given planetary boundaries as a challenge to the core of Protestant theology: Reflecting about the significance of the core confessions of Reformatory tradition, she presents the redemption from sin as a liberation from the pressures of unlimited greed. It needs to be understood as a liberation and a comprehensive conversion, which affects not only individual beings, but the relationship to the whole of creation: The protestant ethics of voluntary self-limitation can be regarded as a crucial contribution to an eco-friendly life-style and the rejection of false Gods of infinite growth and consumption.

---

1   See: William Ripple, Christopher Wolf e.a.: World Scientists warning of a Climate Emergency, In: BioScience, biz088; https://academic.oup.com/bioscience/advance-article/doi/10.1093/biosci/biz088/5610806?search result=1

Ernst Conradie from South Africa reviews five decades of initial eco-theological reflections within World Christianity in which the conviction has emerged that eco-theology offers a dual critique, namely both an ecological critique of Christianity and a Christian critique of ecological destruction. Both are essential, one cannot be neglected at the expense of the other. "Without a critique of Christianity, it becomes an apologetic exercise that overlooks the need for a radical ecological reformation of Christianity and merely reiterates human responsibility towards the environment through notions of stewardship or priesthood. Without a Christian critique of ecological destruction, eco-theology loses its ability to offer any distinct contribution to wider debates. Eco-theology then becomes nothing more than one branch of "religion and ecology" and cannot avoid the traps of self-secularisation." However, his reflections go on to ask the disturbing and really "theo-logical" question like: "What is God really doing now? What is God up to, given what we know already about climate change? Where can signs of God's presence and creative engagement with the world be found *(vestigia Dei)?*"

Dietrich Werner recalls the existing learning journey of ecological learning in the ecumenical movement, which includes both periods of neglect and periods of exciting common discoveries of eco-theological awareness and creational responsibility. The ecumenical movement articulated a substantial concept of "sustainability" already some 20 years before the international debates on UN level came to some similar conclusions. Both the spirit centered cosmological approaches of orthodox theological traditions as well as the insights of the dialogues between historical mainline churches and indigenous African and Asian wisdom traditions have formed a vital part of the ongoing history of an ecumenical emerging tradition of eco-theological reflections and eco-ethics.

Orthodox contributions to an Integral Ecology, based on early insights from Ecumenical Patriarch Bartholomew and his "Religion, Science and the Environment" Conference Series, are highlighted by *Petros Vassiliadis* from Greece, who particularly investigated Orthodox concepts like the "the economy of the Holy Spirit" and the concept of theosis as theological principles, argues that we need a much more inclusive approach to understanding the work of God's grace which includes reconciliation of suffering creation and the healing of a broken world. His article ends with a strong critique of the patriarchal culture which is leading to the suppression both of women and of the nature in affirming Gutierrez in stating: "As long as the patriarchal binary prevails, subjective human development remains defective, with pervasive repercussions in human relations as well as human-nature relations ... There can be no fully integral ecology as long as humanity behaves as the dominant male and treats nature as a submissive female. There can be no lasting social justice, and there can be no lasting ecological justice, as long as human behavior is driven by the patriarchal mindset."

From Roman Catholic perspectives this is complemented by the paper from *Ingeborg Gabriel* (Austria) and *Guillermo Kerber* (Uruguay/Switzerland) who take their start from reviewing the impact of the Pope's Encyclica Laudato Si particularly as the interlinkage between the social and ecological questions as well as the interdependence of all living beings on the planet is concerned. In Laudato Si they also see tentative signs for a first ethics of technology in Catholic Social Teaching which also is combined with a critical but also appreciative view of progress. A key contribution Roman Catholic social teaching has made is widening of the perspective of salvation, which is to include the whole cosmos. This should lead to a new view of creation which sees nature as God's creation in its own worth and in turn requires a fundamental metanoia leading to attitudes of humility over against creation, gratitude for the gifts of life and respect for all what lives in which Christians are to play the role of an avant-garde.

Jochen Motte and *Markus Mühling* deal with the historic significance and ongoing relevance of the Barmer Confession from 1934 in which – as remembered together during an excursion of the Wuppertal conference to the church in Barmen Gemarke – the Confessing Church in the period of the German Church Struggle had articulated resistance over against the imposition of a racist, nationalistic and elitist state ideology as matter of faith and has declared this as a matter of resistance (status confessionis). This is also posing the question of how and to what extend the current global climate crisis poses a similar challenge to the essence of Christian faith today and provokes churches to more distinctly to articulate care for creation as an essential task of their faith witness.

In the section on regional perspectives, two contributions from Latin America provide the start: *Daniel Beros* from Argentina criticizes the "spirit of unlimited growth" as an essential motive of the dominant cultural regime at the global level which ultimately energizes the ecocide which is taking place on our planet, threatening it with the annihilation. Justice by faith – this key principle of reformation tradition – is instead presented as offering a liberating limit, which destroys and puts out of power the mechanisms of unlimitness, as God's incarnation presents the self-limitation of God and his acceptance of the limited character of human life on earth. *Neddy Astudillo* presents a synthesis of 27 years of environmental work and teaching Eco-Theology in six countries in Latin America and the USA to Pentecostal Latino pastors in relating to both of her grandmothers. One – as she explains – is from indigenous background representing the wealth of indigenous Latin American wisdom traditions in relating to nature, the other being from Western background connecting her to the narratives of faith and western science. She comes to the clear conclusion that in Latin America, "the work of healing creation includes the examination and dismantling of our historically inherited principles of colonization, racism, gender domination, etc. If we avoid it, we are prone to committing the same mistakes all over again, even while building new green economies and churches."

Emmanuel Anim (Ghana) and *Kambale Kahongya* (Tanzania) present surprising and critical insights with regard to the role (or lack) of eco-theology in streams of African Christianity: Anim argues that recent Pentecostal movements and particularly some of its charismatic or neo-Pentecostal strands have effectively, in recent time, taken on the "dominion theology" which is inherent in the prosperity gospel, championed by American faith preachers and tele-evangelists. The aspirations of many of these American faith preachers were inspired by the American dream of a superman and highlighted only individual prosperity, freedom and liberty. His thesis is that many African Pentecostal and Charismatic Christians have bought into the dominion theology of the Prosperity Gospel, which presents the most anthropocentric approach to religion and faith and thereby have changed their attitudes to what was considered a 'sacred' environment and sustainable development pattern before. According to *Kambale Kahongya* many African Christians are still not much aware of the urgency and relevance of eco-theological tasks and dimensions in African Christianity. This is because eco-theology was not prioritized in the earlier phases of missionary Christianity and its preaching in Africa or even contradicted by certain types of an of end of the time's theology and an individualistic concept of human salvation. Therefore both a new and advanced ecological reading of the biblical texts as well as a better valorization of some

African cultural values need to be enhanced for contributing to a speeding up of a collective awareness on environmental protection in Africa.

Also six Asian contributions are added which present case studies from Asian churches, starting with *Andar Parlindugan, Daniel Sinaga* as well as *Victor Tinambunan* on the role of interreligious dialogue in preserving the ecological environment to the identification of shortcomings in theological education concerning eco-theological awareness as well as *Theresa Carino* from China on aspects of alternative concepts of growth and ecology of life in China today as well as *Meehyun Chung* from South Korea on major focusses of the South Korea struggle of churches on issues of eco-justice. The reader is also left with a pertinent question from Chinese perspectives: "The world decided to make China its manufacturing hub – 50% of all global production was brought to Chinese factories. All of us have or wear "Made in China" products. The ethical issue this raises is: Whose responsibility is it? In China, some environmentalists argue that western societies and companies who have made China the "factory of the world" have an obligation to contribute to the cleaning up of the environment." (Theresa Carino). From Indonesia also the Muslim scholar *Syafic Hasyim* from the Islamic State University, Jakarta, Indonesia, presents a passionate plea for more trustworthy dialogue between religious communities on Global Climate Change as there is much in Islamic teaching on the attitude of care and respect for "Mother Nature" and obligations of the faithful which can be built upon and which can serve as a common ground for joint action to curb global climate change.

From Europe two contributions from *Henrik Grape* (Sweden) and *Peter Pavlovic* (Belgium) underline the crucial contributions which European churches and networks have made with regard to eco-theological sensitization while at the same time still struggling with the question what is really entailed to live out "Obedience in faith" as mandated by biblical tradition (Pavlovic).

Thematic contributions include a number of unique but also divers thematic insights: Worship is presented as a key area in which ecological formation could take place in thousands of local congregations (*Chad Rimmer*, LWF). The WCC debate on an economy of life and subsequent considerations on an economy of life index and a greed line are presented by *Louk Andrianos* (Greece). New insights from neuro-bio-sciences concerning the nature and learning potentials of animals are recalled as a fundamental challenge to a traditional dominion oriented theology which treats animals only as objects for consumption but not as the "third party in the covenant" (*Bernd Kappes*, Germany). Intercultural insights into new indigenous terms ("Noken") to capture essential eco-theological meaning and relevance and liberate energies for a creation based mission model in the Indonesian context are presented by *Maraike Bangun*. All three last essays from this section bring important insights from eco-feminist reflections pertaining to a learning process to a body-sensitive eco-theology (*Claudia Jahnel*), a Philippino movement towards eco-feminism and its relevance for an earth-based spirituality (*Muriel Orevillo*) as ecological sensibilization in joint women's inter-religious peace-building (*Nadja Furlan Stante*).

The last section collects selected practical case studies on important projects and movements for ecological learning from Western and Eastern Europe (*Anja Vollendorf, Hayarpi Aghankanyan, Karen Nazaryan, Chad Rimmer*), from Africa (*Gloriose Umuziranenge, Geoff* and *Kate Davies* and *Misgana Mathewos Detago*) as well as from Latin America (*Guillermo Kerber, Daniel Beros*) and Asia (*Mathews George*).

Dietrich Werner

The volume concludes with several different language versions of the Wuppertal Call "Kairos for Creation – Confessing Hope for the Earth" which are added as attachment indicating the wide global reception process still going on which this initiative has found already within World Christianity and the membership of WCC. The Barmen Theological Confession from 1934 is added which includes a striking reference to "joyful deliverance from the godless fetters of this world *for a free, grateful service to his creatures*". Also s short introduction into the EKD Study Paper the UN Agenda 2030 as a Challenge to the Churches is provided and finally a key programmatic text from the UN related global interfaith organization *"Faiths for Earth"* which invites church related bodies and networks for full participation in an interfaith learning and action movement expressing a behavioral revolution towards the Earth.

This publication hopes to inspire and deepen emerging ecological renewal and reformation movements in all of Christianity. It is also hoped that the forthcoming assembly of WCC in Karlsruhe 2021 will allow for a substantial discussion of the proposals related to a *Decade for the Healing of Creation* in order to articulate clear priorities for further ecumenical work on these issues in the years to come.

ECUMENICAL LEARNING JOURNEYS

FREEDOM FOR LIMITATION

Protestant theological insights for a culture of sustainability

Ruth Gütter

Exceeding planetary limits as a challenge to the core of Protestant theology

We are living in a time of global crises which have been caused by human beings exceeding many different limits. Scientists speak about the dangers and consequences of exceeding so-called planetary limits in the anthropocene age.[1] Referring to examples such as the destruction of biological diversity and the advance of climate change, they make it clear that the negative consequences of exceeding limits have already brought about irreversible damage to the ecological equilibrium and this fundamentally threatens medium and long term life on the earth.

As early as 1972, the Club of Rome warned that the limits of growth had been reached. The World Council of Churches took up this waking call and, at its assembly in Nairobi in 1975, called for a "just, participatory and sustainable society".[2] This meant that the churches belonging to the WCC were the first in the 20th century to put the concept of sustainability on the global agenda. 1983 the churches within the WCC have replaced the term "sustainability" for inner-church theological reasons by the expression "conciliar process for justice, peace and the integrity of creation".

The United Nations adopted the term "sustainability" with their Brundtland Report in 1987 and the Rio Conference in 1992 as the guiding concept for a development that is ecological, socially compatible and fit for the future, and raised its status to a new, neutral principle of orientation binding on all states with the resolution of 2015 on sustainable development goals,In the 1980s, this conciliar process had a major effect in guiding the ecumenical movement worldwide – including the Protestant Church in Germany (EKD) – and it is still an important ethical principle for orientation on many ethical, global issues in German Protestantism today.[3] With regard to content, the conciliar process has already taken up the questions which are also on today's agenda for sustainability: global just structures and relationships, peaceful and secure conditions and the safeguarding of all created life. Here, too, the member churches of the World Council of Churches were pioneers towards the end of the 20th century and an avant-garde in the social and political discourse.

However, over the past three decades one can observe that elements of discussion which belong inseparably together in the conception of sustainability have become autonomous – including the discussions of ecology, development policy and peace policy. And this has had an effect on the expression of specific theological approaches in Protestantism.

---

1   Johan Rockström, A safe operating space for humanity, in: Nature (2009).
2   Wolfram Stierle, Dietrich Werner, Martin Heider, Ethik für das Leben 100 Jahre ökumenische Wirtschafts- und Sozialethik, 1996 p. 551.
3   Cf. Der Entwicklungsdienst der Kirche- ein Beitrag für Frieden und Gerechtigkeit in der Welt, 1988 ; Umkehr zum Leben, Nachhaltige Entwicklung im Zeichen des Klimawandels, 2009.

So, during the 1980s and 1990s, one could see how theological reflection on creation increased enormously with the growth of the ecological movement. Above all, there was a reaction to the criticism by Lynn White and Carl Amery about the so-called creation mandate in Genesis 1,28 as legitimating the human claim to dominion and anthropocentrism, and there was a plea for a different, attentive, humble and more respectful relation between human beings and their fellow creatures.[4] There can be no doubt that this plea was extremely necessary and still is today. Nevertheless, in many of these reflections on creation in the Protestant theology of the 1980s and 1990s – with the exception of Moltmann's theology – and in the church pronouncements of that period, one misses a link with the second article of the creed which is so central to Protestant theology, namely with Christology and soteriology. Many of those theological approaches and statements do not go any further than reflecting on the mandate of creation in Genesis 1 "fill the earth and subdue it", the "tilling and keeping" in Genesis 2 and a reference to Psalm 24 "The earth is the Lord's".

Over the past ten years, one can observe a change. The memorandum of the EKD on the climate "Umkehr zum Leben – Nachhaltige Entwicklung im Zeichen des Klimawandels"[5] (Conversion to Life – Sustainable development in the light of climate change) of 2009, for example, bases its arguments on the theology of creation, Christology and liberation theology and speaks out in favour of "ethics of enough". In relation to the past two years, mention must be made of the contributions of T. Meireis, E. Gräb-Schmidt and A. Behringer whose arguments relate to both creation theology and soteriology.[6] In Catholic theology, Pope Francis evoked a major response with his encyclical "Laudato Si" and his passionate appeal against the dogma of growth and for an ecological spirituality. "Laudato Si" also contains a convincing combination of the approaches of liberation theology and creation theology.

Therefore, the key question for the reflection which follows is: what is the guiding significance, from a Protestant point of view, of the confession of Jesus Christ and of faith in justification through grace for the issues of sustainability and transformation?

Liberation from sin – Redemption of creation as a whole

As Protestant Christians we believe that God, the creator of heaven and earth, came into the world in Jesus Christ to liberate it from the power of sin. In God's incarnation in Jesus Christ, God's love for his whole creation is revealed in a very special way. There is witness to this love of God for creation already in the Old Testament; for example, in the covenant God makes with Noah and in his promise not to destroy the earth again but to preserve it. God makes this covenant with the whole of creation, not just with Noah (Genesis 9,8-10). It is not just the human beings but also all

---

4   Cf. the reflection on creation theology by Altner, Liedke, Moltmann etc. Cf. Christian Link, Ökologische Schöpfungstheologie- eine Zwischenbilanz, in: Heinrich Bedford-Strohm, Und Gott sah, dass es gut war. Schöpfung und Endlichkeit im Zeitalter der Klimakatastrophe, 2009, p. 29-31.

5   https://www.ekd.de/klimawandel.htm.

6   Cf. Umkehr zum Leben, Nachhaltige Entwicklung im Zeichen des Klimawandels, Denkschrift der EKD, 2009, T. Meireis, Schöpfung und Transformation- Nachhaltigkeit in protestantischer Perspektive, Jahrbuch sozialer Protestantismus 2016, p. 17-50, E. Gräb-Schmidt, Nachhaltigkeit im Zeichen reformatorischer Freiheit, Jahrbuch sozialer Protestantismus 2017, p. 113-129; A. Behringer, Reformation-Transformation-Nachhaltigkeit, Schöpfungsverantwortung als Christusnachfolge, Munich 2017.

Ruth Gütter

their fellow creatures that have a relationship with God![7] Consequently, the renewed relationship with God in Christ is important not just for humankind but for the whole creation.

This dimension of creation theology in the witness to Christ appears time and again in the stories and witness of the New Testament. "He came to what was his own" (John 1,11); in this way Christ followed a path which concerned the whole of creation. This is visible in the descriptions by the Evangelists of cosmic signs which accompany him on his earthly way. There, the birth of Jesus is linked with a new star that appeared in the sky, and his death on the cross with the sun which lost its radiance. Jesus' relation to creation is also made clear in the accounts about his life in proximity to nature. The stories in the Gospels tell how he fasted for 40 days in the desert and repeatedly withdrew into nature to pray. Many of his parables use images from nature (parable of the mustard seed, parable of the multiplication of the seed, of weeds among the wheat, the parable of yeast, etc.); he saw plants and animals with their carefree approach and their dependence on the creator as examples for human beings.[8]

Nevertheless, the question arises whether non-human creation has the same kind of relation with God as human beings. In the first account of the creation, it is only the humans who are said to have been made in the image of God (Genesis 1,26). This would mean that they have a different relation to God compared with their fellow creatures, a relationship which is marked by the ability for dialogue, an ability to reflect and responsibility in relation to God and their fellow creatures. According to the statements in the Hebrew Bible, the ability to respond and the recognition of one's finiteness are what defines human beings.[9] So it is questionable whether our fellow creatures can turn their backs on God in the same way as human beings, i.e. can commit sin. After all, sin essentially means alienation. i.e. no longer living with confidence in God but with the illusion of being able to live in one's own strength without self-limitation and without responsibility towards God and one's neighbours. "Responsibility and self-limitation cannot be separated. Where this is denied, they are perverted into the opposite… It is this perversion that is called sin in the language of faith… The perversion consists of their wanting to take charge of their death by means of their life and, at the same time, losing respect for the lives of others in favour of an unlimited determination of their own lives…"[10] It appears that only human beings as images of God are able to have this kind of alienation from God, their fellow creatures and themselves. But the whole of creation is affected by their ability to sin. Following the flood, the rest of creation is now also subject to perishing. It is no longer "very good" like at the beginning but marked by violence and decay; however, like human beings, it is still under God's assurance of protection and his promises.

In the New Testament letters, there is mention of the presence of Christ in the creation and of his participation in creation: "for in him all things in heaven and on earth were created, things visible and invisible, whether thrones or dominions or rulers or powers – all things have been created through him and for him. He himself is before all things, and in him all things hold together" (Colossians 1,16-17).

---

7   Cf. Georg Hofmeister, Prinzip Nachhaltigkeit! Theologisch-ethische Perspektiven, Hofgeismarer Protokolle 355, p. 17.
8   E.g. the birds of the air and the lilies of the field, Cf. Matthew 6,26-28.
9   Cf. W Huber, Selbstbegrenzung aus Freiheit, Ev Th 52/ 1992 p. 139.
10   Cf. W. Huber, p. 139. See also E. Gräb-Schmidt, who spells out how the limits of human freedom are denied if there is no relationship with God. The debate about both the justification of human beings and about sustainability therefore raises the question anew about the limits to the human power to act. c.f. op.cit. p. 113-114.

Paul understands liberation from the power of sin and death through Christ as clearly relating to the whole of creation. So Romans 8,19-21 states, "For the creation waits with eager longing for the revealing of the children of God; for the creation was subjected to futility … in hope that the creation itself will be set free from its bondage to decay and will obtain the freedom of the glory of the children of God".

So it is a matter of the comprehensive liberation and redemption of a world marked by sin and death. An anthropological, individualistic and spiritual limitation of God's redemptive work in Christ just to human beings and their souls, such as can be found time and again even today in western Protestant churches and their theological history, is not reconcilable with the New Testament witness.[11]

Living in the grace of God – Liberation to comprehensive conversion

Despite all human failings, God has repeatedly shown his love for human beings, accepted them in patience and faithfulness, called them to conversion and given them the chance of a new start. There are many stories about this in the Bible. In Jesus Christ, God revealed his love in a special, unique way and set creation free from the power of sin once and for all by Jesus' suffering and death.

In the Protestant understanding, freedom and liberation are the central characteristics of Jesus' mission. "For freedom Christ has set us free" as Galatians 5,1 says. Faith in Jesus Christ liberates people from worry about themselves which is the core of sin, from the fear of being at a disadvantage, from the effort of trying to put themselves in the place of God. Martin Luther speaks tellingly about sinful people as people "turned in on themselves" because everything revolves exclusively around them. In his lecture on the Letter to the Romans of 1516, Luther describes human beings "…as being so profoundly turned in on themselves that they seize the best gifts for themselves and enjoy them and, in the process, ignore that, in an evil, inward turning and perverse way, they seek everything and even God himself only for their own sakes".[12]

Sin as an unending concern just about oneself appears in many different forms. Today, as Pope Francis urgently points out, it has especially destructive expressions in the form of unlimited greed and numbness to the suffering of others – destructive for human souls, for human relationships and for the wellbeing of creation as a whole. But sin also shows itself in the compulsion constantly to make a good impression or in the tortuous anxieties that one might be worthless.[13] Faith, on the other hand, means allowing oneself to be guided by trust instead of fear, letting go instead of holding fast. Within the protection of God's love, believers have all they need. They no longer need to live at the expense of others and appear in a good light themselves. They live on the fullness of God's gifts and really nothing more than that is needed. That makes them thankful and enables them to pass on what they have received from God. "When this fulfilling joy in

---

11   This view is also clearly stated in the mission document of the WCC of 2013 "Together towards Life: Mission and Evangelism in Changing Landscapes". Cf. p.3; www.oikumene.org/de/ressources/documents/mission-and-evangelisation.

12   Cf. WA 56, 304, p. 22, in a translation by Joachim Köhler, Luther, 2016, p. 178.

13   Cf. Den Wandel gestalten-zum Leben umkehren, Reader der Landessynode der Evangelischen Kirche im Rheinland 2014, p.10.

Ruth Gütter

serving one's neighbour is recognised as the goal of a good life, then one's eyes are opened to see what one really needs."[14]

According to the insights of the Reformation, a faith of this kind is not an achievement but a gift. Receiving this gift gratefully means being liberated from false gods, a radical conversion to a new life, a new creation.[15] "God's gift of righteousness in the life and death of his son Jesus Christ makes it possible and enables us to lead a life in which people are just in their mutual relationships and live in respect for the value inherent in human nature ..."[16]

Faith in the grace of God is not just a matter of the heart and the inner life; it should find expression in the whole life of the believer. "Anyone who speaks about justified persons always has in mind the whole existence of these persons, their attitude to the world and to God".[17] The grace of God changes people radically. Paul understands it as a change of lordship, as death and rebirth: "You must consider yourselves dead to sin and alive to God in Christ Jesus" (Romans 6,11). A life in grace should be evident and prove its worth in a change of practice. Otherwise grace becomes the cheap grace about which Dietrich Bonhoeffer clearly warned us.[18] God's grace is not a comfortable cushion on which believers can take a rest. God's grace is costly grace because it was bought at a high price by the suffering and death of Jesus. Its aim is to renew and heal the earth. Christians devote their lives to the service of this renewing and transforming work of God.

However, they know that they repeatedly fail to live up to what God has called them to be. Nevertheless, they can go on their way with confidence because they rely on God's grace and mercy being greater than their sin and weakness. They believe that, in Jesus suffering and death, the power of sin has been broken and sin and death will not have the last word. Relying on God's grace, they do not despair in face of the enormity of human sin; on the contrary, even when there are setbacks and errors they can always begin again. As Martin Luther understood it, conversion is a life-long process. Therefore, the first of his 95 theses states, "Our Lord and Master Jesus Christ, in saying, 'Repent ye,' (Mt. 4,17) intended that the whole life of his believers on earth should be a constant penance."

Conversion, as described in the witness of the Bible, is thus not only and not primarily the conversion of the soul to God but rather a comprehensive conversion with far reaching consequences for the whole of creation around us. It is a process of new creation with transformative power and significance.

So, faith in Jesus Christ broadens people's perspective to become a perspective of hope. "Within the horizon of God's becoming world and God's becoming human, however, hope unfolds for a renewal of these relationships: for healing in relation to God, for peace in relation to other people and for reconciliation with nature".[19]

---

14 Cf. T. Meireis, Schöpfung und Transformation, in Nachhaltigkeit, Jahrbuch Sozialer Protestantismus 9, p. 45.
15 Cf . 2 Corinthians 5,17.
16 Cf. Umkehr zum Leben- nachhaltige Entwicklung im Zeichen des Klimawandels, Denkschrift der EKD, 2009, p. 110.
17 Cf. E. Gräb-Schmidt, Nachhaltigkeit im Zeichen reformatorischer Freiheit, Jahrbuch sozialer Protestantismus 2017, p. 113.
18 Cf. Dietrich Bonhoeffer, Cost of Discipleship, DBW 4, p. 29-40.
19 Cf. Wolfgang Huber, Selbstbegrenzung aus Freiheit, über das ethische Grundproblem des technischen Teilalters, Ev. Th. 52, p. 139; Cf. also WCC Document "Together towards Life" op.cit. p. 4.

Ethics of self-limitation

If – as was described at the beginning – the boundlessness and immoderateness of human beings have become the greatest contemporary threats to the whole of creation, then conversion today means, above all, the readiness and ability of people to impose limits on themselves.

Such a plea for a healthy self-limitation based on the Christian faith seems to be an excessive demand and a provocation for a society in which unlimited economic growth and unlimited self-realisation are still unchallenged paradigms. It appears to many to be an unacceptable restriction on human autonomy imposed by morality and religion.

But, in reality, freedom and self-limitation are not mutually exclusive opposites. According to the Christian understanding, freedom proves its worth precisely in our being able to limit ourselves responsibly in relation to God and our neighbours. That is exactly what is meant by Luther's dialectical understanding of the freedom of the Christian. "The Christian is a free person and subject to no one. The Christian is a servant of all and subject to everyone."[20]

In relation to today's global crises, that means being able to limit myself for the sake of the rights of other people in the present and future generations, but also for the sake of the rights to life of creation around me. The idea of unlimited freedom is not only dangerous; from a Christian point of view, it is also an illusion. Because I myself am not the result of my own doing but of that of my creator and I also owe my life to that of other creatures. My earthly life is limited in time and space. Recognising my finiteness implies becoming wise (Psalm 90,12). Throughout my earthly life I rely on others and am dependent on them – also on non-human creation. So human freedom is not something absolute but is relational and dialogical. It proves its value in responsibility. And responsibility is also fundamentally something dialogical. Responsibility together with self-limitation, in the Christian view, are only possible in the belief that human beings have already been addressed by God. "That humans have responsibility is not the first thing to be said about them; that is always preceded by their having been spoken to… Because humans have been spoken to before they know how to answer, self-limitation constitutes the first duty of their freedom".[21]

Undoubtedly, the guiding image of sustainability confronts us with the special challenge that our freedom is restricted, not only by responsibility for the rights to life of other people and the rights to life of non-human creation, but also by the rights to life of future generations. Hans Jonas, in his book "Prinzip Verantwortung", has already pointed out this special challenge.[22] We know from experience that people often only react to the consequences of their actions when they feel them themselves and experience them directly. The effects on people who have yet to be born are very abstract and hard to grasp. In the case of responsibility for the coming generation, from a Christian point of view it is not just a matter of some general responsibility for something but decisively of the question before whom I have responsibility. "The fundamental principle of Christian ethics which needs to be recalled today is: I am life only if I am related to other life, to life which extends beyond my own life and which limits it at the same time. This nature of all life is conceived radically in the awareness of God. I am life because I owe myself to God and live on his spirit. This is the basis of freedom which is expressed in consideration for other life. Therefore the possibility of life in the future is a limitation on my actions today."[23]

---

20   Cf. the first sentences in „Von der Freiheit eines Christenmenschen", Weimarer Edition, Vol. 7.
21   Cf. Wolfgang Huber, op.cit. p. 141.
22   Cf. H. Jonas, Das Prinzip Hoffnung, Frankfurt 1979, p. 36.
23   Cf. Wolfgang Huber, op.cit. p.140.

So, because of their faith in Jesus Christ, Christians are called especially to responsibility for the future of human life on this earth and empowered for this. Nevertheless, they are no better than others, do wrong and fail like other people. But they live trusting that they can begin anew time and again and that God supports them in such new beginnings.

"Justification of the Fearful" and narratives of hope

In times of multiple crises and threats, anxieties also increase. Nowadays, they are not the anxieties of the past about a punitive God but fears about the future, about one's own life and that of one's children and grandchildren. They are fears which lead people to cling to maintaining the status quo and to feeling that the necessary changes and transformations are threatening. These are feelings of impotence and of doubt about the significance of one's own actions in view of the major challenges and threats.

What could be the Reformation message today in response to these fears and feelings of impotence? Perhaps it could be translated to convey that we are supported and accepted even in our existential fears and, in precisely that way, can become free and courageous to face the necessary changes. "In times which make many people feel insecure, speaking about the 'justification of the fearful' might be an appropriate translation of the Reformation message for the present."[24]

With precisely this "justification of the fearful", with the acceptance of human beings in their fear and impotence, something new can begin which has been described in many ecumenical documents as "transformative spirituality".[25]

Protestant theology has undoubtedly contributed something to this "transformative spirituality" because "transformative spirituality" is based on fundamental Reformation insights: "liberation from the need to set oneself up as great (grace), redemption from fears of being of no value (being declared just), being able to enjoy because of trusting God (faith)".[26]

People need visions and narratives of hope in order to overcome fears and doubt. This is also true of Christians. The significance of Christian eschatology grows at times when people are wavering between massive suppression and major fears because of apocalyptic scenarios about the future. What visions of the future can provide encouragement in this situation?

After all, the sustainability goals of the UN of 2015, with the telling title "Transforming our World – the 2030 Agenda for sustainable development", are also based on far-reaching positive visions and great determination. Christians are not only empowered by their faith in God, the Creator and Liberator, to cooperate in the "transformation of the world", but also encouraged by the hope of God's coming who wishes to create heaven and earth anew.

The garden of Eden (Genesis 2,4 ff) and the coming city of God (Revelation 21,2-5) are especially effective images of hope in the Bible.[27] The garden of Eden and the city of God are places where God lives in the midst of his creation. They are places of God's presence, of peace and fullness. Such images nourish the yearning for and hope of the coming kingdom of God

---

24   Cf. H. Gorski, Rechtfertigung der Ängstlichen, wie eine evangelische Identität heute aussehen könnte, Zeitzeichen 11/2017 p.21.
25   Cf. above all WCC documents of the past few years, especially "Together towards Life: Mission and Evangelism in Changing Landscapes" op.cit. p.8.
26   Cf. Den Wandel gestalten- zum Leben umkehren, Reader zu Synode der EkiR 2014, p. 10.
27   Cf. T. Meireis, Schöpfung und Transformation, p. 33.

which has already begun on earth with the coming of Jesus Christ and wants to take further shape.

The narratives of hope and peace, which religions have to offer, can become very important for the transformation processes needed now. "Religion is a central element of the contemporary processes of social transformation and conflict. Therefore societies undergoing change, in particular, need a much greater religious literacy...".[28]

Such narratives and images of hope can release energies for the necessary action. Hope of the coming kingdom of God does not discharge people from their current responsibility for the future of the creation but rather strengthens it. "Tomorrow may be the day of judgment. If it is, we shall gladly give up working for a better future, but not before."[29]

---

28 Cf. U. Schneidewind, Religion und Spiritualität, Ressourcen für die große Transformation, 2016, p. 96.
29 Cf. Dietrich Bonhoeffer, Widerstand und Ergebung, DBW 8, p.36 Letters and Papers from Prison, 1953, p. 147.

Ruth Gütter

WHAT IS GOD REALLY UP TO IN A TIME LIKE THIS?

Discerning the Spirit's movements as core task of Christian eco-theology

Ernst M. Conradie

Five decades of eco-theology

Eco-theology emerged as a scholarly discourse in the 1970s,[1] partly in response to growing ecological concerns, expressed for example in the contested report to the Club of Rome on Limits to Growth (1972),[2] partly in response to the equally contested thesis by Lynn White that Christianity is a root cause of the environmental crisis given its deeply anthropocentric orientation.[3] Sources of inspiration to address these challenges emerged from a retrieval of the biblical roots and subsequent history of the Christian tradition, its classic texts, doctrines, moral codes, forms of praxis, saints and leading theologians.[4] For a decade or two eco-theology retained a clear focus, namely reflection on the relationship between "man" and nature, later reformulated as the place and role of humanity within the biophysical environment,[5] or (for some) humanity's significance in cosmic evolution.[6] If anything, eco-theology could be equated with renewed attention to the doctrine of creation, anthropology and environmental ethics.

Since the 1990s eco-theology has become an increasing amorphous discourse – covering a wide array of themes and underlying problems, situated in diverse geographical contexts, expressed in multiple languages, emerging in basically all confessional traditions and schools of theology, covering all the traditional sub-disciplines of Christian theology, trapped in the same old methodological disputes (e.g. between biblical studies and systematic theology, systematic theology and practical theology, religion and theology).[7] Arguments are typically reiterated in different contexts, often in isolation from what emerges elsewhere. At the same time, eco-theology is characterised by global divides – along confessional lines, between the North and the South,

---

1   There were of course precursors to the emergence of ecotheology. See especially Panu Pihkala, Joseph Sittler and Early Ecotheology (Berlin: LIT Verlag, 2017).
2   See Donella H. Meadows et al., The Limits to Growth: A Report for the Club of Rome's Project on the Predicament of Mankind (New York: Universe Books, 1972).
3   Lynn White, "The Historical Roots of our Ecological Crisis", Science, 155 (1967), 1203-1207 (1205).
4 Again one reference may suffice, namely to the now classic study by H. Paul Santmire, The Travail of Nature (Philadelphia: Fortress Press, 1985).
5   It may suffice to mention only one such contribution amongst numerous others, namely by James M. Gustafson, A Sense of the Divine: The Natural Environment from a Theocentric Perspective (Edinburgh: T & T Clark, 1994).
6   See especially the contributions in the tradition of Pierre Teilhard de Chardin and Thomas Berry, especially Brian Swimme and Mary Evelyn Tucker, Journey of the Universe (New Haven: Yale University Press, 2011).
7   From time to time I have offered reviews of such developments. See especially Ernst M. Conradie, "Reformed Perspectives from the South African Context on an Agenda for Ecological Theology". Ecotheology: The Journal of Religion, Nature and the Environment 10:3, 281-314; Christianity and Ecological Theology: Resources for Further Research (Stellenbosch: Sun Press, 2006); "Contemporary Challenges to Christian Ecotheology: Some Reflections on the State of the Debate after Five Decades, Journal of Theology for Southern Africa 147, 106-123.

the West and the East, on issues of gender and sexual orientation and, especially, by reference to contemporary science (especially in the global North) and / or traditional, indigenous wisdom (widespread in the global South).[8] Worldviews clearly play an important role albeit that this category is itself contested and open to confusion.[9] With other theological discourses, eco-theology shares the need to distinguish Christian theology from other forms of theology (especially in the Abrahamic faiths but also with reference to notions of the "Supreme Being" in Indigenous religion), theology from religious studies, the humanities from the social sciences and, in the Anthropocene, the humanities from the natural sciences.

Arguably, throughout the last five decades Christian eco-theology retained both a critical and a constructive task. As I have often suggested, eco-theology offers a dual critique, namely both an ecological critique of Christianity and a Christian critique of ecological destruction. This is similar to feminist theology that offers a feminist critique of Christianity and a Christian critique of patriarchy, and to Black theology that offers a "Black" critique of Christianity and a Christian critique of white supremacy. These dual critiques need to be held together. The genius of Christian eco-theology lies in its ability to maintain this dual critique. Without a critique of Christianity, it becomes an apologetic exercise that overlooks the need for a radical ecological reformation of Christianity and merely reiterates human responsibility towards the environment through notions of stewardship or priesthood. Without a Christian critique of ecological destruction, eco-theology loses its ability to offer any distinct contribution to wider debates. Eco-theology then becomes nothing more than one branch of "religion and ecology" and cannot avoid the traps of self-secularisation.

Such a dual critique would itself become empty without a recognition of the more constructive task of eco-theology. This constructive task is also of a dual nature. This includes both a contri- bution to Christian authenticity and, on that particular basis, also a contribution to public, inter- disciplinary discourse on sustainability[10] – where such a contribution is often highly contested. I will suggest below that the former entails five key prophetic and pastoral tasks, namely to read the signs of the times (the symptoms), to expose the underlying root causes of the problem (diagnostics), to discern the counter-movement of the Spirit, to tell the story of God's work accordingly and to express a prophetic vision of what the world could be and should be like.

An ecological reformation of Christianity

There is something deeply unnerving for Christians, both in the global North and in the global South, regarding the dual critique mentioned above.

On the one hand, the prophetic tradition of speaking truth to power is alive and well, for example in ecumenical calls for climate justice and the recognition of climate debt. The World

---

8   See, for example, Heather Eaton, Introducing Ecofeminist Theologies (New York: T&T Clark International, 2005).
9   See Ernst M. Conradie, "Views on Worldviews: An Overview of the Use of the Term Worldview in Selected Theological Discourses". Scriptura 113 (2014), 1-12; "Ways of Viewing an Evolving World amidst Ecological Destruction", Scriptura 117 (2018), 1-13.
10   This is indeed highly contested. See my contribution to the debate in Ernst M. Conradie "Twelve Theses on the Place of Christian Theology in Multi-disciplinary Conversations" Stellenbosch Theological Journal 1:1 (2015), 375-386.

Ernst M. Conradie

Council of Churches has taken the lead here with sustained statements over several decades.[11] This has helped to ensure that environmental issues are framed as matters of justice (and not merely nature conservation or wilderness preservation). The intricate links between sustainability, peace, health, poverty and gender have to be recognised as "transversals" that are at least dimensions of all other social challenges.[12] These efforts are to be commended. However, on a cautionary note, it is also true that such calls are hardly heard by those in positions of political and economic power so that these all too often come from a safe distance where prophets do not have to carry the consequences of their words.[13] Moreover, Christians do not take the lead here in the sense that environmental activists in the forefront of such challenges to power typically do not align themselves with Christianity. It seems that the divides between right-wing and left-wing Christianity (in the 1970s "evangelicals" versus "ecumenicals") are often deeper on issues of (climate) justice than between Christians and activists in other religious traditions. In fact, one may observe that natural scientists, against their own methodological inclinations, have become the prophets of our day by reiterating warnings over climate change, the loss of biodiversity, ocean acidification and a range of other "planetary boundaries", speaking truth to power. They may be heard, but their warnings are not necessarily heeded and some have been targeted, intimidated and vilified.[14]

On the other hand, orthodox and evangelical Christians may well be concerned that external criteria (ecological sustainability) are applied to critique Christianity. Is this not another form of natural theology, albeit of a progressive kind? This can be circumvented by discovering that ecological concerns are deeply rooted in the Christian tradition, its sacred texts, doctrines, moral codes and forms of praxis. If so, it is not Christianity that is at fault but the ways in which the Christian gospel has been appropriated to legitimise domination. The problem is not the command in Genesis 1:27 but that this command has been gravely misunderstood. However, as the ecological critique of Christianity deepened, this apologetic position became harder to sustain. The Bible may contain sources of ecological wisdom but at least some "grey" texts are deeply ambiguous.[15] The problem does not only lie with the interpretation of Genesis 1:27 but with the harshness of the command itself.[16] Likewise, every aspect of the Christian faith has become contested, for example the emphasis on God's transcendence, human supremacy, dualist views on the soul rather the body, Spirit rather than matter, the "myth" of the fall of humanity and the original "goodness" of creation, anthropocentric soteriologies, divine election, Christocentric exclusivism, eschatological escapism and so forth.[17] This critique is readily extended to Christian ethics, pastoral praxis, ecclesial ministries and especially to Christian mission given its alignment with

---

11   See, e.g. alongside many others, Rogate Mshana (ed.), Poverty, Wealth and Ecology in Africa: Ecumenical Perspectives (Geneva: WCC, 2012).
12   The integral relatedness between poverty and ecology is evident in two South African ecumenical statements, namely The Land is Crying for Justice: A Discussion Document on Christianity and Environmental Justice in South Africa (Stellenbosch: Ecumenical Foundation of Southern Africa, 2002); and The Oikos Journey: A Theological Reflection on the Economic Crisis in South Africa (Durban: Diakonia Council of Churches, 2006).
13   This is my core argument in Ernst M. Conradie, "Climate Change and the Common Good: Some Reflections from the South African Context:, International Journal of Public Theology 4 (2010), 271-293.
14   See the account in Naomi Oreskes & Erik M. Conway, Merchants of Doubt (London: Bloomsbury, 2010).
15   See, for example, Norman C. Habel, An Inconvenient Text: Is a Green Reading of the Bible Possible? (Adelaide: ATF Press, 2009).
16   This is much discussed in literature on ecotheology. The challenge is posted starkly by Norman Habel in his essay "Geophany: The Earth Story in Genesis" in Norman C. Habel & Shirley Wurst (eds): The Earth Story in Genesis (Sheffield: Sheffield Academic Press, 2000), 34-48.

colonialism. Put differently, such an ecological reformation is not only a matter of ethics but also of ecclesiology.[18] A Christian blessing of discourse on sustainability on the basis of a rejuvenated doctrine of creation would not suffice. There is some bitter irony here concerning global divides. While so-called secular North- Western Europe is turning its back on Christianity, the centre of gravity in global Christianity is moving South and East, found especially in the proliferation of multiple forms of Pentecostalism – and to some extent the Americanisation of Christianity. Wherever this has happened, the critique only deepened. In the South the alignment of Christianity with colonialism prompted calls for decolonising Christianity, the heart of the Christian gospel and the Trinitarian core of the Christian faith.[19] In the African context this begs many further questions about the continuity between Christianity and African traditional religion and culture. Some argue for its compatibility, while others resist Christianity as a colonising, divisive religion.[20] Likewise, in the East the Christian faith is scrutinised in conversation with Buddhism, Hinduism and Confucianism.

Calls for an ongoing ecological reformation of Christianity have to be understood in this light.[21] In one of the earliest versions of such a call James Nash observed that this implies both a recognition that Christianity needs to be reformed (or else a reformation is not necessary) and that it can indeed be reformed from within (or else a reformation is not possible).[22] As I have argued elsewhere, such a reformation can be prompted anywhere but the impulse for the reformation then becomes re-appropriated to address other problems so that it soon becomes comprehensive, touching pretty much on all aspects – the biblical texts, the history of the Christian tradition, Christian doctrine, moral codes, forms of praxis, rituals, spirituality and so forth.[23] The Lutheran reformation may have started with malpractices around the selling of indulgences but soon had implications for almost any single aspect of society. Likewise, the Genevan reformation got going by inviting Calvin as a refugee to stay in Geneva, but soon he challenged the authorities for not being welcoming enough to the floods of (often wealthy) refugees flocking to the city.

---

17   My lifetime commitment is to address such issues through monographs such as Hope for the Earth – Vistas on a New Century (Eugene: Wipf & Stock, 2005); An Ecological Christian Anthropology: At Home on Earth? (Aldershot: Ashgate); The Earth in God's Economy: Creation, Salvation and Consummation in Ecological Perspective (Berlin: LIT Verlag) and Redeeming Sin? Social Diagnostics amid Ecological Destruction (Lanham: Lexington Books, 2017).

18   For a discussion from within the African context, see Ernst M. Conradie, Hans S.A. Engdahl & Isabel Apowo Phiri (eds), "Ecclesiology and Ethics: The State of Ecumenical Theology in Africa", The Ecumenical Review 67:4 (201), 495-497, 498-663; also Ernst M. Conradie (ed), South African Perspectives on Notions and Forms of Ecumenicity (Stellenbosch: Sun Press, 2013).

19   For a recent, provocative contribution to this debate, see Ernst M. Conradie & Teddy Chalwe Sakupapa, "'Decolonising the Doctrine of the Trinity' or 'The Decolonising Doctrine of the Trinity'"? Journal of Theology for Southern Africa 161 (2018), 37-53.

20   Teddy Sakupapa. "The Decolonising Content of African Theology and the Decolonisation of African Theology: A Decolonial Analysis", Missionalia (forthcoming).

21   See especially Lisa Dahill & James B. Martin-Schramm (eds), Eco-reformation: Grace and Hope for a Planet in Peril (Eugene: Wipf & Stock, 2016); also Ernst M. Conradie, Elizabeth Tsalampouni & Dietrich Werner (eds), "Manifesto on an Ecological Reformation of all Christian Traditions: The Volos Call", in Dietrich Werner & Elizabeth Jeglitzka (eds): Climate Justice and Food Security: Theological Education and Christian Leadership Development (Geneva: Globethics.net, 2016), 99-108.

22   See James, A. Nash, "Towards the Ecological Reformation of Christianity", Interpretation 50:1 (1996), 5-15.

23   See especially Ernst M. Conradie & Miranda N. Pillay (eds), Ecclesial Deform and Reform Movements in the South African Context (Stellenbosch: SUN Press, 2015).

Ernst M. Conradie

This again had far-reaching implications for every aspect of society and also shaped Calvin's own theology. Given the polemical nature of such a reformation, ongoing theological reflection will necessarily be required for the sake of clarification. This suggests a dialectic between reformation and critical reflection on such reformation.

There is another way in which this dual critique is unnerving. The more the ecological critique of Christianity is emphasised, the less room there seems to be for a Christian critique of ecological destruction. To point any fingers leads to a recognition of more fingers pointing back at the complicity of Christianity. If Christianity is indeed part of the underlying problem, as is widely assumed from the outside, then the most significant contribution that Christians can make to address ecological problems may be to get its own house in order. This may be hard to swallow. If so, it seems that Christians should stop proclaiming that it has a message that can save the world. The question is no longer whether there can be salvation outside the church, but whether there is salvation inside the church,[24] whether the church itself and its message can still be salvaged, whether its decline is inevitable and even needs to be celebrated.

In the forthcoming T&T Clark Handbook of Christian Theology and Climate Change that Hilda Koster and I edited we took this critique as a point of departure, namely to suggest that if North-Atlantic Christianity is indeed associated with the root causes of anthropogenic climate change, then addressing North-Atlantic Christian theology from within may be crucial in order to address climate change.[25] There are alternatives of course, namely to abandon Christianity and to opt for another religion or something like secular humanism.

For Christianity in the global South the challenge is different. Where people have embraced Christianity (as is the case in most of Africa) and with it aspects of Western culture – and American forms of consumerism[26] – it needs to figure out what this really means given the contested and tainted legacy of Christianity and the vibrancy of other religious traditions. In generalised terms, while some resisted colonisation and with that Christianity as the colonisation of consciousness, some have appropriated Christianity in order to survive amidst colonial oppression – and now readily abandon it. Others may have become Christian in order to gain access to the inner secrets of Western culture – and its cultural artefacts in terms of guns, cars, aeroplanes, televisions, computers and cellular phones (and soccer!). The key to such technology may be science and therefore education and behind that modernity, but many surmise (correctly) that the rise of science is partly due to, and partly despite of Christianity.

Yet others have discerned the liberative and inclusive impulse of the Christian gospel. They understood the message better than the Western messengers ever did – slaves better than slave owners, the colonised better than their colonisers, Dalits better than English landlords, those who are gay better than those who are straight. But they may well wonder whether Christianity is really needed in order to maintain such an impulse. This is exacerbated by the bad press that churches often receive, by ecclesial hierarchies, its patriarchal leadership, its alignment with political power, its oppressive teachings on contraception, abortion, HIV, sexual orientation and so forth. Yet, it is also true that many have embraced Christianity deeply as a source of resilience and

---

24   For this comment, see David J. Bosch, Transforming Mission: Paradigm Shifts in Theology of Mission (Maryknoll: Orbis Books, 1991), 384.
25   See Ernst M. Conradie & Hilda P. Koster (eds), The T&T Clark Handbook of Christian theology and climate change (London: T&T Clark, forthcoming).
26   See Ernst M. Conradie, Christianity and a Critique of Consumerism: A Survey of Six Points of Entry (Wellington: Bible Media, 2009).

sustenance and find themselves bewildered when confronted with contemporary challenges. One example is the covenantal promise, symbolised by God's rainbow, that the earth will never again be destroyed through water – that poses an existential crisis of faith for Christians in Kiribati and Tuvalu.[27]

Vision and Discernment

Does, Christianity, then, have any distinctive constructive contribution to offer in collaborative, multi-disciplinary efforts in public forums to address escalating ecological concerns? The question marks in the last sentence and in the title of this contribution signal that the answer should not be taken for granted and that the content of any such answer will necessarily be contested. The priority may need to remain with the dual critique rather than with the dual constructive contributions. I will nevertheless proceed to offer some reflections on the latter. My reflections are shaped by the form of prophetic Kairos theology emerging in South Africa in the 1980s with specific reference to the Belhar Confession (1982/1986),[28] the Kairos Document (1985/1986), the Road to Damascus (1989) and later the Accra Confession (2004). Common to these documents is the recognition of the difference between chronos and kairos,[29] between the ongoing (priestly) tasks of "doing theology" and the prophetic possibility of a moment of crisis where the truth of the gospel is at stake.

The former (priestly) task is necessary in order to keep alive a liturgical vision of the world.[30] Worshippers enter the Christian liturgy with the burdens of the world on their shoulders, as sinners and as being-sinned against, with all their natural theologies, ideologies, idolatries and heresies. They bring with them views and analyses of the world around them and its dominant powers. It is money that makes the world go round; it is the rich, strong, famous, dexterous and beautiful who rule the world. They come with "warped" views of the world[31] as "oh so beautiful" (romanticism), as "red in tooth and claw" (social Darwinism), as natural resources available for exploitation (capitalism), as something so sublime that it is to be worshipped (New Age mysticism), or as a threat to be tamed and brought under human control (ecomodernism). Through the liturgy worshippers may slowly learn to see the world in a new light, in the light of the Light of the world. They may begin to see the world around them through God's eyes, as God's beloved creation, that this messed-up world and the messed-up lives in and around them are nevertheless beloved, so much that for God it is even worth dying for.[32] They may learn to see the invisible, an

---

27   I was first alerted to this in conversation with Clive Pearson and have since picked this up in numerous further conversations, most recently with Upolu Vaai (Pacific Theological College).

28   See especially Daan Cloete & Dirk. J. Smit (eds), A Moment of Truth: The Confession of the Dutch Reformed Mission Church, 1982 (Grand Rapids: WB Eerdmans, 1984).

29   One excellent discussion is by Albert Nolan, "Theology in a Prophetic Mode", in Buti Thlagale & Itumeleng Mosala (eds), Hammering Swords into Ploughshares (Johannesburg: Skotaville Publishers, 1986), 131-140.

30   I developed this more fully in Chapter 2 of The Earth in God's Economy, especially building on the work of Gordon Lathrop, Holy Ground: A Liturgical Cosmology (Minneapolis: Fortress Press, 2003).

31   See Howard A. Snyder, Salvation Means Creation Healed: The Ecology of Sin and Grace (Eugene: Cascade Books, 2011).

32   See the comment by Douglas John Hall: "This world, for all its pain and anguish of spirit, in spite of its injustice and cruelty, the deadly competition of the species and their never wholly successful struggle to survive – this world is the world for which God has offered up his 'only begotten Son'." In The Steward: A Biblical Model Come of Age (Grand Rapids: WB Eerdmans, 1990), 120.

Ernst M. Conradie

intuition deeply embedded in Hebrew, Greek and African sensibilities. They may begin to see the earth in the light of "heaven", in terms of what may become and in a hidden way already is.

This is a deeply counter-intuitive vision. For those with little power in society it may require long services to retrain their eyes, to see that it is really love that makes the world go round, that God's love works through the vulnerability of the cross. For those in positions of power it may take even longer to see that, but they often don't have time for that. Seeing things differently does make a world of difference. In Desmond Tutu's vision, it means to see the beggar as one's brother, the prostitute as one's sister, the rapist as one's uncle.[33] For me it means to see the Dutch Reformed Church in which I grew up, the church that called for and legitimised apartheid, as my mother, even though she is a whore.[34] When believers exit from the liturgy with God's blessing, they are inspired by the vision that a different world is not only possible but has already been established, even though it remains hidden. The "liturgy after the liturgy" enables them to transform the world according to the core identity and characteristics of the Triune God, namely mercy and therefore justice.

Discourse on Christian eco-theology, sustainability, environmental ethics, climate justice and so forth need to attend to many such ongoing (priestly) tasks and arcane disciplines. We need to read and reinterpret biblical texts with an ecological hermeneutics, and we need to recover some and critique other stories from the history (his-story) of Christianity. We need to engage critically with the content and significance of the Christian faith. We need to explore common ethical categories such as justice, rights, duties, responsibilities, values and virtues, what is good and what is right. We need to engage in critical reflection on ecclesial praxis (liturgies, preaching, eco-congregations, pastoral care, ministries, etc). And we need to reflect on God's mission in the world, also in seeking common ground through dialogue with other living faiths. Again, this is both a matter of "ecclesiology" and of "ethics". All of these are necessary tasks to keep the vision alive. In this sense Christian discourse on sustainability not only needs to be sustained (in the imperative) but in another sense also sustains (in the indicative) the daily praxis of Christian communities and the vocations of Christians in society. These tasks can best be sustained by the recognition that it is God's mercy that nourishes and sustains us forever.[35]

The latter (prophetic) task is not always present but needs to be recognised when appropriate.

This requires a dialectic between vision and discernment.[36] I suggest that this typically requires 1) a discernment of the "signs of the time" (if you like the symptoms of the underlying disease), 2) a prophetic critique against ruling powers but also against heresies (a diagnostics of the root causes of the disease),[37] 3) seeking to discern the counter-movements of God's Spirit in

---

33 This is not a direct quotation but builds on Tutu's typical sayings. See for example Desmond M. Tutu, God has a Dream: A Vision of Hope for our Time (New York: Double Day, 2005).

34 I first heard this pertinent comment from a friend Fanie Herholdt but in an inverse form: "The Dutch Reformed Church is a whore, but she is my mother."

35 See Ernst M. Conradie "Is it not God's Mercy That Nourishes and Sustains Us ... Forever? Some Theological Perspectives on Entangled Sustainabilities", Scriptura 116 (2017), 38-54.

36 This is how Charles Wood uses the term "vision", i.e. to indicate a synoptic understanding of a range of data, a grasp of things in their wholeness and relatedness, a seeing of connections. He contrasts this with the need for discernment, i.e. to gain insight into particular situations in their particularity, to appreciate differences, to distinguish. In this way he seeks to overcome misperceptions regarding the relationship between theory and praxis. He argues that vision and discernment are dialectically related. There is no vision without discernment and no discernment without vision. See Wood, Vision and Discernment: An Orientation in Theological Study (Atlanta: Scholars Press, 1985), 67-76.

order to know and follow God's will (the remediating work of God to address what is wrong),[38] 4) to tell, through Christian witness and theological reflection, the story of God's work moving in that direction, and 5) the expression of a prophetic vision of what the world could be and should be like as a critical comment on how the world now is. Indeed, it is this vision (step 5) that enables a recognition of the signs of the time (step 1) – so that this prompts an ongoing spiral of theological reflection.

The fourth of these theological tasks is in my view crucial but also dangerous as any attempt to detect the "finger of God" in human history is fraught with the danger of legitimising narrow group interests. This has left behind a trail of blood and tears throughout the history of Christianity, not least in South Africa.[39] One may retort that there is only one thing that is more dangerous than raising this question of what God is doing – and that is failing to raise it at all. Let me dare to take up this task.

In a time like this … the Anthropocene

In inviting me to offer this contribution Dietrich Werner wrote, "The key question is what is the pastoral, the prophetic and the ethical task and mandate of Christian eco-theology in a context in which the world needs orientation and motivation to avoid a path towards self-destruction." I was intrigued by the question, since it is indeed clear that the world needs orientation and needs to avoid self-destruction. But can Christian eco-theology provide the vision required?

My current work on the ethics of the Anthropocene in the light of Christian discourse on sin confronts me with the truly apocalyptic images found in secular literature related to runaway climate change, tipping points, the collapse of biodiversity, ocean acidification and so forth. These images are of course found in literature, poetry, cartoons and especially films, too, but remarkably also in scientific reports. The images typically confront us with the multiple symptoms and recognising these is crucial to discern the signs of the times. But how should the underlying disease be diagnosed?

One interesting example is the booklet by Naomi Oreskes and Erik Conway, The Collapse of Western Civilization: A View from the Future.[40] They position themselves in the Second People's Republic of China in the year 2393. This is the 300th commemoration of the collapse of the West-

---

37   See my proposal that Christian sin-talk may be regarded, at least from the outside, as a form of social diagnostics. This opens up the possibility of multi-disciplinary conversation on the root causes of ecological destruction since forms of diagnosis are also found in many other disciplines, not just medicine and psychology. Whether sin-talk can be retrieved in the public sphere on this basis requires a more detailed defense. See Conradie, Redeeming Sin? Social Diagnostics amid Ecological Destruction.

38   See Ernst M. Conradie, "What makes the World go Round? Some Reformed Perspectives on Pneumatology and Ecology", Journal of Reformed Theology 6 (2012), 294-305, building on the discussion on a "hermeneutics of nature" by Jürgen Moltmann in Sun of Righteousness, Arise: God's future for humanity and the Earth (Minneapolis: Fortress Press, 2010), 189-208.

39   This has always been an extremely dangerous question, as is well recognized by the South African theologian Jaap Durand in an essay on 'the finger of God' in history, with reference to apartheid theology. See Jaap Durand, 'God in History: An Unresolved problem' in The Meaning of History, Adrio König and Marie Henri Keane (eds) (Pretoria: Unisa, 1980), 171-78.

40   Naomi Oreskes and Erik Conway, The Collapse of Western Civilization: A View from the Future (New York: Columbia University Press, 2014).

Ernst M. Conradie

Antarctic ice sheet in 2093. This led to widespread devastation, the collapse of the global economy and, for example, to the depopulation of Africa. They are tasked to reflect on the question of what went wrong so that people failed to do what was in hindsight so obviously necessary to avoid that crisis. Their conclusion is that the crucial failures could be located in decision making processes at the macro and micro levels in the first few decades of the 21st century. This is therefore a history of the contemporary period from the perspective of the distant future. The decision making processes can be concentrated on two variables, namely the date when carbon emissions peaked and how rapidly such carbon emissions declined after that. This required a transformation of the energy basis of the global economic order from fossil fuels to sustainable alternatives. Since this did not happen timeously, the catastrophe of 2093 became inevitable.

How, then, do we tell the story of our times? What genre is appropriate? This depends on discerning the signs of the time, recognising the symptoms in order to diagnose the underlying disease. A sense of realism requires from us to extrapolate current trajectories. It is indeed unlikely that sufficient political will can be mustered timeously to make drastic cuts in carbon emissions, despite activist campaigns, many good intentions, ample scientific reports and regular Conferences of the Parties. Catastrophic climate change is now virtually certain, declared Clive Hamilton in Requiem for a Species.[41] It is only the degree of catastrophe that can still be engaged with. The truth is that the endless climate negotiations resemble a form of high-stakes gambling in which "catastrophe" is the card that is expected to trump all others.[42] It is the denial of the magnitude and gravity of the situation, more than the biogeophysical trends themselves, that render an "apocalypse" plausible. It is the failure to act upon knowledge that is widely available that is startling.[43] Worse: it is evident that the self-evident character of the threat will not make us change our ways.[44] It is the bourgeois belief in the regularity of the world, that things will always be more or less what they are now, that has inbred a complacency, a madness, a derangement, one that means that large numbers of people will fail to respond despite dire warnings.[45]

One is inclined to say that, as long as life prevails, it can never be "too late" for those alive to make changes and to believe that such changes may and will affect future outcomes. At the same time it is possible to discern when it is indeed too late to achieve particular outcomes or to prevent others. The image often used in literature on climate change is that of peddling a boat in a river just above a waterfall. At some point it can become too late to prevent the boat from going down the waterfall.[46] Often such discernment has also come too late. If alarmist positions may be problematic, so can lukewarm timidity when it over-emphasises uncertainties, downplays risks and defends the prevailing social order against policies that may threaten it.[47] Or, to switch

41   Clive Hamilton, Requiem for a Species: Why We Resist the Truth about Climate Change (London & New York: Routledge, 2015), xiv.
42   Amitav Ghosh, The Great Derangement: Climate Change and the Unthinkable (Chicago: University of Chicago Press, 2016), 149, almost verbatim.
43   In the haunting words of Oreskes and Conway: "While analysts differ on the details, virtually all agree that the people of Western civilization knew what was happening to them but were unable to stop it. Indeed the most startling aspect of the story is just how much these people knew, yet how little they acted upon what they knew." See The Collapse of Western Civilization, 1-2.
44   As noted by Bruno Latour, in Facing Gaia: Eight Lectures on the New Climate Regime (Cambridge: Polity Press, 2017), 73.
45   This is the basic thesis of novelist Amitav Ghosh in The Great Derangement, 36.
46   Will Steffen et al, Global Change and the Earth System: A Planet under Pressure (Berlin: Springer, 2004), 294.

metaphors, Rome may not be burning but Greenland is melting and we may still find ourselves fiddling.[48]

In the history of the Jewish-Christian tradition there are especially three cases where such discernment was required. The prophet Jeremiah recognized that it was too late to prevent the fall of the city of Jerusalem to the Babylonian empire – which happened in 587 BCE – and placed his hope on a God who will start anew. Jesus of Nazareth predicted that Jerusalem will fall again – which happened a generation later in 70 CE due to Roman conquest – and placed his hope in the coming kingdom of heaven. Augustine of Hippo saw the Roman Empire crumbling – and placed his hope in the "City of God".

Following such imagery, the question is therefore whether we are living in such times, in a period before the fall of "Jerusalem".[49] If so, there is a need to realise that the "fall" of the "walls" of Jerusalem (whatever that may mean but Wall Street does come to mind) has become inevitable and then place one's hope not in mere survival but elsewhere, in a vision of a society that may emerge from the ruins of "Jerusalem" after a lifetime of "exile". The so-called "fallist" movement amongst tertiary students in South Africa ("Rhodes must fall!"; "Fees must fall!"; "Zuma must fall!", etc.), indicates that the hope (not the fear!) for the fall of "Jerusalem" may be a vibrant and indeed a militant one. It is the hope for the end of an unjust order.

The task of Christian eco-theology cannot be to scare people with apocalyptic imagery, not least because this is often done for entertainment and hardly ever inspires appropriate responses. The mantle for using apocalyptic imagery has been bestowed on filmmakers, even though they hardly appreciate the pastoral function of such apocalyptic imagery, namely to offer consolation to the victims of Empire: the destructive power of the powerful will not last forever since there is a different power at work in the world, the power of love.[50] There may again emerge a need for coded language to overcome surveillance by the state and in order to encourage those who have gone underground to resist such powers – but that time has not come yet.

Instead, there is a crucial constructive task for eco-theology that is hardly being addressed, namely to reflect on the question what God is doing (if anything!?) in a time like this. In the context of climate change it would amount to a failure of nerve not to address the underlying question that those listening to the story will have: What is God doing now? What is God up to, given

---

47 See Clive Hamilton, Earthmasters: The Dawn of the Age of Climate Engineering (New Haven: Yale University Press, 2013), 112.

48 See Oreskes & Conway, Merchants of Doubt, 265, almost verbatim.

49 To make this more provocative (and playful), it may be helpful to explore biblical analogies to interpret the present moment (kairos). South African theologians have been tempted to do so in changing circumstances. Accordingly, some have likened specific periods to the house of slavery in Egypt, the wandering through the wilderness, the conquest of Canaan, the unruly time of the judges, the establishment of new forms of governance, etc. In each case such comparisons are facile if not dangerous but still symbolically highly effective. In a document published by the South African Council of Churches in 2009 the analogy with the reforms under king Josiah was explored – in a time before it is too late. See South African Council of Churches, Climate Change Committee, Climate Change – A Challenge to the Churches in South Africa (Marshalltown: SACC, 2009). Ten years later some are wondering whether our time is not closer to the experiences of Jeremiah – where the fall of Jerusalem has become inevitable and when he had to place his hope elsewhere. If not, if this may become a self-fulfilling prophecy (as Jeremiah's critics also maintained), how should we interpret our times?

50 See Ernst Conradie, "Appropriate Contemporary Forms of Apocalyptic", in Hille Haker, André Torres Queiruga & Marie-Theres Wacker (eds), The Return of Apocalypticism, Concilium 2014/3, 96-103. See also the many contributions by Barbara Rossing in this regard, including The Rapture Exposed: The Message of Hope in the Book of Revelation (Boulder: Westview Press, 2004).

Ernst M. Conradie

what we know already about climate change? Where can signs of God's presence and creative engagement with the world be found (vestigia Dei)?[51] This requires much theoretical work on notions/images/constructs/models of God[52] and on making sense of any form of divine action in the world.[53] On both of these there is already a sizable literature.

The haunting question then remains: what is God really up to? In the context of climate change, in particular, this is a question filled with anxiety: this message of salvation is confronted by a world clearly in need of salvation, but it may seem that the message itself needs to be salvaged. In a recent essay entitled "The story of God's work: An open-ended narrative" for the forth- coming T.&T. Clark Handbook on Christian Theology and Climate Change I tried to articulate various options for a response to this question instead of offering any affirmative answers. It may help to simply repeat the contrasting possibilities here for the sake of provocation and discussion:

– God is waiting upon humans to change their hearts, habits and minds through mass-religious awakenings. Like in the days of Noah and after the Babylonian exile, there will be a severe crisis, but God promises to save a small remnant through a miracle that will revert global warming, e.g. a series of volcanic eruptions, changes in the ocean currents, cooling off Europe, perhaps introducing a new ice age. Thus God will create a new humanity, one that has acquired a revised set of virtues.

– No mass conversion and no such miracle are to be expected. Instead, God is punishing the world's human population for their folly through a deadly plague that will wipe out most of the population. This allows God to start again with a small remnant in the 22nd century. It may be expected that this will follow the pattern of the oasis of Eden and the expulsion into the desert, the destruction and rebuilding of Jerusalem, the exile and the return from exile. More pertinently, it will follow the dialectic of cross and resurrection, where all the followers of Jesus of Nazareth abandoned him but learned to follow the Way of the cross, inspired by the Spirit at Pentecost.

– God is asking us to do our best to help address climate change through mitigation and adaption efforts and especially to show solidarity with those struggling to cope with the adverse effects of climate change. We should not seek any higher purpose but live our lives before God in God's world as long as that may last – etsi Deus non daretur.

– This is way too timid. As secular commentators agree, only mass social movements can save us now from self-destruction. The current global economic system, based on profi-teering through mass production and mass consumption, is self-destructive. Only religion can provide the counter-vailing moral vision, moral energy and moral leadership to inspire to resist industrialized capitalism. Indeed, a green conversion within Christianity is crucial, precisely given its historical impact. This is what the Triune God is calling for.

– God is asking humans to exercise responsible stewardship of God's good creation. We hu-mans have been entrusted a habitable planet and are the heirs of the rich heritage be-stowed on us through the Jewish-Christian-Muslim tradition. We are now called to safe-guard human civilization (in every of its major forms) and should utilise the technologies

51   See again Moltmann, Sun of Righteousness, Arise.
52   Amongst many other examples the oeuvre of Sallie McFague may be mentioned. See already her Models of God. Theology for an Ecological Nuclear Age (Philadelphia: Fortress, 1987).
53   See, especially, Robert John Russell, Nancey Murphy and William R. Stoeger, Scientific Perspectives on Divine Action: Twenty Years of Challenge and Progress (Berkeley: Center for Theology and the Natural Sciences / Vatican City: Vatican Observatory Publications, 2008).

available to adjust the earth's thermostat through geoengineering. We need to attend to our God-given duty to rule over the earth. This is God's command, for us, today.

- It is now clear, more than ever before, that God is not really the God of the poor, oppressed and marginalized. It is not the meek who will inherit the earth. God is favouring the brave and the clever and will help them to re-engineer themselves in order to escape from a doomed earth through colonizing other habitable planets.
- God is clearly not really concerned about the world after all. What is ultimately important is the salvation of the soul, becoming one with Absolute Spirit more than discerning the movement of the Spirit, gaining Enlightenment more than understanding the physical properties of light. Gnostic forms of Christianity understood God better than those who focus on what is material, bodily and earthly – that are subject to decay and futility anyway. The Anthropocene confirms that God is abandoning the Earth and invites those truly enlightened to escape from this earthly vale of tears. The first step may be to move from carbon-based to silicon-based intelligence.
- God has decided to abandon the covenant with Noah and will allow the human species to become extinct; but like in the past God will start again to renew God's creation with previously despised species such as rats and cockroaches taking the lead. This is after all just punishment for irresponsible human destruction.

Remarkably, God-language is not required to raise these questions or to express these options. They arise no matter how secular one's orientation may be. Needless to say that none of these are really attractive but it does at least raise the question what other answers one would wish to contemplate. To refrain from addressing this question may well be to admit that God is not doing anything (or perhaps is doing something by doing nothing?). This prompts questions not merely about God's existence but also about the identity and character of this God. It is not as if one first needs to provide an account of the plausibility of God-talk and the very notion of a divine being before such questions can be addressed, as if it is possible to outline a generic notion of "God", if this is indeed the best English term to use for something like the ultimate mystery of the world.[54] None of the options above seems to be commensurate with the character of the God of both mercy and justice whom Christians have encountered in Jesus Christ.

Christians do not believe in God for the sake of believing in any available god. From the biblical roots of the Christian tradition it seems (to me) unlikely that some form of dramatic divine intervention is to be expected that would miraculously avert a climate catastrophe. Despite the vehement cry from the crucified Christ that his Father has abandoned him, the Father did not intervene. This non-intervention made room for the slow power of God's Spirit to transform all things. It is unlikely that this is the message a world in need of salvation from self-destruction would wish to hear. The urgency of the crisis prompts more frenetic responses. Is this gospel then good news? This depends upon the way the story of God's work in the world is told by Christian witnesses. Can this story change this world?

This story can evidently be told in many different ways.[55] It can also be messed up in many different ways. One crucial aspect of this story is that it is open-ended; we are telling the story as we

---

54 The two terms that are most widely used in English to translate Yahweh, Elohim and Theos in the biblical roots of Christianity are "Lord" (no comment!) and "God". The etymological roots of the latter are contested but may perhaps be traced to the proto-Germanic guthan, which is also the source of the Dutch god, the German Gott, the Old Norse guð, and the Gothic guþ). The Online Etymology Dictionary suggests that ghutan may be derived from the Proto-Indo-European "ghut-", meaning "that which is invoked" – a sense of awe. See https://www.etymonline.com/word/god (accessed 20 January 2019).

Ernst M. Conradie

are participating within it, with a sense of what has happened in the past, in order to make sense of the present in anticipation of what the future may hold. Story tellers need to hold listeners in suspense, but of course they do not really know the answer either. Yet, if we literally have no clue, we can hardly keep telling the story and should not be surprised if no-one is listening any longer and if many others tell a different story without reference to the Triune God, if not without a whole array of new divinities, demons and monsters. Novelists, film- makers, poets and cartoonists seem perfectly capable of taking over the role of telling the story of where things are going and they do so in rather graphic imagery. There is also the postmodern claim that "history" does not exist, that there is no grand all-encompassing narrative guaran- teeing a sense of history in terms of meaning or direction. If so, not only the "end of history" is to be announced; there never has been any history. But even if there is no history, perhaps there can at least be a story, or stories?

For Christian theology the question then remains: Can this story still be held together as one narrative or are there not only different versions of the story, but also different stories and indeed different gods? For Christians the different versions of the story, the different perspectives from which it may be told, need not be of any concern. They have learned to tell the story from at least three perspectives embedded in the confession of trust in God as Triune. What God did in the time of Moses is not the same as in the time of David, Jeremiah, Jesus or Paul. It may well be that what God is doing in the global North is different from what God is doing in the global South. The story is not only still open-ended; we can only tell it in fragments, over many Arabian nights and then with the awareness that a focus on any one episode may distort the others. Even then, the biblical canon suggests that it is important to see the stories as intertwined with each other. We need to gather together the fragments. At best, the Christian story offers a counter-intuitive liturgical redescription of the universe story, including the story of life (and death) on earth.

Telling the story

In my view one of the crucial tasks of Christian eco-theology is therefore to find coherent ways (plural) of telling the story of God's work in the world. This requires a juggling act in which at least seven "chapters" of the story are kept alive, namely 1) creation in the beginning, 2) on-going creation throughout evolutionary history, 3) the emergence of humanity, its rise and fall, 4) providence (common grace), 5) the particular history of salvation, 6) the formation of the church, its upbuilding, ministries and missions and 7) the consummation of God's work. One crucial problem is how to do justice to God's work of creation and salvation.[56] Another is

---

55   At a recent workshop on the South African Truth and Reconciliation Commission hosted at UWC I was reminded by the different stories that are constructed on land in South Africa. For some this is a story of settler colonialism where land was stolen and simply needs to be given back. Justice demands that there can be no possibility for reconciliation. For others (colonisers) the land was "empty" and available for occupation and exploitation. It is a matter of the survival of the fittest; those with guns and entrepreneurship may rule the world. Likewise, for some (like Steven Pinker) this is a story of Enlightenment and its many material and cultural benefits that have to be spread throughout the world – and are readily adopted by people in Africa in their own interest. One may also argue that some Africans left Africa more than 50 000 years ago, exterminated the Neanderthals, killed off megafauna everywhere – and that some returned more recently thinking that this land also belongs to them. From these versions of the story it is clear how difficult it may be to maintain that it is somehow destiny that brought South Africans together and that they need to become reconciled with each other in order to live together and enjoy each other's company. This is hardly possible amidst current levels of inequality.

to explain whether consummation implies restoration (Reformed), elevation (Roman Catholic), divinisation (Orthodox), replacement (Anabaptist) or recycling (liberalism). There are deep confessional divides here so that this task can only be addressed ecumenically. The task of the juggler is not so much to decide with which cone to start but to keep all the cones in the air. To privilege one is to let the others fall.

In years to come I hope to contribute to ecumenical collaboration in addressing this task through a series of twelve edited volumes with contributions from the global South and the global North, the West and the East, involving senior scholars and emerging voices. My hope is that if such a juggling act can be maintained, the seven chapters together may offer an interpretative lens through which the story of our times may be told.

---

56 For a more detailed discussion, see my Saving the Earth? The Legacy of Reformed Views on "Recreation" (Berlin: LIT Verlag, 2013); and chapter 5 of The Earth in God's Economy.

Ernst M. Conradie

ECO-THEOLOGY – ELEMENTS OF THE LEARNING JOURNEY IN THE ECUMENICAL MOVEMENT

Wuppertal Lecture

Dietrich Werner

1. Eco-Theology – Elements of the Learning Journey in the Ecumenical Movement

1.1 The neglect and the discovery of the ecological dimension in the ecumenical movement
The ecumenical movement grew as a renewal movement for the social witness of the churches and their unity in the shadow of two devastating world wars in the 20th century. Its major focus in its beginning period in the 20th century was reclaiming the Lordship of Christ over against both the church and the world as the world of nations was in a state of complete disorder and chaos in this period: The phase after the First and the Second World had underlined how much nationalism, denominational disunity and ethnocentrism could lead to devastation within the global community and in each national state. Thus in this period the reordering the life of societies and of the relations between nations was a major concern, not so much the harmony between humankind and nature. The theme of the first Ecumenical Assembly Amsterdam in 1948, "Man's Disorder and God's Design", was reflected in terms of the relations between nations, people and denominations. Discovering the unity of both the churches and the unity of humankind after a period of devastating wars was at the heart of the ecumenical vision unfolded; relations between humankind with nature did not present a major focus yet in the period of the foundational years of the ecumenical movement. One can therefore argue that by and large the early ecumenical movement – at least before 1961 –remained within the framework of a mainly anthropocentric perception of Christology and Ecclesiology and also moved towards a predominantly positive appreciation of the role of science and technology in modernity which were seen as liberative forces after decades of destruction.

The classical criticism of the American historian Lynn White Jr.[1] that western Christianity to a large extend has remained uncritical to the expansionist and domination oriented attitudes of Western culture towards both nature and indigenous people during the colonial and industrialization periods, that it got married with secularist world views too easily and therefore Judeo-Christian civilization is the root of the ecological crisis, can be regarded as of critical relevance also for some major trends in the first phase of the ecumenical movement in the 20th century until the 60ies.

However, there were a few incidents already in the early period of ecumenical discourse in the period of the fifties which reflected an early hint towards the need for a creation theology as forming an essential part of a "theology of the world", which was a major focus of the early ecu-

---

1 White, Lynn Townsend, Jr. "The Historical Roots of our Ecological Crisis." Science 155 (10 March 1967): 1203-1207.

menical discourse on nature and history. It was affirmed for instance during the WCC assembly in Evanston 1954 that "this world, disfigured and distorted as it is, is still God's world. It is his creation, in which he is at work, and which he sustains in being until the day when the glory of his new creation will fully appear."[2]

The discovery of ecology as an integral dimension of ecumenism came about in the 60ies as a result of three factors:

a) the influence of orthodoxy and its cosmocentric ecclesiology/pneumatology,
b) the beginning dialogue between faith and natural science and
c) the insights of modern biblical scholarship on the creation narratives and modern schools of thought (like process theology).

During the New Delhi assembly 1961 the debate on the relation between nature and grace brought about challenging remarks by Joseph Sittler, arguing that a new kind of ecumenical theology is required which should focus not only on the relationship between salvation and human history, but also on salvation and nature (discussing aspects of the cosmological tradition of Christology in the New Testament tradition, based on Kol 1,15-20).[3]

The Orthodox theologian Paul Evdokimov in 1964 in a Faith and Order conference continued this line in unfolding an ecclesiology of love with and for the whole of creation ("a human heart which is full of compassion for the smallest pain which is inflicted to any created being in God's cosmos").[4]

The Uppsala assembly in 1968 with its theme "Behold, I make all things new" affirmed a dynamic understanding of God's presence and work in the whole of creation: "The living God is the creative force within everything that is constantly renewing all things."[5]

The Church and Society conference 1970 in Geneva, two years before the Club of Rome Report "Limits to Growth"(1972) , under the title "The future of Humanum in a scientific-technical world" for the first time in ecumenical history articulated the tension between ecology, human progress and development and demanded for a "global policy of environmental protection" (Frederick H. Knelmann, Montreal, and Ernst von Weizsäcker, Carlson Blake).[6]

1.2 The birth of the ecological concept of sustainability

It should not be forgotten easily that the ecumenical discourse of church representatives, scientists and concerned environmentalists gave birth to the global concept of sustainability some years significantly before the UN conference on Environment and Development in Rio in 1992: It was the Bukarest Conference in 1974 on the "Role of Science, Technology for Human Development"[7] which offered the birth place of the ecumenical concept of Sustainability (almost 20 years before

---

2   Evanston Assembly 1954, Report on „Christians in the Struggle for World Community", in: Art. "Creation", in: Dictionary of the Ecumenical Movement, (Nicolas Lossky a.o. eds), WCC, Geneva 2002, p. 271; also: Walter William van Kirk: International Affairs – Christians in the Struggle for World Community, in: Ecumenical Review, Volume7, Issue1, October 1954, p. 42-48.
3   Steven Bouma-Prediger, Peter Baken (eds): Evocations of Grace. The Writings of Joseph Sittler on Ecology, Theology and Ethics. William Eerdmanns, Grand Rapids, 2000.
4   See also: Paul Evdokimov: The Sacrament of Love, St Vladimirs Seminary Pr, 2011.
5   The Uppsala report 1968: official report of the Fourth Assembly of the World Council of Churches, Uppsala July 4-20, 1968, WCC, Geneva 1968.
6   See: Church and Society From Here to Where? Technology, Faith and the Future of Man. Report on an Exploratory Conference, Geneva, 28 June-4 July 1970. Ed. by David Gill, Geneva, WCC 1970.
7   Search for a Just and Sustainable Society: WCC Conference on Science and Technology for Human Development, Bucharest, Romania, 24 June –2 July 1974, WCC, 1974.

UN Rio Conference!).[8] Sustainability at this stage was described as a pattern of development in which environmental pollution is kept well under the capacities of the eco-system to absorb pollution; in which utilization of non-renewable energy resources is lower than what can be made available as new resources; human activities are to be held within the boundaries of natural climate conditions.[9]

It was both before, during and after the assembly in Nairobi 1975, that the voice of the Australian biologist Charles Birch was prominent in promoting new viewpoints of sustainability: He specifically argued that ecological liberation is not a distraction from the social liberation of the poor, but both belong together and are integrally linked with each other. His work was closely related also to processes leading to the famous MIT conference 1979 on Faith, Science and the Future in which 900 leading ethicists and scientists were participating. [10]

The Nairobi Assembly in 1975 articulated the concept of "just, participatory and sustainable society" (JPSS) which was a response to the growing recognition of the persistence of poverty and misery and at the same time of the limits of and threats to the earth's capacity to sustain human life.[11] Unfortunately, the WCC central committee decided in 1979 not to accept the findings of the JPSS advisory committee due to doctrinal and ethical controversies between some church delegations.[12]

It were the follow up of the Nairobi conference and the preparations for the MIT conference 1979 in the GDR churches which led to the formation of an independent ecological movement in East Germany which still was under socialist and atheist rule (meetings in Luckow and Erfurt, Heino Falcke and others), which –in interconnection with other factors –paved the way for peaceful civil society revolution and the overthrow of the Socialist government at the end of the 80ies (1989 Fall of Berlin Wall) – an indication of the tremendous significance of the conciliar process for really making a lasting impact of the current world order at that stage and therefore not being in vain.[13]

1.3 The birth of the conciliar process for justice, peace and integrity of creation

The conciliar process for justice, peace and integrity of creation can be regarded as the major phase in which concepts of sustainability entered the mainstream of ecumenical social thinking, became an integral part of any conceptual thinking on justice and peace and also inspired a broad based ecumenical mass movement for something like a comprehensive socio-political transformation of economy and society. The history is well known: It was during the Vancouver assembly in 1983, that East German church delegates proposed the calling of a Genuine Universal Christian Council.

8   Vgl. Hans Joachim Döring: Sustainability und Ökumene, in: Brief zur Orientierung im Konflikt Mensch-Erde, Heft 54, 2000, S. 26-30, in: http://www.oekumenezentrum-ekm.de/attachment/97805e02a6bf11de99800bf9 f2dbda49da49/c1f6f928b90911de9472bb634039d34ed34e/sustainability.pdf.

9   See the key texts on the concept of a sustainable society in: Science and Technology for Human Development. The Ambiguous Future and the Christian Hope. Bucharest June 24-July2, 1974, in: Anticipation No 19, November 1974, p. 4ff, in German language in: Wolfram Stierle/Dietrich Werner/Martin Heider: Ethik für das Leben. 100 Jahre Ökumenische Wirtschaftsethik, Rothenburg 1996, S. 550ff.

10   See also: http://oikoumene.net/home/hostudies/gerecht.book/one.book/index.html?entry=page.book. 1.2.9.1

11   See also: Roger S. Gottlieb: The Oxford Handbook on Religion and Ecology, Oxford University Press 2006, p. 134ff; John B. Cobb, Jr.: Sustainability. Economy, Ecology and Justice. Wipf and Stock Eugene 1992, p. 84ff.

12   See: http://oikoumene.net/home/hostudies/gerecht.book/one.book/index.html? entry= page.book.1.2.9.

13   Stephen Brown: Nachhaltigkeit und die Umwelt: Wie die ökumenische Bewegung half, den Umweltprotest in der DDR zu mobilisieren, WCC 2015, in: https://www.oikoumene.org/de/press-centre/news/sustainability-and-environment-how-the-ecumenical-movement-helped-mobilize-ecology-protest-in-east-germany.

The WCC Central Committee then decided "to engage the member churches in a Conciliar Process of mutual commitment (covenant) to justice, peace and the integrity of creation" and that this project should be a priority for World Council programs. The foundation of this emphasis should be confessing Christ as the life of the world and Christian resistance to the demonic powers of death in racism, sexism, caste oppression, economic exploitation, militarism, violations of human rights, and the misuse of science and technology. Ecumenical study and action on the ecclesiological, spiritual, and socio-ethical implications of this commitment process should be organized.

Some further work on aspects of theology of creation within the conciliar process was done during major ecumenical consultations in Amsterdam 1987 and in Granvollen 1988: the notion of the "disintegration of creation" and the "need for reintegration God's creation" were spelled out and a critique was articulated of the senseless exploitation of the natural resources as a consequence of the unlimited human mastery over creation which for centuries had been justified also by Christian dominium terrae theologies.[14] This was a major phase in which new insights of pioneering eco-theologies were incorporated into the ecumenical discourse (Paul Evdokimov, Jürgen Moltmann, Douglas J. Hall).

At the same time the dynamic of the conciliar process did not remain to the academic theological discourse, on the contrary the framework of the conciliar process developed into a major platform on which political, social and ecological demands were jointly articulated by Christians for substantial reforms: The regional assemblies for JPIC (Stuttgart, Dresden, Assisi 1988) articulated key demands for ecological transformation of societies, culminating in the first European Ecumenical Assembly in in Basel (1989). This "EEA1" can be regarded as the first comprehensive ecumenical church assembly in European contexts since 1054 at all and articulated a pioneering vision for the renewal of Europe in the context of ecological sustainability: Basel even demanded for a "new ecological world order" and a dramatic reduction of energy consumption patterns in western societies, including the renunciation of the nuclear energy option – which until now was put into practice on a political level only by the German government.

1.4 Granvollen 1988: WCC consultation on integrity of creation

The theological conference of WCC in Granvollen, Norway, probably was one of the most productive and theologically creative consultations on eco-theology in the ecumenical history. "For the first time in any consistent manner, the documents (of Granvollen) demonstrated the church's readiness to consider the creation for its own sake and not only as the setting for the human drama".[15] Remarkable and worth recalling is also the list produced there of possible deviations and distortions which have hindered a comprehensive eco-theological approach in the life of the churches so far and need to be overcome in developing a holistic approach to a Trinitarian theology of creation. The Granvollen study Report highlights the following:

- Theological reductionism, based on an individualized and spiritualized conceptualization of salvation which tends to believe that everything will solve itself once people are converted;
- Natural science based, technological hybris assuming that the ecological crisis fundamentally is a technological problem to be solved with technological means only;
- Leaning towards a romantic reconceptualization of nature, assuming that a back to untouched nature and pre-technological life-styles will solve the problems of modernity;

---

14 See: Art. "Creation", Douglas John Hall, in: Dictionary of the Ecumenical Movement, WCC Geneva 2002, p. 274; also: D.J. Hall, Imaging God: dominion as Stewardship, Grand Rapids 1986 .
15 Douglas J. Hall, in: Art. Creation, in: Dictionary of the Ecumenical Movement, p. 274.

Dietrich Werner

- Resignation-based neo-apocalyptic perceptions which view the ecological crisis as pre-sign of the final end of this world to come soon for only the faithful to be rescued;
- Utopian temptations which project an ideal world without problems, perfectionist and ideal, without any temptations for sin and evil, jumping over the internal contradictions even within ecological life-styles;
- Fatalistic attitudes which articulate an attitude – whether in religious or in political rhetoric, that we cannot do anything as the world cannot be changed anymore;
- "Not my problem"-attitudes which perceive ecological issues as a challenge only for the industrialized countries or for a certain group of people, but not for oneself and one's own people.[16]

It would be worth looking more deeply into the root causes, weaknesses and detailed processes which led to the feature that the conciliar process for justice, peace and integrity of creation while unleashing a lot of potential and energy for articulating a new vision of sustainability in the long run did not maintain the strength to keep eco-theological concerns at the top priority level of the global ecumenical movement. However, the culmination of the conciliar process in the so-called Seoul convocation on JPIC in the year 1990 produced the first ever Ecumenical Social Creed of all Christian churches together. From the 10 Affirmations of the Seoul Convocation two focussed explicitly on Creation.[17] Conflicts and tensions continued between those in the ecumenical movement who would put integrity of creation first and those who argue that justice issues are the first priorities to be dealt with by ecumenical and development organizations. There were internal structural problems within the conciliar process: Considerable un-simultaneity of learning processes continued between the different regions of the world and different denominational environments. Sometimes there was a lack of clear follow up and monitoring mechanisms concerning implementation. The predominant focus on general statements with confessing language sometimes made it not easy to get churches engaged in concrete political objectives. A major global priorization of environmental policies as well as eco-theology and therefore direct historical link and continuation of the conciliar process has only come with the Encyclical of Pope Francis on Laudato Si in 2015.

However: Sometimes the success is even beyond what was deliberately planned for within ecumenical circles: It can well be argued that it was secularized versions and elements of the ecumenical discourses within the conciliar process which directly and indirectly inspired the later process at UN levels, which later led to the Rio Summit on Environment and Development in 1993, the Paris Global Climate Summit and subsequently the UN Agenda for sustainable development (2015).[18]

1.5 Ecumenical Accompaniment for the global climate change discourses
Shortly after the Seoul Convocation on the JPIC theme there was the Canberra assembly of the WCC in 1991 under the theme "Come Holy Spirit, Renew the whole creation": This was the first assembly with an overall ecological theme – a unique chance and tremendous challenge! As bush

---

16 A German version of these possible temptations and misleading theologies from the Granvollen Report can be found in: Wolfram Stierle/Dietrich Werner/Martin Heider: Ethik für das Leben. 100 Jahre Ökumenische Wirtschaftsethik, Rothenburg 1996, S. 539ff.

17 See for the whole context: Ernst Conradie: Christianity and Earthkeeping: In search of an inspiring vision, Sun Press Stellenbosch, 2011, page 72ff; see also: http://oikoumene.net/home/hostudies/gerecht.book/one.book/index.html?entry=page.book.1.5.1.

18 Beat Dietschy: Der konziliare Prozess und die Agenda für nachhaltige Entwicklung, in: Jahrbuch Diakonie Schweiz 1 (2017), S. 33ff.

fires were ravaging in eyesight from the assembly venue and the whole tragic story of the aborigines and the suppression of their harmonious ways of relating to nature in the processes of western colonization and conquest were in the air, the imperative to review classical doctrines of human mastery over nature and to move towards a comprehensive new eco-theological approach were quite strong. The reports of section I and II are still worth reading which produced strong results in terms of the eco-theological work in Canberra.[19] A key conviction which had been articulated already in Granvollen was taken up in Canberra and set the tone for a new understanding also of a life-centered economy which was gaining momentum within the ecumenical discourse: "Growth for growth's sake is the strategy of the cancer cell."[20]

Since the Canberra assembly also the political engagement in lobbying work towards global climate change issues took on a new urgency and priority: Since the WCC 1991 consultation on climate change in Gwatt a permanent climate change working group of WCC has accompanied all the international negotiations on climate change. Since the United Nations Framework Convention on Climate Change was adopted in 1992, the WCC was also present at all UN climate change conferences.

Highlights in the work after Canberra included the 1994 Johannesburg conference which produced the Study on "Accelerated Climate Change: Signs of Peril, Test of Faith"[21] as well as the David Hallmann Report on Climate Change for Porto Alegre which was produced as part of the Mandate for the Justice, peace and Creation Team at the 1998 Harare Assembly.[22]

6. Other fields of ecumenical engagement in eco-theology

The brief survey given here can only highlight general trends such as the observation that major engagement in the WCC in the 90ies was devoted to issues of climate change: This is also affirmed by the fact that after the III. European Ecumenical Assembly (EEAC III) in Sibiu in 2007, an intensification of the work of European Christian Environmental Network (ECEN), which was founded in 1998, took place. It could be critically asked to what extend other similar regional Christian Environmental Networks have followed and were founded in Asia, Africa and Latin-America. Perhaps this is a task to be considered by this Wuppertal conference.

However there were also other thematic fields which gained attention, if not with the similar attention and energy due to lack of staff and resources, so still these other fields were also gradually becoming more visible. Only recently therefore ecumenical commitments can be noted to other areas like the following:

– In 2007 the Johannesburg conference focused on issues of bio-technology and genetic engineering and for the first time made churches aware of the huge task of interrelating the discourses on technology and the discourses on justice as part of their public theology efforts.

---

19   See Canberra Report Section I and II, in: http://oikoumene.net/eng.home/eng.global/eng.canberra91/eng.canber.2/index.html.

20   Again quoted by Konrad Raiser: Adress to the UN Summit on Social Development Copenhagen 1995, in. Ec Rev 47 (1995), p. 385.

21   Accelerated Climate Change: Signs of Peril, Test of Faith 1994, in: The Church and Climate Change, EcRev 49 Vol. 2, April 1997.

22   See David G. Hallmann, The WCC Climate Change Programme. History, Lessons, Challenges, in: Climate Chance, WCC, 2005, in: https://www.oikoumene.org/en/resources/documents/wcc-programmes/justice-diakonia-and-responsibility-for-creation/climate-change-water/climate-change/@@download/file/Climate_Change_Brochure_2005.pdf.

Dietrich Werner

- Since 2006 (Porto Alegre) also major engagement unfolded in water issues, which lead to the Ecumenical Water Network, (EWN) as an expression also to make visible the churches engagement in the International Decade on "Water for Life" 2005-2015.[23]
- There was little engagement in the last decades on issues of bio-diversity, only a new statement was tabled at the WCC ExCom in May 2019 which highlighted the enormous challenges ahead in this area.[24]
- In 2016 a major ecumenical conference at the Volos Academy in Greece came up with the Volos Manifesto for a genuine "Ecological Reformation of Christianity": Radicalizing the Reformation tradition by calling for a twofold critique, namely both a deeper Christian critique of the root causes of ecological destruction and an ecological critique of forms of Christianity which have not recognized the ecological dimensions of the Gospel.[25]
- A lot could be reflected about how the conciliar process on justice, peace and integrity of creation which had three elements, including a strong emphasis on creation, was transformed and continued in 2013 Busan assembly into the ecumenical pilgrimage on justice and peace, which had only two elements, namely justice and peace.[26] However, the recent period in the ecumenical discourse in the last decade can tentatively also be marked positively by a growing convergence between ecumenical social ethics, ecumenical missiology and ecclesiology in terms of the recognition of the significance of a comprehensive cosmological or ecological approach to both unity, mission and prophetic service of the churches:

The International Ecumenical Peace Convocation in Kingston, Jamaica, (2011) was marking the Conclusion of the Decade to Overcome Violence, 2001–2010: The "Ecumenical Declaration on Just Peace" articulated a trinitarian understanding of peace, including "peace with the earth". In its statements one could read: "Violence as embedded in current processes of globalization is by no means limited to the human community, but it has become more clearly than ever before to what extent the environment, climate, and indeed the whole of God's creation are being affected and are suffering violence."[27] Thus the culmination of the Decade to Overcome Violence can be also regarded as the beginnings of an ecological just peace ethics.

Some similar transformations and positive trends can be observed in the ecumenical discourse on mission which has taken up the notion of an ecological or cosmocentric understanding of mission much more strongly. The Manila conference from 2012 in its new mission statement "Together Towards Life"[28] emphasized strongly: "Mission is the overflow of the infinite love of the Triune God. God's mission begins with the act of creation. Creation's life and God's life are entwined. The mission of God's Spirit encompasses us all in an ever-giving act of grace. We are

23 https://www.oikoumene.org/en/resources/documents/assembly/2006-porto-alegre/1-statements-documents-adopted/international-affairs/report-from-the-public-issues-committee/water-for-life.
24 https://www.oikoumene.org/en/press-centre/news/wcc-executive-committee-global-biodiversity-crisis-reaches-urgent-level.
25 https://www.globethics.net/-/ecotheology-conference-in-greece-and-manifesto; https://www.oikoumene.org/en/resources/documents/other-ecumenical-bodies/manifesto-on-an-ecological-reformation-of-all-christian-traditions.
26 See on this also: Fernando Enns, Behutsam Mitgehen mit Deinem Gott. Der ökumenische Pilgerweg der Gerechtigkeit und des Friedens als Neuausrichtung der ökumenischen Bewegung, in: https://wccpilgrimage.org/de/trittsteine/was-ist-ein-pilgerweg/materialien/wccpil grimagesite-app-staticdocument-1/@@images/file.
27 See on Kingston Jamaica: https://www.oikoumene.org/en/resources/publications/copy_of_JustPeaceCom panion2ndEd_SAMPLE.pdf.
28 https://www.oikoumene.org/en/resources/documents/commissions/mission-and-evangelism/together-towards-life-mission-and-evangelism-in-changing-landscapes.

therefore called to move beyond a narrowly human-centred approach and to embrace forms of mission which express our reconciled relationship with all created life."

Ethics of Sustainability – challenges in the global ecumenical debate on eco-theology

Looking back to a rich, divers and complex history of ecumenical discourses on eco-theology and ethics of sustainability which cannot fully present here, one cannot refrain also from arriving at certain overarching general critical questions, pointing to challenges, tensions and dilemmas the ecumenical movement has and had to wrestle with in coping with both a 2000 years of history of different Christian doctrines concerning the relation between humanity and nature as well as different languages applied and used in the different church traditions in current context. Critical questions pointing to these challenges can be articulated as follows:
– How is it possible to relate contextuality of eco-theological reflections with catholicity in ecumenical approaches to eco-theology, common global focus and targeted regional goals for joint lobbying work?
– How can the ecumenical movement and the churches engaged in it ensure comprehensiveness in eco-theological reflection with equal immersion in the different subject areas of eco-theological ethics as there are so many? (eco-theology and ecological ethics; ecology and economy for life; ecology and ecclesiology; ecology and genetic engineering; eco-ethics and earth system sciences; eco-ethics and issues of water, oceans and atmosphere; eco-ethics and nuclear energy and waste issues; eco-ethics and seeds in agriculture; eco-theology, spirituality, value-change and cultures; eco-ethics and population growth; eco-theological ethics and animal ethics; eco-ethics and agriculture/nutrition)
– How does it become possible and effective to relate the ecumenical witness of churches in areas of eco-theology and sustainability with the strategic lobbying activities of specialized ministries, namely of ACT Alliance?
– How has the ecumenical movement managed to relate major ecumenical Christian discourses both to secular UN discourses and also – which still is another issue – interfaith discourses in eco-ethics and sustainability studies? (like: Faith4Earth and UN -Environment processes; Great Transition Global Network of Global Scenario Group; Laudato Si Alliance: Protect the Earth – Dignify Humanity Initiative; World Future Council)?
These critical questions remain on the common agenda of this consultation as well as the discourse of those who want to shape the future impact of the eco-theological discourse in the ecumenical movement.

Apart from these general critical questions pointing to structural and thematic challenges we can summarize our reflections on the learning journey of the eco-theological discourse in the ecumenical movement in briefly pointing to
– Five common core convictions reached so far in the international ecumenical discourse on eco-theology (a)
– Five major shortcomings identified in the current global discourse on sustainability (b) and to
– Five urgent priorities for future ecumenical commitments in eco-theology and ethics of sustainability (c)

These short thesis-like propositions are offered here to stimulate common discussion and debate in the future ecumenical discourse:

a) Five common core convictions reached so far in the international ecumenical discourse on eco-theology
1) The earth is not just the property of human beings, but the mirror of God's glory.
2) The Christocentric focus of the ecumenical movement has been widened to a trinitarian and cosmological perspective.
3) An integrated ethics for life (ethics of sustainability) based on the interrelatedness of justice, peace and integrity of creation/care for creation is at the core of the ecumenical pilgrimage of justice and peace.
4) The unity of the church, unity of humankind and unity of all creation need to be seen as belonging together.
5) The misunderstandings of the traditional theology of the dominium terrae need to be overcome.

b) Five major shortcomings identified in the current global discourse on sustainability
1) There are contradictions between the economic goals and the ecological goals in the SDG Agenda from 2015: Which goals dominate the UN process?[29]
2) An alternative growth concept is still under –or ill-defined and indicators for growth measurement are politically not agreed: What kind of growth within the planetary boundaries do we want?[30]
3) A new definition of value and the implementation of the polluter pays principle is still lacking: What value do we pay for (market value, ecological value, cultural value)?
4) The reconciliation and integration between ecology and legislation is insufficient: Who cares and fights for the rights of nature? How to strengthen the strategic links between Ecology and Jurisprudence? How to get churches more visible engaged in the ongoing UN dialogues on Harmony with Nature?[31] How to mobilize for Earth Jurisprudence?[32]
5) Education for sustainability and health – Who prepares a broad revolution in ETCF education?[33]

c) Five urgent priorities for future ecumenical commitments in eco-theology and ethics of sustainability
1) The growing inter-generational and inter-contextual/regional conflicts around impacts of climate change: Who pays for ecological costs?
2) Assaults against the very fabric of biological live – genome-editing and patenting of seeds in

---

29   See Ernst Ulrich von Weizsäcker/Anders Wijkman u.a.: Bericht des Club of Rome 2018: „Wir sind dran. Was wir ändern müssen, wenn wir bleiben wollen", S. 90ff.
30   See for instance: Martin R. Stuchtey, Per-Anders Emkvist, Klaus Zumwinkel: A Good Disruption. Redefining Growth in the Twenty-First Century, Bloomsbury,. London 2016.
31   See the series of international dialogues since 2011: http://www.harmonywithnatureun.org/dialogues/.
32   See the debate on Earth Jurisprudence in the Global Alliance for the Rights of Nature (GARN), in: https://therightsofnature.org/principles-of-earth-jurisprudence/.
33   See: Dietrich Werner/Elisabeth Jeglitzka (eds): Eco-theology, Climate Justice and Food Security. Theological Education and Leadership Development. Globethics.net Geneva 2005, in: https://www.globethics.net/documents/4289936/13403236/GE_Global_14_web.pdf.

the name of agricultural productivity: Who decides on the extent to which science and technology manipulate the essence of creation?[34]

3) Threats against biodiversity on earth: Towards a theology of eco-responsible land use and waste disposal: How do we clean up toxic waste from the lands and the plastic from the oceans?

4) Digitization and acceleration of the loss of memory of the dignity and ecological integrity of life – the need for new narratives and rituals to sustain spiritual value change towards sustainability: How do we cope and reflect on the long-term consequences of the digital information revolution on both of the ecological and the psychological systems? Or to be put positively: Which narratives can still inspire, motivate and sustain a mass-conversion to sustainable lifestyles in times of apocalyptic trends?

5) How to break the circle of growing meat production, increasing health threats and environmental degradation? – Towards an ecological nutrition revolution: How to change what humans eat?[35]

Kairos for Creation – How to Mobilize People's Passion for the Planet?

In bringing this paper to a close we can only tentatively point to some directions and needs which underline the practical, strategic and conceptual nature of the Wuppertal conference which is mandated to make common suggestions on how to deepen and continue the ecumenical engagement in issues of eco-theology and ethics of sustainability in the years to come after the next WCC assembly. We are all sure that we need a re-priorization in the work of the churches and the ecumenical movement as the global climate change has become an undeniable global life risk challenge for the whole of humanity as well as the inhabited planet. Continuing business as usual will not do as we live in a global unprecedented and accelerating ecological crisis.

One of the first priorities this conference has to wrestle with is to find a common answer to the question: What is the key and main theological challenge in the context of the planetary ecological crisis?

How can we speak of the presence of God as Creator, Sustainer and Redeemer of the whole of the inhabited cosmos in the apocalyptic context of a manmade crisis of the earth's sustaining planetary ecological systems? What sources do we have of our common hope? Eco-theology which does not give hope, is not proper Christian creation theology. How to renew our sense of hope if we simultaneously listen to the ongoing promise of the biblical God, that the rhythms of summer and winter, frost and heat, sowing and harvest will never cease and at the same time listen to language of the climate scientists who argue that the very essence of the natural rhythms and balances which sustain live and its continuation on this planet is deeply disturbed?

We need to spell out what is the nature of the „Kairos for Creation" which we feel strongly has come at the beginning of the second decade of the 21st century as the window of opportunity in which we still have the chance of fundamentally changing the course of history and current rates of global warming is a rather short, limited one and time flees faster that we can imagine. We do

---

34 On the debate see: https://www.the-scientist.com/bio-business/companies-use-crispr-to-improve-crops-65362; and the campaign of Vandana Shiva: https://www.lifegate.com/people/lifestyle/monsanto-india-seed-patent-vandana.

35 See the debate for instance in: Meat Atlas – Facts on Figures about the animals we eat, Boell-Stiftung 2014, in: http://www.fao.org/fsnforum/resources/fsn-resources/meat-atlas.

Dietrich Werner

not just want to produce abstract doctrinal statements but we want to contribute to mobilizing People's Passion for the Planet in every continent of this precious world. We can do this only if we convincingly argue from a faith perspective making our distinct value the special asset we have to bring into the global discourses. We need to answer the question: What is the Basis of Hope in a Time of Despair?

Might be we should learn from the example of the tradition of various Kairos-Theology statements in various contexts during last years which actually have both a sound and critical analysis of the political and ideological context as well as a deep theological reflection and basis both to brought together organically: We could dream of a new Global Kairos for Creation Call or Document which could be formulated in some closeness or analogy to the South African Kairos Document from 1985.

It could spell out common and new eco-theological convictions in similar steps as applied to the South African Kairos Statement:

1) The Moment of Ecological Truth has come: It is important and a challenge today to both listening to the cries of the poor, listening to the cries of the earth as well as listening to the cries of the prophets (scientists) of today.

2) The Moment of Ecclesial and Ecumenical Truth has come: It is important and a challenge today hat the Global Church is divided in its ecological commitments, integrity and common goals and attitudes.

3) The Moment of Theological Truth has come: It is important and a challenge today to strengthen the discernment of three types of theology as there are also false prophets and theology or religion can be misused to justify scenarios which irreconcilable with the belief in God as Creator of all:

There are Conventional World theologies/theologies of excuse (market centred and business as usual theologies; relativization and cosmetic adaptation approaches, negating climate change theologies, anthropocentric domination theologies);

There seems to be Barbarization scenario and Break Down theologies (nationalist theologies of a fortress world; apocalyptic and escapist theologies of a breakdown and spiritualistic individual refuge of sectarian groups);

There are also different approaches to proper theologies of transformation towards a great transition to eco-communalism or new values of sustainability which the ecumenical movement has inspired in the past and should continue to inspire in the future.[36]

We will be able to provide motivation and orientation for people in reviving their passion for the planet, if we articulate the basis of hope in a time of despair in a way which addresses and spells out all the our key dimensions of a new ecumenical approach to eco-theology which have been articulated in the history of the ecumenical discourse outlined here:

- **The Prophetic dimension** of a new ecumenical eco-theological paradigm: de-constructing false religious and secular claims in the understanding of the role of humans in the whole of inhabited earth; announcing key values of a new ecological civilization in accordance with the Covenant of God with all Creation.

- **The Priestly dimension** of a new ecumenical eco-theological paradigm: dealing with the pastoral dimensions of providing energy and motivation for eco-social transformation today;

---

36   See on the Great Transition Scenarios approach: https://www.greattransition.org/.

- **The Kingly dimension** of a new ecumenical eco-theological paradigm: translating key ethical dimensions in a new system of legislation for nature and Earth Jurisprudence
- **The Wisdom dimension** of a new ecumenical eco-theological paradigm: Recollecting and harvesting indigenous and regional cultural elements of wisdom tradition for a new art of life within planetary boundaries and learning for sustainable life-styles from ancient Christian and pre-Christian wisdom traditions.

The distinct potential of such an international consultation on issues of eco-theology and ethics of sustainability is to enable churches and church-related agencies to learn from each other where and how engagement in eco-theology is needed and growing in different sectors of World Christianity. It is also to articulate a concern for more strategic planning for the future of eco-theological and ethical work in the global ecumenical movement. There is a sense of urgency in what the scientists tell us – despite all ongoing denial of human induced climate change – as the time given to us to change the course of human civilization and the system of carbon fossil fuels might be quite limited a period. We should consider a re-priorization of ecumenical efforts which need to pool and unite efforts of joined learning, common lobbying work and concrete commitments and changes in local action. "Integrity of creation" –the key-word from Vancouver 1983 should be a top priority again, in close interconnection with issues of peace and justice. Currently the devastating effects of ongoing global climate change are about to reverse, destroy and contradict all global efforts put in poverty alleviation and development in the past 60 years. We need to consider something like a global ecumenical decade of ecological learning, stimulating a new passion for creation and a joint new culture of mobilizing religious resources for the care of creation. If the recent study of ETH Zürich[37] scientifically and politically is affirmed that global reforestation plans could well have an unexpected positive impact on curbing global CO2 emissions and reduce global warming, each local church would have a major task to become an agent of cultivating a new consciousness of respecting and nurturing trees as one of the most precious gift to bring down emissions from fuel to zero, to contribute its significant contribution in the global movement of faiths for the earth[38] and to provide a glimpse of hope for the suffering earth.

Appendix: Current eco-theological initiatives of the World Council of Churches 2019 (Louk Andrianos)

The World Council of Churches (WCC) has been working on care for creation for many decades and its eco-theological initiatives have been started as early as 1970. The present world development model is threatening the lives and livelihoods of many, especially among the world's poorest people, and destroying biodiversity. The WCC ecumenical vision is to overcome this model based on over-consumption and greed. The concept of sustainable communities, care for creation, sustainability and climate justice are the main concerns of the eco-theological works of the WCC through its Diakonia and Witness (DW) on Ecological and Economic justice (EEJ).

The programmatic objective of current eco-theological initiatives of WCC-EEJ are to strengthen the common prophetic voice of member churches and ecumenical partners in promoting life

---

37   See for instance: https://www.theguardian.com/environment/2019/jul/04/planting-billions-trees-best-tackle-climate-crisis-scientists-canopy-emissions; https://www.science news.org/article/planting-trees-could-buy-more-time-fight-climate-change-thought.
38   See: https://www.unenvironment.org/about-un-environment/faith-earth-initiative.

Dietrich Werner

dignity, rights and justice in economy, ecology, climate change, water, food, health and healing, children, youth and gender-related issues.

Economic and ecological issues are interlinked and inseparable. Eco-theology at the WCC refers to theological reflections and actions on both ecological and economic issues. The focuses of eco-theological activities of the WCC are threefold: (a) Theological reflection and interfaith cooperation on economic and ecological justice; (b) Transformative education for economic and ecological justice, and (c) Advocacy and Accompaniment for Economy of life and Climate justice. Examples of the current projects in each area of eco-theological activity of the WCC_EEJ are the following.

I. Theological reflection and interfaith cooperation on economic and ecological justice
- On indigenous spiritualities and theologies of the Oikos: common reflection with the WCC Indigenous Peoples reference group on climate justice and theologies of the Oikos (common home).
- On contextualizing care for creation, climate justice and linking ecological and economic justice: Publication of working papers on theologies of the Oikos from eco-theological conferences and other workshops in the Ecumenical Review journal of the WCC.
- On Climate Change and Human Rights at the Geneva Interfaith Forum in collaboration with the Franciscans International and Brahma Kumaris.
- On the Celebration of Season of Creation (SOC) in collaboration with the Global Catholic Climate Movement (GCCM), Anglican Communion Environmental Network, World Evangelical Alliance, ACT Alliance, Lutheran World Federation (LWF) and WCC Spirituality.
- On Faith and Ethical Perspectives for the Conference of Parties (COP 25) of the UNFCCC: in collaboration with Geneva Interfaith Forum on Climate Change and Human Rights.
- On the Christian Right, Populism, and Climate Change: Conduct of a workshop to explore the links between Christian fundamentalism, populism and false climate change narratives.
- On ethics of sustainability, eco-theologies and models of eco-churches in different contexts in collaboration with EKD, BFW, LWF etc.

II. Transformative education for economic and ecological justice
- Training on Economy of Life, care for creation, sustainability and climate justice during the meeting of the WCC Working Group on Climate Change in collaboration with the WCC Mission from the Margins and Pacific Conference of Churches (PCC).
- Ecumenical School on Governance, Economics and Management for an Economy of Life (GEM school) in collaboration with the World Communion of Reformed Churches (WCRC), Council of World Mission (CWM) and Lutheran World Federation (LWF).
- Eco-School on water, food and climate justice in collaboration with the EWN (Ecumenical Water Network), the EAA (Ecumenical Alliance Advocacy) –Food for Life, and the World Student Christian Federation (WSCF).
- Webinars on Food, Health and Trade Online in collaboration with WCC EAA –Food for Life and WCC-Health and Healing.
- Conduct of the biannual conference on Ecological Theology and Environmental Ethics (ECO-THEE) at the Orthodox Academy of Crete in Greece on the theme of "Ecological racism and prophetic voices for ecological crisis" on September 23-26, 2019.
- Conference on the "Future Life in the Arctic" bringing together church leaders and Indig-

enous representatives to discuss common agendas of justice, peace and climate change as a follow up to the Icelandic conference.

- Conduct of the biannual conference on Sustainable Alternatives for Poverty Reduction and Eco-justice (SAPREJ) with academic institutions and NGO acting in Africa, Latina America and Pacific islands for 2020.
- Dissemination of the "Roadmap for Churches, Congregations and Communities towards an Economy of Life and Eco-justice": a tool kit developed by (late) Pastor Norman Tendis in early 2019 for WCC member churches.

III. Advocacy and Accompaniment for Economy of life and Climate justice
- Advocacy for economic and climate justice at the UN High-level Political Forum on the SDGs in New York, USA.
- Advocacy for climate justice at the UNFCCC COP 25 in Chile.
- Contributing to "Oikotree" workshop and pilgrim team visit addressing "extractivism" in collaboration with WCRC, CWM and Franciscans International.
- Advocacy at the New International Financial and Economic Architecture (NIFEA) Interfaith Consultation on Just Finance and Debt and engagement with international financial institutions and faith based organisations.
- Dialogue on the theme "Stronger Together" with Faith-based Entrepreneurs in Europe in collaboration with Geneva Agape Foundation.
- Engagement in the UN Forum on Business and Human Rights in Geneva, Switzerland with ACT Alliance and LWF.
- Development and dissemination of the Oikos IQ (interactive quizzes) online application to promote deeper awareness of the impact of contemporary lifestyles to the natural environment and to the global earth sustainability.

INTEGRAL ECOLOGY IN THE WITNESS OF THE ORTHODOX CHURCH

The CEMES Ecological Project[1]

Petros Vassiliadis

1.

After the Holy and Great Council (2016) our Center of Ecumenical, Missiological and Environmental Studies "Metropolitan Panteleimon Papageorgiou" (CEMES) started their ecological project, dedicated to Patriarch Bartholomew, the "Green Patriarch," focusing both in praxis and in theory/theology, further developing the notion of "integral ecology".

They first convened an International Conference on "Integral Ecology" (2016),[2] starting at the same time the "SMILE" ecological project, a music world tour (2016-2019)[3] and the "Green Smiles" book for young people (2019).[4] And finally, setting up an Inter-Orthodox Ecumenical Post-Graduate Program with Ecological theology as a core course, and special ecological specialization[5].

2.

There are two understandings of "Integral Ecology": one secular and another one religious. On the secular level the term "Integral Ecology" was first used by Michael E. Zimmerman early in this millennium,[6] and it was based on Ken Wilber's "Integral Theory", which was an attempt to place a wide diversity of theories and thinkers into one single framework. It was for this reason

---

1   A paper read at an international ecumenical conference preparing for the 11th Assembly of WCC in 2021, entitled "Together towards Eco-Theologies, Ethics of Sustainability and Eco-Friendly Churches" (Wuppertal, June 16-19, 2019).
2   http://cemes-en.weebly.com/2016-integral-ecology.html. Cf. also my article "The Witness of the Church in Today's World: Three Missiological Statements on Integral Ecology, in https://www.academia.edu/28268455; and N.. Dimitriadis, "Integral Ecology: Mission of God, Mission with the "Other", and Mission Towards Nature in a Multi-Religious World," *Antonianum* 91:4 (2016), pp. 1077-1090.
3   https://www.huffpost.com/entry/a-greek-rock-stars-message-to-humanity_b_591f7841e4b07617ae4cbc19?fbclid=IwAR2TkJQNunRbu3Rd1kFneJQgTeMaWIu_WXkPvPfUTLmK2hOVaI86kc2LUSQ&guccounter=2
4   https://www.facebook.com/cemes.thess/posts/1243232595853721
5   https://hum.ihu.edu.gr/index.php/en/courses/masters/master-in-orthodox-ecumenical-theology
6   "Integral Ecology: A Perspectival, Developmental, and Coordinating Approach to Environmental Problems," in *World Futures: The Journal of General Evolution* 61, nos. 1-2, (2005), pp. 50-62. Cf. also Sean Esbjörn-Hargens, & M. E. Zimmerman, "Integral Ecology," in J. B. Callicott, & R. Frodeman, (eds.) *Encyclopedia of Environmental Ethics and Philosophy*, New York: Macmillan (2008); and Sean Esbjörn – Hargens and M. E. Zimmerman, *Integral Ecology: Uniting Multiple Perspectives on the Natural World,* Integral Books (2009). Cf. also *Michael Zimmerman, Heidegger and Wilber on the Limitations of Spiritual Deep Ecology,* 2003.

that it is also called a "theory of everything,"[7] because it draws together already existing separate paradigms into an interrelated network of approaches. It was launched early in the 1970s, with the publication of his *Spectrum of Consciousness* that attempted to synthesize eastern religious traditions with western ideas. Wilber›s Integral Theory, because of its strong syncretism, has been applied only in a limited range of domains, and though it attracted attention in specific subcultures it was widely ignored both in academia,[8] and in theology.

A completely different trajectory was followed within the Christian ecumenical domain, which during the cold war integrated peace and justice. On a theoretical level, the ecumenical movement for almost half a century had being examining justice and peace as inseparable entities, when the superpowers at that time were stubbornly prioritizing them in differing and opposite ways.[9] The unit "Justice and Peace" of WCC was later expanded to also include ecology, using the religious understanding of "integral ecology". Thus, the "Justice and Peace" unit was renamed JPIC (Justice, Peace and "Integrity" of Creation). It was the time the Ecumenical Patriarchate started its conscious involvement in the ecological crisis. Therefore, the contribution of the Orthodox in this wider than earlier perspective of JPIC can hardly be underestimated. It is not an exaggeration to underline that Patriarch Bartholomew was the first in the religious domain to have shown an ecological concern,[10] which preceded the series of ten conferences on Religion and Ecology organized by Yale University professors Mary Evelyn Tucker and John Grim and held at the Harvard University Center for the Study of World Religions, though of course many scholars of religion by the 1990s begun to generate a substantial body of literature discussing and analyzing how nature is valued in the world's various religious systems.[11]

---

7   C. Macdonald, in *Integralis: Journal of Integral Consciousness, Culture, and Science*, Vol. 1, No. 0.

8   Cf. Markus Tomislav, *Pitfalls of Wilberian Ecology: A Critical Review of "Integral Ecology"*, 2009. Also Frank Visser, "Assessing Integral Theory: Opportunities and Impediments," *Integral World*, 2010.

9   During the 22nd session of the United Nations Human Rights Council (HRC, 24 February -22 March, 2013) in Geneva, a symposium was organized by the WCC in collaboration with other Christian organizations, interfaith networks and civil society groups. It was moderated by Dr Guillermo Kerber, WCC program executive on Care for Creation and Climate Justice, who in his concluding remarks called action for climate justice an "ethical and spiritual imperative". From this perspective, he said, the WCC, other faith-based organizations and a broad coalition of non-governmental organizations are calling on the HRC to establish a Special Rapporteur on human rights and climate change.

10   His All Holiness, the Ecumenical Patriarch Bartholomew of the Orthodox Church is the leading spirit of "Religion, Science and the Environment" movement, which was originally conceived in 1988 on the Isle of Patmos, at a meeting of environmental and religious leaders. It was established out of concern for the water environment of the planet, which covers seven-tenths of the earth's surface. This concern is both theological and scientific, and one of the underlying purposes of the movement is to establish common ground on the implications and imperatives of this ecological crisis between representatives of faith communities, professional scientists, and environmental NGOs. Cf. also Maria. G. Sereti's recent article, "The Contribution of Ecumenical Patriarch Bartholomew to the Configuration of an Ecumenical 'Integral Ecology,'" in *The Ecumenical Review* 70, 4 (2018), 617-626, which focuses on Ecumenical Patriarch Bartholomew's environmental actions. According to Patriarch Bartholomew, the ecological problem affects all humankind, and above all has a painful impact on the poor and the weak. The message of the Ecumenical Patriarch is one of solidarity and humanity for the marginalized and the poor. The Eucharistic vision and that of integral ecology, urges us to look after nature and people and fight against exploitation, poverty, and hunger.

11   Cf. Mary Evelyn Tucker, Worldly Wonder: Religions Enter Their Ecological Phase <u>Open Court</u>: Chicago, 2003. Dieter T. Hessel – Rosemary Radford Ruether (eds.), Christianity and Ecology: Seeking the Well-being of Earth and Humans. Cambridge, MA: Harvard University Press, 2000. Cf. also in the Greek literature Elias Oikonomou, Theological Ecology. Theory and Praxis (Θεολογική Οικολογία, Θεωρία και Πράξη), Athens 1994.

Petros Vassiliadis

These actions, initiatives and expressed views in the top level of Orthodox hierarchy are shared by the wider ecumenical movement, which few years ago came to the conclusion that "various aspects of climate, ecological, financial, and debt crises are mutually dependent and reinforce each other. They cannot be treated separately anymore.[12] "The people of faith" discern the fatal intertwining of the global financial, socio-economic, climate and ecological crises accompanied in many places of the world by the suffering of people and their struggle for life. Far-reaching market liberalization, deregulation, and unrestrained privatisation of goods and services are exploiting the whole Creation and dismantling social programs and services and opening up economies across borders to seemingly limitless growth of production."[13] In short, all Christian traditions slowly, but steadily, started being concerned about two interrelated aspects of globalization: ecology and economy, both stemming from the Greek word *oikos* (household), and both carrying inherently the notion of communion *(koinonia)*, all basic terminology of the Orthodox tradition, and not simply the Greek. [14]

3.

In both the secular and religious understanding the rise of the notion of "integral ecology" coincides with the period of the transfer from modernity to post-modernity. Christianity in order to meaningfully and effectively exercise its mission in today's pluralistic – modern and/or post-modern – world it is necessary to proceed to a certain encounter with modernity.[15] If today this encounter is possible, and even desirable – despite the tragic events of Sept 11, and the ensuing awful war against terror, which resulted in the escalation of violence after the unilateral establishment of a Muslim caliphate (ISIS) – this is because of the undisputed transition of our culture to a new era, the *post-modern* era that brought with it the resurgence of religion in the public domain.

This resurgence of religion is undoubtedly both a threat and a hope. It is a threat if the fundamentalists – certainly on the part of the ISIS, but not only and exclusively – assume uncontrolled power. However, it is a hope if religion is willing, or allowed, to exercise its tremendous potential and power to bring back moral values, and if recreate, and originate new images of what means to be human in a just, peaceful and sustainable universe through an integral ecology.

It was for this reason that Christianity slowly but steadily – Catholicism after Vatican II and the Orthodox Church quite recently[16] – unanimously endorsed this encounter. Either reluctantly,

---

12   § 10 of the 2013 WCC appeal: *Economy of Life, Justice, and Peace for All: A Call for Action* (Geneva).
13   *Ibid.* Cf. also Elias Oikonomou, "Holistic Ecology. The Vital Triangle (Ecology-Economy-Ethics)" in http://www.diplomatikoperiskopio.com/2010/12/h-o.html (retrieved 28.7.2016)
14   Pope Francis made the most thorough analysis of this connection in both his Apostolic exhortation *Evangelii Gaudium,* and his recent encyclical *Laudato Si.*
15   Cf. my book *Unity and Witness: A Handbook on Inter-Faith Dialogue,* Epikentro Publishing: Thessaloniki 2007; and its predecessor *Postmodernity and the Church. The Challenge of Orthodoxy,* Akritas: Athens 2002. By and large, there still exist a aloofness between religion and modernity, which is caused not only by the former' rejection of the latter, and the negative attitude toward the whole range of the achievements of the Enlightenment; but also by the obstinate persistence of the adherents of modernism – and of course the democratic institutions that come out of it – to allow historic and diachronic institutions, like religion, to play a significant role in the public life, without being either absorbed or alienated by it, with the simple argument that derive their origin in the pre-modern era.
16   In the *Message* of the 2008 Synaxis of the Primates of the Autocephalous Orthodox Churches (the ultimate authority of the Orthodox Church, until the convocation of the Holy and Great Council of the Orthodox Church, in Crete 19-26 of June 2016), disseminated *urbi et orbi,* it is mentioned that "efforts to distance religion from societal life

or as an established fact, religion even in the West is being accepted as far too important for human existence to be excluded from public life.[17] All these affirmations were on the ecumenical agenda of Christianity since the 1963 World Mission Conference in Mexico. It was there that ecumenical Christianity replaced the negative assessment to modernity by a more positive one.[18] Since then most of the earlier models of evangelization of the whole world were completely abandoned.[19] The new understanding of Christian mission is not any more limited to such terms as *Christianization, verbal proclamation, evangelization, conversion* etc. in their literal and exclusive sense; they were replaced by a variety of much more inclusive terms, like *witness* or *martyria, public presence, inter-faith dialogue, liberation, integral ecology,* etc.[20] And what I consider as the most optimistic development in religious history, the Church – in collaboration with other religions – began to address the human sin in the structural complexities of our world, and started ministering the socially poor and marginalized of our societies in their contexts, what is generally described as "Global South." Above all Christianity entered into a constructive dialogue with pluralism and at the end of the road with modernity and/or post-modernity, thus making her presence visible in the society.[21]

---

constitute the common tendency of many modern states. The principle of a secular state can be preserved; however, it is unacceptable to interpret this principle as a radical marginalization of religion from all spheres of public life."(§ 7).

17   Max Stackhouse in his entry on "Politics and Religion," in the well-known *Encyclopedia of Religion,* has stated that: "authority in all civilizations is incomprehensive without attention to religion". Politics is the theory of an on-going exercise of power, of coercion that includes legitimized violence. Politics also addresses religious issues and makes religious statements. But on the other hand, religions very often take up political stance and engage in political action. People expect from religions not only private views, but also final solutions to shared problems. This expectation means that they anticipate from them some sort of acts of power, not only affirmations of conscience. After all, almost all religions integrate the private and the public. Sociologically speaking religion produces political consequences, shaping attitudes and ideas that make an impact on issues of public policy. Obviously, this happens because it comprises what people *do* together, not just what they believe in the privacy of their hearts. In other words, religions functions socially. From an Orthodox viewpoint on politics see my (Politics in) "Orthodox Christianity," in J. Neusner (ed.), *God's Rule. The Politics of World Religions,* Georgetown University Press, Washington DC, 2003, pp. 86-105.

18   Quite rightly D. Keramidas characterizes modernity as the rebel child of the medieval Christianity, thus speaking of an integral witness ("Christianity in the post-Constantinian Europe. From a Return to Christianity to a Return of Christians" (Ο Χριστιανισμός στη μετακωνσταντίνεια Ευρώπη. Από τη μεταστροφή στο Χριστιανισμό στη μεταστροφή των χριστιανών»), in *Synthesis* 2013/2, 75.

19   This is not to say that Christian churches no longer organize evangelical campaigns or revival meetings; in fact, many Christians are still asked to take up conversion as their top priority mission. We must confess, however, that the traditional terminology (*mission, conversion, evangelism* or *evangelization, christianization*) still have an imperative validity and are retained as the *sine qua non* of the Christian identity of those Christian communities which belong to the "evangelical" stream of the Christian faith. What I mean is that all churches on the institutional level are coping in one way or the other with the questions of many contexts, many religions, many cultures and systems of values – what we call *pluralism* or the effects of *globalization.* Rather than proclamation alone, the Christian churches are now exploring in their own ways a different understanding of "Christian witness".

20   Cf. *Common Witness. A Joint Document of the Working Group of the Roman Catholic Church and the WCC,* WCC Mission Series, Geneva 1982; the WCC document *Common Witness and Proselytism;* also I. Bria (ed.), *Martyria-Mission,* WCC Geneva, 1980. Even the *Mission and Evangelism-An Ecumenical Affirmation,* WCC Mission Series: Geneva 1982, ²1985, is an attempt to correctly interpret the classical missionary terminology. A comprehensive presentation of the present state of the debate in J. Matthey, "Milestones in Ecumenical Missionary Thinking from the 1970s to the 1990s," *IRM* 88 (1999), pp. 291-304. The New Mission Statement recently (2012) endorsed by the Central Committee of WCC, will be discussed later, together with the "Call for Action 2012", also from WCC.

21   In the recent New Mission Statement, entitled *Together Towards Life: Mission and Evangelism in Changing Landscapes* it is clearly stated: "The church lives in multi-religious and multi-cultural contexts and new commu-

4.

Speaking for the Orthodox tradition, God in God's own self is a life of communion and God's involvement in history (and consequently our religious responsibility) aims at drawing humanity and creation in general into this communion with God's very life.[22] This ultimate expression of *koinonia* (communion) and love – in the framework of "integral ecology" and through "inter-faith" encounter – is transmitted to the whole world not as doctrinal statements (dogmas) or ethical commands, but as a communion of love. This concern for the entire created world and the openness toward the faithful of other religions is also reinforced by the unique Orthodox anthropology, expressed in such terms as *theosis* or deification.[23] The human nature is not a closed, autonomous entity, but a dynamic reality, determined in its very existence by its relationship to God. Determined by a vision of how to "know" God, to "participate" in His life, and of course to be "saved" neither by an extrinsic action of God nor through the rational cognition of propositional truths, but by "becoming God", this anthropological notion is much more inclusive to non-Christians, even to non-believers, and much more relevant to the social, economic and environmental issues, than the old conventional missionary attitude.[24]

On the basis of "the economy of the Holy Spirit" we believe that God uses not only the Church, but many other powers of the world for God's mission *(missio dei)* for the salvation of humankind and the entire creation. After all, God's Spirit, the "Holy Spirit", who is the "Spirit of Truth," "blows wherever He/She wills" (Jn 3:8, leading us to the "whole truth" Jn 16:13), thus embracing the whole of cosmos. According to the Biblical *Magna Carta* (Mt 25), God judges humanity with criteria other than the conventional religious ones. With the "Economy of the Spirit" the narrow (or canonical) boundaries of the Church are widened, and all cultural (and religious) superiority syndromes and arrogant missionary behaviour give their place to a "common witness", an "integral ecology" and a humble "inter-faith dialogue".

---

nication technology is also bringing the people of the world into a greater awareness of one another's identities and pursuits. Locally and globally Christians are engaged with people of other religions and cultures in building societies of love, peace and justice. Plurality is a challenge to the churches and serious commitment to inter-faith dialogue and cross-cultural communication is therefore indispensable." (§ 9).

22 Cf. Ion Bria (ed.), *Go Forth in Peace* Geneva 1987, p. 3.

23 More on this in my (as an editor) *Orthodox Perspectives on Mission*, Regnum series: Oxford, 2013.

24 This rapprochement with people of other faiths does not mean a naïve affirmation that all religions are the same, or that a new "world religion", a *Pan-religion*, is needed or is at hand, as it is feared or claimed by the ultra-conservatives from all religions. On the contrary, the inter-faith dialogue and co-operation are necessary, exactly because the various religious traditions are different and promote different visions of the reality. The inter-faith dialogue is an "encounter of mutual commitments and responsibilities" on the common goal of humanity to restore communion with God, which would inevitably also lead to a "communion of faithful from different religious traditions". After all, this is the ultimate goal of the divine economy, as it is clearly stated in the Christian Bible (cf. Eph 1:10, Col 3:11 etc). The aim of today's inter-faith dialogue has nothing to do with the naïve experiment in Chicago at the end of the 19th c. (1893) with the World's Parliament of Religions, the ultimate goal of which was "to unite all religions against irreligion", This initiative came out of the conservatives of the so-called "American awakening". 100 years later, in 1989, the new inter-religious initiative was motivated by the new "mission paradigm", which for the Christians was theologically based on the "economy of the Spirit". In this gathering, again in Chicago, the person who gave the keynote addresses, and prepared the famous document: *Towards a Global Ethic: An Initial Declaration,* was the Roman Catholic professor of Tübingen, Hans Küng.

5.

The most important characteristic of the connection between inter-faith dialogue and integral ecology, from an Orthodox (and authentic Christian in general) point of view is that it considers the "other" a real partner in, and not just an "object" of, mission.[25] It does not simply aim at decreasing the enmity and the hostilities between people of different religions – this is what the secular powers in the world are interested in, just for the stability of the present world order and *status quo*. Most importantly, however, the inter-faith dialogue is being promoted and with full determination pursued, in order to build upon what is left unfinished in modernity by the so-called "secular condition". And the main areas where the "modern paradigm" failed to succeed – in addition to the spiritual and material welfare of the people, the degradation in social and moral values, its inability to enforce a lasting just peace on earth – was its inability or unwillingness to preserve the natural environment, God's καλή λίαν creation, and its surrender to the rules of the dominant world economic system. In other words, modernity's inability to pursue *integral ecology* and *just economy* in a meaningful and sustainable way.

This failure or shortcomings of modernity in justice, peace, the integrity of creation, and the world economy, is to a certain extent the result of individualism, one of the pillars of modernity, and the ensuing absolute, unconditioned, uncontrolled freedom of the individual in all aspects of life (legally protected freedom in accumulating wealth regardless of the actual effects on the environment, sexual freedom etc.), heralded as the new faith after the Enlightenment. Looking at the ambivalence of modernity many Christian theologians insist that there must be a criterion to judge what should be saved from the values and achievements of modernity and what should be overcome. For with the free-market economy, especially in its latest neo-liberal form, the argument goes on, the power balance changed and modernity from a midwife of human rights became their murderer. On the basis of the old principles of modernity, the present world economic system is increasingly falling back into totalitarian trends. Only if the world listen again carefully and gleans from the shared wisdom of the Christian social ethics and other ages-old ethical and religious traditions, can the positive values of the "modern paradigm" be renewed and revitalized, and thus be accepted by the faithful. It is for this reason that we speak of *liberation of modernity*, of *just economy* and of *integral ecology*.

6.

Integral ecology is inconceivable without further development of what is most dear in modern Western societies: *The Universal Declaration of Human Rights*. In view of the inconclusive effects of all the last International Conventions on Climate Change it became clear – at least in Christian circles – that human rights are awfully ineffective, if they are not accompanied by "human responsibilities".

More and more Christians from all quarters nowadays believe that the values and principles that form part of a common world ethic need not only be publicly declared, they also require an international legal endorsement; they should be more effectively integrated into the work of the UN system and major international legal institutions, even if integrating such values and prin-

---

25   More on inter-faith dialogue in N. Dimitriadis' Ph.D. dissertation, submitted in the Department of Theology of the Aristotle University of Thessaloniki under my supervision (2009), entitled Theological and Religious-Historical Approach to Inter-religious Dialogue in Contemporary Mission (Θεολογική και θρησκειολογική θεώρηση του διαθρησκειακού διαλόγου στη σύγχρονη ιεραποστολή).

ciples requires significant reforms to leading organs and agencies of the UN.[26] The struggle of Christians to promote a Universal Declaration of Human Responsibilities is not just a diplomatic initiative aiming at introducing in the world agenda Christian moral values at the expense of the values of modernity and the democratic achievements of the Enlightenment. It came out of pressure not only by the Orthodox, but also by prophetic and charismatic figures and theological movements for social and ecological justice from a faith perspective. "Economic justice" is a concept developed by the churches and the ecumenical movement towards achievement of global justice through advocating for equitable sharing of resources and power as essential prerequisites for human development and ecological sustainability.

Long before a universal concern (political, scientific etc.) and advocacy for the dangerous effects of the climate change was developed, Christian sociologists and theologians put a critical question to their Churches: Do they have "the courage to engage with the 'values' of a profit oriented way of life as a matter of faith, or will they withdraw into the 'private' sphere? This is the question our churches must answer or lose their very soul," declared a WCC consultation of Eastern and Central European Churches on the problem of economic globalization at the dawn of the 3rd millennium.[27]

7.

The two persons who have immensely contributed towards the above described integral perspective of the Church's mission are undoubtedly His All-Holiness the Ecumenical Patriarch Bartholomew,[28] and more recently His Holiness Pope Francis. The former with his global ecological endeavour and his sensitivity for the environment, God's creation, his ecological initiatives, both at a liturgical level (establishment of the feast of the protection of God's creation on September 1) and at a scholarly and theological one (the series of the international ecological conferences) that have rightly given him the nickname "Green Patriarch." The latter by his overall treatment of the structural evil in the Apostolic Exhortation *Evangelii Gaudium* (2013), and the Papal encyclical *Laudato Si* (2015).[29]

---

26   The inter-faith document: *Faith, Shared Wisdom, and International Law*, insists that "a Universal Declaration of Human Responsibilities that would stand beside the Universal Declaration of Human Rights" is a *sine-qua-non* for a just, peaceful and sustainable universe. Action has already been taken that the Secretary General of UN "acts to advance acceptance of a statement of shared ethical values and that the document be introduced into the General Assembly for debate and adoption". And the document goes on: "To this end religious and other ethically based institutions should work with legal and political authorities…in order to develop a higher level of public understanding and awareness of commonalities in values between the major religious and ethical traditions, while fully respecting religious, ethnic and cultural diversity".

27   Rogate Mshane, *Globalization*. WCC-JPC, presented in the Harare WCC Assembly. See also *The Responsibility of World Religions for Ecology, the World Economic System, and the International Law*.

28   Among the various presentations on Patriarch Bartholomew's ecological views I isolate those of his most authentic interpreter, his ecological advisor Prof. Dn. John Chryssavgis (J. Chryssavgis (ed.), *On Earth as in Heaven: Ecological Vision and Initiatives of Ecumenical Patriarch Bartholomew* Fordham University Press, New York 2012; idem (ed.), *Bartholomew: Apostle and Visionary*, GOARCH, New York 2016; idem and B.V. Foltz (eds.), *Toward an Ecology of Transfiguration: Orthodox Christian Perspectives on Environment, Nature and Creation*, Fordham University Press, New York 2013).

29   In the Encyclical *"Laudato Si,"* Pope Francis paid from the very beginning a tribute to his "beloved Ecumenical Patriarch Bartholomew, with whom we share the hope of full ecclesial communion" (§ 7). Pope Francis

8.

I will limit myself in the remaining time, to very few quotations from the Orthodox conciliar document *The Witness of the Church in Today's World,* adopted by the Holy and Great Council of the Orthodox (2016), an event of great magnitude which is indisputably credited to Patriarch Bartholomew.[30]

The extraordinary and long-awaited by all Holy and Great Synod of the Orthodox Church, a conciliar event of such a magnitude that had not been convened in Eastern Christianity since the 7th Ecumenical Council, dealt with integral ecology mainly in its mission document. Without denying the importance of all the other agreed documents, the one on mission is of utmost and extraordinary significance, because the Church exists for the world (humanity and environment alike), and not for herself. Entitled: *The Mission of the Orthodox Church in Today's World* this document refers to ecology as follows: "The yearning for continuous growth in prosperity and an unfettered consumerism inevitably lead to a disproportionate use and depletion of natural resources. Nature, which was created by God and given to humankind to *work and preserve* (cf. Gen 2:15), endures the consequences of human sin: '*For the creation was subjected to futility, not willingly, but because of him who subjected it in hope; because the creation itself also will be delivered from the bondage of corruption into the glorious liberty of the children of God. For we know that the whole creation groans and labors with birth pangs together until now* (Rom 8:20-22).

The ecological crisis, which is connected to climate change and global warming, makes it incumbent upon the Church to do everything within her spiritual power to protect God's creation from the consequences of human greed. As the gratification of material needs, greed leads to spiritual impoverishment of the human being and to environmental destruction. We should not forget that the earth's natural resources are not our property, but the Creator's: *The earth is*

---

continued: "Patriarch Bartholomew has spoken in particular of the need for each of us to repent of the ways we have harmed the planet, for "inasmuch as we all generate small ecological damage", we are called to acknowledge "our contribution, smaller or greater, to the disfigurement and destruction of creation". He has repeatedly stated this firmly and persuasively, challenging us to acknowledge our sins against creation: "For human beings... to destroy the biological diversity of God's creation; for human beings to degrade the integrity of the earth by causing changes in its climate, by stripping the earth of its natural forests or destroying its wetlands; for human beings to contaminate the earth's waters, its land, its air, and its life – these are sins". For "to commit a crime against the natural world is a sin against ourselves and a sin against God". At the same time, Bartholomew has drawn attention to the ethical and spiritual roots of environmental problems, which require that we look for solutions not only in technology but in a change of humanity; otherwise we would be dealing merely with symptoms. He asks us to replace consumption with sacrifice, greed with generosity, wastefulness with a spirit of sharing, an asceticism which "entails learning to give, and not simply to give up. It is a way of loving, of moving gradually away from what I want to what God's slightest detail in the seamless garment of God's creation, in the last speck of dust of our planet" (§ 8 & 9). An excellent analysis of Pope Francis' encyclical, with all the conservative reactions to it and the necessary appraisal to Patriarch Bartholomew, in Guillermo Kerber, "Ecumenical Background and Reactions to *Laudato Si*," *VOICES* n.s. 39:2 (2019), pp. 63-75.

30   On Pope Francis' encyclicals and the WCC New Mission Statement, under the title *Together towards Life: Mission and Evangelism in Changing Landscapes* (2013), and the closely related to the new mission statement "Call for Action", prepared by the committee "Poverty-Wealth-Ecology" of the AGAPE process focusing on eradicating poverty, entitled: *Economy of Life, Justice, and Peace for All: A Call for Action,* see my "*The Witness of the Church in Today's World: Three Missiological Statements on Integral Ecology*" (academia.edu/28268455). There, I also made some passing references to the declaration of an inter-faith initiative with the name: *Faith Shared Wisdom and International Law.* It was produced by the most serious global movement initiated in Asia, called: *Initiative on Shared Wisdom (ISW)–Thought and Action for a Sustainable Future.*

Petros Vassiliadis

the Lord's, and all its fullness, the world, and those who dwell therein (Ps 23:1). Therefore, the Orthodox Church emphasizes the protection of God's creation through the cultivation of human responsibility for our God-given environment and the promotion of the virtues of frugality and self-restraint. We are obliged to remember that not only present, but also future generations have a right to enjoy the natural goods granted to us by the Creator".[31]

9.

If one wants to neutrally assess all three ecological contributions from a mission theology perspective, the Papal encyclical *Laudato Si* offers a more detailed, scientifically solid, and well documented presentation of an ecclesially sound "integral ecology." In addition, the LS is the only document that *expressis verbis* speaks about "integral ecology."[32]

The ecumenical mission statement TTL is making a consistent use of the inter-connectedness of ecology with economy, something that Pope Francis had thoroughly examined in his *Evangelii Gaudium*, and frequently repeats in *Laudato Si.*

Finally, the Orthodox conciliar mission document is a short exposition in a Dorian style of the main views expressed in the *Synaxeis* of the Primates of the Orthodox Churches, based mainly on the various speeches of Patriarch Bartholomew.[33]

As a matter of fact, however, all Christian traditions slowly, but steadily, started being concerned about the two interrelated aspects of globalization: ecology and economy. Which means, that it is time to move beyond "eco-theology", even beyond simple "ethics of sustainability," concentrating more on "eco-justice," in fact towards developing an "integral ecology" in future theological education.[34]

---

31   Chapter 6 § 10. See also a shorter reference in the *Message of the Synod:* "It is clear that the present-day ecological crisis is due to spiritual and moral causes. Its roots are connected with greed, avarice and egoism, which lead to the thoughtless use of natural resources, the filling of the atmosphere with damaging pollutants, and to climate change. The Christian response to the problem demands repentance for the abuses, an ascetic frame of mind as an antidote to overconsumption, and at the same time a cultivation of the consciousness that man is a "steward" and not a possessor of creation. The Church never ceases to emphasize that future generations also have a right to the natural resources that the Creator has given us. For this reason, the Orthodox Church takes an active part in the various international ecological initiatives and has ordained the 1st September as a day of prayer for the protection of the natural environment" (§ 8).

32   In my critical assessment of Pope Francis' *Evangelii Gaudium,* at a symposium to honor him and Patriarch Bartholomew, I stated that "it marks – finally I want to believe – the removal of the last (in my opinion important) obstacle for the unity of Christians, and the union of the traditional Eastern and Western Churches. In any case, history will record in the future, that contemporary Christian world, and not only the Catholic Church, is divided in the pre-papal encyclical "*Evangelii Gaudium*" of November 24, 2013, and after that. My assessment may seem too optimistic, even unrealistic, but it is perfectly in line with the vision of the great Christian leader Patriarch Athenagoras, at times even with minor openings of the Catholic Church, but also the dynamic ecclesiastical policy of the current Ecumenical Patriarch Bartholomew".

33   E.g. *Address in Santa Barbara, California* (8 November 1997); cf. John Chryssavgis, *On Earth as in Heaven: Ecological Vision and Initiatives of Ecumenical Patriarch Bartholomew*, Bronx, New York, 2012. Also, his *Message for the Day of Prayer for the Protection of Creation* (1 September 2012); his *Lecture at the Monastery of Utstein,* Norway (23 June 2003); and his closing remarks at the Halki Summit I, Constantinople (20 June 2012): "Global Responsibility and Ecological Sustainability".

34   By "integral ecology" we mean a new paradigm in theological education with regard to eco-theology. Up to this very moment environmental issues were approached not as *theologia prima,* but as urgent practical issues, i.e.

10.

Allow me to end my presentation with one critical remark that is considered extremely important in the integral ecological project of CEMES. And this was something that was actually missing from the Orthodox, but also of the global ecumenical Christian, understanding of integral ecology: the anthropological dimension: the male *and* female interrelatedness and its consequences for integral ecology. That was one of the conclusions of a previous project of CEMES, which was initiated after our international conference 4 years ago, on "Deaconesses, ordination of Women and Orthodox Theology", held in our headquarters in Thessaloniki and co-organized with two other Orthodox academic institutions: The Holy Cross Orthodox Theological School of Boston USA and the Department of Theology of the Orthodox Theological School of Thessaloniki, Greece.[35]

An eminent Orthodox scholar, Metropolitan Kallistos of Diokleia (Ware) has recently made the following remark: "Undoubtedly, in the 21st century ecclesiology will continue to theologically concern us. But it is my belief that there will be a shift in the central focus of theological

---

a *theologia secunda,* to be dealt with on the basis of a "theology from above," mostly retrieved from the traditional fundamental theological resources (biblical, patristic, systematic etc.). Our small experience has shown that our authentic Christian theology in all its various disciplines (biblical, liturgical, dogmatic, ethical, patristic, systematic) is permeated by eco-theology.

35   More on this in cemes-en.weebly.com. Cf. also other aspects presented at the last IOTA conference in Iasi, Romania, last February 2019. Frances Kostarelos' paper, "Orthodox Christian Theology, Ecology, and Sustainability", based on ethnographic research conducted among Orthodox Christian farmers and householders in Lerna, a coastal settlement in the Southern Peloponnese, Greece. In Lerna, Orthodox teachings and practices interact with and enliven everyday farming and household routines. This research applies a dialectical approach and theory, directing attention to collective symbols as they interact with wider political and economic contingencies and environmental constraints and possibilities. The approach draws on symbolic anthropology (Geertz 1973; Bourdieu 1977; Douglas 1993) and cultural ecology (Kardulias and Shutes et al 1997). Following Kardulias and Shutes (1997), attention is directed to human interaction with the environment. This study also draws on a multifunctional perspective (Brouwer 2004) directing attention to meaningful local knowledge, stewardship, and heritage articulated in farming practices and village institutions. The paper seeks to shed light on local agricultural knowledge and practices worthy of note in discussions of climate change and sustainability. Also, Frederick Krueger, "Orthodox Theology, Climate Change and Respect for Animals", who suggested that Orthodox Christians possess an elaborate theology of creation that can address global climate change and a host of other issues. This theology defines a world in which human purpose is to transform and transfigure God's creation. This transformation becomes a prerequisite for the transfiguration of the larger creation. Despite this inheritance Orthodox communities typically fail to fulfil their theology of creation. This failure includes the ability to maintain awareness of the sacred that fills all creation. As we embrace forgotten dimensions of our faith, we may address climate change, respect for animals and restore a forgotten ascesis. The present degradations to creation are foretold in Isaiah's depiction of a suffering world. Healing inspiration is found in the patristic emphasis on human responsibility 'to serve and preserve the earth.' In the Orthodox Liturgy, we find 'Thine own of Thine own, we offer to Thee, on behalf of all and for all.' Returning creation back to God recalls the divine mandate to restore a cosmological vision and sacramental relationship to the earth. And finally, Dr. Christina Nellist, "Eastern Orthodox Christianity and Animal Suffering", who advanced the opinion that the Eastern Orthodox church has the potential to develop a theology which tackles the subject of animal suffering. There is considerable debate on protection and care of the environment, but very little is said about the need to care for and protect the individual animals within that environment, with even less commentary on their suffering. There are positive comments which denounce cruelty, but there is also ambiguity regarding our use and relationship with animals. This paper aims to address this lack of engagement by providing an anamnesis of an alternative, though less prominent Orthodox tradition. This tradition promotes compassionate relationships with animals. Friendly relationships with animals is acknowledged as a positive act and their suffering viewed as being against God's will. It is suggested that by causing harm to animals or by our indifference to it, human salvation is jeopardized.

Petros Vassiliadis

research from ecclesiology to anthropology. Actually, there are many signs that such a shift has already begun. The key question now and in the future is not just: 'what the Church is', but also and more fundamentally: 'what the human being is' ".[36] There is a similar concern in the Roman Catholic Church (and of course in other Christian Churches). The Roman Catholic social doctrine recognizes that an adequate theological anthropology is required for social/ecological justice, but so far shows an ambivalent admixture of natural law and patriarchal ideology. If man and woman complete each other in both Church and society, why is patriarchal male headship still enshrined in the Church hierarchy, given that man and woman are fully homogeneous in their "whole being"?

This is, of course, something that has been consistently pursued by the secular "eco-feminist" movement. And it has been long stemming from a patriarchal ideology of male domination and female submission, which for many scholars was the consequence of the Augustinian doctrine of the original sin.[37] It is, however, also a Christian (and Orthodox ecclesiastical) ecological concern. This is not about what women (or men) want. This is about discerning what Jesus Christ wants for the Church in the 21st century, for the glory of God, for integral human development, for integral humanism, and for integral ecology in light of an adequate theological anthropology, based on the authentic, though latent, tradition of the Church, and not just on the historically established one.

"As long as the patriarchal binary prevails, subjective human development remains defective, with pervasive repercussions in human relations as well as human-nature relations….There can be no fully integral ecology as long as humanity behaves as the dominant male and treats nature as a submissive female. There can be no lasting social justice, and there can be no lasting ecological justice, as long as human behavior is driven by the patriarchal mindset".[38]

***

Thank you for listening to the (or rather an) "Orthodox voice." For despite the Holy and Great Council achievements Orthodoxy is not yet with one voice, "One" Church; to some she looks more like a confederation of independent Orthodox Churches and less a One, Holy Catholic and Apostolic Church.

More in

(a) cemes-en.weebly.com for some of our ecological activities,

and

(b) https://www.huffpost.com/entry/a-greek-rock-stars-message-to-humanity_b/591f7841e4b07617ae4cbc19?guccounter=1&fbclid=IwAR2TkJQNunRbu3Rd1kFneJQgTeMaWIu_WXkPvP-fUTLmK2hOVaI86kc2LUSQ, for its reception by the secular press (where the "Smile" project is at the end).

---

36   (Metropolitan of Diokleia) Kallistos Ware, Η Ορθόδοξη Θεολογία στον 21ο αιώνα (*The Orthodox Theology in the 21st Century*), Indiktos: Athens, 2005, p. 25.

37   TOB 31, based mainly on Genesis 3:16. See also my article "St. Augustine as Interpreter of St. Paul and the problem of Human Sexuality (Ο ιερός Αυγουστίνος ως ερμηνευτής του Αποστόλου Παύλου και το πρόβλημα της ανθρώπινης σεξουαλικότητας)," in academia.edu/1992336/.

38   From a working draft (22 December 2015) – among so many others, encouraged by Pope Francis' willingness to promote gender equality in his Church – by Luis T. Gutiérrez, entitled: "Gender Balance for Integral Humanism & Integral Ecology".

ECO-THEOLOGY AND HUMAN RESPONSIBILITY: A CATHOLIC PERSPECTIVE TO THE ECOLOGICAL AND CLIMATE CRISIS

Ingeborg G. Gabriel / Guillermo Kerber

Abstract
In this article, building on the statement presented by Ingeborg G. Gabriel, and the comments offered by Guillermo Kerber at the Wuppertal Conference, we will first highlight the relevance of Pope Francis' Encyclical Laudato si' (LS) on "Care for our Common Home" in the context of Roman Catholic Social Teaching. We will then argue for an ethics of eco-responsibility in dialogue with other religious and non-religious actors, as well as scientists and finally stress some contributions a Christian eco-theology can make in our view in the present situation.

Catholic Social Teaching on Ecology: Papal engagement after a (too) slow start

The papal encyclical *Laudato si*[1] published in June 2015 had for long been awaited. When the encyclical was released, especially from the international and scientific communities there were strong voices of praise.[2]

There were references to the ecological question in other ecclesial documents,[3] papal as well as those from regional Bishops Conferences before, but the subject remained at the margins.[4] The clearest statement on the ecology crisis could be found in an early text: the final statement of the Global Synod of Bishops in 1971 *De iustitia in mundo*, which was issued one year before the decisive Report of the Club of Rome on the "Limits of Growth" that initiated global discussions on ecology. This document already stresses the close link between the ecological crisis and the situation of the poor, which is the main focus also of *Laudato si'*. It moreover emphasised the close connection between these crisis and a Western model of consumption that cannot be universal-

---

1   http://w2.vatican.va/content/francesco/de/encyclicals/documents/papa-francesco_20150524_enciclica-laudato-si.html [14.07.2018].
2   Christiana Figueres, Executive Secretary of the UNFCCC expressed "Pope Francis' encyclical underscores the moral imperative of urgent action on climate change to lift the world's most vulnerable people, protect development, and spur responsible growth". Former UN Secretary General Kofi Annan commented " As Pope Francis reaffirms, climate change is a widespread threat ... I congratulate the pope for his moral and ethical leadership. We need more than such inspired leadership".
3   John Paul II's Message on the 1990 World Day of Peace: Peace with God the Creator, peace with all of Creation, http://w2.vatican.va/content/john-paul-ii/en/messages/peace/documents/hf_jp-ii_mes_19891208_xxiii-world-day-for-peace.html (14.08.2019)
4   It is interesting to note the relevance of the consideration of the ecological crisis in the Latin American Bishops conference in Aparecida in 2007, as Cardinal Bergoglio (now pope Francis) was the chairman of the drafting committee. See, e.g., the following sections: 2.1.4 Biodiversity, ecology, the Amazon, and the Antarctic; 3.5. The good news of the universal destiny of goods and ecology, https://www.celam.org/aparecida/Ingles.pdf (14.08.2019)

ized and therefore must be considered unjust.[5] However, the engagement of the Roman Catholic Church remained, considering the magnitude of the problem, notwithstanding local and regional activities and statements as well as the statements of Pope John Paul II for the World Day of Peace 1990, unfortunately insufficient.[6] One can only speculate about the reasons for this disappointing response of the highest authority of the Roman Catholic Church to the ecological crisis. Since she is a centralized institution it certainly reflects last but not least the world views of the recent popes: For Pope John Paul II it was the fight against communism which was at the centre of his pontificate and indeed he decisively contributed to the fall of the Iron Curtain. Pope Benedict XVI' main focus was the struggle against the secularization of Europe. So it needed the global view of Pope Francis as well as his strong social impulse which is closely linked to the ecological question, for the Catholic Church to speak up on ecology with a strong and distinctive global voice and recognize the priority of the issue. In the introduction to *Laudato si'* (LS) the Pope thereby refers to *Pacem in terris*, the testament of of Pope John XXIII, which he wrote in view of the possibility of a nuclear war in 1963. There could not be any stronger statement with regard to the urgency of the issue.[7]

We want in the following to focus on three points to be found in *Laudato si'* that in our opinion deserve particular notice and may be inspiring also for the common endeavour.

1. The encyclical strongly stresses the interlinkage of social (poverty, migration) and ecological issues (climate crisis etc.). In one of its most famous phrases the encyclical urges us to equally hear the "cry of the earth and the cry of the poor" (LS 49.[8]".

The links between social and ecological issues are an expression of another phrase that appears several times in Laudato si': Everything is interrelated, interconnected (LS 70, 92, 117, 120, 137, 142, 240).

Ecology, therefore, is not only a question of securing a natural environment and natural resources for future generations, but also for the poorer ones of this earth, who *already now* suffer more gravely than others from ecological destruction and climate change. Thus, to cite but one example, the rise of the sea level which continues with unexpected speed, "can create extremely

---

5   "Furthermore, such is the demand for resources and energy by the richer nations, whether capitalist or socialist, and such are the effects of dumping by them in the atmosphere and the sea that irreparable damage would be done to the essential elements of life on earth, such as air and water, if their high rates of consumption and pollution, which are constantly on the increase, were extended to the whole of humanity. 12. The strong drive towards global unity, the unequal distribution which places deci-sions concerning three quarters of income, investment and trade in the hands of one third of the human race, namely the more highly developed part, the insufficiency of a merely economic progress, and the new recognition of the material limits of the biosphere--all this makes us aware of the fact that in today's world new modes of understanding human dignity are arising. (IM 11), vgl. http://www.iupax.at/index.php/140-1971-world-bishopssynod- de-iustitia-in-mundo (20.10.2018).

6   https://w2.vatican.va/content/john-paul-ii/en/messages/peace/documents/hf_jp-ii_mes_19891208_xxiii-world-day-for-peace.html (access 28/8/19)

7   With regard to the following reflections see I. Gabriel, *Die Enzyklika Laudato si'. Ein Meilenstein in der lehramtlichen Sozialverkündigung,* in: IKaZ 44 (2015), 52-65.

8   Similar affirmations are made in LS 14, 53 and 117. The phrase, set in italics , mirrors the title of the book on theology and ecology authored by Brazilian liberation theologian Leonardo Boff *Cry of the earth, cry of the poor* (New York, Orbis 1997). Original edition in Portuguese: *Ecologia: grito da terra, grito dos povres* (São Paulo, Attica 1995). See G. Kerber, *Latin American and Ecumenical Insights in Laudato Si',* The Ecumenical Review, Vol 70, Issue 4, December 2018, p. 627-636.

serious situations, if we consider that a quarter of the world's population lives on the coast or nearby, and that the majority of our megacities are situated in coastal areas (LS 24)." Most of these nearly 2 billion people are poor and cannot afford costly technical means to protect themselves.

We are, therefore, confronted with a threefold ethical problem of ecological justice: a) the endangered livelihood of future generations; b) the endangered livelihood of present poor populations; who, as has to be added, 3) have not contributed to the problem in the first place because they have sofar consumed far less than those who could afford to do so. Thus climate change and this is indeed scandalous, hits worst in places where people live who did not cause it.

In addition to this focus on the interlinkage of the social and ecological questions as well as the interdependence of all living beings on the planet the encyclical contains the first ethics of technology in Catholic Social Teaching combined with a critical but also appreciative view of progress. Without technological progress – we have to realistically admit – the presently 7, 7 billion people worldwide (a number that will increase according to moderate estimates by 2050 to 10 billions) would not be able to survive. We thus do need technological progress together with an economic thinking that favors qualitative growth and, even more important, that includes natural resources in its theory. One of the main problems at present is that we lack adequate economic models which properly take into account the gigantic changes that have occurred during the past three decades because of technically and politically induced globalization. The dominant economic theories largely exclude ecological and social effects, which are seen as externalities. We need to understand the simple fact that we live in "finite world"[9] and cannot rely on infinite growth, e. g. a permanently growing economy.[10]

2. Secondly, with regard to its argumentation strategy Laudato si' follows the See-Judge-Act methodology that was recommended in 1961 by Pope John XXIII in his Encyclical *Mater et Magistra* for the Social Teaching of the Church[11]. This methodology has an earlier history with Catholic Action movements (of workers, students, intellectuals, etc.) since the first half of the 20th century and it was one of the main contents of liberation theologies in Latin America in the 1970s. [12]

In Laudato si', according to this approach, the first chapter, *What is happening to our home* (See), lists the different expressions of the ecological crisis: pollution, climate change, the water crisis, the loss of biodiversity. These expressions are closely related to poverty and inequality that reach planetary dimensions (LS 48).

The second moment of the methodology (Judge), includes the following chapters of Laudato Si', *The Gospel of Creation* (Chapter 2), *The human roots of the ecological crisis* (Chapter 3), *An integral ecology* (Chapter 4). In it, Pope Francis starts by recognizing that the ecological crisis is

---

9   I .Gabriel (with P. Steinmaier-Pösel), *Gerechtigkeit in einer endlichen Welt*, Ostfildern 2. Aufl, 2014.

10   I. Gabriel (together with P. Kirchschläger and R. Sturn), *Eine Wirtschaft, die Leben fördert. Wirtschafts- und unternehmensethische Reflexionen im Anschluss an Papst Franziskus*, Grünewald: Ostfildern, 2. Aufl. 2019.

11   John XXIII, Encyclical *Mater et Magistra*, Citta del Vaticano 1961, §236: "There are three stages which should normally be followed in putting social principles into practice. First, one reviews the concrete situation; secondly, one forms a judgment on it in the light of these same principles; thirdly, one decides what in the circumstances can and should be done to implement these principles. These are the three stages that are usually expressed in the three terms: see, judge, act."

12   A very good analysis of the use of the methodology in theology is provided by Clodovis Boff's 1978 doctoral thesis (Louvain University), published in English as "Theology and Praxis," in which he presents the different mediations: socio-analytical (see), hermeneutical (judge), practical (act). See also Guillermo Kerber, Etica social ecuménica y la encíclica Laudato si', Didaskalia XLVI (2016), p. 55-72.

complex, hence the search for a response must include an intense dialogue between science and religion that can be fruitful for both (LS 62-63). Then the pope develops a theology of creation, an indispensable instrument to respond to the crisis from the Christian perspective (LS 65-100). In analysing the human roots of the ecological crisis, the pope affirms that an effective response to the crisis must address in particular the technocratic paradigm (LS 106ff), excessive anthropocentrism (LS 115ff) and the financial and economic system (LS 189ff) that destroy the earth and deepen the inequalities. The integral ecology proposed in Chapter 4 is based on a leitmotiv of the encyclical that everything is closely related (LS 137). Integral ecology includes the principle of the common good, human rights and justice between generations as some of its essential contents (LS 156-162).

The analysis of the current situation of the planet and the discernment illuminated by the Bible lead to the third moment (Act), developed in Chapter 5, *Some guidelines and action points* and Chapter 6, *Ecological education and spirituality*. On Chapter 5, the pope reaffirms the need for a change of direction and urgent action at the international (LS 164-181) national (LS 176-181) and personal levels (LS 203ff). These changes are the expression of a profound conversion marked by joy, peace and liberating sobriety, central elements of Christian spirituality (LS 223).urthermore, by combining scientific arguments with ethical and theological ones, Laudato si'follows the Pastoral Constitution of Vatican II *Gaudium et spes* in a rather creative manner. It is worth remarking that despite the clear recognition of the seriousness and urgency of the problems the encyclical never reverts to alarmism or an apocalyptic tone, which the Pope considers rightly to be counterproductive. The intention of the text rather is to give hope and stimulate useful action despite of the magnitude of the problems.

3. A key word all along the encyclical is dialogue, to which the entire Chapter 5 (LS 163-201) is devoted. Dialogue is the precondition for the joint efforts needed to mitigate ecological problems, a dialogue that includes natural scientists, politicians, civil society as well as faithful of all religions, so as to make some headway with regard the "bold cultural revolution" (LS 114) demanded. This also requires an efficient promotion of the position of the Roman Catholic Church on ecological issues, which often has been a deficit as ideas have often been better than their public dissemination. In the case of *Laudato si'* the presentation as well as the timing were well chosen the encyclical tuning in perfectly with the ecological efforts of the international community. Thus, the adoption by the UN-General Assembly of the Sustainable Development Goals (SDG's), which replaced the Millenium Goals of 2000, took place in September 2015. At this occasion the Pope also addressed the UN asserting delegates of the support of the Roman Catholic Church in its effort. The following Conference of Parties (COP 21) of the United Nations Framework Convention on Climate Change (UNFCCC) in Paris in December 2015 was able to reach an (albeit in the meantime contested) agreement against all expectations. This shows that it is worth reflecting on the Kairos so as to combine efforts with the international community to make them more successful.

An Ethics of Eco-responsibility in Dialogue with Other Religious and Non-Religious Thinkers and Actors

The ecological state of emergency which has developed over the past decades because of overconsumption of a part of the world population, technological developments and population growth requires a new ethics that includes nature into all its reflections and thus can guide human actions in the age of ecological crisis. This has been the main thesis of *The Imperative of Responsibility: In Search of Ethics for the Technological Age* by Hans Jonas first written and published in German in 1979.[13] In it Jonas analyses the shift in paradigm brought about by modern technologies. Whereas until the present age it was man who found himself at the mercy of a largely untamed nature, it now is nature itself, i. e. the natural environment, that is threatened by mankind. This fundamental change because of its magnitude and novelty has still not been sufficiently recognized and anchored in the human mind. The imperatives Jonas proposes is valid also today: Are my actions with regard to consumption, production as well as the ecological regulations (micro, meso and macrolevel decisions) compatible with the conservation of nature and with it the life of future generations? To this an aspect also must be added which is often overlooked: the intragenerational effects of ecological devastation: Are my actions compatible with eco justice for those who are poor and who are affected more gravely by them despite the fact that they have not contributed to natural and climate degradation? Are my actions compatible with peace, regional and global, which is and will be even more endangered by conflicts over natural resources, e. g. water, in many parts of the world?

One of the central questions of Jonas with regard to the direction natural science and technology need to take is: What is the aim of technological inventions? Can the risks they entail be calculated sufficiently? Will they bring about major improvements for human life or only minor amelioration, which do not justify the invention and production of new goods.[14] Because of economic competition it is practically impossible for companies and their Research and Development departments today to follow this conservative principle of risk aversion. To reach this aim the position of political actors, national as well as international, needs to be strengthened so as to counterbalance the effect of economical activities and act for the common good (a demand also frequently made in LS). A further question, not yet posed by Jonas, is that it will be imperative to reduce the worldwide consumption of energy and therefore of goods, whereby the rich as well as the richer nations need to go ahead and develop life styles that can serve as a good example. This may seem utopian but Christians and the Christian Churches could here be major promotors of sufficiency and a more ascetic style of consumption. To give but one example: According to the latest Special Report of the IPCC 10% of global CO2 emissions are the result of food waste.[15] If one combines this with the fact that in the EU a scandalous 50% of food are wasted, one realizes that personal change from an ethical point of view is imperative.[16] Without linking questions of

---

13   Hans Jonas, *Das Prinzip Verantwortung. Versuch einer Ethik für die technologische Zivilisation*, Frankfurt 1979 (*The Imperative of Responsibility. In Search of an Ethics for the Technological Age*).
14   The poem „Der Zauberlehrling" (the sorcerer's apprentice) by Johann Wolfgang von Goethe written in 1827 shows that the dilemmas of modern technology could be discerned at the beginning of the Industrial Revolution.
15   https://www.de-ipcc.de/media/content/Hauptaussagen_SRCCL.pdf Report of 8th August 2019 (access 28/8/19).
16   http://www.europarl.europa.eu/news/de/headlines/society/20170505STO73528/lebensmittelverschwen dung-in-der-eu-infografik vpm 2017 (access 28/8/19).

sufficiency and sustainability of goods with those of life style and consumption the ecological crisis cannot be solved or even mitigated. Central issues are besides food waste, mobility, meat consumption and digitalization. There is still hardly any discussion about the fact that digitalization and robots besides other negative effects will drive up energy consumption to new hights. We still behave as if there were no limits to growth and consumption, the internalization of an ethics of eco-responsibility remaining anything but weak. This has last but not least to do with the fact that the present public eco-discourse is trapped in sometimes overlapping, at any closer look ideology driven ideas: Thus, the public debate continues to suffer from technological overoptimism and the widespread illusion that new technological inventions and improvements will be able to solve human and therefore also ecological problems as they have done, more or less efficiently in the past. This mentality often goes hand in hand with the idea that progress is guaranteed by evolution, an ideology which replaces or underpins other progressist narratives of modernity.[17] In its stricter variants it is combined with a deterministic world view which is highly seducing because it allows us to just put our heads in the sand. Evolution will go on and therefore nothing can happen to us. This mindset easily furthers irresponsibility and can even lead to outright inhuman ideas. In an article on climate change the columnist of the Economist wrote unabashedly: "Unfortunately such adaptation (to climate change IG) has always meant large number of deaths. Evolution works that way."[18] And there is a third trap – the romantic dream of an intact nature we only have to return to by developing holistic lifestyles untouched by modern technologies. As much as we have indeed to change our patterns of consumption and initiate a courageous, ecological revolution (LS 142) and as much as we have to find life styles that are more humane and more in accordance with leading real personal lives, ideas have to stand the test to whether they are in agreement with the further development of all mankind.

All these ideas, to be clear, contain some truth: We need technological progress to feed and cloths the earth population. Without a large range of technologies in all fields of life, the present world population which is about ten times than that of the pre-industrial age, will obviously not be able survive. And it is indeed necessary today to develop more holistic and sufficient alternative lifestyles which are in closer relation with nature and scale down energy consumption. However, without a new mentality with regard to nature which makes us see it with new eyes and understand that we are its stewards and guardians and thus carry responsibility for its future, major changes will not be possible.

Possible Contributions of a Christian Ecotheology in Theory and Practice

For Christians in particular an ethical approach and action will be embedded in the wider framework of Christian faith and therefore needs to be reflected by eco-theology.

It has become standard to attribute (at least some) of the fault for the present ecological disasters to Christianity. These accusations are based on a half-verse to be found in Genesis: "Be fertile and multiply, fill the earth and subdue it." (Gen 1,27) There are several reasons why this lacks in plausibility. The argument stated most often is that philologically the Hebrew word *raddah*, to subdue, does not mean arbitrary domination but good kingly rule. In this sense it is also

---

17   See the bestsellers of Yuval N. Hariri or Steven Pinker, to name but two highly popular authors, who peddle such ideas with great success.
18   Adapting to Climate Change, in: The Economist, 27th November 2010, 13.

Ingeborg G. Gabriel / Guillermo Kerber

interpreted by the second (and older) creation narrative according to which men and women are to be guardians of the creation which is depicted as a garden (Gen 2,5). More important, however, it seems that the paradigmatic change Hans Jonas speaks about could by no means be foreseen in the 6th century BC. The accusation thus is anachronistic. To this has to be added that it constitutes a kind of inverted biblicism to interpret highly complex historical developments of two and a half millennia in this linear way, whereby the fact that those who hold this view often also defend the equally widespread opposite idea that Christianity was and is inimical to scientific and techno-logical progress. To the contrary the the monotheistic world view has a strong focus on ethics and therefore on the care for the other as a brother and sister because God as creator of the earth and its sustainer is the one who gives the laws, demands justice and love and wants humans to flour-ish. It is with this basic insight in mind (which by the way is shared by all monotheistic religions) that a Christian eco-theology and ethics can be developed. Some of its main pillars should be:[19]

A widening of the perspective of salvation which is to include the whole cosmos. Climate change teaches us in an almost experimental way that our actions influence not only other hu-mans in a positive or negative way but also the whole universe (cf. Romans 8.19-22).

This should lead to a new view of creation which sees nature as God's creation in its own worth. This change of mentality requires a fundamental metanoia in which Christians are to play the role of an avantgarde. Whereas the modern world view degrades nature to pure mate-rial which has (so Immanuel Kant) a price and not dignity, a Christian world view includes by definition all creation, albeit without falling into pantheism. Creatures are different in their duties and rights. Dignity is indeed a human quality only. It is essentially linked to freedom and with it responsibility. But this does not mean that the other creatures are at the arbitrary disposal of men. As St. Augustin writes: "It is not with respect to our convenience or discomfort, but with respect to their own nature, that the creatures are glorifying their artificer."[20]

Out of this new world view for which nature constitutes not only an object but an integral part of creation which we have to care for we need to consciously develop new ethical attitudes from the Christian tradition (which can also be shared with others, religious or not).[21]
Today some of them seem to be particularly crucial:[22]
- *Humility against hybris*: Humility has been a central Christian virtue since antiquity. Etymo-logically the term stems from *humus*, the Latin for earth, just as the Hebrew word *adama* means earthling and thus links humans to the earth. Man, thus is a biological and therefore mortal and limited being. He and she depend on others, as well as on nature and with it his/ her creator. This view is largely at odds with a modern world view which reagards man as his own lord. This is indeed a form of hybris. To recognize that this view is false constitutes humil-ity and can be a first step to a new lifestyle.

---

19   Cf. extensively: I. Gabriel, *Die Ökologie als Frage nach dem Neuen Menschen,* in: Michael Biehl/Bernd Kappes/Bärbel Wartenberg-Potter (Hg.), Grüne Reformation. Ökologische Theologie, Hamburg 2017, 83-108.
20   Cited in Charles Taylor, *A Secular Age,* Cambridge 2007, 342.
21   David Hallman proposed the following spiritual values for justice and sustainability: gratitude, humility, suf-ficiency, justice, love, peace, faith and hope. See David Hallman, *Spiritual Values for Earth Community,* Geneva, WCC, 2000. We have developed some of these perspectives in G. Kerber, Caring for Creation and Striving for Climate Justice: Implications for mission and spirituality, International Review of Mission, Volume 99, Number 2, November 2010, p- 219-229.
22   For more extensive treatment cf. I. Gabriel, *Fascinated with Domination: The Dark Side of Modernity, its Eco-logical Consequences and how to deal with them ethically and spiritually,* in: G. Müller-Fahrenholz (ed.), Peace on Earth and Peace with the Earth. Serving the Goodness of God's Creation, Geneva 2008, 113-135.

- *Gratitude versus greed*: Gratitude constitutes another central of not the Christian virtue *par excellence*. To be grateful to God and others as well as to nature for what He has done for us and for what it gives us means the recognition of the fact that man is not his own maker. Moreover, it creates bonds between all living things. It is a way to humbly recognize the interdependence of all things. This constitutes the opposite of an arrogant and illusionary individualistic attitude of autarky. It teaches us to accept limits and resist an attitude that wants to have more material things at all cost at the expense of others and nature (in Greek this vice is called *pleonexia*). It is this form of greed which lies at the heart of our present lifestyle and which affects us negatively. It tends to destroy inner and outer peace. *Eucharistia* – Thanksgiving as the central Christian liturgical celebration could be at the heart of this development of this new attitude of gratitude.
- *Human dependence and the importance of grace*: Closely connected with humility and gratitude is the recognition that man is not alone in the universe, that he can turn to the Other, God and that this is not debasing him/her but uplifting. As Pope Francis writes at several occasions we urgently need God's grace and inspiration to find a way out of the disaster humanity got itself into.

It is worthwhile to reflect further on these and possibly other attitudes as the basis of a new worldview and an ecological reformation which has to be followed by deeds which may be small but which will improve our insights and help us to bring about greater deeds, laws and regulations so as to contribute to overcome the ecological crisis or at least mitigate its dire effects and thus give hope to others.

In fact the ecological and climate crisis have led to joint interfaith statements and actions that, stressing the ethical commonalities of faith communities, alert and propose common actions to deal with these interlinked crises. The centrality and sacredness of life, the care for the earth and for the most vulnerable, and the critiques of exploitation and overconsumption are some of the common values many faith traditions share. When coming together to express their convictions and decide common actions, faith leaders and activists have been reinvigorated and a synergy has been created. This has not been done in isolation from other actors. Especially with civil society, religious actors have developed for many decades a strong international advocacy work, based on their ethical convictions. [23]

---

23   We have analysed in detail this action in G. Kerber, International advocacy for climate justice, in R.G. Veldman, A. Szasz and R. Haluza-Delay, (eds.) *How the World's Religions are Responding to Climate Change: Social Scientific Investigations,* Abingdon: Routledge, 2013, p. 278-294.

Ingeborg G. Gabriel / Guillermo Kerber

THE CONFESSION OF BARMEN: ITS SIGNIFICANCE 1934 AND TODAY

Jochen Motte

Eighty-five years ago, from 29-31 May 1934, the 139 members of the first Reich synod of the Confessing Church met in the church of Gemarke in Barmen, one year after the National Socialists had taken power in Germany. Communists and Social Democrats were being brutally persecuted; Jewish citizens faced discrimination and prejudice. The seventh of April 1933 marked the adoption of the "Aryan paragraph" by the Reichstag, which among other things provided for Jewish officials, professors, and pastors to be dismissed from their posts. Democracy was functionally abolished. Human rights and citizens' rights were violated. Books by outlawed authors were banned and burned. The first concentration camps were built.

Most Germans welcomed this development, as shown in the monument in the pedestrian zone in front of the Barmen Gemarke Church. Most of the figures are depicted as hailing Hitler, with only a small group turning away and gathering around the bible.

(From https://www.ekd.de/11294.htm)

Many Christian men and women were open to "positive Christianity", as the National Socialists referred to it in their platform. They joined the faith movement of "German Christians" who had gained a broad majority within the churches in 1934. This movement supported combining Christianity and National Socialism in a manner that was supposed to be structurally completed on 27 September 1933 with the centralization of Germany's "Landeskirchen" and the appointment of a "Reichs Bishop".

The resistance of the "Confessing Church" formed in opposition to these developments. Most of the Christians who assembled in Barmen in 1934 were concerned not with resisting National Socialism itself, much less solidarity with its victims, but rather with preserving the independence of the church against the claim from the German state to interfere into church affairs and to get control.[1]

"Church should remain church and not conform to the demands of the time: the Führer principle, the ideology of blood and soil, the Aryan paragraphs, the new state's claim to totality. The demands were broadly affirmed for the political sphere but not for the church."[2] It was against this backdrop that the Theological Declaration of Barmen was adopted.

Although the confession of Barmen was not directed primarily against the state, it was understood by the same as a criticism and an interrogation. Thus the Theological Declaration also had an inherent political effect, to the extent that it theologically questioned the state's totalitarian claim to power.

The fifth thesis of Barmen states that the task of the state is to use the threat and exercise of force to effect justice and peace in an unredeemed world. Furthermore, it declares that "We reject the false doctrine that the Church could and should recognize as a source of its proclamation, beyond and besides this one Word of God, yet other events, powers, historic figures and truths as God's revelation."

Barmen and the birth of the Confessing Church marked the beginning of the churches' many conflicts over supremacy within the Protestant Church in Germany, known as the "Kirchenkampf". There were also individual voices within the Confessing Church that called for political resistance to National Socialism as well as solidarity with its victims. Among the best known of these are the theologians Dietrich Bonhoeffer and Karl Barth.

It is very significant for the later history of the effects of the Barmen Theological Declaration that the confession was adopted jointly by members of the Lutheran, Reformed, and United Churches, which was not at all common at the time. One example of the fundamental importance the Confession continues to have is that theologians of the Evangelical Church in the Rhineland are ordained not only according to the confessions of the early church and the Reformation, but also to the Theological Declaration of Barmen. In the Reformed Church and the Protestant Lutheran Church in Northern Germany, the Barmen Theological Declaration is part of the confessional foundations of the Church. In other churches it has become part of the constitution. Article 1(3) of the Evangelical Church of Germany (EKD) constitution endorses the decisions taken by the Barmen Synod for all member churches.

The Barmen Theological Declaration has had an impact within the worldwide ecumenical movement as well, especially in combating racism and apartheid in South Africa. In his article about the reception of Barmen in South Africa, Nico Koopmann has written that "Barmen and the 'Kirchenkampf' started to function as liberating symbols of confession and resistance, for the emerging discourse of Black Theology in South Africa."[3] As Koopmann sees it, Barmen not only gave rise to the *Belhar Confession*, but also paved the way for the wider reception of Belhar.[4]

---

1   See „Vorwort", Günter van Norden, Paul Gerhard Schoenborn, Volkmar Wittmütz, in Wir verwerfen die falsche Lehre. Arbeits- und Lesebuch zur Barmer Theologischen Erklärung und zum Kirchenkampf, (1984) p. 9f.
2   Loc. cit., p. 10.
3   Nico Koopmann, "The Reception of the Barmen Declaration in South Africa", Ökumenische Rundschau, (2009) p. 62.
4   Loc. cit., p. 65.

Jochen Motte

Also worthy to be mentioned in the broader context of the reception of Barmen is the 2005 Declaration of the Reformed World Community of Churches in Accra: "Covenanting for Justice: *The Accra Confession*", which comprehended "confession" as a continuous ecumenical process that determines the social-ethical agenda of the churches. Nevertheless, the declarations stated in the context of Barmen remain limited to the confessional family of the Reformed Churches.

In the history of how the Barmen Declaration has been received, the question has often been raised as to whether Barmen should not motivate more courageous confession in the face of new challenges. At a conference for the fiftieth anniversary of the Barmen Theological Declaration, the theologian Jürgen Moltmann gave the following answer to what the difference was between the confessional situation of 1984 and 1934:

"One could say that in 1934 it was 'errors' that were 'ravaging' the Protestant Church in Germany and 'shattering' its unity, as stated in the introduction to the Barmen Theological Declaration. Since 1945, however, we have dealt with 'errors' that go beyond the *unity of humanity* that God intends."[5] Moltmann focuses in particular on the division of the world into the first, second, and third world, which has condemned a portion of humanity to misery and the threat of nuclear war, which could lead to the annihilation of humanity and the destruction of the natural foundations of life.

In addition to these threats, it is clear that today we must also keep in mind the destructive effects that climate change is having on human livelihoods. But Moltmann, in his list of man-made hazards, already named environmental destruction as one of the central challenges of our time: "That's why we reflect and ask ourselves: What does the Barmen Declaration say, and what does it lead to, in the face of the destruction of the third world and its natural environment by our expansive economic power?"[6]

Because Moltmann believed that the errors were located within the church as well as outside it, even back in 1934, he asked the following question of the five hundred participants at the conference in Barmen: "Are we able to confess? Are we willing to confess? Will we confess Christ as the one Word of God here today, where Christ is *waiting* for our presence, our word, and our deed?"[7]

Given this history, what impulses from Barmen in 1934 can reach us today, when the consequences of climate change threaten the whole of humanity? And can the confessional format chosen in Barmen still be relevant?

This question is being asked against the backdrop of the changing ecumenical discourse on justice, peace, and the integrity of creation. For example, the *Conciliar Process for Justice, Peace and Integrity of Creation* was initially influenced by covenants – such as at the WCC World Convocation in Seoul in 1990 – in which the participants renewed their commitment to this covenant.[8] The delegates believed that the alliance had been broken by injustice, war, and environmental destruction. The covenant led to a struggle against injustice in order to promote peace and the integrity of creation. In such a hermeneutic context, the "confession" category is more than appropriate.

---

5   Jürgen Moltmann, „Einführung", in: Bekennende Kirche wagen. Barmen 1934 – 1984 (1984) p. 19.
6   Loc. cit., p. 20.
7   Loc. cit., p. 22.
8   See WCC World Convention, Message of the World Convocation on Justice, Peace and the Integrity of Creation, (1990) – http://oikoumene.org/eng.home/eng.global/eng.seoul90/eng.seoul.1/index.html

Just a few years after Seoul, however, these categories broadly receded or were transformed, as the Orthodox churches in the WCC grew more self-assured, the Christological concentration – long shaped by theology of the West – became less important, and the WCC opened its membership to free-church and Pentecostal movements. The process started as early as the Decade to Overcome Violence adopted at the Eighth Assembly of the WCC in Harare and continued in Porto Alegre, up to and including the Pilgrimage for Justice and Peace adopted at the Tenth Assembly in Busan. "Commitment is no longer the issue here: instead, the member churches and the recipients of the message are invited to join this journey. The path is not described; instead, God is called upon to show the pilgrims the way. Above all, however, the chosen image of the pilgrimage – an original element of Catholic tradition rejected by the Reformation, a path to a holy site for the purpose of atonement of the fulfillment of a vow – shifts to become the focus here. Elements of spirituality, mediation and contemplation come to the fore. Struggle, resistance, and protest against the system transform into a decidedly spiritual movement of Christians advocating for justice and peace. How justice and peace will specifically be realized is not defined from the beginning; the reply is requested of God, and must spring forth anew in each process of pilgrimage."[9]

In 1934, Christians in Barmen saw themselves as challenged to confess because of what they believed was a threat to their existence as a church of Jesus Christ. Today Christians worldwide are challenged in the face of a global crisis, in which the future existence of life on this planet hangs in the balance.

In today's multi-confessional and multi-contextual world community of Christians, there may be many ways to respond – just as Barmen then was only one response from Christians of a certain confessional character in a particular historical context. There will also be many forms of expression, of which a confession is only one of several possible choices. All the same, given the challenge we face today, it is worth the trouble and effort to share a common message – to global Christianity, the community of nations, and the world – founded on faith and biblical witness. Inside and outside Christianity, there are some who have no response for the life-threatening consequences of climate change and environmental destruction, and others – worse still – who spread misleading and false messages.[10]

It is to be hoped that the delegates to the Eleventh Assembly of the WCC in 2021 will seize this opportunity. I would be delighted if this 2019 International Conference in Wuppertal, Barmen could give them an incentive to do so.

---

9   Jochen Motte, "Advocacy for Justice, Peace and the Integrity of Creation as an Element of Missionary Activity from 1993/96 to the Present Day", in "Mission Still Possible?" Global Perspectives on Mission and Mission Theology, ed. by Jochen Motte and Andar Parlindungan (2017) p. 89.
10   See, e.g., Meghan Mayhew Bergman, "What Would Jesus Do? Talking with Evangelicals about Climate Change", in The Guardian, 19. December 2018 – https://www.theguardian.com/environment/2018/dec/19/talking-with-evangelicals-about-climate-change-south.
"I spoke with people of faith in Alabama, Mississippi, Georgia, Florida, South Carolina, North Carolina and Virginia, and it became clear that the primary barrier to climate action is the fact that it's been yoked with the liberal agenda. Climate activist and author Anna Jane Joyner, whose father is the pastor of a megachurch in North Carolina, writes that she grew up lumping 'environmentalists in with hippies and liberals and all the other people who were probably going to hell …'. Dr Lucas Johnston, a professor of religion and environment at Wake Forest University, explains that 'there is a longstanding antipathy toward environmental sentiments in Christian, and especially evangelical circles, because they have, for centuries, been imagined as pernicious and dangerous, and possibly bordering on paganism'."

ECO-THEOLOGY AND PERSPECTIVES FROM THE TRADITION OF BARMEN

Markus Mühling

'Jesus Christ, as he is attested for us in Holy Scripture, is the one Word of God which we have to hear and which we have to trust and obey in life and in death.
We reject the false doctrine, as though the church could and would have to acknowledge as a source of its proclamation, apart from and besides this one Word of God, still other events and powers, figures and truths, as God's revelation.'[1]

1. The confessional and symbolic weight of the Barmen Declaration, particularly of Barmen I, can not only be explained by its historical success – i.e. by its success in the totalitarian situation in Germany in the 1930ies, and by the fact that it served as a kind of template for other declarations of confession later on –, but by being an answer to an inherent problem of modernity and postmodernity.

2. There are two features inherent in modernity that led to postmodernity: 1. Every realm – ethics, politics, religion and principially reason, too –, had become a matter of human or social cultivation or choice, and can be seen as at human's disposal. 2. Reason should be seen the only universal denominator. This causes contradictions and to perceive and to live under these contradictions is the signature of post-modernity. In the course of history, it has been revealed that there is no universal basis for reason; therefore, also reason is in the need of being orientated and in the need of being cultivated. The post-modern answer is that this can happen predominantly in two ways, in a constructivist one (a), and in a fundamentalist one (b):

(a) It can simply be claimed that also reason is an object of voluntarily human cultivation. In this case, societies become constructivist, and it seems that humans are in the position of the voluntarist God of late-scholasticism: They can and have to choose whatever is true, whatever is good, and whatever is beautiful.

(b) It can also be claimed that there are specific fundaments that orientate reason, and that – due to the universal claim of reason – these fundaments have to be spread over all aspects of the life-world: Examples of fundamentalism are as well empiricist naturalism, as reductive historism, or the different ‚religious' fundamentalisms, which see their fundaments in different sacred texts. The problem with fundamentalism is not, however, that it is claimed that there are fundaments at all, but that it is claimed that these fundaments are at human disposal. In this feature lies a danger: In that case, everything that can be derived from the fundaments can be conceived or taught. And anyone, who will not follow, is seen either as not owning the cognitive capacities (he or she is 'ill') or as an intentional opponent (he or she is 'evil'). What is traditionally called 'fundamentalism' is

---

1   The Barmen Declaration, in ASSEMBLY, THE OFFICE OF THE GENERAL (Hg.), The Constitution of the Presbyterian Church (USA), Part I: Book of Confessions, Philadelphia 2004, 245–250, 248.

therefore a phenomenon of misplaced fundamentals: The fundamentals are identified at a place where they open the road to human manipulation.

The outcome of both answers is a simultaneous pluralization: Whereas in pre-postmodern periods different paradigms of rationality followed in a succession of sequences, in the present days they appear all at once.

3. The Barmen Declaration is the church's answer to this post-modern condition: It acknowledges that any kind of reason or rationality is in the need of being orientated or informed, but it denies that this kind of orientation is in any kind at human disposal: It claims in Barmen 1 that the only standard or canon of rationality is the incarnated word of God, the bodily appearance of the eternal logos, the second person of the Trinity that is Godself. In doing that, it detracts systems of reason or knowledge of human voluntarily choice, be it individual or cultural, and at the same time it prevents any kind of fundamentalism, be it natural reductionism or literal fundamentalism, by claiming that the only true fundament, the incarnated Word, is a *person* that is not at human disposal. The appropriate answer to the incarnated Word that informs reason and rationality is therefore neither choice – as in constructivism – nor submission – as in fundamentalism, but faith and confession. And faith and confession are no subjects of human will. Without being passively convinced, without fiducia, faith and confession are impossible. On the one hand, submission presupposes to oppress one's wishes; but faith is an alteration of affections, with the effect that one feels 'delight and love' (Luther). On the other hand, choice presupposes a realm of alternatives. But in faith as a mode of perception, truth, and value, one's will is bound by feeling and perception. Therefore, any possible alternatives are not antecedent to faith, but appear in the framework of faith.

4. It is this feature of the Barmen Declaration – that it confesses any kind of rationality and any kind of human cultivating activity as dependent on the person of the incarnated Word – that enabled its historical success in the 1930ies and that enables its critical function in the face of the challenges of the global ecological crisis.

5. In confessing the eternal Word as *incarnated* in the person of Jesus Christ, it acknowledges that rationality is neither a matter of mind nor of matter: Incarnation means the priority of bodliness. Mind and matter are abstractions from that. Humans are in continuity to other non-human animals and other bodily creatures. According to Gregersen, the incarnation has to be seen as a „deep incarnation",[2] if it is an incarnation at all: it permeates the whole creation. The fact that God the eternal logos became man means by implication that he became foxes, sparrows and dust, too. No distance of mind and matter separates human beings from creation. Whereas in the quasi-religion of reductionist naturalism curiosity is seen as the only virtue, and care is seen as delegated to other responsibilities (political ones), bodiliness implies that the virtues of curiosity *and care* are only different but inseparable sides of the same coin.

6. In confessing the *eternal Word* as incarnated in the person of Jesus Christ, it acknowledges the inherent and essential relationality of bodiliness and rejects atomism and individualism: In the same manner as the eternal Word is only the eternal word due to its eternal relationships of love

---

2   Cf. GREGERSEN, NIELS HENRIK, Deep Incarnation. Why Evolutionary Continuity Matters in Christology, Toronto Journal of Theology 26 (2010), 173–188.

from and with Father and Spirit, also creation is a nexus of internal, bodily relations, not an accumulation of individuals. No spatial distance separates the lives on earth. Therefore, re-assessing the weight of Barmen 1 in the times of the ecological crisis means to confess that spatial distances are no restriction of human responsibility to care.

Furthermore, to see the incarnated Word as bodily incarnated means that economic and immanent Trinity are entangled: We are living in the story of the Trinity, and also the nexus of bodily relations contributes to the identity of God. Christianity is – if it is classifiable at all – a kind of panentheism,[3] for in him we live, and move, and have our becoming (Act 17:28).

7. In confessing the eternal Word as incarnated in the *person* of Jesus Christ, Barmen enables and restricts human activity and responsibility to curiosity and care, since a person cannot be by any way at another one's disposal. Persons are always Whence-and-Whither-becomings[4]: They are constantly in becoming, never finished, and they only become in solidarity from and to other persons and the natural world. As humans, we are not so much blobs or points entering relationships of a network, but developing knots in a woven meshwork. As humans, we are no human beings, but human becomings. Therefore, ecological solidarity is commanded, since it fits to our ontic constitution. However, in the communication of the mutual relationships, also the particularity of persons and personal transcendence appears. As a result it is part of ecological solidarity to respect that the further course of mutual becoming is not at human disposal: The global ecology in its becoming is *no system*.[5] Its course of becoming is *not driven by an algorithm*, that is or could be discovered. We do not have to behave primarily intentional in setting ends in regard to cultivating nature, but we are in the need of behaving attentional, in perceiving and constantly accommodating our own becoming in solidarity with non-human creatures. Therefore, humans do *not* have the task of the preservation of creation. The talk of the preservation of creation was an understandable first reaction from churches to the appearance of the ecological crisis in the 1970ies and 1980ies. Nevertheless, this talk only reflected the modern overestimation of human cultivation, the old modern titanism that led exactly into the ecological crisis, which has become a global one today. Preservation of creation is primarily a divine and trinitarian work. From the perspective of Barmen, not the preservation of creation, but only *collaboration with and contribution to the preservation of creation* is a meaningful human task.

8. Therefore, any attempts of geo-engineering relying only on the claim that nature is seen as a system appear not without danger in the light of Barmen.

However, also the contemporary and popular talk of sustainability is not without danger. 'Sustainability' originally came from the economics of forestry. In distinction to other agricultural economics, in forestry it is clear that a generation can only earn its income if their predecessors have set the basis. And it is also clear that the succeeding generations can only earn something if the present generation does not exploit the forest. Thus, the term sustainability is an excellent one

---

3 Cf. Mühling, Markus, Post-Systematische Theologie 1. Denkwege – Theologische Philosophie, Leiden – Paderborn 2020, ch. 21.
4 Cf. Mühling, Markus, The T&T Clark Handbook of Christian Eschatology, New York – London 2015, 206.
5 Cf. for the problems of thinking in systems Mühling, M., PST 1, ch.1. In the case of ecology and the misleading talk of ‚eco-systems“ cf. Ingold, Tim, The Life of Lines, London – New York 2015, 155. The decisive problem with the term ‚ecology‘ is, that it is bound since its use in Erich Haeckel to a specific kind of ontology, that should be questioned by phenomenological reasons.

in order to stress not only the spatial, but also the temporal dimension of ecological responsibility. This is without doubt an advantage. Moreover, in shifting this concept from forestry to all other branches of human economics, a hidden eschatological aspect appears: Whereas in the economics of forestry, only the specified future of one's children and grandchildren matters, in the broadening of the concept to all fields of economics one has to care for an unspecified future: Therefore, an eschatical[6] reservation appears. We simply have not to care for the very near future of 50, 100 or 500 years, but for a future that cannot be measured. Also, this is an advantage of the use of the concept of sustainability, and interestingly this is a feature where the eschatological expertise of theologians can contribute directly to understand and shape global economics of sustainability. However, sustainability still is a concept of economics, and it still follows economic rules like profit maximisation and economic growth. If the principles of profit-maximisation and economic growth are spread over large periods instead of being restricted to one generation alone, nothing is won. Profit maximisation and unrestricted growth are still mechanisms of a behaviour that treads the natural world only as a matter that has to be shaped by the human mind – the common mistake of both, capitalism and Marxism. From the perspective of Barmen, stewardship and the solidarity of mutual love also towards and from the natural world have to replace these old attitudes. Accordingly 'sustainability' alone won't make it.

9. In confessing the eternal Word as incarnated in the person of *Jesus Christ*, Barmen acknowledges a particular universality of an ecological ethics. Therefore, it is an excellent example of how a global pluralist ethics can work: It is decisive that one is bound to a particular narration and that any kind of ethics is bound to a particular tradition. In our example, this is the tradition of the church as confessing Jesus Christ as being incarnated in a constitutive-relational manner. Hence, the origins and the basis of such an eco-ethics are particular. However, in claiming that this particular Jesus Christ is the incarnated, bodily reason of creation, responsibility and care of confessing, Christians concern the whole bodily world. Responsibility and care find no boundary in religions and traditions. It cannot be restricted to members of the same religion, as long as it does not become a contradiction.

In that – providing an *ethos* that is based in particular, grown traditions with universal, unrestricted implications in engagement – Barmen is an excellent template for pluralist societies: No abstract theism, no abstract humanism, and no abstract 'world ethos'[7] can maintain and acknowledge a global pluralist society. All these are expressions of misplaced universality: universality in the basics instead of universality in the outcome. Any kind of universality of basics suffers automatically from the mistakes of constructivism or reductionism. Thereby it denies the real plurality of the life-world. Therefore, not the construction of one single global eco-ethics should be the aim. Also, Barmen cannot be the basis for such a single united eco ethics. That would be a *contradictio in adiecto*. On the contrary, Barmen should be a motivation to develop particular *ethe* (pl.) on the basis of local traditions with universal, unrestricted implications.

10. Although the Barmen Declaration is gained from the insight that reason has to be informed by particular narrations, and although it is sceptical against any kind of natural reductionism, it is not sceptical against science as such or against natural philosophies. In pronouncing bodili-

---

6   Regarding the distinction between ,eschatic' and ,eschatological' cf. MÜHLING, M., Handbook of Christian Eschatology, 38.
7   Cf. KÜNG, HANS, Projekt Weltethos, München ¹³1996.

ness of reason, relationality of life, and regarding the fact that life is a matter not of being but of becoming, it provides many points of contact to non-theological ideas that could be helpful in behaving in the face of the global ecological crisis. Among these non-theological ideas that meet the specific Christian implications of Barmen, are e.g. the theory of affordances in the ecological psychology of James Gibson,[8] the non-anthropocentric anthropology of lines of becoming by social anthropologist Tim Ingold,[9] the theory of the extended mind,[10] phenomenology of the body,[11] the theory of the ecological brain,[12] an extended evolutionary theory as e.g. in the theory of niche-construction,[13] and of course an economics of sustainability.

11. During the history of the last 50 years of eco-theology, the churches learned that the role of man is due to Gen 1,28 not so much like an exploiter or sovereign, but has to be modelled in terms of stewardship. Here I cannot present this meaningful model in detail. However, I want to stress an inspiring feature of this model. The 'steward', in English, is not only the house-keeper, but also the *waiter*, who serves the guests: In the framework of an anthropology of continuation to non-human becomings this means: being stewards in the sense of waiters and waitresses for one-another, and for the creatures of nature; isn't that a wonderful image for the role of humans in creation?

12. At last, back to Barmen 1: The decisive point in the confessional and symbolic weight of Barmen is, that it concerns the identity of the *koinonia* of the church. Therefore, it does not have only an impact for the society (in the 20th century) or for the nexus of nature (today), but it relates this external ethical dimension to the internal identity claims of the church. Whoever is not following the confession cannot be seen as part of the church; and any community which is not confessing according to Barmen 1 cannot be seen as a church. Therefore, the relation between the confession of Barmen 1 and its eco-theological ethical impacts is a logical implication or a necessary condition. And this means in return, that the eco-theological engagement, described in this paper, is a logical replication or necessary condition for a community to be a church: Whoever speaks, 'I love God', and is exploiting the organism of creation, is truly a liar.

In its historical framework, the Barmen Declaration had to be seen together with the Stuttgart declaration of guilt. This is also true in a theological sense: To alter things presupposes to confess one's guilt. And since we are whence-and-whither becomings, we – our generation – we are always 'older than ourselves'[14]. As a result, we have the task first of confessing our guilt, which is that our ancestors' overestimation of humanity in the period of classical modernity led to colonialization and an ethics of exploiting nature. We also have to confess that we have inherited guilt in the heritage of this unholy encounter of some of the worst branches of modernity with Christian

---

8   Cf. GIBSON, JAMES JEROME, The Ecological Approach to Visual Perception, New York – London 2015.
9   Cf. INGOLD, T., Life of Lines.
10   Cf. CLARK, ANDY/CHALMERS, DAVID J., The Extended Mind, Analysis 58 (1998), 10–23.
11   Cf. e.g. MERLEAU-PONTY, MAURICE, Phenomenology of Perception, London–New York 2002.
12   Cf. FUCHS, THOMAS, Das Gehirn – ein Beziehungsorgan. Eine phänomenologisch-ökologische Konzeption, Stuttgart ⁴2013.
13   Cf. MÜHLING, MARKUS, Resonances: Neurobiology, Evolution and Theology. Evolutionary Niche Construction, the Ecological Brain and Relational-Narrative Theology, Göttingen – Bristol (CT) 2014.
14   WALDENFELS, BERNHARD, Bodily Experience between Selfhood and Otherness, Phenomenology and the Cognitive Sciences 3 (2004), 235–248, 242.

theology. Thereby, we perverted the story of the gospel, of the word incarnated, and thereby we have violated our own identity claims. Therefore, I have a wish; a wish that could perhaps be an outcome for the World Council of Churches' general assembly in 2021: Let us formulate a confession of guilt, where we are confessing that in stressing the *dominium terrae* as mastery of mind over matter, of human interests over non-human creatures, we perverted the proclamation of the gospel, we perverted the image of the triune God in creation, and we perverted our own identity and becoming as the people of God.

The Barmen Declaration, in Assembly, The Office of the General (Hg.), The Constitution of the Presbyterian Church (USA), Part I: Book of Confessions, Philadelphia 2004, 245–250.

Clark, Andy/Chalmers, David J., The Extended Mind, Analysis 58 (1998), 10–23.

Fuchs, Thomas, Das Gehirn – ein Beziehungsorgan. Eine phänomenologisch-ökologische Konzeption, Stuttgart ⁴2013.

Gibson, James Jerome, The Ecological Approach to Visual Perception, New York – London 2015.

Gregersen, Niels Henrik, Deep Incarnation. Why Evolutionary Continuity Matters in Christology, Toronto Journal of Theology 26 (2010), 173–188.

Ingold, Tim, The Life of Lines, London – New York 2015.

Küng, Hans, Projekt Weltethos, München ¹³1996.

Merleau-Ponty, Maurice, Phenomenology of Perception, London–New York 2002.

Mühling, Markus, Post-Systematische Theologie 1. Denkwege – Theologische Philosophie, Leiden – Paderborn 2020.

Mühling, Markus, Resonances: Neurobiology, Evolution and Theology. Evolutionary Niche Construction, the Ecological Brain and Relational-Narrative Theology, Göttingen – Bristol (CT) 2014.

Mühling, Markus, The T&T Clark Handbook of Christian Eschatology, New York – London 2015.

Waldenfels, Bernhard, Bodily Experience between Selfhood and Otherness, Phenomenology and the Cognitive Sciences 3 (2004), 235–248.

Markus Mühling

REGIONAL PERSPECTIVES

JUSTICE BY FAITH AND ECO-JUSTICE

Contours of a life in the Spirit before the ecocide (of the) unlimited

Daniel C. Beros

In memory of my brother in Christ and college Dr. Pedro Kalmbach

Introduction

The starting point for the following reflections on Christian "spirituality" in our current context is grounded in the thesis that sees in the "spirit (of the) unlimited" an essential motive of the dominant cultural regime at the global level, under the prevailing rule of financial capitalism. According to our point of view, it is that spirit that ultimately energizes the authentic ecocide that is taking place on our planet, threatening it with the annihilation. From this background, we propose to show the concrete form in which, in front of the deadly tyranny of the unlimited, to the faith there has been promised in Jesus Christ the irruption of a "liberating limit". And as, with the permanent renewal / revolution that takes place through the justice by faith, the essential contours of a life in the Spirit become manifest, expressing itself as a resilient and solidary commitment to eco-justice. While traveling down this road, we will converse, without pretending to be exhaustive, with analogous ideas about spirituality and "ecological conversion", as developed by Pope Francis in his very important Encyclical Letter "*Laudato si*".

The tyrannical régime of the unlimited

Our place in the world is the southern cone of South America. Here, the multinationals that control the extractive exploitation that they call "agro-industry" or "agribusiness", celebrate the virtual dissolution of the limits of the old national states due to the establishment of a "United Republic of Soy".

Now, that propaganda fiction does not consist only in calling "republic" what essentially operates as a tyranny or a dictatorship. The "green spot" on the map of Latin America hides, above all, the very serious mortgage that leaves behind itself the advance of the transgenic desert: plundered wealth, expropriated and / or poisoned peoples, devastated ecosystems, corrupt institutions. That is the violent reality associated with the neocolonial cartographic transformation that is promoted in our subcontinent -among other factors- in the heat of the victorious war cry: "Soy knows no borders".

When attention is paid from our location and concrete experience in the south of the world to the symbolic and discursive operations around which the propaganda and marketing of companies such as *Syngenta* or *Samsung* pivot, it is possible to notice, in that privileged topic, the remarkable recurrence of an essential motive of the globally dominant cultural régime, referring to the unlimited, to that which knows no limits. This is how the figure of an immanent order that aims to establish itself as absolute, seeking to appropriate of any other alterity with material and symbolic violence, is manifested exemplarily in the leitmotiv of a major American software company, *Netsuite*, specializing in international finance and trade: "One system, no limits".[1]

The crucial meaning of the "spirit of the unlimited" within the framework of our globalized civilization, hegemonized by the powers of financial capitalism -which we have developed on our part on another occasion[2]-, has found in several ways an outstanding treatment in the Encyclical Letter "On care for our common home", by Pope Francis.[3] In this regard, a series of key paragraphs are particularly important, in which the magisterial text seeks to identify "the human roots of the ecological crisis" (Chapter III), focusing on: "I. Technology: creativity and power" (LS § 102-105), "II. The globalization of the technocratic paradigm" (LS § 106-114), "III. The crisis and effects of modern anthropocentrism" (LS § 115-136).[4]

In the type of "phenomenology of the spirit" of the unlimited that is sketched throughout various passages of the encyclical, at the time of characterizing the phenomenon as a whole, a series of rather rationalistic notes prevail, which we suspect relate to its basic anthropological conception, essentially indebted to the classical tradition. Therefore, from that perspective, above and beyond all "disease" consigned to human freedom (§ 105), even so, the ability "of going out of ourselves towards the other" is attributed to it. Consequently, the encyclical letter holds that "Disinterested concern for others, and the rejection of every form of self-centeredness and self-absorption, are essential if we truly wish to care for our brothers and sisters and for the natural environment. These attitudes also attune us to the moral imperative of assessing the impact of our every action and personal decision on the world around us." (LS § 208).

---

1   A relevant observation, which makes it possible to locate approximately the historical matrix that gave the mobile density for the first time, related to the remote origins of Western individualism and the extension of private property and money throughout Eurasia from approximately 800 BC, notes that: "…the pre-Socratic philosophy, beginning in Miletus, the first fully monetarized polis, is essentially determined by the thought of the money subject. Those thinkers – from Thales to Parmenides, but first of all Anaximander, who produces the concept of the unlimited (*apeiron*) to designate the One in the Plural – are consciously understood as individuals. His fundamental question points to the One in the Plural, just as one can transform money into all merchandise…" Ulrich Duchrow "El posicionamiento de Lutero hacia el individualismo del moderno sujeto del dinero" in: Martin Hoffmann, Daniel C. Beros, Ruth Mooney, *Radicalizando la Reforma. Otra teología para otro mundo*, Buenos Aires / San José CR, Ediciones La Aurora / Editorial SEBILA, 2016, p. 162.

2   For the first time in: Daniel Beros, "El límite que libera. La justicia ajena de la Cruz como poder de vida", en: Daniel Beros / Pablo Ferrer (Comp.), *Con la mirada en el Mesías, de la mano del pueblo. Libro en homenaje a Néstor Míguez*, Buenos Aires, ISEDET, 2014, pp. 81-104. The article was later received in the series "Die Reformation radikalisieren / Radicalizing Reformation", by Ulrich Duchrow et al. Cf. Daniel C. Beros, "Die befreinde Grenze. Die fremde Gerechtigkeit des Kreuzes als Macht des Lebens ", in: Ulrich Duchrow / Hans Ulrich (Eds.), Befreiung vom Mammon / Liberation from Mammon, Berlin, LIT, 2015, p. 187-212.

3   In different analytical-descriptive contexts of the factors that determine the current "ecological crisis", the pontiff resorts more than 30 times to categories that revolve around a group of concepts that refer to (the loss or suppression of) "limits" and the "unlimited" (or, equivalently, to the opposite "finite" – "infinite").

4   In one of the key passages of the chapter and of the encyclical as a whole (LS § 106) it is possible to observe exemplarily the relevance of the problem of the unlimited in papal discourse. There, it is emphasized that the fundamental problem "it is the way that humanity has taken up technology and its development *according to an undifferentiated and one-dimensional paradigm*". In relation to this, the letter argues that to this scheme corresponds "a concept of a subject who, using logical and rational procedures, progressively approaches and gains control over an external object. This subject makes every effort to establish the scientific and experimental method, which in itself is already a technique of possession, mastery and transformation." And later he concludes: "This has made it easy to accept the idea of infinite or unlimited growth, which proves so attractive to economists, financiers and experts in technology. It is based on the lie that there is an infinite supply of the earth's goods, and this leads to the planet being squeezed dry beyond every limit." (the italics are our).

Daniel C. Beros

In contrast to this view, which has as its counterpart a notion of sin that remains on a rather moralistic plane ("errors, sins, faults and failures", LS § 218), if the imprint of the biblical and reforming tradition is followed, it is necessary to emphasize that this "spiritual" motive identified in the "root" of the ecological crisis is expressed above all as *abysmal desire* (for the) unlimited. In the current stage of civilization, governed by technological and military power at the service of global finance, it is maximized and fed into to such a magnitude that it has come to represent the real threat of the annihilation of all creation – its first victims being the poorest and most vulnerable. To that desire the New Testament gives the name of "concupiscence of the flesh2 (see Ga. 5,13ff.).

The Reformation described in the light of the Scriptures the hermetic closure in the economy of that unlimited desire of the human being that held in view in the context of the expansion of European mercantilism and colonialism, as *incurvatio in se ipsum* and, to its supposed "self-determination", as a product and expression of its *servo arbitrio*. In the same sense, to speak today of the human being as subject, supposes returning to put in focus the etymological meaning of the Latin word *sub-iectum*: "put under", "subservient", "subjected". For in its blinded devotion to the "spirit of the unlimited", that the globally imposed system does not cease to update as the infinite greed for capital and "natural resources", the human being tyrannically *governs* the world in as much as it is *tyrannically governed*. That is the paradoxical tyranny that, through multiple mediations, so well described in the encyclical letter, "have caused sister earth, along with all the abandoned of our world, to cry out, pleading that we take another course" (LS § 53).

Now, if the diagnosis that we have just outlined of the current human and civilizational reality captures in essence "what is real" (*quod res est*)[5], beyond all other grateful appreciation for the very significant contribution of the encyclical letter in the promotion of a serious debate in relation to multiple relevant aspects (the relationship between the poor and the fragility of the planet, the conviction that in the world everything is connected, the criticism of the "self-centred culture of instant gratification", etc.), related to the ecological crisis, in regards to our specific topic, we ask ourselves: how appropriate is it to formulate a possible response from Christian spirituality to that clamor and complaint based on an appeal to the basic attitude of "self-transcendence" of human beings? Would not we thus run involuntarily and surreptitiously the danger of further cementing "the spirit of the unlimited" by way of its religious or theological self-justification? Where could we expect then "*another* direction"?

The justice by faith: a liberating limit

In our opinion, a first and valuable indication in relation to that question is offered to us by the simple beginning of the liturgy of community worship, which is celebrated every Sunday in our own community of faith, the Evangelical Church of the Río de la Plata. There the believers are invited to listen and confess with the psalmist the common hope in the *coming*, in the *advent* of God: "From where will my help come? My help *comes* from the Lord, who made the heavens and the earth" (Ps 121.2).

From this perspective, the opening of the hermetic world of the human being and its institutions takes place in the event through which *God's very self breaks into the world* by the force of

---

5   See the thesis 21 of the "Heidelberg Disputation", in: *Obras de Martín Lutero* (Tomo I), Buenos Aires, Paidós/ El Escudo, 1967, p. 42.

God´s Spirit, upon pronouncing the "Word of the Cross" (1 Cor. 1 , 18). In this Word, God's unparalleled love for the world in God´s strange wisdom and justice, in its characteristic "madness" becomes manifest to us: as a proclamation of God´s unconditional solidarity with the "no one" or "nothing", victims of the unlimited desire for appropriation and domination of the world by the *homo peccator*, and at the same time, as unrestricted condemnation of the victimizing powers of those who seek to be "someone" by surrendering themselves blindly to him.

Who by faith allows to avail for him or herself that Word and justice of *God*, which is issued by the free judgment and decision *of God* in the resurrection of the Crucified, justifies God in *God's* reasons (see Ps. 51,4). Renouncing thus, without reservations or conditions, his or her own interests, calculations and arguments, this person stops living from his or her own judgments and possibilities, in order to live from the possibilities and justice of the One who "gives life to the dead and calls into existence the things that were reduced to nothing, that they may live" (see Rom 4:17).

For this reason, with the justice of the faith -that lives only from the *iustitia aliena crucis*, and thus concretely lets "God be God"[6] in God's Word and judgment, consummated through God's own radical *self*-limitation (E. Jüngel)[7] – the Spirit of grace establishes the "liberating limit" through which she (the Holy Spirit) manifests herself as the *power of life*. Because through the Spirit the triune God paradoxically *creates* a redemptive path, which opens in hope for those who live (and die) imbricated in the sacrificial violence that the idolatry of the unlimited propitiates.

On the background of what has been said up to now, it is fitting to resume the conversation with the ideas developed by the encyclical *Laudato si* in regards to the possible contribution of Christian faith and spirituality in the face of the arduous challenges posed to humanity by the growing aggravation of the ecological crisis. Particularly where in the letter it is affirmed (LS § 75):

> "A spirituality which forgets God as all-powerful and Creator is not acceptable. That is how we end up worshipping earthly powers, or ourselves usurping the place of God, even to the point of claiming an unlimited right to trample his creation underfoot. The best way to restore men and women to their rightful place, putting an end to their claim to absolute dominion over the earth, is to speak once more of the figure of a Father who creates and who alone owns the world. Otherwise, human beings will always try to impose their own laws and interests on reality."

The aforementioned paragraph raises the connection between the concept of God and the human problematic of power, violence and limits in a way that is quite analogous to ours. However, if one considers the remarkable christological and soteriological "deficit" that we seem to be able to verify throughout the encyclical[8], "the figure of a Father who creates and who alone owns the

---

6   See the work of Philip S. Watson, *Let God be God. An interpretation of the Theology of Martin Luther*, Eugene (OR), Wipf & Stock Publishers, 2000. Only then will that human being be left behind who "by nature cannot want God to be God; rather, he wants him to be God, and God is not God" according to the acute and concise description offered by Martin Luther in Thesis 17 of the "Disputation against Scholastic Theology" (1517).

7   See Eberhard Jüngel, „Gottes ursprüngliches Anfangen als schöpferische Selbstbegrenzung. Ein Beitrag zum Gespräch mit Hans Jonas über den 'Gottesbegriff nach Auschwitz'" in: Eberhard Jüngel, *Wertlose Wahrheit. Zur Identität und Relevanz des christlichen Glaubens*, Múnich, Chr. Kaiser, 1990, pp. 151-162.

8   Within the framework of the encyclical letter, the Christological references are concentrated in section VII "The gaze of Jesus" (LS §96-100), of its Second Chapter "The Gospel of Creation", where a rhetoric of the *exemplum* of the earthly Jesus predominates as an archetype of a healthy bond with creation, rather than that of the *sacramentum* as a mediator of salvation (aspect not only restricted, but somewhat dissociated from the first).

Daniel C. Beros

world" that would be as such "the best way to restore men and women to their rightful place, putting an end to their claim to absolute dominion over the earth", shows itself to be in essentials equally indebted to classical metaphysics, sharing with that tradition -at least in virtue of our concrete question- all its problematic.

Limiting ourselves to only two of the main aspects, one might ask: when "re-proposing" that concept of an "almighty God" in the terms mentioned, would not humanity be presented with a "human, all too human" figure of the divine, one that would run the risk of enabling a dynamic of speculative feedback of that "will to power" that "knows no limits" in its "self-referentiality", which it is proposed to counteract? And if what is desired to propose is the "figure" of a "Father who creates and who alone owns the world", would this not run the risk of that kind of "iconic" mediation of the divine, about which the second commandment warns (Ex. 20, 4s.), making it an easy prey to the subtle and gross operations of manipulation and instrumentalization of that same unlimited will of power?

Life in the Spirit – in the service of eco-justice

From what has been pointed out in the previous paragraph it is clear that the "change of course" (*metanoia*, Mk 1,14ss) lies above all in "suffering" again and again that *verbum crucis* (1 Cor. 2,2), in "allowing oneself to be pulled into the path of Jesus Christ, into the messianic event" (D. Bonhoeffer)[9]. Thus the believers enter into an ineffable becoming, into a permanent renewal / revolution of their whole existence. Driven by the Spirit of God, they open themselves to God's reign, to God's call to live a life of communion and solidarity with those who had lost, and who have now rediscovered themselves in Jesus Christ: to God and to neighbor, beginning with the most neglected among the others human beings and with the suffering creation[10] – that groan as one, in ardent longing for the manifestation of the daughters and sons of God (see Rom 8, 18ff).

Therefore, if we follow the trail of that biblical reforming theology, what is involved is to be incorporated into that "school of the Holy Spirit" in which Mary herself learned to give witness to the God of the Promise, who, with the coming of God's justice and cruciform work, "lowers the high and raises the fallen; breaks that which is something and from that which is nothing creates that which God loves".[11] For only to those who expose themselves unreservedly to this concrete becoming in the history of God with God's people and creation, offering themselves as instruments of justice, to them will also be given the capacity to indicate that place where it is possible to await the *manifestation of the new* in its transforming and renewing power: the new creature and creation of God in Jesus Christ (2 Cor. 5,17).

That eschatological *topos*, to which the promise of the renewed irruption of the justice of God is associated, lies where the mutual testimony of the Word of the Cross takes place —as a sacramental anticipation of a renewal that includes and is expanded to all of creation. The way of life

---

9   See Dietrich Bonhoeffer, *Resistencia y sumisión. Cartas y apuntes desde el cautiverio*, Salamanca, Sígueme, 1983, p. 253.

10   Here we assume the suggestion of Wanda Deifelt, in: "Out of Brokeness, a new Creation. Theology of the Cross and the Tree of Life", en: *Eco-Reformation*... p. 60

11   See Martin Luther, "El Magníficat (1521)", in: *Obras... (Tomo VI)...* pp. 377-436; for the discussion of the principles of a theological epistemology based on a rereading of this text of the Reformer, see: Daniel C. Beros, "Fuera de lo cual no se enseña otra cosa que apariencias y palabrería...", in: *Cuadernos de Teología XXX (2011)*.

that is recreated over and again in this *topos* becomes decisively manifested as *vita passiva* (passive life) – as a life that is constituted "suffering" the cruciform Word.[12] Now, because it is precisely a creature of that Word (*creatura verbi*) -and not of other words that it purports to say to itself-, the community of those that follow that has been called to be the Church, is urged to give witness of the promised advent of the foreign justice of which she herself lives to the whole of creation, in the broad, cooperative, "ecumenical" pursuit of *eco*-justice, that is: of a renewed fidelity, solidarity and commitment in favor of both the right to a dignified life for the poor (*economy*) as well as of the care of all creation (*ecology*).[13] This resistant, compassionate and tangible witness, materialized in the different spheres in which it develops its personal and collective existence (church, politics, economy, education, culture, science, etc.), is an inherent and inseparable expression of the justice of faith. Such are the essential contours of its life in the power of the life-giving Spirit of the "crucified messiah".

If we briefly resume our dialogue with the thought of the encyclical letter regarding the contribution of Christian spirituality in regards to the need for an "ecological conversion" (LS § 216-221), it is equally necessary to ask whether its accent, put on cultivating in people "adequate motivations", "internal incentives", "virtues", animated by a "mysticism", which proposes to follow the "model" of Francis of Assisi (LS § 10-12; § 218ss), does not have a potentially problematic character. Here we believe to observe a certain eschatological and ecclesiological deficit, which leads us to ask about the conditions of possibility of an authentic overcoming of the self-referentiality of the religious subject, not being sufficiently clear the critical-communicative constitution of the ethical dimension of the believing experience (and not just its community projection, LS § 219), in the same line as with what was indicated in the previous paragraph.

Brief final reflexions

Returning to our place in the south of the world, we cannot but welcome the timely contribution of the encyclical letter *Laudato Si* in relation to the serious and urgent challenges posed by the current ecological crisis which, driven by the "spirit (of the) unlimited", threatens to destroy "our common home" (*oikumene*). Our critical observations do not prevent us from celebrating other aspects of enormous value, which manifest a growing convergence, such as the one that sustains the indissoluble relationship between justice for the exploited peoples of the earth and for the devastated creation.

In the light of the changes in political regimes that have taken place throughout Latin America in the last decade, marked by the enormous capacity for manipulation and intervention of the global hegemonic powers – as shown by the Pope's recent statements on the phenomenon of *lawfare*, juridical war[14] –, it is essential not to dissociate either the environmental damage of the

---

12   On this topic see: Daniel C. Beros: "¿Qué es el hijo del hombre ... para que lo visites? Reflexiones en torno al ser humano en perspectiva teológica", in: Daniel C. Beros, Jorge Luis Roggero, David A. Roldán y Flavia Soldano Deheza (Comp.), *Dios, ser humano, mundo. Entre la filosofía y la teología*, Buenos Aires, Editorial de la Facultad de Filosofía y Letras de la Universidad de Buenos Aires, 2016, pp. 137-154.

13   I make use of the term in the sense enunciated by Guillermo Kerber, in: "Ecología y cambio climático: perspectivas ecuménicas", in: Eusebio Lizarralde y Alfredo Salibián (Comp.), *Ecoteología. Aportes desde el ecumenismo*, Buenos Aires, Dunken, 2013, p. 34.

14   https://www.americamagazine.org/faith/2019/06/04/pope-francis-judges-there-no-justice-when-there-in-equality.

Daniel C. Beros

foreign imposition (silently endorsed by the "international community") of pseudo-democratic regimes that – through extreme financial liberalization, aggressive extractive opening and excessive external indebtedness – sacrifice on the altar of a "deified market" (LS § 56) their entire peoples and countries, reissuing the colonial drama.

At the expense of whom or of what will our states pay such a mortgage? What kind of ecumenical spirituality would be ours, what would be our justice, if we should propose to listen to "the groans of creation" without recognizing committedly "in, with and under" them the "cry of the poor", which never ceases to rise to the sky clamoring for justice, and vice versa?

INTER-RELIGIOUS COOPERATION IN ECO-ETHICS A LATIN AMERICAN EXPERIENCE

For Together towards Eco-Theologies, Ethics of Sustainability and Eco-Friendly Churches

Neddy Astudillo

Introduction: *This is a personal reflection from 27 years of environmental work and teaching eco-theology in six countries in Latin America and the USA to Pentecostal Latino pastors. The course I taught was effective in introducing people to theological and biblical resources that can undergird a way out of the environmental crisis. For the matters of this presentation, I am focusing on the values and eco-theology that need to be in place when a church decides to engage in environmental issues alongside people from other faiths. These are churches who are ready to reconsider and even amend their relationships and ways of valuing the world. I begin with a narrative, that is part of my own personal story, but it can be the story of almost every Latin American.*

As a Latin American, I am a mestizo woman. On the paternal side of my family, I had two very distinct grandmothers. One, an immigrant, a European woman, who people say liked bathing in milk to keep her white skin beautiful. The other, an indigenous woman, of lands and a nation forgotten, who enjoyed bathing in the river so as not to lose her relationship with Earth.

I am the daughter of both grandmothers, both live within me.

One connects me with stories of courage, adventure, commitment, science, and the Christian faith. And she also connects me with stories of dominion, invasion, class and racism.

Through her story, I met the Church. Her story opened my path to becoming a Presbyterian pastor. Her white skin has given me privileges and power. Meanwhile the Church has given me knowledge to recognize their limits, and the importance of using them for the common good.

The story of my indigenous grandmother connects me with stories of nature, ancient wisdom, survival. Her story also manifests itself in my spirituality. It connects me with Earth, the ocean, the dream world, animals, birds, and human right struggles. Her story opened my path to becoming an eco-theologian.

In my work with GreenFaith[1], a coalition of interfaith partners in action for the Earth, and teaching eco-theology, I have come to understand how the stories of my grandmothers are still at play in the dynamics, causes and the solutions of the environmental crisis in Latin America; and what type of values, attitudes and theologies need to be in place when the Church is ready to engage with environmental issues.

Since today's environmental problems have arisen out of one dominant culture imposing itself over others, the answers to today's environmental problems need to include a dialogue among the diversities of cultures, peoples and spiritualities present in our context, appreciating the gifts that each can bring to solve them.

---

1   https://greenfaith.org.

As Pope Francis in his Encyclical, Laudato Si', also points out:

> "We need a conversation which includes everyone, since the environmental challenges we are undergoing, and its human roots, concern and affect us all... We require a new and universal solidarity... Everyone's talents and involvement are needed to redress the damage caused by human abuse of God's creation. [22] All of us can cooperate as instruments of God for the care of creation, each according to his or her own culture, experience, involvements and talents." (14). [2]

In a later verse (63) Pope Francis also mentions the need of respect for the various cultural riches of different peoples; including their interior life, spirituality, science and wisdom.

In contrast to centuries past, the solutions to today's challenges will not emerge from a single way of interpreting and transforming reality, i.e. Western dominant worldviews.

Eco-ethics in Latin America

Over the last decade, I had the opportunity to teach eco-theology in diverse seminaries and settings in Latin America and the USA. All participants except one shared in common our mestizo culture. We may have been raised in a western culture or the Christian faith, but we all retained childhood memories of living closer to nature.

Many people in Latin America live their lives integrating a diversity of cultural and religious expressions available to them and do so essentially without questioning whether something is Christian or not, indigenous or not, environmentally correct or not.

In class, every time we read the Bible from a place of environmental concern and began to look for its ecological sensitivities, most participants recognized for the first time, even though they had read these passages before, that some of the Biblical stories were similar to experiences shared by their indigenous and peasant grandparents. The school system had taught them to disregard those experiences and label them as superstition, and the church, that "in order to be Christian they needed to stop being indigenous". Reading Scripture using environmental lenses, provided new insights, revealed that earlier experiences were valuable for our Christian faith, and supported so called secular[3] ecological concerns.

To care about the environment, it turned out, was to be a good Christian.

> "I have discovered that the river of my childhood, the place I understood as important for my community, and a source for our needs for food, turned out to be a specialty of God's creation."[4] (Guatemala)

---

2 http://w2.vatican.va/content/francesco/en/encyclicals/documents/papa-francesco_20150524_enciclica-laudato-si.html.

3 The ecological sensitivity had not been learned at the church. Some had just been curious from a young age, by being raised in the countryside, closer to nature. Most had seen the changes in their environment along the years. The rivers of their childhood memories were now polluted or ran dry.

4 As shared in my Doctor of Ministry Thesis: "Ministering with the Earth: Towards an Ecological Liberating Christianity in Latin America", a professional project submitted to the Theological School of Drew University, page 70.

Neddy Astudillo

My emphasis is that we need to give our church members the same permission: to let ourselves be moved, lose our fear, and look with wonder at God's creation. Not because we might otherwise lose thousands of church members to other religions and environmental organizations, but because of a very real human-spiritual need, deep within our soul, pretty much present among our church members, still.

Our way of knowing engenders ways of valuing, relating, and acting in the world. It leads to ethical issues and practices.
As Senegalese poet Baba Dioum once said, *"We only protect what we love. We only love what we understand."*[5] This connection with the natural world can also give birth to curiosity about the human structures that damage the other, and strengthen the will to act with courage, to block destruction and protect life, even to the point of giving our life, if necessary.

Creating space for nature and interfaith dialogue in our faith communities are matters of environmental justice.
Some of the greatest spiritual experiences people have, regardless of their faith, happen in the natural world. These experiences connect people with nature and therefore are potentially helpful in providing a common stage on which Christians can dialogue with people of other faiths who have similar stories and also want to consider the importance of nature for our faith and the future of the planet.

The view that peasant and indigenous experiences have no value must be a matter of the past. It has no place in an Eco-Ethic.
Allow me also to add that the mentality that devalues the experience of women, indigenous peoples, or any other human being who is set apart and subjugated to the whims of a dominant other, has no place in the Eco-Ethic either.

An Eco-Ethic considers all these voices as part of God's creation, equally valuable, and sacred. The Interfaith work considers the other as a real partner, no longer an object of conversion or domination.

The healing of Creation runs through the veins of human justice and reconciliation.
In Latin America, the work of healing creation includes the examination and dismantling of our historically inherited principles of colonization, racism, gender domination, etc. If we avoid it, we are prone to committing the same mistakes all over again, even while building new green economies and churches. Unless all voices are sitting at the table and standing at the pulpit, there still no eco-ethic.

We need to be a church that seeks inspiration in the other, including the marginalized Earth; a church willing to challenge its own traditions, a church that discovers the presence of the Living God in the world and with the world.

---

5   http://assets.wwf.org.uk/downloads/learn_tigers_autumn_2008.pdf.

An opportunity

In a stroke of divine grace, in spite of human sin, the environmental crisis is providing us a way to reconsider who we are and those of us that need, redirect our footsteps. As human beings, we share a common story and responsibility with all people (Genesis 2:15). We exist interdependently with each other and the natural world (Joel 2:18-27), and have a common need to care for life (Deuteronomy 30:19). If we do not ground ourselves in these principles of our faith, and act upon the wisdom of our tradition, the human made environmental crisis will force millions, without discrimination, to suffering and death.

The report of the UN Intergovernmental Panel on Climate Change (IPCC)[6] gives us less than 12 years to amend our shortcomings. Those of us involved in this work for over 25 years may wonder where we failed. The inaction of the Church is not the result of spending too much time in nature, neither perhaps from spending enough time relating with each other as people of faith.

We have come to a time when the question is not if caring or praying for Earth is part of our faith, which is what most of our work focused on in the last few years. We know Earth, clean water, clean air, stable climate is important for human survival, if not also our faith's.

The question now is how we put our environmental values into action as people of faith, with whom do we act, and what specific actions are most urgent and meaningful now, to save Earth as we know it, and ourselves. Interreligious cooperation is certainly a step in the right direction. It is time to join forces with other people of good will and faith. The task is too great for any one religion, one culture, one community to tackle the environmental crisis alone. The crisis will meet us all at one point or another; and when it does, it better finds us united, collaborating, as resilient communities.

We need communities of faith living out the values of interdependence, solidarity, wonder, love for the natural world; and curiosity and respect for other people's wisdom and spiritualities. As Pentecostal pastor Edgar Castaño Díaz from Colombia said recently, during an interview, and after hearing about the urgency of protecting Tropical Rainforests and the rights of indigenous peoples as forest's best guardians, for reversing climate change:

"I understand, this is no longer a matter of evangelization, but of survival of the planet" (Interfaith Rainforest Initiative, 2018)[7]

Perhaps, we do need to approach each other and this historical moment as a matter of evangelization, but of a different kind of evangelization.

"I have been learning the importance of praying even for the rains!" said another Colombian pastor, sharing lessons from her ministry with peasants impacted by droughts.

"Our churches invested many years on teaching the Gospel and how to arrive to Heaven, but very little was ever said about protecting the Earth", said Pastor Jaime Berruecos, during the launching of the Interfaith Rainforest Initiative in Colombia.

---

6   https://www.ipcc.ch/sr15/.
7   https://faithsforforests.com/wp-content/uploads/2019/09/Interfaith_Evangelical_V3.pdf (page 5).

Neddy Astudillo

To develop a Christian ecological ethic, the church needs to focus on sharing the good news of Christ with all creation (Mark 16:15, John 10:10).

An ecological ethic can grow out working together in ministries of reconciliation, interreligious dialogue and cooperation, environmental justice, protecting tropical forests and the rights of indigenous peoples to self-determination; divesting from fossil fuels, supporting local organic farmers, welcoming climate refugees, living simply, eating lower in the food chain, and using our religious influence to demand governments to pass environmental policies that support sustainable means of transportation, agriculture, waste management, water and energy use. We can do all of these actions alongside interfaith partners.

How else we share the good news of Christ for Creation will depend on how Earth cries out in each locality, awaiting the revelation of the sons and daughters of God.

To develop an Eco-Ethic in a time of environmental crisis, Christians must trust that our active witness to the love of God for all Creation, will directly contribute to the ministry of reconciliation Jesus Christ came to establish on Earth (Colossians 1:15-20).

Looking at Earth from a Christian eco-theological perspective[8]

One of the theological proposals that seems most pertinent now – inspired on a desire to heal the damage done to Earth and Earth's creatures, respects our Latin American cultural diversity and grows from the roots of our Judeo-Christian tradition, is Eco-Spirituality.[9]

Eco-Spirituality proposes experiencing God in a Pneumatic way: God the Father, Son and Holy Spirit, living in and among us; as the Spirit that not only sustains human beings but gives life to all creatures (Job 34: 14-15; Ps 104: 29-30); inspiring the daughters and sons of God to be Church, manifesting and liberating Creation from the oppression to which Creation has been subjected (Romans 8: 19-23a).

Through an eco-spirituality, we can continue to participate in the universal reconciliation founded on Jesus Christ. Its end is not only the salvation of human souls, but the whole universe (John 3:16). Nothing exists outside of God, just as we do not exist independently of the rest of creation. The Christ presence in the world, from a pneumatic point of view, is what makes it possible for us to find life and salvation[10] in a moment of solidarity, in the community, in tenderness, among women and indigenous peoples, in Earth herself[11].

As human beings, we were made from the dust of Earth (Gen 2: 7), as so were the other creatures (v 19). Our salvation might require, in part, that we live in communion with all. As the

---

8 This segment has been adapted for the purpose of this material. Its content was published as part of a longer chapter on "Mis abuelas y la Reforma Protestante. Forjando una nueva Reforma junto a la Tierra." in the book "Reforma religiosa y transformación social", Editorial SEBILA, San José, Costa Rica, 2017.

9 Part of this approach was published in the journal Ecumenical Presence No. 71, January-April 2011, but has been modified for the purposes of this writing.

10 In an article written by Ivone Gebara in 1999, for Diez Palabras claves sobre Jesús de Nazaret, She proposes that when Jesus invites his disciples to admire the lilies of the field and find wisdom in them, Jesus was opening new paths of salvation.

11 Ivone Gebara, "¿Quién es el 'Jesús liberador' que buscamos?" in: *Diez Palabras Claves Sobre Jesús de Nazaret*. Estella, Navarra: Editorial Verbo Divino, 1999, 167.

image of God (Gen 1:26), we are called to reflect the God who self-limits, exists and creates in community (Gen 1: 11-12)[12]. From God's own unity in diversity, God invites us to live in union with others, co-creating, healing, sustaining. Under this spirituality we exist not only because we think, but also because we feel[13]; and we accept the limits of our domain (Gen 2: 15-16), so life can flourish.

From this spirituality, we are part of nature. With nature we live, suffer, die, and receive salvation (Ecclesiastes 3: 17-22, Joel 2: 21-22). Nature is our neighbor and from the beginning, together we are "very good" (Gen 1:31). If nature was ever cursed because of human sin, Christ delivered us from such condemnation (Gal 3: 13-14). Regardless of our ability to dominate Earth, the Earth is God's and everything that dwells in it (Psalm 24:1). Any efforts to dominate nature outside of these values will be futile, for we are foreigners and strangers on the Earth (Lev 25:23).

Our call is to experience Earth as our partner (1 Kings 17: 2-6; Nm 22: 23-30; Gen 2: 18-20); and sister (Gen 9: 8-11), as St. Francis of Assisi recognized nature to be. Throughout history, God has decided to reveal God's glory in the natural realm (Ex 3: 1-6; 19: 16-19; 20: 18-21; Lk 3: 21-22), not only in human history; and although nature is not the same as Godself, the Spirit of God inspires and enlightens us to discern Earth's messages and this makes nature our teacher (Prov 6: 6-8, Job 12: 7-11), and the means by which, Christians might find a piece of our salvation.

> "He said to his disciples, "Therefore I tell you, do not worry about your life, what you will eat, or about your body, what you will wear. For life is more than food, and the body more than clothing. Consider the ravens: they neither sow nor reap, they have neither storehouse nor barn, and yet God feeds them. Of how much more value are you than the birds! And can any of you by worrying add a single hour to your span of life? If then you are not able to do so small a thing as that, why do you worry about the rest? Consider the lilies, how they grow: they neither toil nor spin; yet I tell you, even Solomon in all his glory was not clothed like one of these. But if God so clothes the grass of the field, which is alive today and tomorrow is thrown into the oven, how much more will he clothe you—you of little faith! And do not keep striving for what you are to eat and what you are to drink, and do not keep worrying. For it is the nations of the world that strive after all these things, and your Father knows that you need them. Instead, strive for his[c] kingdom, and these things will be given to you as well.

> "Do not be afraid, little flock, for it is your Father's good pleasure to give you the kingdom. (Lk 12:22-32)

Eco-Spirituality is based on a Creator God and an experience sensitive to the divine in a marginalized Creation. Eco-Spirituality as a moral standpoint can help us redeem our stories, restore the damage committed against many peoples, against fields and mountains, rivers and oceans, and against the forgotten gifts of legions of grandmothers--like the African women of my motherland, whose gifts I can feel when I dance.

---

12   Professor Catherine Keller, in an Eco-theology class at Drew University proposed an alternative version to Genesis 1: 9, 11, 14, 24, 26. Where we normally interpret as the Trinitarian expression of God, another equally valid vision is the possibility that God in each of these moments is inviting the earth to create with God and the earth responds in obedience.

13   In the seventeenth century, the philosopher René Descartes (France), became famous with his great phrase: "I think, therefore, I exist", placing the existence of the human being, in the mind.

Eco-spirituality roots us in the place and with the people we live with. It enriches our whole life, and moves us to fight for life, our own life, while Earth can also partake in the Good News of Jesus Christ (Mk 16:15).

Suggested materials/publications for further reading

Ramirez, Jose Enrique, ed, *Reforma religiosa y transformación social, Aportes desde América Latina en occasion de los 500 años de la Reforma Protestante*; San José, C.R., Sebila, 2017.

Rasmussen, Larry L. *Earth Honoring Faith, Religious Ethics in a New Key*; New York, NY, Oxford University Press, 2013.

Kerber, Guillermo. "Climate Change and Southern theologies: A Latin American Insight" in *Horizonte, Bello Horizonte*. Vol. 8, No. 17, April/June 2010.

Kearns, Laurel and Catherine Keller, eds., *ECOSPIRIT: Religions and Philosophies for the Earth*. NY: Fordham University Press, 2007.

Gebara, I. *Longing for Running Water: Ecofeminism and Liberation*. Minneapolis: Fortress Press, 1999.

ENVIRONMENTAL SUSTAINABILITY AND ECO-JUSTICE: REFLECTIONS FROM AN AFRICAN PENTECOSTAL

Emmanuel Anim

Introduction

Environmental pollution and degradation as a result of human activities have been a major concern at the turn of this century. Although concern about adverse human activity is not new, the last two decades have seen an increasing global concern and this has also been clearly captured in the Sustainable Development Goals (SDGs). Osborn observes that four major issues in particular have become focal points for public anxiety about the impact on the environment. These include, "the realization that, through hunting and the destruction of natural habitats, the human race has been responsible for the extinction of many plant and animal species"[1]. Secondly, towards the end of the 1950s, concerns were shown about "the effect of industrial and agricultural pollution on the environment". The 1960s placed attention on "related issues of population, pressure and resource depletion".[2]

Concerns have been raised about the human capacity to "modify the climate through the Greenhouse Effect and the damage we are doing to the ozone layer"[3]. A related issue is our impact on ecosystems, which fundamental assumption is a rhythm of interdependence of living creatures in any given environment. Osborn further observes that the ecosystems are complex and interdependent to the extent that there are no clearly defined boundaries between them even for ecosystems which are separated by thousands of miles. There is therefore the need to think in terms of a global ecosystem.[4]

Osborn rightly observes that human beings tend to modify the environment in their own favour, and this has often resulted in devastating consequences on the environment and ultimately on human life itself. Several factors may account for this attitude and actions, among them include, the desire for pleasure, self-aggrandizement, or national glory, a concern for the good of mankind and human advancement[5].

---

1 Osborn, Lawrence. *Stewards of Creation: Environmentalism in the light of Biblical Teaching* (Oxford: Latimer House, 1990), p.3.
2 Osborn, *Stewards of Creation,* p.3.
3 Osborn, *Stewardship of Creation,* p. 3.
4 Obsborn, *Stewards of Creation,* p. 3.
5 *Ibid.*

The Perceived Culpability of African Pentecostalism and Sustainable Development

Dietrich Werner has brought to our attention that the issue of ecological transformation and eco-theology is not a new theme in African theological discourse. He goes on to outline the various ecumenical conferences and seminars on the subject[6]. One of the key issues Werner raises in his paper is the old augment that Christianity may be held at least in part, for the ecological crisis in Africa because of its doctrine of creation and particular theology of "dominion" which has led to the disenchantment of nature[7] African scholars such as Sindima, Werner observes, "view the introduction of Christianity in Africa as a factor which weakened human ability to interpret and reconstruct the systems of values and norms that give meaning to the lives of Africans"[8]. It is observed that in many primal societies in Africa, the earth was seen as a mother, a fertile giver of life. The forest, the sea and rivers were endowed with divinity, and humans were subordinate to it. The ancestors were considered as the custodians of the moral and spiritual laws of the land or the community and the chiefs and other community leaders were principal managers of the natural resources to preserve their sanctity and to serve the needs of the people in the community. The unborn children were also considered members of the community[9] and therefore any decision and activity of the present must necessarily consider the children of the future. However, Osborne draws our attention to a publication in the Time Magazine, which sates that:

> The Judaeo-Christian tradition introduced a radically different concept. The earth was the creation of a monotheistic God, who, after shaping it, ordered its inhabitants, in the words of Genesis: 'Be fruitful and multiply, and replenish the earth and subdue it: and have dominion over the fish of the sea and over the fowl of the air and over every living thing that moveth upon earth. The idea of dominion could be interpreted as an invitation to use nature as a convenience. Thus the spread of Christianity, which is generally considered to have paved the way for the development of technology, may at the same time have carried the seeds of the wanton exploitation of nature that often accompanied technical progress".[10]

This criticism was first popularized by the American historian Lynn White. He begins by laying the blame for our present environmental problems squarely at the door of western science and technology. This leads him to examine their historical origins and he comes to the conclusion that, 'since both our technological and our scientific movements got their start, acquired their character, and achieved world dominance in the Middle Ages, it would seem that we cannot understand their nature or their present impact upon ecology without the particular presuppositions of the Christian doctrine of creation. Thus White looks critically at the Judaeo-Christian Scriptures as interpreted by Western Christianity.

---

6   See Werner, Dietrich. "The Challenge of Environment and Climate Justice- Imperatives of an Eco-Theological Reforms of Christianity in African Contexts", Unpublished Paper, Humboldt University of Berlin, 2018, pp1-20.
7   Werner, "The Challenge of Environment and Climate Justice",p.2.
8   Werner, The Challenge of Environment and Climate Justice", 3.
9   For a good elucidation of the role of ancestors and the view of the unborn child in traditional African cosmology, see Mbiti, John. *African Religions and Philosophy* (London: Heinemann, 1976), pp. 75-91.
10   The *Time Magazine*, January 2,1989, p.17ff, cited in Osborn, Stewards of Creation,p.7.

In particular, Osborne attacks the doctrine of human dominion over nature and the belief that human beings are made in God's image. He believes that the former reduces nature to a human utility, its sole purpose being to minister to our physical needs. 'God planned all of this explicitly for man's benefit and rule: no item in the physical creation had any purpose save to serve man's purposes'. The latter sets man apart from nature, presenting him as a demigod manipulating passive matter. My position builds on the framework of White's assertion and I argue further that recent Pentecostal movements and particularly of its charismatic or neo-Pentecostal strand have effectively, in recent time, taken on the dominion theology which is inherent in the prosperity gospel, championed by American faith preachers and tele-evangelists. The aspirations of many of these American faith preachers were inspired by the American dream of a superman, individual prosperity, freedom and liberty. My thesis is that many African Pentecostal and Charismatic Christians have bought into the dominion theology of the Prosperity Gospel, which presents the most anthropocentric approach to religion and faith and thereby have changed their attitudes to what was considered a 'sacred' environment and sustainable development.

In his critique of Western missionary activity, in Africa, Chinua Achebe argues that the Whiteman did not understand our culture neither did he appreciate the peoples' customs and religious considerations. These elements provided the framework and principles which defined not only the identity of the people but also their sense of community, preservation and continuity of life itself. By ignoring the religious significance which underpinned cultural values, Achebe maintains that "the white man is very clever. He came quietly and peaceably with his religion. We were amused at his foolishness and allowed him to stay. Now he has won our brothers, and our clan can no longer act like one. The missionary by his preaching and attack on the religious apprehensions and culture of the African people has "put a knife on the things that held us together and we have fallen apart"[11] This is how the book gets its name!

The attitude and reactions of early missionaries to African people and culture largely lies in the "consensus of Christian Europe at the beginning of the 20th century that the primal religions of the world, usually designated at the time by the term 'animism' were backward and degraded as the people who practiced them…These religions were held to be the farthest removed from Christianity, at the bottom of a scale of religions that rose through polytheism, to monotheism, with Christianity being the highest and most civilized monotheistic faiths.[12]" These narratives were influenced by early European view of the world, where Europe was perceived as Christian and divinely favoured. This perception "largely unchallenged for over three hundred years, was to be fundamental to the European Christian perception of other peoples even into the 20th century, and in particular to the missionary perception of peoples of primal religion"[13]

African Traditional Religion, Pentecostalism and Dominion Theology

The dominion theology as espoused by the Pentecostal/Charismatic church in Africa is basically a brand of the American Faith Gospel, sometimes also referred to as the Prosperity Gospel. The basic assumption of the Prosperity Gospel is that, God wills the best for all his children and this

---

11   See Achebe, Chinua. *Things Fall Apart* (London Heinemann, 1958), pp.124-125.
12   Bediako, Gillian. "Primal Religion and the Christian Faith: Antagonists or soul-mates", *Journal of African Thought Christian Thought,* Vo. 3, No.1, June 2000, p12.
13   Bediako, Gillian, "Primal Religion",p.13.

finds expression in wealth, good health and long-life.[14] Material wealth or conspicuous consumption is considered a success in life and a sign of God's blessing.

Prior to early missionary activity, African societies were held together by a belief in God, the divinities, and ancestors who were regarded as custodians of the moral and spiritual laws of the land (better understood as "unseen" but active policemen and judges who could not be bribed). Creation was seen as sacred just as God was holy. These traditional beliefs informed the moral and ethical values that shaped the consciousness of the people in relation to their immediate environment. They also guided people's social, political and economic activities and conserved the environment. Land was given a "human" name (Asaase Yaa), meaning it had life and begat life. These considerations caused traditional people to treat the land and environment with respect. This largely underpinned the African concept of "sustainable development" and well-being. The Pentecostal belief in God empowering believers to harness their God-given potential, take dominion (Gen. 1:26), and exploit the available natural resources, such as gold and diamonds to their benefit without recourse to any moral or ethical obligations, has set in motion a destructive behavior to the environment.

Pentecostals and many other Christians in Africa consider African Traditional Religion as idol worship and must be done away with. The divinities in ATR are "demons" and the "gods" are fallen angels. However, adherents of ATR see the lesser gods as children or messengers of God and the ancestors as living and active mediators between the living and the gods, who then send their petitions to God Almighty. Adherents of ATR make sacrifices and pour libation as a form of prayer to God (*Onyame*) through the ancestors and the gods for protection, prosperity, good health, longevity and fertility or procreativity. The concept of prosperity and a good life is also embedded in African traditional religion and culture but here, wealth is regulated as rich people were also expected to justify the source of their wealth and conspicuous consumption was also frowned upon. The wealthy man was also expected to take good care of his children and relatives as also his service to the community.

Understanding African Traditional Religion(s) (ATR)

ATR is a primal religion; by this we mean it has no immediate or apparent relationship with other primal religions or to any of the major world religions, such as Christianity, Islam, Hinduism, nor Buddhism. African Traditional Region has no founder or any holy scriptures[15]. It has no missionaries. People are simply born into it, and they carry it with them wherever they go, not to propagate it but to live it. The life of the African is simply intertwined with his or her religion; it is the way he or she lives. John Mbiti rightly observes that:

> Having no sacred scriptures, it has been able to move with the times, and it has produced no religious controversies. People are free to hold different views and beliefs without the danger of being accused of heresy or falsehood. On the other hand, since there are no

---

14 See Anim, Emmanuel. *Who Wants to be a Millionaire?: An Analysis of Prosperity Teaching in the Charismatic Ministries (Churches) in Ghana and Its Wider Impact.* (Unpublished PhD Dissertation, All Nations Christian College/The Open University, UK, 2003).

15 Mbiti, John. *Introduction to African Traditional Religion* (London: Heinemann, 1975),pp.13- 15.

Emmanuel Anim

sacred books, we cannot tell precisely what African Religion may have been five hundred years ago and how far it may differ today from what it was many centuries ago.[16].

In the African traditional cosmology, the universe is both visible and invisible. It is created by God and is sustained by Him, whilst man is at the very centre of the universe. There is the belief that power and order exist in the universe and as long as this order is not disturbed there will be peace, harmony and progress. The following are some essential elements of African traditional religion and culture:

There is Moral Order Among People

The understanding here is that there is moral order which guides the activities and character of people in society. Kofi Asare Opoku describes African spirituality as one in which "relationships are not limited to humans, for there is an interconnectedness between humans and the world around them". Opoku rightly observes that in the past, African spirituality was characterised by an attitude of reverence for aspects of nature considered sacred."[17], and indicated that this had far reaching and serious ecological consequences. It is believed that God is the one who gives the moral order to ensure people live in peace and harmony with one another. Moral order helps people to know or determine what is good or evil. It helps people understand what is right or wrong and determine what is true or false. Customs and institutions arise out of this moral order to safeguard the life of the individual and the community as a whole. It is also the basis upon which society formulates its values and allegiances.

Religious Order in the Universe

God did not only create the universe. It is also believed that the laws of nature are controlled by Him either directly or through his servants (gods and divinities). The morals and institutions of society such as chieftaincy institutions are thought to have been given by God or sanctioned by him. To this end, any breach of such morals or lack of respect for the institutions is regarded as an offense against God, and the departed members of the society (ancestors) who are regarded as the custodians of the moral and spiritual laws of the land.

Taboos

There are taboos which strengthen the observance of the moral and religious order. Taboos and rituals exists to preserve and maintain the earth on which humans live[18]. There are taboos on virtually every aspect of life: words or speech, food, dress, relationships, marriage, burial, work, etc. Punishments for breaking taboos come in the form of social ostracism, misfortune, or death. It is believed that if people did not punish the offender, then the invisible world will take that responsibility. This belief reinforces the religious order in which God and other invisible beings are thought to be actively engaged in this world.[19]

---

16   Mbiti, *Introduction to African Traditional Religion*, ,p. 15.
17   Opoku, K. Asare, "Cooking on two stones of the earth? African spirituality and the socio-cultural transformation of Africa", Journal of African Christian Thought, Vol. 13, No. 1 (June 2010), pp3-9, cited in Howell, Alison, African Spirituality and Christian Ministry: 'Discerning the Signs of the Times' in our Environment and Community", *Journal of African Christian Thought*, Vol. 20. No.1, June 2017, p. 15.
18   Howell, Alison. "African Spirituality and Christian Ministry: 'Discerning the Signs of the Times' in our Environment and Community", *Journal of African Christian Thought*, Vol. 20. No.1, June 2017, p. 15.
19   See, Mbiti, John. *An Introduction to African Religion* (London: Heinemann, 1975), pp. 10-53.

Myths and Proverbs
African myths and proverbs are coded languages which need careful interpretation for their essence and value. They often conceal the truth to the foreigner but the wise person was expected to understand. Myths and proverbs remain the treasure and heritage of the community and must be preserved at all times by passing them on to the ensuing generations. Gillian Bediako highlights the significance of myths and argues that primal religions and Christian faith have a unique phenomenological affinity, illustrated historically also in the emergence of new religious movements in each area of encounter between Christian faith and primal religion. Bediako points to Harold Turner, who suggests a "phenomenological reason for the historical linkage between primal religion and Christianity in an essential 'affinity', expressed in the experience of many who responded to early missionary preaching that the Gospel message was 'what we have been waiting for'. Turner sought to overturn the negative image of primal religion by highlighting the 'profundities of myth and world-view, the richness of symbol and the sheer spirituality' that characterize many primal religions"[20].

Pentecostalism and African Traditional Religion: Abiding Tensions and Animosity

Pentecostals argue that any relationship with the gods and the ancestors brings curses upon the person and obstructs their progress. Pentecostal spirituality offers one power over the gods, ancestors, and other evil entities such as witches. To be a true Christian and to succeed or prosper in life is to "make a complete break with the past" (with the gods, ancestors, and related beliefs)[21]. It is believed that this is the only way that one can have favor with God and prosper. All this is made possible by fasting and prayer and having faith in Christ. The faith in Christ is expressed through positive confession and the faithful giving of tithes and offerings as "seed" money, upon which God would multiply the money in double-fold or even more. Key proponents of the prosperity gospel include, Kenneth Hagin, Fred Price Kenneth and Gloria Copeland, John Avanzini, and until very recently Benny Hinn, who has renounced prosperity gospel as an "offense to God and the Holy Spirit" and that it was wrong to put a price on the gospel for personal gratification.[22]

Secondly, the new faith, as understood in Pentecostalism takes the believer "outside the system's boundaries". Meaning that the believer no longer comes under the authority and regulations of the traditional culture and religious apprehensions as prescribed by ATR. In the latter, resources were considered limited and a "common good" which must be shared by all members of the society as in the case of many peasant societies. Foster argues that a principle accounting for much of the behavior of people in peasant societies is a cognitive orientation that "Good" or wealth is limited and not expandable. [23] "The members of every society share a common cognitive orientation which is, in effect, an universalized, implicit expression of their understanding of the 'rules of the

---

20   Bediako, ".Primal Religion", p. 14.
21   See, Meyer, Birgit. *Translating the Devil: Religion and Modernity Among the Ewes in Ghana* (Africa World, 1999).
22   A recent YouTube release has Benny Hinn making such confessions. See " Benny Hinn REPENTS of prosperity gospel", https://youtu.be/10k4YyGzBFI.
23   Foster, G. M, "Peasant Society and the Image of Limited Good", *American Anthropologist*, Vo l. 67, 1965, p.298. In anthropology, "limited good" is the theory commonly held in peasant or traditional societies that there is a limited amount of "good" or resources to go round. Thus, amount of money or resources available are limited or finite and therefore every time one person profits, it is at the expense of another.

game' of living imposed upon them by their social, natural and supernatural universe"[24]. In recent African Pentecostalism, it appears the God of the Bible is "privatized," and He works according to the measure of one's faith in Him. Poverty is synonymous with sin, a lack of faith and a curse. The down side of this theology, among others is that adherents of Pentecostalism and prosperity gospel now take matters into their own hands and work for their own individual prosperity without recourse to any social or sound religious ethics. It can be observed that the corruption index in Africa rises with the countries where there is a mass appeal and following of Pentecostal and Charismatic Christianity. The situation is more disturbing in Ghana where environmental degradation; pollution of water bodies by activities of "galamsey" or illegal mining has bedeviled a country that prides itself with about 72% Christians and a good majority of them follow the Pentecostal and Charismatic theology of dominion and prosperity. Galamsey is an illegal mining activity usually in such of gold and diamond. The impact of galamsey on mining communities cannot be overemphasized. Many people have lost their lives and water bodies severely polluted with chemicals. Children as young as six(6) years have been involved by fetching water to assist with the process instead of going to school. The involvement of children in this activity of galamsey means that these children end up dropping out of school in search for quick money. Alison Howell, brings this into sharp perspective when she quotes from Addo-Fening in an interview:

> The involvement of children in mining not only means that they do not go to school, it also led to increasing immorality and disrespect towards parents and the elderly. Children and teenagers with access to money from gold do not necessarily use this for their education. It is creating a class of children and teenagers who have the ability to go to market and buy food for themselves rather than eat with their parents. The level of insolence is shown where teenagers, through what they can earn from gold and *sakawa* can afford a car. So why should they respect an elderly person who doesn't even own a bicycle?"[25]

The Church of Pentecost has taken this matter very seriously and in the last 12 months has launched an extensive campaign in the country to address the problem of sanitation and environmental care. The Church has since engaged civil society and government through consultations and various campaigns. In November 2018, the Church of Pentecost launched a 5-year environmental campaign programme in collaboration with the Zoomlion waste management company in Accra. The event which was attended by government officials and church leaders sought to tackle key areas such as education on the environmental crises and attitudinal change, cleaning up exercises in partnership with the District and Municipal Assemblies and the Zoomlion company across the country. Others include community-based initiatives related to the environment and sanitation.

Pentecostalism and Sustainable Development: The Case of Ghana

In popular Pentecostal/Charismatic theology, wealth defines success and is the evidence of God's favour upon the believer. Time is linear and development is personalized. It is observed that the removal of traditional value systems and ethics were often not replaced by any meaningful biblical values and principles and this created a moral and ethical gap. A theology of "dominion" without responsible stewardship brought unintended, destructive consequences on the environ-

---

24   Foster, "Peasant Societies", p. 293.
25   Cited in Howell Alison.

ment and the ecosystems. For example, in traditional peasant societies, farmers were not allowed to clear their farmlands beyond fifty meters to the nearest river or stream. This in some villages were considered a taboo or unacceptable practice and the offenders could be brought before to local chief or traditional elders for questioning. In the same way women were advised to avoid the use of the stream or rivers during their menstrual period for hygienic purposes. It is also known that in most traditional African communities, famers would have one day in the week which was considered a taboo to work in the farm except to go for food for the household. Fishermen have a similar situation where a day, usually Tuesdays in the case of the Ga and Fanti people who work along the coast were considered a non-working day. In the Christian tradition, this would be considered a Sabbath. These and similar considerations have been observed among the indigenous and tribal peoples in the USA and Canada as well as the Maoris in Aotearoa-New Zealand, the Aborigines in Australia and the tribal people in many countries in Asia. These indigenous people tend to have utmost respect for the environment and ecosystems and try to keep their economic and social interests within the limits of sustainability and renewal of the earth.[26]

It is without doubt that the 17 Sustainable Development Goals as agreed by the United Nations provide us with an excellent framework, which could guide our human aspirations and quest for sustainable development. The need to end poverty in all its forms everywhere cannot be overemphasized, so also is the goal to "ensure healthy lives and promote well-being for all at all ages." However, our attention is drawn to the need to "ensure sustainable consumption and production patterns." But it is the goal to address environmental issues by taking "urgent action to combat climate change and its impact" which best draws our attention to life below water and the need to conserve marine resources. Human life, as discussed earlier, is intertwined with the ecology. We are part of a system that constantly needs to renew itself. For this reason, we have to "protect, restore and promote sustainable use of terrestrial ecosystems, sustainably manage forests, combat desertification, and halt and reverse land degradation and halt biodiversity loss."[27]

Urbanization and Sustainable Development in Ghana

African societies are becoming increasingly urban and this comes with new challenges. The case of Ghana provides us with a classic example of what has taken place in the last 7 decades as illustrated below in the last population census taken by the Government.

Urbanization in Ghana (Settlements of 5000 or more)[28]	
Year	Percentage of Urban Population
1931	9.4%
1948	13.9%
1960	23%

---

26   Abraham, K.C. "A Theological Response to the Ecological Crisis" in Hallman, David (ed). *Ecotheology: Voices from South and North*(Eugene, Oregon: Wipf & Stock, 1994),p.65.
27   See United Nations Sustainable Development Goals.
28   Jacob Songsore, "Urban Transition in Ghana: Urbanization, National Development and Poverty Reduction," Dept. of Geography, University of Ghana. Accessed at: http://pubs.iied.org/pdfs/G02540.pdf

Emmanuel Anim

1970	28.9%
1984	31.3%
2000	43.9%
2010	50.9%
2017	55.3%[29]

The 2010 population and housing census reveals a historic shift. As can be seen from the above table, for the first time in 1984, more Ghanaians live in urban areas than in rural[30]. This is a marked change from the life of our parents and grandparents, and the trend continues. Many factors account for the increasing migration of people from the rural areas to the urban communities. These include the lack of an equitable distribution of resources to the rural areas and apparent lack of jobs and good educational and health facilities. For example, between 2000 and 2008, the Greater Accra attracted 84% of total investments (including agriculture). The city accounts for 44% of all people engaged in industry and 66% of all manufacturing output. Greater Accra is the country's most developed region and has the least proportion of the poor.[31] As of 2000, 655 foreign companies were headquartered in Accra.[32] However, by migrating to the cities, many of the people end up in even worse situations as they soon find out there are no jobs and the cost of living is also very high. Such people end up in shanti towns where sanitation challenges are also compounded. Records indicate that malaria is the leading cause of death in Ghana.[33] On average, two to three children die each day as a result of the disease,[34] while $6.6 million is lost in productivity each year.[35] The Kaneshie market, which is one of the largest commercial areas in Accra generates about 22 tons of garbage a day.[36] Ashiedu-Keteke is one of the most densely populated areas of Accra, with sometimes more than eleven people in a household.[37] Urban migration therefore has implications for sustainable development and ecological justice.

29   2017 data from: Central Intelligence Agency, "Ghana," *The CIA World Factbook 2018-2019* (New York: Skyhorse Publishing, 2018), 34135 (e-book).
30   2010 Population and Housing Census: National Analytical Report. Accra: Ghana Statistical Service, May, 2013.
31   George Owusu and Samuel Agyei Mensah, "A comparative study of the ethnic residential segregation in Ghana's two largest cities, Accra and Kumasi," University of Ghana (Online: Springer Science-Business Media, LLC, 2011), pg. 338.
32   George Owusu and Samuel Agyei Mensah, "Segregated by Neighbourhoods? A Portrait of Ethnic Diversity in the Neighbourhoods of the Accra Metropolitan Area," University of Ghana (Online: Wiley Online Library, 2010), 512.
33   Ghana Health Service, "The Health Sector in Ghana: Facts & Figures 2017," p. 56. Accessed at: Ghanahealthservice.org.
34   Ghana Health Service, p. 56.
35   Justice Nonvignon, *et.al.*, "Economic burden of malaria on businesses in Ghana," *Malaria Journal*, 2016. Accessed at: https://malariajournal.biomedcentral.com/track/pdf/10.1186/s12936-016-1506-0
36   *Daily Graphic*, "Remove this heap of refuse," May 10, 2008.
37   The World Bank, The City of Accra: Consultative Citizens' Report Card (Washington, DC: 2010), p. 11.

Cosmology and Development: What is the church not doing right?

In this paper, I would like us to understand cosmology, not from a scientific perspective but from a religious and anthropological perspectives. What comes to mind immediately is world-view – weltanschauung – a particular philosophy or view of life. In other words, the worldview of an individual or group of people, which reflects their particular and fundamental cognitive orientation. It implies an existential and normative postulates or point of view and helps us to understand their value systems. Worldview is also essential in understanding one's identity and approach to wealth creation, fullness of life and sustainable development.

In his book, the Primal Vision- Christian Presence amid African Religion, John Taylor observes:

> Christ has been presented as the answer to questions a white man would ask, the solution to the needs that Western man would feel, the Saviour of the world of the European world-view, the object of the adoration and prayer of historic Christendom. But if Christ were to appear as the answer to the questions that Africans are asking, what would he look like? If he came into the world of African cosmology to redeem Man as Africans understand him, would he be recognizable to the rest of the Church Universal? And if Africa offered him the praises and petitions of her total, uninhibited humanity, would they be acceptable?[38]

The late Professor Kofi Abrefa Busia, a sociologist and lay preacher of the Methodist Church Ghana, and former Prime Minister of the Republic of Ghana, observed:

> For the conversion to the Christian faith to be more than superficial, the Christian church must come to grips with traditional beliefs and practices, and with the worldview that these beliefs and practices imply. "It would be unreal not to recognize the fact that many church members are influenced in their conduct by traditional beliefs and practices, and by the traditional interpretation of the universe. "The new convert is poised between two worlds: the old traditions and customs he is striving to leave behind, the new beliefs and practices to which he is still a stranger. The Church would help him better, if she understood the former, while she spoke with authority about the latter.[39]

S.G. Williamson came to the same conclusion when he wrote that "there is a sense in which both Christianity and African culture face a crisis."[40] This crisis finds expression not only in the theology and identity of the African people but also their value systems and ethical considerations. Africa is one continent where the numerical growth of Christianity is equally matched by the rise of corruption and ecological degradation. In Ghana for example, the government has been struggling especially in the last decade or so to stop the practice of illegal deforestation, mining and pollution of water bodies. The government seems to be loosing the battle and had appealed to the churches and other religious bodies to assist in fighting this crisis. These considerations bring us to the hermeneutics of creation and the role of humankind in the mist of God's divine purpose for his creation. Fallen human beings have corrupt minds which is naturally alienated from the purposes of God (Romans 3:23).

---

38   John V. Taylor, *The Primal Vision* (London: SCM Press Ltd, 1963), p. 16.
39   Kofi Abrefa Busia, "The African World View," in Christianity and African Culture: The Proceedings of Conference Held at the Accra, Gold Coast, May 2nd – 6th, 1955, Under the Auspices of the Christian Council (Accra: Christian Council of the Gold Coast, 1955), p. 4.
40   S. G. Williamson. "Introduction," *Christianity and African Culture*, p.v.

The gospel of salvation is not only directed to the redemption of mankind but also for the rescue of all creation (Romans 8:22-23). The pollution of our water bodies means the extinction of aquatic organism and life, whilst birds, insects and animals who forage and sustain the ecology by their activity of procreation and pollination may be cut short or destroyed through deforestation. Poor sanitation has resulted in millions of dollars spent on the treatment of diseases such as malaria and sedentary, not counting the number of lost hours for productivity as a result of people who are sick from malaria and could not go to work. These and many other problems lead us to consider the thoughts of Kwame Bediako, regarding our understanding of the gospel and the Great Commission. He observes, "the gospel of salvation which comes through Jesus Christ has more to do with the nations and the things which make nations, than it has often assumed." Bediako goes on to explain that we have become so used to regarding the Gospel as concerned with individuals that we are much less alert to its "fundamental relationship to those elements and dimensions of our human existence which designate as culture – language, social values, cultural norms, religion, political organization, ethnic identity, technology, arts and craft and economic activity." In this process, the tendency has been to reduce the Gospel to a category we regard as purely spiritual and has no reference to our culture or way of life. The danger here is that Christianity at best becomes an overlay of already existing worldviews and mentalities. Thus, the Great Commission must be understood as not just about the conversion of individuals, numbers and statistics however essential these may be, but more importantly, to know that it is about the conversion of the things that make a nation. This obviously has reference to our "spiritual environment, the world of the spirits, of ancestors, of the departed and the realm of the invisible, which many still affirm is real. The Great Commission therefore, Bediako argues, is about "the conversion of cultures, and conversion is not the overlay upon our old habits and attitudes and fears, of some regulations and traditions and solutions which do not answer to our needs". Rather, true evangelization and conversion is "turning to Christ all that He finds when He meets us, and asking that He cleanse, purify and sanctify us and all that we are, eliminating what He considers incompatible with Him. That is what the Great Commission is about, the disciplining of the nations."[41]

Conclusion

It is without doubt that perilous events in our generation draws our attention to understand and act decisively on the ecological crisis, particularly the threats of climate change that confronts us. The rapid depletion of non-renewable natural resources raises the question of our responsibility to future generations. Poverty is a function of ecological crisis. Sometimes the poor and marginalized are driven out of their habitat in the name of development. Uneven distribution and use of natural resources raises issues of equity and justice. Unless the poor and marginalized have alternate sources of food and basic needs such as fuel and shelter, they will also exploit and destroy whatever natural resources are within their reach. This is the case with the rapid depletion of forests and illegal mining called "galamsey" in Ghana. It is important to look at the ethical, socio-cultural, religious and theological dimensions of the problem and address them appropriately. The recent initiative of environmental care campaign by the Church of Pentecost in Ghana is laudable and must be emulated by all religious bodies.

---

41   Bediako.Kwame, "What is the Gospel" *Transformation*, Vol. 14, No. 1,(January/March 1997), ,pp1-4.

I have sought to explain that many factors account for dismal attitudes to the environment in Africa. In the past traditional religious beliefs and cultural practices had values and principles that ensured the preservation of the environment and natural resources. The value and respect given to nature found expression in the myths and metaphors that described the earth in human terms such as "mother", and other natural elements such as the the vegetation and rivers also assumed a divine nature which called for reverence and preservation. The people in the past, by indigenous wisdom, understood that humanity was dependent upon the ecology for its own survival and that treating the environment with respect and dignity was a form of worship to God who in his wisdom created them. Thus African traditional people saw themselves as stewards of God's creation and by respecting the handiworks of God one showed respect to God.[42]

It is without doubt that "we need to evolve a form of spirituality that takes seriously our commitment to the earth. Matthew Fox has coined the phrase 'creational spirituality'...Its hallmark is a deep awareness of God's gifts and presence in his creation"[43] This is precisely what defines the African primal spirituality, which sees God's presence in all his creation but Western theology understood this as "pantheism", an anathema to true worship of God. After nearly two centuries of Christian presence in Africa, south of the Sahara, there still seems to be a moral gab, which can only be explained in the absence of engagement of the received Christian faith and primal worldview and traditions.

In his response to the question, "What is the Gospel, Kwame Bediako helps us with a good analysis of how evangelism and mission has been conducted in the past, which still leaves much to be desired. The whole idea of conversion is a narrative that needs to be evaluated. Christians have often been taken out of their African context in its cognitive orientation without a replacement of a biblical understanding of conversion as a function of transformation and sustainable development. To multiply and subdue the earth (Genesis 1:26-28) is not a call for humans to exploit the resources of the earth for their individual benefit but for a common good that also calls for responsible management or stewards of those resources. It is without doubt that stewardship is at the heart of humanity's role in God's creation. "The earth is the Lord's, and everything in it, the world and all who live in it" (Psalm 24:1). When we think of development, we must contemplate whose language it is and what that means. Whatever God created and said it was very good (Genesis 1:31) must receive very good attention. As salt of the earth and light of the world (Matthew 5:13ff), Christians are enjoined to set a good example by showing the way we ought to live in God's world. Stewardship of God's creation is therefore a missiological imperative which the Church cannot ignore.

REFERENCES

Abraham, K. C. "A Theological Response to the Ecological Crisis" in Hallman, David (ed). Eco-theology: Voices from South and North(Eugene, Oregon: Wipf & Stock, 1994).

Achebe, Chinua. Things Fall Apart (London Heinemann, 1958).

---

42 See Achebe, Chinua. *Things Fall Apart* (London Heinemann, 1958), pp.124-125.
43 Abraham, "A Theological Response to the Ecological Crisis", p. 74.

Anim, Emmanuel. Who Wants to be a Millionaire?: An Analysis of Prosperity Teaching in the Charismatic Ministries (Churches) in Ghana and Its Wider Impact. (Unpublished PhD Dissertation, All Nations Christian College/The Open University, UK, 2003).

Bediako, Gillian. "Primal Religion and the Christian Faith: Antagonists or soul-mates", in Journal of African Christian Thought, Vo. 3, No.1, June 2000.

Bediako. Kwame, "What is the Gospel" Transformation, Vol. 14, No. 1,(January/March 1997).

Foster, G. M, "Peasant Society and the Image of Limited Good", American Anthropologist, Vo l. No. 67, 1965.

Howell, Alison, African Spirituality and Christian Ministry: 'Discerning the Signs of the Times' in our Environment and Community", Journal of African Christian Thought, Vol. 20. No.1, (June 2017).

Mbiti, John. Introduction to African Traditional Religion (London: Heinemann, 1975).

Mbiti, John. African Religions and Philosophy (London: Heinemann, 1969).

Meyer, Birgit. Translating the Devil: Religion and Modernity Among the Ewes in Ghana (Africa World, 1999).

Nonvignon, Justice, et.al., "Economic burden of malaria on businesses in Ghana," Malaria Journal, 2016. Accessed at: https://malariajournal.biomedcentral.com/track/pdf/10.1186/s12936-016-1506-0

Opoku, Asare, K. "Cooking on two stones of the earth? African spirituality and the socio-cultural transformation of Africa", Journal of African Christian Thought, Vol. 13, No. 1 (June 2010).

Osborn, Lawrence. Stewards of Creation: Environmentalism in the light of Biblical Teaching (Oxford: Latimer House, 1990), p.3.

Owusu, George and Agyei Mensah, Samuel "A comparative study of the ethnic residential segregation in Ghana's two largest cities, Accra and Kumasi," University of Ghana (Online: Springer Science-Business Media, LLC, 2011).

Owusu, George and Agyei, Samuel Mensah, "Segregated by Neighbourhoods? A Portrait of Ethnic Diversity in the Neighbourhoods of the Accra Metropolitan Area," University of Ghana (Online: Wiley Online Library, 2010).

Songsore, Jacob, "Urban Transition in Ghana: Urbanization, National Development and Poverty Reduction," Dept. of Geography, University of Ghana. Accessed at: http://pubs.iied.org/pdfs/G02540.pdf

Taylor, John, The Primal Vision (London: SCM Press Ltd, 1963), p. 16.

Busia, Kofi Abrefa, "The African World View," in Christianity and African Culture: The Proceedings of Conference Held at the Accra, Gold Coast, May 2nd – 6th, 1955, Under the Auspices of the Christian Council (Accra: Christian Council of the Gold Coast, 1955),

Werner, Dietrich. "The Challenge of Environment and Climate Justice- Imperatives of an Eco-Theological Reforms of Christianity in African Contexts", Unpublished Paper, Humboldt University of Berlin, 2018.

ECO-THEOLOGY IN AN AFRICAN PERSPECTIVE: WHY THE DELAY TO EMBODY ECO-THEOLOGY IN AFRICAN CHRISTIANITY?

Kambale Jean-Bosco Kahongya Bwiruka

1. Introduction

Known as a form of constructive theology that focuses on the interrelationship of religion and nature, particularly in the light of environmental concerns, eco-theology starts generally from the acknowledgment that there is an intimate connection between Christians' faith in God as Creator, and how Christians treat the rest of the Creation. It explores the interaction between ecological values such as sustainability and the human domination of nature.[1]

The historical statement of Lynn Whyte[2] in 1967, that the western Christianity was the most anthropocentric religion the world has known, still differently appreciated. It has led to what has been called "Ecological Complaint", consisting in accusing Christianity to promote the idea that the human dominates nature and therefore can use it for his needs.[3] Some have reacted defensively, arguing that Christianity is more concerned about ecology than it is supposed to be.[4] However in an African perspective, many facts could be seen as part of Whyte's concern.

More than a half century since Whyte's statement and all the discussion which followed, can we then assume that Christianity has further integrated the whole creation as part of human existence even part of the divine worship, and that, the environmental promotion as well as concern have embodied the daily life of Christians?

Obviously the universal discourse about climate change and environmental protection have positively increased worldwide in the recent decades. Even relevant international actions have been initiated. However, all these efforts are, in my opinion, still unevenly distributed, not only due to the difference in geographic regions whereby the western countries are seriously aware and taking the lead, but also due to the political influences whereby the impulse from the religious perspectives in the African context is still very poor in this regards.

This analysis is based on the observation in the central African countries (Rwanda, Kenya, Tanzania, D R Congo, etc.)[5], where the attitude of political leaders have shown more impact than the

---

1   Valerie Brown, "the Rise of Ecotheology" in http://unitingearthweb.org.au/about-us/1-what-is-ecotheology. html, consulted on 30th May 2019.
2   Lynn White, « The Historical Roots of our Ecological Crisis », Reprinted in A. E. Lugo & S. C. Snedaker (Eds.) Readings on Ecological Systems: Their Function and Relation to Man, New York: MSS Educational Publishing, 1971.
3   Gale Cengage, « Ecotheology », Encyclopedia of Science and Religion, see also on http://unitingearthweb.org. au/about-us/1-what-is-ecotheology.html, consulted on 30th May 2019.
4   «What is Ecotheology», on http://unitingearthweb.org.au/about-us/1-what-is-ecotheology.html, consulted on 30th May 2019.
5   Since ten years now Rwanda have make an important progress in reducing the importation and the use of plastic bags. Kenya have followed, but the experience have not yet been very successful. The case of DR Congo is

theological discourse on eco-theology. Nevertheless, the contribution of the church in promoting and supporting the development projects involving environment protection still is very crucial. The most questionable aspect, in my view, is the awareness of the congregants in different churches on the whole issue related to eco-theology. It seems that Christians are not aware enough of the need to promote the whole creation. This lack – better weakness – of awareness could be considered as result of connection of different factors to be identified, since the destruction of the nature is taking a high and dramatic speed, while the riposte is still very dangerously slow.

My first thesis is that historically, the discourse on eco-theology was not prioritized in the earlier kerygmatic content of Christianity in Africa. It was even somehow contradicted by the frequent reference to eschatology, the end-time theology, and to soteriology, especially the individual human salvation. Secondly, methodologically, the discourse on eco-theology is today more present in the higher level of the church organizations, involving more church leaders and academic scholars, but has not yet spread to the Christians on grass root level through a daily liturgy. Third, theologically, new reading of the biblical texts in association of better valorization of some African cultural values related to the traditional strategies of keeping harmony in the universe, could contribute to speed up the collective awareness on environmental protection, in order to mitigate the gap between the rhythm of destruction and the until now suggested solutions.

I will start with a study case done at the Université Libre des Pays des Grands Lacs de Butembo (ULPGL-Butembo) in 2016, by Gilbert Lusenge, a pastor of the Baptist Church in Central Africa (CBCA), one of the member church of the United Evangelical Mission (UEM) in Africa.[6]

2. Case study: Moderate commitment of the Baptist church (CBCA) towards the plantation of eucalyptus trees.

The research was based on the role of the church in the protection of the creation, a critical approach of the commission of Justice Peace and Integrity of the Creation (JPIC) toward the promotion of planting eucalyptus trees in Butembo city.

2.1. Butembo city statistics

Butembo is one of the cities of North-Kivu Province in the Democratic Republic of Congo. It is located at more than 280 km North of Goma, capital city of the province, and at 54 km South of the city of Beni. Butembo is at 1381 meters above sea level with an area of 190.34 km². The population was estimated to be 917 625 in 2015, with a density of 4821 inhabitants per square kilometre. The temperature is 18-28 grade.[7] The religious landscape of Butembo is dominated by the Roman Catholic Church and protestant churches, which are mostly members of the Baptist denomination.

---

more complicated, since for insecurity reasons, all the territories are not ruled by the government. Very recently the government of Tanzania have stopped the use and the importation of plastic bacs. The deadline was on the 1st June 2019, this can be seen in the whole country as an important decision. Earlier, the production of charcoals was very limited, and submitted to particular regulations and restrictions.

6   Gilbert Lusenge, *Le rôle de l'église face à la sauvegarde de la création en ville de Butembo. Approche critique de l'action de la commission Justice Paix et Sauvegarde de la Création*, inédit, ULPGL-Butembo, 2016.

7   See also „Butembo City", on https://en.wikipedia.org/wiki/Butembo. Consulted on 2nd June 2019.

Kambale Jean-Bosco Kahongya Bwiruka

2.2. Background of eucalyptus plantation in Butembo

Plantation of eucalyptus trees is not an innovation in North-Kivu Province today. Until the end of the colonial time in 1960, the region had some plantations of eucalyptus already. But the use of eucalyptus was limited to specific needs such as protecting the dirt roads from erosion, burning bricks and tiles for building purposes, fire wood in the factories, covering no fertile areas, etc. During the next two decades, until the years 1980, local traders increased the plantation of eucalyptus, but its uses had not changed that much yet. Though they used it in drying coffee and tea in factories before exportation, in this period, at least, eucalyptus wood was not used as domestic fire wood because of its massive smoke production. Rather, wood from the large forest and other tree varieties were more appreciated in this regard, even in building the walls of wooden houses. The eucalyptus could only be used for carpentry, where it was most needed.

In the 1990s, a drastic change occurred in the plantation and the use of eucalyptus trees in the region. Various factors contributed to this negative change. On one hand, economically, the coffee price dropped on the world market, and in the region a terrible disease destroyed the coffee plantations, which was the major income generating resource for many families. All the farms were then converted into eucalyptus plantations.

On the other hand, politically, eucalyptus plantations had been used to try to escape the insecurity. Still in the 1990s, the large natural forests of North-Kivu were cut off for breeding farm needs. Livestock was therefore the new income generating resource. But since 1994, due to the constant presence of national and foreign rebel groups in the farms, the farmers had no more access to their livestock. They then transformed their breeding farms into eucalyptus plantations. In the same time, other people sold their family lands to rich people, while they could migrate to the cities looking for more security. Since the new owners of the land could not exploit it directly for the same insecurity reasons, they could only protect their new property by planting eucalyptus trees on it. In this business, churches were not an exception. Most of them, in order to secure their land from several ownership conflicts and land grabbing, they covered it with trees, among them eucalyptus. In this setting, the relevance of the concern risen by Pastor Gilbert Lusenge about the role of the church in addressing the impact of eucalyptus tree in Butembo City can be understood.

2.3. Negative impact of the eucalyptus tree in Butembo

Scientifically, it is known that the eucalyptus trees destroy the soil, making it more acidic and therefore sterile. Even a number of animals and birds disappear from that ecosystem. This is the sad situation experienced in Butembo since a while, but with an aggravation of erosion in two different types: the first being the rainfall erosion. This is one of the consequences of eucalyptus having solidified the soil, making rain water flow quickly on the ground provoking terrible floods. The second type is the soil erosion provoked by wind, which prevents the constitution of fertile soil.[8]

The impact of the eucalyptus trees on human health in Butembo is also visible in the regional warming and the increase of female mosquitos provoking malaria. Up to the 1990s, the minimum annual average temperature was between 15 and 18 degrees, but in 2016 the minimum has increased from 18 to 20 degrees. This change of 2 degrees is enough to create a favorable environment for mosquito growth.

According to the report of *Agence Prince France 2010*, mosquitos don't survive under the tem-

---

8 Gilbert Lusenge, Op. Cit., p.10.

perature of 15 degrees.[9] This can be proved in Butembo because before the year 1990, the city was considered as a kind of refuge for people suffering from malaria. They could move from the warm territory of Beni and come to spend some weeks in the cold weather of Butembo, expecting to be healed from malaria by the cold weather. What they did not know was the correlation between mosquitos-malaria and weather. Otherwise, Malaria was not known in Butembo city as reported by Kasereka Ndalutwa, the Health supervisor of Butembo health zone. "The urban Health Zone of Butembo has registered a big number of Malaria cases which did not exist before in Butembo city".[10]

In the last decades, the cases have constantly increased. In 2010: 4.497 cases were reported; in 2011: 4.541 cases, in 2012: 4.358 cases, in 2013: 4.329 and 2014: 3.989. The drop in 2014 was the result of the distribution of insecticide-treated mosquito nets to the population.[11] This result appears on the chart here below.

2.4. Awareness of the church on the negative impact of eucalyptus tree

As social actors in the field of health care, the church leaders are perfectly aware that the degradation of the health situation is a result of climate change. For that reason, the Synod of the Baptist Church has decided, in 2010, that its commission on Justice Peace and Integrity of Creation (JPIC), which in principle was established in each protestant church under the umbrella of the Église du Christ au Congo (ECC) since 1993, should help the church in fighting all kinds of injustice, promoting human rights. In particular, the Synod insisted on the fact that climate justice and environmental protection should be brought on the daily agenda of each congregation. And the budget to implement this program should be elaborated in each congregation. The goal of this decision was to raise awareness of Christians and church leaders on the environmental issues and to mitigate the negative impact of climate change. Therefore, the commission should involve all the structures of the church in training and actions to promote tree planting in respect of biodiversity and initiating various techniques for environmental protection.[12]

In addition, the Baptist Church has dedicated one week for special teaching, preaching and implementing specific actions in the field of Justice Peace and Integrity of Creation. The program is prepared by the leadership of the commission and it is followed in liturgy of the whole week in all congregations.[13] So elaborated, it sounds very perfect. On the higher level of the church administration, people are aware of the danger of climate change and are really committed to make significant changes in practical ways. But how does Gilbert sees the reality?

Five years after the Baptist church had integrated the environmental issues in its liturgy through the JPIC Commission, Gilbert Lusenge considered that the commission was really committed in the issues of peace building, human rights protection, and advocacy for justice, etc. but the fields of environmental protection and climate justice were still poorly addressed. Concrete measures to restrict the plantation of eucalyptus trees in Butembo for example, were not yet elaborated. Therefore, people still plant it considering only the short term advantages that it provides, like quick growth, firewood, building material, etc.[14]

---

9   See also, N. Barette et L. Daleau, *Climat, future et conséquences,* Université, 2011, p.9.
10   Kasereka Ndalutwa, Registre des données sur le cas du paludisme et des décès dus au paludisme en zone de sante urbaine de Butembo, 2010-2015.
11   Gilbert Lusenge, Op cit., pp. 14-16.
12   Compte Rendu de la 33e AG de l'ECC/3-CBCA, Kikyo-Butembo 6-11.9.2011, p.16.
13   Mwongozo Kuhusu Mwaka wa Matengenezo na Ufuasi Bora 2019, CBCA, Goma, 2018.
14   Gilbert Lusenge, Op. Cit., p.38.

In this region where insecurity has reigned for decades, it doesn't surprise that the work of the Baptist JPIC commission was more visible in the field of human rights protection and not strongly on the eucalyptus tree, which furthermore, is not yet perceived by many as a green desert! It seems to be a choice between two priorities, one touching, in short run, directly people's lives, and the other one touching the nature, heading of course finally and in long run to humanitarian disaster. Such an assumption would not mean that the church is doing nothing in the field of environmental protection. Many projects are run in this regards. But people on grass root level, are still considering them more as development projects than environmental protection strategies.

Such ambiguity in the positive commitment of the church leadership towards the climate change and the delay, or rather, the weakness in implementation of concrete plans are not rare in the African context. And this is not the experience only on the microcosm level of a local church, but also on the macrocosm level of regional organizations of churches.

3. The impact of eco-theology in a Regional church organization

In 2016, church leaders of the UEM African member churches, especially from Rwanda, Tanzania and the Democratic Republic of Congo, adopted a number of recommendations about climate change. In a working document[15], they committed themselves to:
- Include and strengthen climate justice and environmental protection in the church Agenda and develop a policy to make Climate change a crosscutting issue and mainstream it in all church programs;
- Cooperate with other Churches and Institutions (NGOs, the government...) in addressing climate change issues wherever possible;
- Create a network of churches in the Great Lakes Region to promote climate justice and environmental protection, facilitate exchange and dissemination of relevant materials and network on youth action plan and environmental projects.
- Promote the production and the use of improved cooking stoves, filters and renewable energy;
- Promote conservation agriculture for land restoration through agro forestry, reforestation, and other modern land friendly farming techniques;
- Integrate eco-theology/theology of creation and environment in theological and other training programs including development programs ...

During the evaluation of the implementation of these recommendations two years later, the church leaders had realized that:
- Climate justice and environmental protection have been part of the annual agenda of all Churches in different aspects: liturgy, action plan of different groups in churches, trainings, etc.
- Church leaders are supporting climate justice, promotion activities and are playing a key role (in advocating and bringing in other stakeholders like the government, NGOs and other partners).
- Seminars to sensitize and mobilize communities in promoting climate justice protection are continuously being done by Churches, (e.g. tree planting, using energy saving stoves, solar home systems, waste management, rain water harvesting projects and environmental friendly agricultural practices, etc.).

---

15   Workshop on the Role of Churches in Addressing Climate Change, Nyamata, Rwanda, 16 – 18 March 2016.

Despite these successful stories, the initiative is still facing very big challenges such as:
- Limited skills and expertise in implementing some environmental activities.
- Limited financial capacities which reduce the intervention of churches in some cases.
- Due to some contextual reasons, some projects are not always very feasible (like governmental policy, availability of local resources, etc.)
- Less involvement of some pastors in projects related to climate justice.[16]

The above challenges mentioned by the African regional church leaders do not clearly present theological orientation being one of the obstacles of understanding the communion between human beings and the whole creation. They don't even refer to the African culture or traditions to be the causes. They rather refer to environmental expertise, financial issues, political context, and to particular lack of interest for some pastors. Pastor Gilbert Lusenge, in his case study of the eucalyptus in Butembo, did not mention these reasons, he rather referred to the priority of the JPIC commission, that it's more active on the justice side than the environmental one. Why do environmental concerns lag behind in being integrated into collective thinking in the church? Why are some pastors still taking distance from the issues related to climate justice? Many reasons can be mentioned.

4. Reasons of late integration of eco-theology in African Christianity

After having observed the situation in one church organization, and working in an international church organization addressing the environmental concern, I would then come to develop my thesis to explain the delay of the integration of eco-theology in African Christianity.

4.1. Eco-theology as victim of the earlier kerygmatic communication of the African church
My first thesis is based on the historical content of the kerygmatic communication in the earlier Christianity in the African context.

For a very long period, the kerygmatic proclamation of Christianity in Africa was focused on soteriology, individual human salvation, without much link to the entire creation. eco-theology was therefore not prioritized and was even sometimes contradicted by the frequent reference to eschatology.

The theological understanding of "global salvation" which involves – *each person, the whole person and the whole creation* –, seems to be a recent and very late theological development and liturgical orientation in African Christianity. It's still not yet well elaborated. The creation was always presented, not as a divine project of which the creator was proud – as to say it is good –[17]: creation was rather presented mostly as only useful for the human welfare.[18]

In such a world conception, the human will consider nature as his property and can endlessly harvest its products for his own consumption, his own good, and his own salvation. This personal salvation has dominated the minds to such an extent that some Christians have become arrogant and individualistic, thinking only about themselves, attaching less value to the non-human world. And whenever these natural resources have been exhausted by human overexploitation, people

---

16   Evaluation of the implementation of the UEM Recommendations for Climate Change since 2016, Shyogwe-Muhanga, Rwanda, 14-16th November 2018.
17   Genesis 1,25.
18   Genesis 1,29-30.

and land become very poor. As a consequence, animals and humans – if they are not killed by hunger and other disasters – migrate to other places for a better life.[19] That's where the wrong understanding of "dominion"[20] becomes a destructive motif for nature and humanity.

The Kenyan theologian Andrew R. Mukaria, reflecting in 2013, on the silence of the church towards the ecological crisis happening at the Mau forest complex, which is a very important ecological feature in Kenya, mentioned this attitude as *spiritual motif*. It is a 'religious worldview that, if not outright hostile to the natural world, is at the very least unconcerned with its state of existence.' The motif is "predicated on a vision of the human spirit rising above nature in order to ascend to supra-mundane communion with God." This worldview leads to the perception that the destruction of this world equals to salvation or does not affect the personal salvation.[21]

In addition to this spiritual motif, the earlier kerygmatic communication of the Christianity in Africa was dominated by an *eschatology orientation* with negative impact to the perception of the nature. The constant representation of the world in a contradictory dualism: material and spiritual (earth-heaven), present world and the world to come, the timely limited world and the eternal world, the corrupted and paradisiac world, etc. have ended up dividing the African Christian worldview into a perishable world, represented by the world in which we live now, devilish and fallen[22], on one hand, and on the other hand, the unperishable divine world which is to come, waiting for the Parousia.[23]

In this regards, the study of Andrew Mukaria has shown that in the Kenyan context, the kerygma of Parousia (next coming of Jesus Christ), have developed an *escapist eschatology* consisting in minimizing attention on the life (earthly), and its afflictions in favor of rather singular focus on the world to come. It holds the view that the believers are indeed strangers and foreigners on the earth,[24] living as those just passing through, with eyes fixed on the eternal city God has prepared for them, then believers may be justified to pay little attention to a homeland that does not belong to them (that is the present homeland-earth).[25] With such an attitude, some Christians believe that "human beings have no responsibility in what is happening; rather, they should assist by exhausting the earth's resources to speed up the coming of Christ".[26] Even if some could not consider that they have a role in exhausting the natural resources for eschatological reasons, Andrew Mukaria states that still they will attribute the degradation of the environment to the "will of God" or "Mapenzi ya Mungu", a divine order, where God is in control and human beings have nothing to do.[27]

Although I have not yet personally met such conception, honestly I find it very irresponsible and devastating. In the Democratic Republic of Congo, natural calamities are sometimes rather considered by some Christians as signs of the end-time. The eschatology theology has built in the

---

19   Robert Minani Bihuzo SJ (ed), *Migration in and out of Africa. Jesuits Ministry Outlook*, Nairobi, Paulines Publications Africa, 2015, p.26.
20   Genesis 1,28.
21   Andrew R. Mukaria, Theological ambiguity: A challenge to a constructive Ecotheology in Africa, 2013.
22   Revelation 6,14-17.
23   Revelation 21,1-4.
24   1Peter 2,11, Hebrew 11,13-15., etc.
25   Andrew R. Mukaria,
26   Andrew R. Mukaria, Theological ambiguity: A challenge to a constructive Ecotheology in Africa, in *International Journal of Current Research*, Vol.5, Issue 5, pp.1255-1261, May 2013. Available on https://www.academia.edu/3462529/Theological_ambiguities_A_challenge_to_a_constructive_ecotheology_in_Africa, consulted on 30th May 2019.
27   Andrew Mukaria, Op. Cit.

Christian mindset a belief that they are the last generation to live on earth – *Kizazi cha mwisho* – many Christians believe that the end-time is very close and that the environmental crises are evident signs of it, referring to a literal interpretation of the apocalyptic biblical texts in the gospels and the Revelation.[28]

4.2. Eco-theology a discourse in high spheres of the church

My second assumption is related to the communication approach on eco-theology. In my view, eco-theology has been until now a discourse in high leadership spheres of the church, and the message has not yet reached the African Christianity on the grass roots level. Likewise, many initiatives are done on an academic level, books are written and put in libraries, and conferences are held in higher spheres of the society, etc. but most of these important activities are not transmitted to the low levels of society, in order to meet people in their daily lives and activities.

On the side of the church, very good decisions have been taken by synods, assemblies, etc. regional organizations, etc. But the appropriation of all these initiatives by the congregants can be done only if this knowledge is fully and perfectly integrated in the daily church liturgy, not only one week per year. I mean, the hymn book, the songs of choir groups, the daily prayers, the biblical texts to be read, even the preaching should be impregnated by ecological concerns and valorization. Then the development of economical, and social activities on the grass root level should be promoted in the way that the human regains his understanding that he belongs to the nature and therefore, has a huge responsibility of protecting the nature, as his own life. But, since the church cannot impose its view like the political leaders in the region, training, teaching, preaching and interacting will be the best tools.

4.3. Revalorization of eco-theology through a new reading of the Bible and better consideration of African traditions

My last thesis is based on an intercultural theological approach. There is a need of a new reading of the biblical texts in association of better valorization of some African cultural values related to the traditional strategies of keeping harmony in the universe. This connectivity of biblical and cultural theology could contribute to speed up the collective awareness on environmental protection, and try to mitigate the distance between the higher rhythm of destruction and the very slow speed of until now suggested solutions towards the climate change.

The recent change in the kerygmatic communication of African Christianity referring to a global salvation is still very new and not well integrated in the collective mindset. However, theologically, this global understanding of salvation is clearly developed in the bible. For example, the apostle Paul links the fall of human beings with the suffering of the whole creation. Therefore, the creation itself is waiting for salvation.[29] For the apostle, there is no individual human salvation without the general salvation of nature, since the human fall has resulted in the fall of the whole creation. A second text which can be mentioned is the salvation of the biblical city of Nineveh motivated not only by the big number of people unable to distinguish their right hand from their left, but also because of the multitude of animals in the city.[30] For Christians, such biblical texts and many others, should be utilized to speed up the integration of the whole creation in the liturgy as well as in the hymnology and in the practical life of the church.

---

28   Luke 21,25-28.
29   Roman 8,19-23.
30   Jonas 4,11.

Kambale Jean-Bosco Kahongya Bwiruka

There is also cultural potential which could be useful in the process. The African concept of *bondedness of life*, mentioned by the Malawian Hervey Sindima, is of such African richness. Bondedness is based on the consciousness that all creatures are part of all others, that humans share a common destiny with nature.[31] So, for Malawians, in the human sphere, the process of life achieves fullness when humans are richly connected to one another, to other creatures, and to the earth itself. Humans realize their own fullness by realizing the bondedness of life.[32] This conception shared by many African cultures can be really relevant to promote Ecotheology in African Christianity. This consciousness of mutual connectivity of human and non-human, is the result of the perception that, the nature is not an empty impersonal object or phenomenon, rather it is full of religious significance. God, who is invisible, becomes visible in and behind these objects and phenomena. They symbolized or are the manifestation of the invisible world. The invisible world presses hard upon the visible: one speaks of the other, and African peoples see that invisible universe when they look at, hear or feel the visible tangible world. So the physical and the spiritual are two dimensions of one and the same universe.[33]

Historically, this traditional African perception was deeply challenged, even destroyed in the time of colonialism and Christianization. Sindima states that with the imposition of Western cultural views, the African hermeneutical process, by which African people appropriated their own heritage, became so impaired that the Africans ceased to understand their world through their own cultural system or through the symbolic interpretation given by their cosmology. Today, pursues Sindima, this impairment prevents the traditional concept of the bondedness of life from being an organized logic informing African life and practice.[34] He then suggest that African Christians should rediscover traditional African values and rethink Christianity in an African way.[35] In this way, African tradition is rich and still has a lot to offer to Christianity, for example the traditional system of keeping harmony within the universe.

Another African cultural richness that Christianity can refer to in promoting eco-theology could be the idea of maintaining harmony or balance between the two spheres of universe – visible and invisible –, and among all beings. This is, according to Laurenti Magesa, the Kenyan author of culture and theology, the most important ethical responsibility for humanity, and it forms the basis of any individual's moral character. Even more significantly, however, it determines the quality of life of the human community in the universe and the quality of the universe in itself.[36] Without harmony, greed, selfishness and exploitation – in a word, chaos – set in and triumph over universal moral order. Chaos does not imply simple disorder; it risks putting relationships between the two spheres of the universe on a collision course, inviting great suffering for the human community.

To emphasize the connectedness between humanity and creation and to ward off the chaos that might ensue if this bond is not respected, African Religion erects a system of totem and ta-

---

31   Harvey Sindima, "Community of Life: Ecological Theology in African Perspective" in https://www.religion-online.org/article/community-of-life-ecological-theology-in-african-perspective, consulted on 30th May 2019. See also Charles Birch, William Eaken and Jay B. McDaniel (eds.) Liberating Life: Contemporary Approaches in Ecological Theology, Orbis Books, Maryknoll, New York 10545, 1990, pp. 137-147.
32   Harvey Sindima, Op. Cit., p.6.
33   John S. Mbiti, *African Religions & Philosophy*, East African Educational Publishes Ltd., Nairobi, 2015, p.55-56.
34   Harvey Sindima, p.3.
35   Harvey Sindima, p.6.
36   Laurenti Magesa, *African Religion. The moral traditions of abundant life*, Nairobi, Pauline Publications Africa, third reprint, 2011, p.73.

boos. A totem is any species of animal or less often a plant or species of it, or even in some cases, a force of the nature, such as rain, water or lightning, which is perceived to have a special relationship with a given clan. A totem is seen to incorporate or be an expression or representation of an ancestor of the entire clan. Different clans cannot have the same totem. The totem is understood to have responsibility of protecting the clan. But the obligation is mutual: if the totem cannot harm its tutelaries, the members of the clan must also not kill or harm it in any way. If the totem is an animal, the member of the clan cannot eat its meat. This prohibition is the taboo, which is perceived to contain within a certain assumed danger, that always has repercussions against anyone who transgresses it.[37]

In an eco-theological perception, I could say that the system of totem connects human and non-human in a mutual respect, acceptance and protection. It contributes also to protect biodiversity. I still remember since my childhood, some species of bird and animals that I was forbidden to kill or to eat. They were considered to belong to our families as totems, some from my father's clan and others from my mother's clan. But today, nobody is considering totem, since from the African Christian view, cultural traditions and beliefs were labeled as paganism. African Christianity still can refer to such a system not as totem, but as a mean of setting limits in human consumption and developing new connections to the nature which is unfortunately disappearing.

5. Conclusion

African Christianity has a delay in reacting to the climate change. However enormous efforts are taken, but face obstacles of a different nature. These obstacles can be, first, the historical context characterized by a theological orientation which separates humans and the rest of the creation, presenting only humans to be the most important creature. The revalorization of the global salvation is the way out of this.

Second, the nature of approaches used until now has led to the problem of keeping the discourse on eco-theology in the higher spheres of society and church organizations. More efforts should be put on the work on the grass root level, to involve the entire church, and the entire society, so that the speed of the positive change can be enhanced.

Last, the African traditional practices could cease to be globally labeled as "paganism", but considered as initiative potential to enrich the understanding of interconnectivity between human beings and nature. This will encourage African Christians to feel not ashamed or guilty when referring to their own traditional conception system.

6. Bibliography

Barette, N. et Daleau, L., Climat, future et conséquences, Université, 2011.

Birch, C., William Eaken and Jay B. McDaniel (eds.) Liberating Life: Contemporary Approaches in Ecological Theology, Orbis Books, Maryknoll, New York 10545, 1990.

Brown V., "The Rise of Ecotheology" in http://unitingearthweb.org.au/about-us/1-what-is-eco-theology.html, consulted on 30th May 2019.

---

37   Laurenti Magesa, *Op. Cit.*, pp.74-75.

„Butembo City", on https://en.wikipedia.org/wiki/Butembo. Consulted on 2nd June 2019.

Cengage, G., « Ecotheology », Encyclopedia of Science and Religion, see also on http://unitinge-arthweb.org.au/about-us/1-what-is-ecotheology.html, consulted on 30th May 2019.

Compte Rendu de la 33e AG de l'ECC/3-CBCA, Kikyo-Butembo 6-11.9.2011.

Evaluation of the implementation of the UEM Recommendations for Climate Change since 2016, Shyogwe- Muhanga, Rwanda, 14-16th November 2018.

Lusenge, G., Le rôle de l'église face à la sauvegarde de la création en ville de Butembo. Approche critique de l'action de la commission Justice Paix et Sauvegarde de la Création, inédit, ULPGL-Butembo, 2016.

Magesa, Laurenti, African Religion. The moral traditions of abundant life, Nairobi, Pauline Publications Africa, third reprint, 2011.

Mbiti, John S., African Religions & philosophy, East African Educational Publishes Ltd., Nairobi, 2015.

Minani Bihuzo, R. SJ (ed), Migration in and out of Africa. Jesuits Ministry Outlook, Nairobi, Paulines Publications Africa, 2015.

Mukaria, A. R., Theological ambiguity: A challenge to a constructive Ecotheology in Africa, in International Journal of Current Research, Vol.5, Issue 5, pp.1255-1261, May 2013.

Mwongozo Kuhusu Mwaka wa Matengenezo na Ufuasi Bora 2019, CBCA, Goma, 2018.

Ndalutwa, K., Registre des données sur le cas du paludisme et des décès dus au paludisme en zone de sante urbaine de Butembo, 2010-2015.

Sindima H., "Community of Life: Ecological Theology in African Perspective" in https://www.religion-online.org/article/community-of-life-ecological-theology-in-african-perspective, consulted on 30th May 2019.

«What is Ecotheology», on http://unitingearthweb.org.au/about-us/1-what-is-ecotheology.html, consulted on 30th May 2019.

White, L., «The Historical Roots of our Ecological Crisis», Reprinted in A. E. Lugo & S. C. Snedaker(Eds.) Readings on Ecological Systems: Their Function and Relation to Man, New York: MSS Educational Publishing, 1971.

Workshop on the Role of Churches in Addressing Climate Change, Nyamata, Rwanda, 16 – 18 March 2016.

MAPPING RECENT MAJOR ECO-THEOLOGICAL INITIATIVES FROM SCANDINAVIAN PERSPECTIVES

Henrik Grape

Let me start with a little reflection on the term "eco-theology". The headline of the session allocated to me reads "*Mapping recent major eco-theological initiatives – Exploring the ground*. This is a title which is fine and understandable. This needs to be done. At the same time, after being interested in eco-philosophy and eco-theology since I stumbled over the concept as a young student at Uppsala University in 1980, I have some problems to label some kind of theologies as "eco-theology" and others as not.

I think that any theology of today must take the context seriously. Humanities largest question of today is how we shall live together on an Earth that – as we now know – has boundaries that we as human beings started to transgress.

This is a totally new situation. We live in the aftermath of a huge transformation during the last century with great improvements on many fields of human life like health, technology, science communication etc. And those in power have a mindset still coined by the last century in their understanding of development and building society. Add to this a quadrupled or so, increase of inhabitants of the earth, and you see which challenges we are facing.

A theology that is living must face this new situation. Sometimes it is called eco-theology, but that might lead us wrong. It may point in a direction that this is a special form of Theology for green geeks or those who just like to be out in the nature for recovering. A middle class hobby!

I know that this is not the case about those who think of themselves as eco-theologians. My point is that every contemporary theology must have a reflection over what the gospel means in a time of urgency to act on climate change and other systematic ecological challenges. It must reflect upon what it means to be church in a time when bio diversity is being lost at a rate that will have great impact on human life in the coming days.

Every theology of today must in some way respond on the justice aspect on how to transform a society from an extractive, accumulative and economic growth-oriented track to a just transition, to a circular and sharing society that respects the planetary boundaries and also taking care of the most vulnerable. And those might be the poor, coming generations or Creation itself.

So with that said, I will try to sketch a picture on how this challenge is met in the context of Churches in Sweden with a focus on Church of Sweden.

The issue of environment has gone from being a small activist based group inside church of Sweden to a main stream work that is embraced by most of the congregations but not always actively working on today.

In the tradition of issuing Bishops letters from the Church of Sweden bishop synod, a first letter was written in 1989. It was the bishop of the diocese of Linköping, Martin Lönnebo, who took the initiative together with Stefan Edman, a Swedish biologist and "adult educator" and also an advisor to the Swedish prime minister.[1] The text was issued as a letter from the bishops of Church of Sweden. This was the first step that focused on the relation between theology and environment. It was one part about theology and some church fathers and another part on contemporary environmental issues. It was a start.[2]

In 1992 as a response to the call from WCC group attending the Rio meeting and picking up the challenges from Rio summit 1992, a voluntary network around environment in Church of Sweden saw the light of day. Very small financial resources but a lot of will and spirit gathered the enthusiasts in Church of Sweden to push for an environmental agenda for the congregations. All from the start it was important to keep to connection between theological reflection and more concrete action. To keep in mind what is the church identity in this environmental work. This was not formulated by people from the academia or professional theologians, it was driven locally and invited local parishes and congregations to reflect on both the biblical text and the environmental context. This was a challenge for many and still is. The challenge for the theologians in the congregations, like pastors, was to not be an expert or authority on environment issues but to reflect on environmental problems and share thoughts. For those driven by a will to concrete action the challenge might been to reflect upon theological implications of environment.

For this work a tool was constructed called Environmental Diploma for congregations work on sustainable development. At start it was a simple model with check lists. This was developed to a more complicated audit scheme with a standard to fulfill. That involved to do an analysis of the status of the congregation when it comes to the environmental impact and setting goals/targets for the work and after that evaluation and follow up. Even the standard, that was to some extent similar to the industrial methods like ISO 14001 or EMAS system, was developed and tailored between 2000 and 2004 by people employed at the national office of church of Sweden. Today we have it as a free tool for congregations to voluntary use and it comes with rather low costs. But, the important part of this project is that it should combine a theological reflection with a more structured work for the practical work to lower the environmental impact of the activities of the congregation.

This is the important part if we look at it from a theological perspective; to combine reflection with action. And this is also the hard part. Some are more interested in the hands on work and not too happy about doing the reflections. Some are more or less lost in the practical parts but enjoy the reflections.

I think of this as a pattern for the Swedish context on eco-theology. It is often locally initiated and builds on a common reflection on how we as local church should, in our local context respond to the ecological issues that we meet. That means that we have many different initiatives and network with different ways of taking the challenge.

But I want to exemplify what has been happening during the last decades that can give a picture of the eco-theological work in Sweden

I will start with the Uppsala interfaith climate summit in 2008. As a part of the preparations for a good outcome of the Copenhagen COP in 2009 the Archbishop of Uppsala initiated a summit for faith leaders from all great traditions to meet and to sign a climate manifesto named "

---

1   See also: http://www.hammarbykyrkan.nu/boktips/stefan-edman-martin-lonnebo-jordens-och-sjalens-over-levnad
2   See: https://www.svenskakyrkan.se/klimatbrevet; https://lutheransrestoringcreation.org/reflections-on-swedish-bishops-letter-on-climate-change/

Henrik Grape

Hope for the future! "[3] (and this is ten years before "Fridays for Future") . The content of the manifesto was both appeals to the global political leadership as commitments from people of faith. [4]

You can always debate about how useful or instrumental these kinds of documents really are but one effect is that for those involved it starts many other processes. For church of Sweden this was the start of divesting from fossil fuels[5], which means coal and oil. This was finalized in 2014 when the natural gas was out of the portfolio as well.

The chain effects from preparing and making statements are often underestimated. For church of Sweden the Uppsala interfaith manifesto meant that climate change was identified as a main stream church subject. It was regarded as a theological subject that must be reflected. The strategy to keep a theological reflection together with concrete action was paying back in some sense. But we should also keep in mind that the development aid is a part of Church of Sweden, now called Act Church of Sweden, at the same time pushed for climate action. This also influenced the church to reflect more on eco-theological issues. I think that the last lines of the manifesto pretty much sums up were we were at that time:

> "As religious leaders and teachers, we want to counteract a culture of fear with a culture of hope. We want to face the climate challenge with a defiant optimism to highlight the core principles of all major sacred traditions of the world: justice, solidarity and compassion. We want to encourage the best science and political leadership. We commit or communities to fostering a spirit of joy and hope in relation to the greatest gift given to us all – the gift of life" Uppsala Interfaith Climate Manifesto 2008

The Christian Council of Sweden formed a climate change group in the beginning of 2000. Within this group the different member churches shared their work on environmental issues and arranged seminaries on the topic. It was also the group who shared and promoted the Creation time/Season of Creation material for many years. Even though this is not even now fully embraced by all churches and congregations it is growing. After some years, in 2013, a common document for all the member churches in the Christian Council was formulated. *Protect the Earth that God loves*[6] is the name of the document and was endorsed by the board of Christian Council and formulates common understanding of climate change and our Christian tradition.

2014 the Church of Sweden bishops synod released a Bishops letter on climate change. It is little booklet with a short summary of the science of climate change, a short recapturing on what in human behavior and understanding means to the problem and some theological reflection as well as some calls to the political leadership as well as commitment and calls to the congregations to act on climate change.

This letter manifested the climate issue as a genuine theological issue that we as church cannot have in our reflections on being church in the 21 century. Later this year an updated edition will be released.

At the same time there are at least three different Swedish eco-theological networks that meet regularly and discuss different aspect of theology/being church and the different sustainable issues that we stand in front of. From members of those networks different publications have come

---

3 See: https://www.oikoumene.org/en/press-centre/news/uppsala-manifesto-demands-action-on-climate-issues
4 See also: https://www.svenskakyrkan.se/Sve/Bin%c3%a4rfiler/Filer/4b2c2f28-bedb-44cc-90be-b83efe397b9b.pdf
5 See: https://gofossilfree.org/church-of-sweden-completes-full-divestment/
6 https://www.diakonia.se/en/Info/News--Publications/Latest-news/booklet-climate-development/; https://www.skr.org/wp-content/uploads/2018/10/protect-the-earth-that-god-loves.pdf

out. One was released by the most northern diocese with the title Sustainable life with a special focus on what this means in an Arctic context. Another diocese have by their bishop done extended courses in eco-theology for all the pastoral workers in the diocese and at the same time investing in solar cells at some of the roofs of their buildings. In the most southern diocese in Sweden in the town Malmö, close to the Danish capital Copenhagen, a congregation did a special work on the altar flowers and called it the The Altar table of solidarity.

I could go one with different small things that is happening and mostly not synchronized. They are driven very much by the local context but often inspired by the more national contributions like the bishops letter or the Christian Councils text or Season of Creation.

Last I want to share with you the Storforsen appeal. In 2015 , after years of discussions Church of Sweden together with the Canadian Council of Churches finally gathered church leaders from different churches in Canada and the Nordic countries together with indigenous people of the Arctic. It was on Future of Life in the Arctic – The Impact of Climate Change. Indigenous and Religious Perspectives[7] And it underlines that

"Climate justice for the Arctic is a spiritual issue, and the power to change comes from spiritual sources. Climate justice is intergenerational, needs to include the peoples of the Arctic, and calls for common but differentiated responsibilities."

It also point out the important contributions from indigenous people

"The ancestors and Indigenous Peoples bear witness to a worldview, spiritual relationships with the land, animals, water, and the Creator, and traditional practices. We believe these are indispensable resources for addressing climate change."

The appeal from Storforsen[8] is a unique document formulated by church leaders and indigenous together after sharing stories about what we see and hear. I think that indigenous outlook on the world and the spiritual traditions is much needed to transform our world to a more sustainable and equitable world.

"We have gained a new respect for the interconnectedness of spirit and nature. For example, berry picking is itself a spiritual practice; it connects us to the land and its spirit. This seasonal and community activity illustrates and reminds us of the way to live together in our common home (oikonomia, economy, or rules for thehousehold): sharing and equity, the participation of all, respect for the land, and the enjoyment of its fruits."

This I my very short and fragmented illustration of what eco-theology that I can observe from the Swedish context. Of course there are other things that happens. More books and writings are evolving, we are looking for opportunities to work together with universities around these issues, we have an interfaith cluster group on water with Stockholm International Water Institute a and other things. To sum it up I could say that eco-theology is growing but not always under the label of eco theology, more as a theological answer to the urgent questions of today.

---

7   https://www.councilofchurches.ca/news/arctic-future/;   https://www.oikoumene.org/en/press-centre/news/churches-address-impact-of-climate-change-on-indigenous-peoples-in-the-arctic
8   https://seors.unfccc.int/applications/seors/attachments/get_attachment?code=31PH3RDTUOGN3MOS9GAIFZ6QBSVR8QL2

THE ROLE OF INTERRELIGIOUS DIALOGUE IN PRESERVING THE ECOLOGICAL ENVIRONMENT

Indonesia as an Example

Andar Parlindungan / Daniel Sinaga

In this millennial era, issues of preserving an ecological system have become trendy global topics. This is due to the problems of justice and the integrity of creation particularly concerning the inter-generational Justice. Everyone has the right to enjoy a decent life, including the next generation which also has the right to enjoy the created things by God in this world. The question is what will we leave as an inheritance to the next generation when the environment is left unprotected?

The issue of this global environment has been discussed in June, 1992 in the Summit Conference in Rio de Janeiro held by the UN (United Nations Organization). Delegations from many countries have raised the issue of the degradation of the global ecosystem due to the massive industrial revolution which has a fatal effect on human life globally. Ecological degradation with the effect of climate change worsens the life conditions of communities. The people whose lives rely directly on natural resources are most susceptible to sufferings by the climate change. Policies by the UN are obviously to protect people who are exposed to physical suffering by climate change so that they can enjoy their rights to experience a decent life.

The procedures of dialogue on the ecological system have been set up by a UN council called the United Nations Framework Convention of Climate Change or UNFCCC that was specially established to tackle and arrange frameworks globally to address climate problems. The arrangement was made in the Conference of Parties (COP) where the stakeholders from government and non-government bodies met to design the frameworks. In 2015, the 21st COP in Paris was one of the milestones to show this global movement in which about 189 countries had ratified what is called the Paris Agreement with the target ambition of 1.5 degrees. The interesting event of the COP in Paris was that the meeting was also supported by International Religious Organizations for Humanity such as Act Alliance, Islamic Belief, Bhramakumaris, Fransiscan International and so on.

In spiritually based movements, there are NGOs, Green Faith that work to educate people about the problems of climate change. The organizations which have existed since the Earth Summit of 1992 in Rio have made great changes especially in the spiritual education in the teaching of religions. In the 23rd COP in Bonn, the Green Faith proposed three changes of lifestyle with the motto "Walk on Earth Gently" such as a) reducing the family emission, b) reducing transportation emission and c) reducing meat consumption. The three points are the key factor to deal with the life changes because when the climate changes, the lifestyle should also be adapted to it so that people can live in balance.

Significant Roles of Indonesia for Climate Justice

The Eco-Theology conference, which was held in Wuppertal from 16 to 19 June 2019, discussed intensively about the roles of inter-religious communities on how the ecumenical and religious communities should support and struggle for this process. In particular, the churches and our ecumenical movement should be aware that the Christian communities live together with the pluralistic societies such as in Indonesia. For the Indonesian, diversity is God´s grace for the nation. It is naive and inadequate if the churches are still imprisoned with exclusive fantasies that the struggle for climate justice can be handled only through their ecumenical movements. The global churches must expand their ecumenical movements into interreligious movements through awareness education, joint agreements for a concrete action against all forms of environmental destructions in Indonesia and globally. Therefore, this question is always relevant for me on why the roles of Indonesia are very strategic to fight for climate justice?

Indonesia as the largest Muslim population in the world consists also of multi-religious and cultural societies such as Christianity, Buddhism, Hinduism, Confucianism and hundreds of local religions. As a country with the number of more than 250 million inhabitants, the vivid roles of Indonesian populations are quite strong in several social political instruments. However, the roles of Indonesian populations and governments in climate issues have been questionable. We have to mention some cases of systemic environmental destructions where many devoted religious communities live. It is reported that the statistic of forest fire damage has increased rapidly in Sumatra and Kalimantan provinces, the air of Jakarta is claimed to be the worst in the world, and the cases of land grabbing of indigenous people for palm oil plantations and large-scale business ventures. Those cases have proven that Indonesia is still unware of the realities of our mother earth. Religious communities in Indonesia fail to create a vivid awareness on protecting and preserving God´s creation. Dr. Kambale Kahongya (DR Congo) and I shared our non-western experiences on preserving the earth in a public discussion in *Kirchentag* (German church convention) 2019 in Dortmund. We shared our ideas that the absence of environmental awareness in Asia and Africa is inseparable from the realities of massive poverty of the entire religious populations in the global south. Unfortunately, consumers of environmental damage in the global south are the populations who live in Europe and North America. In our understanding, the matter is ecology and sustainability is how to stand for justice, equality and equity. As long as our world stake holders are not seriously reforming our global economic systems, which are still dominated by neo-liberalistic and capitalistic economic orientations, so our struggle for climate justice will always end in vain. I agree with Prof Petros Vasiliadis who emphasized an interrelation between ecology and economy in his presentation in the conference of Eco-Theology in Wuppertal. He says: "The ecumenical mission statement is making a consistent use of the inter-connectedness of ecology with economy, something that Pope Francis had thoroughly examined in his *Evangelii Gaudium* and frequently repeats in *Laudato Si*."[1] Issues of climate justice must be seriously linked to equitable socio-economic policies, so that the religious communities are encouraged to formulate a joint movement to resolve these challenges. Moreover, if we base our ecological concerns on economic systems and justice, conversations of interfaith theology and the roles of the faith based organizations are becoming

---

1   Petros Vassiliadis, *Integral Ecology in the Witness of the Orthodox Church*, Eco-Theology Conference in Wuppertal, June 16-19, 2019.

remarkable, because the whole religious societies are affected by economic and social injustice in their regions in Indonesian.

Nonetheless, we witnessed serious efforts in the President Jokowi´s administration to work on climate justice which have involved various elements of the religious communities. Without joint participation among religious societies and faith based organizations, commitments to proceed the climate justice´s campaigns will only be a matter of conversation on the table. Indonesia, during the President Jokowi's administration (2014-2019), in particular has taken many important roles in saving the environment. In the COP meeting in Paris, Indonesia expressed its participation in ratifying the Paris Agreement. In following the spiritually based movement like Green Faith, in 2015 the Minister of Environment and Forestry, Dr. Siti Nurbaya with religious prominent figures endorsed the establishment of Standby Earth Movement led by Prof. Dr. Din Syamsuddin. This movement is the realization of the participation by interreligious organizations in setting up dialogues about the ecological environment. The guests who were present in the event were from the Indonesian Council of Ulema (ICU), Buddhist Monk Council, United Indonesian Churches (UIC), Hindu Council, Indonesian Chinese Religious Council, Nahdlatul Ulama (NU), Muhammadiyah, and Indonesian Mosque Council. They declared the movement in the International Peace Day on the 21st of September 2015.

In 2017, the ICU started a program called Eco-Mosque established through their website which provides directions in building a more ecologically friendly mosque according to the teachings of Islam. Meanwhile, the UIC itself issued out programs of Nature Friendly Churches (UFC) carried out by the Council of Field Workers of the UIC in 2013 by adopting the program implementations of Green Church from the Canadian Center for Ecumenism. Although the books of instructions have been published, however, the implementation has become a big challenge. Still few people know about the above-mentioned documents and so the progress of the programs is very slow. The writer has particularly observed the churches as members of the UIC which have conducted many activities concerning the enviromental protection, however, they were exclusively done. Ideally, such actions and activities should be performed inclusively because environmental protection is the duty of all people together.

In the 23rd COP, it is expressed that spiritual leaders should be the models to bring the people to make changes. A spiritual leader must be a key model of life to other people both in behavior and lifestyle. Therefore, in saving our ecological environment and climate change, we expect the spiritual leaders to understand and recognize what should be done together to solve the problems of injustice. In the various contexts in Indonesia, the dialogues among the high level people should be continued on the grassroot level of people so that the dialogue brings greater positive impacts. There have been interfaith activities to learn about tolerance and peace among human beings, however, interfaith dialogue about ecological environment means that we as humans not only live peacefully among ourselves but also with the ecological environment (Psalm 96:11-12 and Hadith Ahmad bin Hambal[2]). One strategy that I could suggest in our theological conference is to formulate fundamental theological statements for a friendly environment. It invites the role of religions and also their worshippers to have a dialogue and dia-praxis, actions as climate protection strategies must be seriously followed by all faith-based institutions and actors. Mutual dialogues of the holy scriptures on human responsibility for God´s creation is highly needed because one fundamental religious mission in the world is to transmit the positive impacts of reli-

---

2   "Whoever kills a child, cuts a fruiting tree, kills an animal to take its skin, kills farmers or parents who did not join the war, then he will not return in a state of wealth".

gions and beliefs in order to sustain and maintain our life and the life of our future generations. A theological dialogue on climate change can become an effective approach for deepening dialogue for more extensive, strategic and relevant issues about the role of *Dakwah* and Mission in the Muslim and Christian communities. Therefore, such a conference with participations of diverse faith-based institutions and academicians is strongly encouraged in the near future.

The efforts to construct interfaith dialogue should be performed not only once but also continuously so that people can understand their duties and responsibilities to protect the environment. Spiritual leaders should be the frontline guards to lead the followers to adopt the sustainable, millenial lifestyle. This is our commitment to reach a sustainable life in the various contexts. We believe that there will be new movements in Indonesia which focus on the present millenial lifestyle that produces more sustainable life. Through interfaith dialogue it is expected that the discussion can be significantly carried out and continued until the target of the motto "Walk Gently on Earth" is successfully reached.

ALTERNATIVE CONCEPTS OF GROWTH AND THE ECOLOGY OF LIFE IN CHINA TODAY

Theresa C. Carino

Let me begin by giving a brief overview of the context in China today. To say that the lives of the Chinese have been heavily impacted over the last 40 years in the midst of rapid change is an understatement. The economic and technological reforms created a paradigm change for the Chinese people. We celebrate the fact that it has lifted 800 million farmers out of poverty in a short span of 40 years. But the cost was immense, especially to the environment. For many Chinese people, the state of the environment is a serious existential problem.

China's environmental damage

Seven years ago, I researched on the impact of Amity's water projects in Guizhou and Guangxi, which are among the poorest provinces in China. Here are some statistics on water pollution:
- 2007: 30,000 rural children died annually from diarrhea in China
- 2009: more than one-third of rural residents in China lacked access to safe drinking water
- 2 million people drank water high in arsenic
- 63 million people were at risk from fluoride poisoning
- 2013: it was finally publicly admitted that there were 350,000 new cancer patients every year and many came from "cancer villages", near sources of pollution.[1]

Water pollution comes from industry and intensive agriculture such as fertilizer and pesticide runoff and intensive animal production enterprises. There are also other statistics to show the extent of pollution in soil, water and air and its impact on the Chinese population and environment which this paper will not elaborate on.

China's pollution is a global issue: Whose responsibility is it to fix this?

Suffice it to say that industrial pollution is a major problem in China, where massive, low-cost manufacturing has taken priority over environmental protection. It has been pointed out by Chinese anthropologist Dan Smyer Yu that "China is a global factory. However you consume, whatever you consume, pay attention to the label 'Made in China.' So each of us has a responsibility for the environmental practices in China. China's environmental issue is a global issue. We have to take responsibility, each of us."[2]

---

1 These statistics are found in Theresa Carino & Ying Xie, "Water and sanitation in six villages in Guizhou and Guangxi Provinces, China: a critical perspective" in SPECIAL ISSUE: Water Suppy and Sanitaton as 'Preventive Medicine': Challenges in rapidly growing economies, *Water International* Vol 38 Number 7 November 2013, 954-966.
2 Dan Smyer Yu, Director Himalaya Research Center, Yunnan Minzu University. See Dan Smyer Yu, *Ecological Civilization Proceedings, International Conference on Ecological Civilization*. Ecologicalcivilization-ibook compressed. Yale Center, Beijing. June 16, 2015, 20.

The world decided to make China its manufacturing hub – 50% of all global production was brought to Chinese factories. All of us have or wear "Made in China" products. The ethical issue this raises is: whose responsibility is it? In China, some environmentalists argue that western societies and companies who have made China the "factory of the world" have an obligation to contribute to the cleaning up of the environment. Chinese activist Ma Jun founded an NGO, the Institute of Public and Environmental Affairs (IPE), to fight factory pollution by means of transparency, accessible data, and public information. He makes a list of polluting companies in China then IPE takes its concerns to the global level, to customers of the polluting factories. For instance, IPE has contacted big buyers, including Nike, Walmart, Gap and H&M when it found that its Chinese suppliers have not been compliant with environmental regulations. They were then the ones who put pressure on their Chinese suppliers.[3]

Chinese Environmentalists: transformative values and ethics emerge by integrating learning with practice

a. Focusing on the practical and the existential
Most Chinese environmentalists tend to focus on the practical, not the philosophical. For them, it is an existential issue. Zhao Zhong who is leading the fight to save the Yellow River says: "It is not a question of whether I like or not like living here. This is where I live," he said. "I will do what I can."[4] Today, green groups constitute the largest and most developed sector of China's nascent civil society. Activists like Zhao Zhong are on the leading edge of environmental campaigns bringing about a remarkable evolution in how people in China think about watchdogs, the public sphere, and government accountability.

b. Changing mindsets and values through practice and collective reflection:
Some Chinese NGOs have been doing consciousness raising and educational work such as the Shangrila Institute for Sustainable Communities. According to its Director Liu Yunhua, her NGO started a project called "Water School China" and has worked with more than 130,000 students across four river basins. She believes that learning comes through practice: "only when everybody takes action, when everybody starts to think and everybody puts their heart in things—that it is only then that we can see a hope, a change, in the future."[5] Social learning, she contends, is required to build a way for people to reflect together on shared values and ethics, and to deconstruct what is currently being practiced, so that something new could be constructed. Being ecologically aware, and not wanting more, are concepts deeply rooted in Chinese traditional culture. Learning emerges from projects with children, with the community, with nature reserves, with monaster-

ies, with government, and with businesses. These can be great platforms to engage this kind of learning, and to engage in a kind of social movement or people's movement.

---

3   Fred de Sam Lazaro, In China Environmental Ethics http://pulitzercenter.org/reporting/china-environmental-ethics downloaded Nov. 17, 2017| PBS Religion & Ethics NewsWeekly.
4   Christina Larson, "China's Emerging Environmental Movement" in Yale Environment 360,
June 2, 2008 (Yale School of Forestry & Environmental Studies).
5   Li Yunhua, Ecological Civilization Proceedings, International Conference on Ecological Civilization. Ecologicalcivilization-ibook compressed, Yale Center, Beijing. June 16, 2015, 19.

Theresa C. Carino

Developing role models of Ecological Civilization

Some scholars have held up Yunnan Province as a role model in building ecological civilization in China. It is part of the eastern Himalayan region recognized as one of the top 10 biodiversity hotspots of the world. One of the richest natural genetic pools in the world, it hosts the greatest number of biological species of any province and has one tenth of China's forests. In 2009, provincial leaders formally issued a plan called "Ecological Health as the Foundation of the Province." Three important aspects of promoting an ecological civilization were identified: ecological *consciousness*, ecological *protection systems*, ecology *conserving behavior*." According to Chinese anthropologist Dan Smyer Yu, what seems to be more important is to spread *ecological culture* and cultivate *ecological consciousness* paying attention to how we consume and what kinds of choices we make.[6]

Yu also speaks of the need for a *cosmo vision* based on smaller, viable communities. Given Yunnan's ethnic and ecological diversity he proposes that ecological civilization should encompass efforts to identify and revitalize "native peoples' existing ecologically sustainable modes of being which are grounded in their ancient environmental knowledge and practices."[7] It means a willingness and commitment to relearn and experiment with new meanings and applications of the eco-spiritual wisdom of both ancient and modern origins in a renewed appreciation of the Earth as a "living being".

Earth as a Living Being and the Ecological Temple Network

The notion of the Earth as a "Living Being" is common to both Buddhism and Daoism. This belief undergirds many of the efforts by Chinese FBOs to conserve the environment. The Chinese Daoist community, for example, has set up a Daoist Ecological Temple Network, consisting of more than 200 online members.

Since 2008, this network, which was established through collaboration with ARC (Alliance of Religions on Conservation, headquartered in London) has been adding ecological dimensions to all Daoist businesses and industries. One example is the sale only of low pollution incense sticks. The network has effectively reduced the burning of candles to just three electric ones per temple. It has also reduced the use of rhino horns and bear bile in traditional Chinese medicine and plan to eliminate their use. There is a strong effort to eliminate the use of ivory.

The network has called for more environmentally friendly forms of annual pilgrimages as millions of Chinese visit sacred mountains and temples every year. Other efforts include:
1. Ecological education and training
2. Advocating simpler lifestyles
3. Building ecological temples
4. Building and maintaining a Daoist Ecological Protection Network

---

6   Ecological Civilization Proceedings, International Conference on Ecological Civilization. Ecologicalcivilization-ibook compressed. p 21.
7   Ibid. p 22

Traditional Chinese perspectives and Christian eco-theology

It is acknowledged that Confucian teaching is the most influential in Chinese social ethics. Lai Pan-chiu states that unlike the Judeo-Christian understanding of the universe, Confucianism tends to understand the "genesis" of the universe in terms of "give-birth" rather than "create". The universe is thus conceived as a living system, analogous to the growth of an organism and does not presuppose an external and personal agent of creation. The "creation" of the universe is not seen as a single act that was completed a long time ago, but as a continuous process taking place here and now. In this cosmic process of "continuing creation" (creatio continua), the human being is entrusted with the role of assisting the work of Heaven or Dao or Nature in the renewal or transformation of lives as well as maintaining the order and harmony of the universe.[8]

"In other words, in the process of achieving the eventual, perpetual Great Harmony, some sort of confrontation, conflict, strife or hatred is unavoidable. According to this view, there is no natural harmony to be preserved and true harmony should be reconciled harmony."[9] The virtue of Heaven embodied in the production, renewal, and reproduction of life will bring forth an orderly and harmonious universe, with the assistance of the human being, including human spiritual cultivation, culture and even political activities.[10]

It is important to note that this Confucian understanding of harmony is quite different from that of Daoism. According to Daoism, the Dao is universally present, life-giving and life sustaining, but its "action" is characterized by "non-intervention" or "without action". The Dao silently "brings forth" a harmonious universe spontaneously, effortlessly, and in accordance with the natural course of all things. The active involvement of human culture, especially social and political institutions, will tend to be considered as artificial, against nature, intrusive, and potentially damaging.[11]

Thus, due to their different understandings of the roles of cultural activities and political institutions in the actualization of cosmic harmony, Daoism tends to understand harmony in terms of natural harmony, whereas Confucianism would prefer to understand harmony in terms of cultural harmony.[12]

Responding to the rise of nationalism and scientism in China during the 20th century, some Chinese theologians, particularly those influenced by liberal theology or the "social gospel", attempted to defend the Christian doctrine of creation against the scientific challenges, and to reinterpret the doctrine of salvation with regard to the Christian contribution to the salvation of the nation.[13] Most of them tended to adopt a Christo-centric approach to theology and focused on the personality of Jesus or the kingdom of God as an ideal society in Jesus' preaching. Although theologians such as Zhao Zichen (also known as T. C. Chao) and Wu Leichuan (also known as Wu Zhenchun) did make some comparisons between the Christian and traditional Chinese ideas of cosmos / creation / nature, the cosmic dimension of salvation remained ignored and the doctrine of salvation remained largely disconnected from the doctrine of creation in their theologies.[14]

8   Lai Pan-chiu, Harmonious Society and Environmental Protection: Legacies and Challenges of Chinese Christian Theology in Theresa C. Carino (ed) *Christianity and Social Development in China*, Hong Kong, Amity Foundation, 2014, p 98.
9   Ibid. p 100.
10   Ibid.
11   ibid.
12   Ibid.
13   Ibid. 104.
14   Ibid.

The Cosmic Christ and ecological justice

With the establishment of the People's Republic of China in 1949, and especially after the 1970s, the theological mainstream of the church in China has affirmed the value of humanity, the present world, and the Christian participation in society. *Agape* is emphasized as the most fundamental attribute of God's essence expressed in creation, providence, redemption and sanctification. A related emphasis is on the immanence of God, affirming that all good things originate from God and therefore Christians should learn to appreciate all the good things taking place outside the Church, because they too come from God's love.[15] In terms of Christology, the key concept is the notion of the "Cosmic Christ," which implies that Christ is God incarnate and that human beings may seek redemption, renewal and reconciliation in him. As Christ is cosmic, God's redemption is universal.[16] According to Lai Pan-chiu, Bishop K. H. Ting's concept of the cosmic Christ may become the cornerstone for the further development of a Chinese Christian theological response to the issues of a harmonious society and environmental protection.

Speaking in 1995, Bishop K. H. Ting, strongly criticized a Christianity that would turn a blind eye to ecological destruction:

> People have done a poor job of watching over and safeguarding God's world; rather, they fell forests, burn timber and oil. All this destroys the ecological balance. The Third World has suffered the most. This damage to the globe for their own self-interest by a minority of people, this theft of the right of the majority to sustain existence and enjoy a good life, takes many forms. To take an example closer to home, in Chinese society today, corruption – the use of public resources for personal profit – is rife. A Christianity which turns a blind eye to all this, one which thinks all this bears no relation to the gospel, which believes the gospel is concerned only with personal salvation, is not a two-legged Christianity, but a lame one.[17]

Approaching the problem from a global viewpoint, Ting saw pollution as mainly coming from the industrialized, developed countries and causing great harm in the developing ones. As early as 1990, he had said: "The work of healing the planet has grown beyond the work of a single factory, region or nation. We can only approach it from a global standpoint. There is a very unjust state of affairs in the world today—the majority of pollution comes from the industrialized developed countries and many developing countries reap a great deal of harm from this."[18] He stressed that:

> "Cutting down the forests, polluting the air, contributing to the rise in the earth's temperature are also forms of murder, though not as obvious as shooting someone. Ignoring the ecological balance is destruction of God's creation; it leads imperceptibly to the deaths of countless innocent people. The natural world is suffering and cries out to us."[19]

---

15   Chen Zemin, Christ and Culture in China: A Sino-American Dialogue, *Chinese Theological Review* 6 (1993), 85. See also K.H. Ting, God is Love: Speech while on a visit to the Hungarian Church, October 5, 1986 in Janice Wickeri (ed) *Love Never Ends: Papers by K.H. Ting*, (Nanjing: Yilin Press 2000) 266-70.

16   K. H. Ting, Creation and Redemption (1995) in Janice Wickeri (ed) *Love Never Ends: Papers by K.H. Ting*, (Nanjing: Yilin Press 2000) 477-83.

17   Ibid 481.

18   Ibid.

19   Ibid. 401.

At an earlier speech given in 1990 at a global consultation on Development and the Environment held in Moscow[20] Ting had emphasized the multi-cultural and multi-religious context of China and the importance of working with people of different faiths and of no faith: "Among China's one billion people, there are Buddhists, Muslims, Taoists and Christians, both Catholic and Protestant. Our religious beliefs are all different, but when it comes to the environment, we all feel this is an important question tied to the continued existence on this planet of our common humanity."[21] He continues:

> To safeguard our earth, we need to unite with others who have the same goal. Anywhere you look, there are religious believers and non-believers, or those who believe differently from ourselves. But in matters of faith we can have mutual respect. Toward all those who are involved in improving the environment and developing the economy, we should be welcoming, grateful, supportive and cooperative. We express this idea in one short phrase in Chinese: "Seek the common ground while reserving differences."[22]

Attitudes of churches today

Today, in churches across China, there is a seeming lack of concern when discussing ecology or environmental issues. It could be partly due to a theology that focusses on evangelization and church planting. The lack of concern could also reflect a sense of helplessness and the attitude that it is the government's responsibility and it is the government that has the resources and capability to address such serious problems such as preventing desertification, reducing the use of coal for energy, afforestation and so on. Today, China reportedly has the most wind turbines and solar panels in the world and probably is also producing the most electric vehicles. There have been extensive reforestation efforts with very visible results in southwest and northwestern China. There has been the gradual restoration of wetlands and biodiversity in some areas. More recently, there have been campaigns to reduce food wastage. In last year's training of local church leaders in diaconia, it seems that ecology and food security is something very new to them in relation to diaconia.

In an online survey by a faculty member of Jinling Seminary that attracted 20,000 respondents in 2018, he discovered that all respondents, both Christians and non-Christians, ranked ecology last in a list of important social issues. Topping the list were children, the disabled, the elderly and women. Ecology was way down the list. Obviously, there is a need for more awareness raising.

All this raises the question of "who" should be addressed in eco-theologies? What is the connection between theology and the practice of churches? Is there a connection and has there been an impact on ecological practices and social behavior? Any collection of articles on eco-theology needs to show the close connection between theology, ethics and praxis. Obviously, this is a serious issue. At least on one level, it is essential that it be part of the curriculum of seminaries.

Can churches or church congregations be part of the solution rather than a problem? For instance, in China, the building of mega churches and tall edifices, imitating western style archi-

---

20   K. H. Ting, Caring for God's Creation in Janice Wickeri (ed) *Love Never Ends: Papers by K.H. Ting*, (Nanjing: Yilin Press 2000) 399-401.
21   Ibid. 399.
22   Ibid. 400.

Theresa C. Carino

tecture, is becoming commonplace in some urban centers. Chinese Christians believe that these represent 'real churches' and do not want them to be mistaken for Buddhist or Daoist temples.

In contrast, we see the opposite trend in the practice of Daoist followers: the ecological temple network is advocating preservation of the environment and have rules about renovations and expansions of temples that consider the impact on the environment.

China's case shows that in a multi-cultural context it is important to approach environmental concerns in a multi-religious way – through inter-faith dialogue and cooperation on some of the key concerns. It is not enough that different religions try to do something on their own, there has to be a joint, concerted effort that can gain momentum and make a difference.

Environmental laws and their non-enforcement

In China itself, there are hundreds of good environmental laws that have been in place at the national and local levels for decades. However, for many years, the Ministry for Environmental Protection has not been able to adequately implement or enforce these laws. The reasons indicate that environmental issues are more than just legal issues—they are also political, social, and philosophical issues. Important factors, identified by scholars, include the role of capital, interest groups, the prevalent development model, and an anthropocentric worldview and values.[23]

According to Zhang Xiaode, director of the Center for Ecological Civilization at the Chinese Academy of Governance, "the most difficult issue of implementing ecological civilization is to overcome vested interest." A Greenpeace report, for instance, states that eighteen major international and Chinese companies, including Shell and Sinopec, broke China's "most basic" pollution law because they failed to publish pollution information "after they were found guilty of irregularities in discharging sewage."[24] Some local governments have joined hands with the companies in resisting environmental protection in the name of developing the economy. For instance, in May 2010 the government of Anhui province's Guzhen county removed six local environmental protection officials—including the bureau chief—from their posts.[25] Other places began to follow suit, with the result that the biggest polluters and energy consumers are now protected by local governments. Some scholars have also noted that it is "China's reliance on external capital and foreign investment that has generated a weakening influence on China's environmental regulation."[26]

Conclusion

While the focus of Chinese environmental groups has been on China itself, there is perhaps less attention and concern paid to the destruction of forests and ancestral lands in other countries. With its Belt and Road Initiative, China has a share of responsibility for preserving the environment and human rights of local communities affected by mining, dam building and other infra-

---

23   Zhihe Wang, Huili He and Meijun Fan, The Ecological Civilization Debate in China. *Monthly Review 2014*, Volume 66, Issue 06 (November), Accessed at http://monthlyreview.org/2014/11/01/the-ecological-civilization-debate-in-china/. Retrieved 20 August 2016.
24   Ibid.
25   Ibid.
26   Ibid.

structure projects in these countries. There is increasing evidence that some Chinese companies have turned a blind eye to these concerns or are totally out of touch with local communities. Although the topic of CSR has been brought up on media, this is too limited and done with a lot of caution within China. The pressure on companies to address these issues will more likely have to come from organized communities in the affected countries.

The Universal Periodic Review Report of 2018 "Violation of Human Rights of Indigenous population in the Amazon Basin by (the) Chinese Investments" by a coalition of NGOs supported by Rainforest Foundation in Norway and the Mott Foundation have listed the areas in several Latin American countries that have been affected by Chinese investments: Venezuela, Colombia, Ecuador, Peru, Brazil – mostly caused by dams, mining, and oil extraction. To say the least, some of the worst damage to the environment and the displacement of large numbers of people has come from mining and deforestation from large and small companies.

The corporate social responsibility agenda remains limited in scope and effectiveness.

Far greater attention must be paid to the notion of corporate accountability and the way business interests influence public policy.[27] Obviously much of the problem has to do with power relations. Increasingly, corporate interests have taken over in governance on a global scale. In the Philippines, for instance, it was very obvious and open for all to see, how corporate mining interests dictated who would become Secretary for the Environment. During the appointment of the cabinet secretary, an active and well known environmentalist, she could not be confirmed because of the business lobby lined up against her.[28]

From very early times: China's rulers had recognized basic environmental principles. There were laws/regulations against hunting young animals, or against land reclamation where it could lead to flooding. Most important was the idea that the Confucian state was responsible for the welfare of the people. Environmental disaster was one of the signs of misrule and blamed on the emperor. Thus there is a long history of imperial attempts to control and regulate the environment. Irrigation systems and dams were big projects undertaken by Chinese rulers as the great rivers often broke their banks and caused destructive floods. The Chinese also altered their environment greatly at different times in history – e.g. the Great Wall, the North-South Canal, the Dujiangyan Irrigation System, rice terraces. [29]

In today's China, leaders are influenced by Western anthropocentric approaches to ecology and more important, still focused on the modernization of Chinese society. They are promoting globalization and the building of massive infrastructures along the Belt and Road. There has to be a way to determine their ecological impact and the costs – not only the economic benefits – if there will be a solution to our current ecological crisis. Perhaps what is needed will be nothing short of a seismic shift from the current paradigm of unlimited growth towards sustainable development.

---

27   UN Research Institute for Social Development, *Combatting Poverty and Inequality: Structural Change, Social Policy and Politics* 2010.
28   Gina Lopez, an active environmentalist, despite being a scion of a powerful family, failed to be confirmed as Secretary of the Environment in the Philippines in 2018.
29   Robert Weller, Chinese Cosmology and the Environment, in David A. Palmer, Glenn Shive and Philip Wickeri (eds), *Chinese Religious Life*. New York: Oxford University Press, 2011, 124-138.

Theresa C. Carino

References

Carino, Theresa & Xie, Ying. Water and sanitation in six villages in Guizhou and Guangxi Provinces, China: a critical perspective in SPECIAL ISSUE: Water Suppy and Sanitaton as 'Preventive Medicine': Challenges in rapidly growing economies, *Water International* Vol 38 Number 7 November 2013. 954-966.

Chen, Zemin. Christ and Culture in China: A Sino-American Dialogue, *Chinese Theological Review* 6 .1993. Holland, MI: FTESEA. 85.

Lai, Pan-chiu. Harmonious Society and Environmental Protection: Legacies and Challenges of Chinese Christian Theology in Theresa C. Carino (ed) *Christianity and Social Development in China*. Hong Kong, Amity Foundation. 2014. 95-116.

Larson, Christina. China's Emerging Environmental Movement in *Yale Environment 360*, June 2, 2008. Yale School of Forestry & Environmental Studies.

Lazaro, Fred de Sam. China Environmental Ethics available at http://pulitzercenter.org/reporting/ china-environmental-ethics downloaded Nov. 17, 2017.

Li, Yunhua. Ecological Civilization Proceedings, International Conference on Ecological Civilization. Ecologicalcivilization-ibook compressed. Beijing: Yale Center. June 16, 2015. 19-20.

Ting, K.H. God is Love: Speech while on a visit to the Hungarian Church, October 5, 1986 in Janice Wickeri (ed) *Love Never Ends: Papers by K.H. Ting*. Nanjing: Yilin Press 2002. 266-70.
Creation and Redemption (1995) in Janice Wickeri (ed) *Love Never Ends: Papers by K.H. Ting*. Nanjing: Yilin Press 2000. 477-83.

UN Research Institute for Social Development. *Combatting Poverty and Inequality: Structural Change, Social Policy and Politics.* 2010.

Wang, Zhihe, He, Huili and Fan, Meijun. The Ecological Civilization Debate in China. *Monthly Review 2014,* Volume 66, Issue 06 November. Accessed at http://monthlyreview.org/2014/11/01/the-ecological-civilization-debate-in-china/ Retrieved 20 August 2016.

Weller, Robert. Chinese Cosmology and the Environment, in David A. Palmer, Glenn Shive and Philip Wickeri (eds), *Chinese Religious Life*. New York: Oxford University Press, 2011. 124-138.

Yu, Dan Smyer. Ecological Civilization Proceedings, International Conference on Ecological Civilization. Ecologicalcivilization-ibook compressed. Beijing: Yale Center. June 16, 2015. 20-22.

REGIONAL APPROACHES TO ECO-THEOLOGY IN KOREA: DIFFERENT FOCUSES AND EMPHASES

Meehyun Chung

Abstract

I would like to locate my theological thoughts as being shaped by my perspective as a Korean protestant theologian, grown up in the most progressive Presbyterian Church in Korea, educated in a center of Feminism in Korea, further having studied in a center of reformed theology in Europe. I then worked in a Swiss international Christian organization, and now I live and teach in Seoul in South-Korea.

Korea was colonized by Japan a non-Christian country in the first half of 20th Century. Thus, Korea wasn't contaminated by the form of Christianity which is combined with colonialism. Christianity helped liberate people from fear in the face of nature and spirits. Generally, instead of fear of nature people have started to treat it as an object of development. Although environmental crisis didn't begin with the introduction of Christianity which is connected to Western science and modernity, militant Christian thoughts and militarism have led to environmental destruction.

The most current burning issue on the Korean peninsula regarding environment is the micro-dust issue, which poses very serious challenges to our economy, culture and society. Our chronic problem is the division of the country which causes general on-going propagation of anti-communism and dualistic tensions among the people and the two Koreas. Due to the military tensions between the two Koreas there are many political incidents and events which negatively impact the people. The ongoing construction, relocation and expansion projects related to the US American military basements are still continuing and they are work in progress. Just to mention some examples: There is the US Military Base in Pyeongtaek, the US naval base in Gangjeong village on Jeju Island, the Terminal High Altitude Area Defense (THAAD) weapon system in Sangju and so on. South Korea still is a highly militarized country. Progressive Churches are working together with other faith communities, in order to change the focus that still rests on military solutions for the most part and instead to encourage new forms of how to cultivate peace and to promote life.

As a result of this militarization generally, farming communities and the nature, including land and ocean, are constantly endangered, destroyed and violated against by inflicting extensive environmental damage.

Generally speaking, Korean Protestant churches are still predominantly anthropocentric in their theological orientation. Instead of a universal 'green' salvation, they are preaching a narrow anthropocentric and individualistic 'red' salvation through blood of Christ. Green salvation refers to an inclusive restoration.

The World Council of Churches has produced fine publications on environmental matters like the booklet *Together Towards Life. Mission and Evangelism in Changing Landscapes.* In this ecumenical mission statement from Manila there is a new perception of mission that includes nature which is very interesting for us.[1] Unfortunately, this document has not generated much interest at the level of local churches in Korea. Ecumenism itself is not a predominant theme among ordinary Church settings in South Korea, rather a topic among small progressive church circles or discussed at the level of the National Church council (NCCK). Due to the hierarchical structure of the Catholic Church, *Laudato si'* may very well have more impact in Korea (in the case of Hansalim Movement).

And the Orthodox Church is small in terms of number, still generally relatively invisible in Korea. Protestant theologians have an increasing interest in a cosmic approach to Orthodox theology in order to correct the lack of ecological awareness in Protestant Korean Churches.

My contribution[2] is composed in four parts to show some examples of how Korean Churches have become engaged in eco-theological actions and reflections:
–   The Case of Militarism and deconstruction in South Korea
–   The Example of Churches: The case of PROK (The Presbyterian Church in the Republic of Korea) regarding protests against economic greed of humans in the case of Geyang mountain
–   The case of the Y- Green movement in Yonsei University
–   The case of the Samae Church as an example of a local church movement for the threefold love of God, love of work and love of farm village

The Case of Militarism and deconstruction in South Korea

After the second war of Imperialism many countries in the Global South suffered under interior war, which was related to colonial heritage. In the Korean case an ideological conflict between Communism and Anti-communism based on the Cold War caused the Korean War. Since then due to the militaristic tensions between the two Koreas there have been many political incidents and events. They are mostly related to militaristic constructions like the US Military Base in Pyeongtaek[3], the US naval base in Gangjeong village on Jeju Island,[4] the Terminal High Altitude Area Defense (THAAD) weapon system in Sungju and others. Progressive churches worked together with other faith communities, not focusing on military solutions but on the challenge of how to cultivate peace and promote life.

In order to keep the status quo of the world political line combined with a tendency of Korean dependency on US militaristic politics, Korea's deep division of the country remains. If the current status of "a cease fire agreement" is not changed into either a non-aggression agreement or even better "a permanent peace treaty" constant fear of potential war in both Koreas and a culture of dualistic destruction remain. This kind of dominant culture of destruction prevents eco-friendliness on the Korean peninsula. This particular political crisis and context justifies having a militaristic system and promotes a culture of militarism. For the sake of national security the democratic movement or issues of ecological and economical justice remain behind. And greed-driven military expenditure and business dominate instead.

---

1   Joo-seop Keum(ed.), *Together Towards Life. Mission and Evangelism in Changing Landscapes* (Geneva: World Council of Churches, 2013).
2   Additional material for my power point presentation see http://www.credo.or.kr/jmh_sub_connect.html
3   Cf. Meehyun Chung, *Reis und Wasser* (Berlin: Frank & Timme, 2012), 163.
4   Cf. Meehyun Chung, "Seeking the Lost Three fold Thoughts: Relationships with God, Earth and Human Beings," *Madang. International Journal of Contextual Theology*, 22(2014, 12), 128.

The Example of Churches: The case of PROK regarding protests against economic greed of humans in the case of Gyeyang mountain

Gyeyang Mountain in Incheon city is located on the west coast of Korea. In 1989 Lotte Construction Company had planned to build a golf course after they bought a huge land of 2,570,000m² in the Gyeyang mountain area. A pastor of the Presbyterian church of the republic of Korea and another NGO member for environmental movement took initial action against this construction plan of Lotte Conglomerate since 2009. Rev. Yoon In-Joong, a pastor in Incheon Presbytery of the PROK, spent his time and energy in the high branches of a 20-metre pine tree on the slopes of Gyeyang Mountainin order to protest against the golf club project. Regardless of temperatures of even minus 10 degrees celsius and lower local ministers and lay people of the PROK and many NGO members joined the struggle to preserve the natural beauty of Gyeyang Mountain.

The former major of Incheon city approved in 2009 to construct the golf course, however his successor changed the plan in order to protect the environment. Lotte Conglomerate sued against this decision of the city. After several trials the supreme court announced its final decision in October 2018 not to allow the construction of the golf course. Instead, the area should be used as a park for common good and sustainability.

The case of the Y- Green movement in Yonsei University

The Green Campus movement was launched in Korea as a sort of eco campus movement regarding energy and water saving etc. It has been developed to feature awareness building and education and to contribute in a region which became more lively since the establishment of The Korean Association for Green Campus Initiative (KAGCI)[5]. Yonsei University hosts this KAGGI and takes initiative for actions and implementation. There are many initiatives of students to implement Green Campus projects although they are mostly small-scale projects.

The case of the Samae Church as an example of a local church movement for the threefold love of God, love of work and love of neighbor

The Samae Church is located on Samae Campus of Yonsei University on the Hillside of Gobong Mt in Ilsan, a satellite city. This Land was donated to Yonsei University in 1989 by Pastor Minsoo Pai, who was a Presbyterian and a leader of an independent movement under Japanese colonialism, and his wife Soonok Choi. The spirit of 'Samae' comes from the vision of Pastor Minsoo Pai who wanted to promote work for a farming village through Christian Spirit. 'Samae' literally refers to "love God, work and neighbor". Samae Church seeks for God's truth and freedom and aims to practice God's love in daily life as an eco- friendly congregation.

One of the burning issues is development of this property. Recently the board of trustees of the University made a Memorandum of Understanding with a construction conglomerate for

---

5   It is composed by 58 Universities. The goal is to implement and to practice green movement in management, education by promoting participation of staffs and faculties and developing environmental friendly infrastructure. However, due to financial matters this movement lags behind in terms of prioritization.

development. The descendants of the donors and members of the Samae Church insist that this precious land should be kept as a place to commemorate Pastor Pai's spirit publicly for Christian educational purposes in the light of the gospel. They also state that it should remain a public space where the beauty of nature is preserved and people can practice their Christian live and work in harmony with and respect for nature. The donor's family strongly insists that this land is not to be the object of profit oriented development for University. Samae Church member try to protect this place as an ecological sanctuary, and as a place for Christian education towards the reign of God where all creation enjoy completely peace and life.

Overall, eco-awareness is increasing in people's minds. But, so far, the majority of Christian communities do not have a serious interest in this matter. If Christian people get better educated about environmental needs, our good system of nationwide networking an active movement could be very helpful, especially since this is a vital neutral issue beyond ideological conflicts and religious orientations.

CHRISTIAN IDENTITY APPROACHING CLIMATE CHANGE IN A DIALOGUE WITH SECULARITY

Peter Pavlovic

What is the content of Christian hope? Indivisibility of hope and faith

Climate change is becoming a political, economic and security issue defining 21st century. It is widely acknowledged that climate change is an ethical issue. Hope becomes in this regard one of the central terms that are discussed. Climate change is along with being ethical at the same time a theological issue. What is needed in considering the theological stance as the starting point for an authentic and effective churches' action, is the clarity in theological standings and theological language related to ecological concerns. This includes precision in relating theological and ethical concerns and distinct ethical and theological approaches to the question of hope and its specific features in time of climate change.

In focusing the attention on hope, its' content and scope, the Bible underlines that it is not possible to understand hope without clarifying the content of faith. Hope and faith are intrinsically related. If we want a new hope in time of frustration, we need to look at quality of faith.

A fresh look at the major New Testament document – the letter to the Romans document outlines Paul's view on an action of faith in secular society. Paul sends the letter to, at that time, the political centre of the world and formulates in it, following the argumentation of Jacob Taubes, an outline of a new political theology, a new type of an approach to the hostile and kindless world. Paul's key formula in his masterpiece of political theology is *'the obedience of faith.'* In the context of Rome of the 1st century AC, its culture, rules and politics it is *'the obedience of faith'* the central formula, which he puts into the sharp opposition to *'the obedience of law,'* the major achievement of Roman politics and social life.

An insistence on *'the obedience of faith'* and the political theology based on this assumption raises questions about the quality and the format of politics as well as theology. In looking at most of current style and way of doing politics and if wanted to be serious about Paul and his understanding of the relationship between faith and politics in the context of current challenges, we might probably expect from Paul an advice like: to be the church is not to be an improvement of current ways of doing politics, but much more a peaceful, steadfast and reliable alternative to the politics. This alternative is to be developed not in an isolation from the world and politics but in a dialogue. Adding to that and in coming back to understanding of hope in the spirit of the apostle Paul: reading of Paul leads to the confidence that, faith and *'the obedience to faith'* makes, in spite of current difficult and messy situation, in spite of many challenges, including those ecological, in spite of frustrations and disappointments, sense. In this sense Paul's formula: *'endurance/faith produces character, and character produces hope'* (R 5:4) opens new horizons and offers a new language in talks about hope. At the bottom line of this approach is a conviction that it is primary through faith, through our endurance, determination and reliability how we can provide an authentic and truthful witness about the world we are living in. Through our way of life, through respect of the world with its beauty and its limits, as well as through dealing with close and distant neighbours, including the victims of climate change.

What does it mean for the life of a Christian?

Consequences of deliberations about faith and hope, their content, relevance and their implications framing the succeeding actions can be illustrated in 3 examples:

Freedom and modesty
Are we allowed to consume food, energy, natural resources as much as we want? Are we allowed to behave as rulers of the world and forgetting that at the same time we are called to stewardship?

Justice, fairness, interrelation, solidarity and compassion
Climate science confirms that latest in 20st century humanity entered in the era of anthropocene. Humanity is not anymore a passive observer of earths development, but an active contributor, an actor shaping the earth and forming conditions for life. There is a number of proves demonstrating how this is happening. Christian insistence on active justice, solidarity, interrelation, respect and compassion, as well as the call to respond through a thankful action to the gift of creation instead of dominating and plundering the world offer theological instruments for a response to ecological challenges we need to face and endorse in its own way signs of interdependence not only in interpersonal relations, but at the same time in relation between humans and the earth.

Rights, ownership and hope
Hope belongs to qualities of transitive nature; it is not possible to possess hope it's value is in sharing. In this respect hope stands in an opposition to the idea of rights. Christian hope is not to be possessed, but transmitted.

Conclusions

Paul's formula of '*the obedience of faith*' poses a particular challenge especially in the context of increasing calls of theologians of the 21st century for an engaged public and political theology. On the way there is a lot of the need for clarifying of what kind of politics, as well as what kind of theology do we need to talk about.

Challenge of climate change is an opportunity for exploring concrete implications of the normative commitments of Christian faith. Challenge of climate change, reaching the limits of earth's capacity and challenge of environmental degradation is an opportunity in which the church must engage the world for the sake of its own actualization and renewal and in a constant effort for actualised and living content of faith in the world of today.

Peter Pavlovic

ISLAM AS GOD'S MERCY FOR THE UNIVERSE (RAHMATAN LIL ALAMIN)

A Crucial Need for trustworthy Dialogue among Religious Communities on Global Climate Change

Syafiq Hasyim

Introduction

Climate change is becoming a global phenomenon and an experience for every people, especially religious believers. The world population – regardless of religion, ethnicity, geographical area – is now facing similar problems of climate change everywhere, such as floods, disaster, water crisis, scarcity of food, abnormal season-change, unpredicted weather and many others.

We are in a dilemma: on the one hand, the increasing world population means that we should also increase production and consumption which are good and energizing for the extension of prosperity and welfare, but all these things, on the other hand, can at the same time become the root-causes of environmental damage that has an impact on climate change.

Climate change is not a single phenomenon, but it relates to many aspects; economic, political, social, cultural and theological. The attitude and behavior of believers for instance can contribute to negative changes in the climate. Seen from economic, social and cultural perspectives for instance, the lifestyle of believers in terms of production, consumption and many other issues can also contribute to worsening the sustainability of world health. The most important theological aspect of climate change is the inattentive attitude of religious leaders and scholars on environmental issues.

I would like to mention some theological rationalities from Islamic writings, which could contribute to our mutual co-operation and discussion on the theme of climate justice. I want to start by stating that the Muslims in Indonesia in general have not contributed much to the issues of climate justice and environmental protection. However, the Nahdlatul Ulama (NU), as the largest Muslim organization in Indonesia, a Sunni Islam movement in Indonesia following the Shafi'i school of jurisprudence which was founded already in 1926, stands already in a critical position against the Indonesian government to erect an atomic reactor in Jepara, Indonesia. According to the NU, this project must be rejected, as it was understood as a form of human greed to damage the nature of Allah´s beautiful creation for the following generations.

Human Being and the Universe

Relations among the humans, nature, and God have been regulated in Islam. *Habluminallah* tells of human relations with Allah by obeying His commands and prohibitions. *Habluminannas* is a relationship among human beings, and Habluminal 'alam, is an Islamic concept for preservation of the environment and nature.

The Koran explains several important meanings of the Mother Nature. Out of a total of 57 words that say 'Jannah' (heaven), 45 of them can be interpreted as 'forest'. The beauty of Heaven is described by "green forests, dense, full of beautiful fruits and flowing rivers that are clear and cool". In addition, many Islamic literatures in the Koran and Hadith explain the importance of maintaining (planting) trees with a great reward for those who practiced them.

> "Neither does a Muslim plant a tree, nor does he plant a plant, then the tree or plant is eaten by birds, humans or animals but becomes alms" (Hadith Bukhari and Muslim narrated by Anas bin Malik)

> "It is not a Muslim to grow plants unless what is eaten from him is alms, what is stolen from him is alms, what is eaten by wild animals is alms, what is eaten by birds is alms, and what is taken by others is also alms, or in other word is alms to the end of doom" (Muslim hadith narrated by Jabir bin Abdullah)

> "If the end of the world is about to happen, while you have date palm seeds, so if he is able to plant before the end of the world, then he should plant it." (Hadith narrated by Ahmad)

> The Prophet Muhammad uttered, "Whoever plants a tree, will surely be rewarded as much as the tree and its fruit" (narrated by Abu Ya'la)

It is even prohibited to cutting down trees during the war:

> "Whoever kills a child, cuts a fruiting tree, kills an animal to take his skin, kills a farmer or a parent who did not join the war, then he will not return in a state of wealth" (Hadith narrated by Ahmad bin Hambal)

In Islam, acts of environmental or natural destructions can be categorized as acts of *hirobah* (act of war). The Muslims are asked to protect the environment by planting trees and preserving the earth as divine practices that never break until the end of time (the afterlife).

The Noble Human Beings

Humans are created by Allah as the noblest creature among the other creatures (*insanul kamil*): "We have certainly created man in the best of stature" – At Tin: 4. Allah has emphasized the glorious meaning of becoming a human being on the earth as the most ultimate creation compared to the other creatures as the gift of Allah (humans are given knowledge, reason and the best form that is not given to other creatures of His creation):

> "And We have certainly honored the children of Adam and carried them on the land and sea and provided for them of the good things and preferred them over much of what We have created, with [definite] preference" (Al-Isra 70)

Distinctive religious teachings with regard to the human position within creation are also found in various other parts of the Koran. Some of them are written as follows:

> "And He has subjected for you the night and day and the sun and moon, and the stars are subjected by His command. Indeed in that are signs for a people who reason" – An-Nahl 12.

"And it is He who subjected the sea for you to eat from it tender meat and to extract from it ornaments which you wear. And you see the ships plowing through it, and [He subjected it] that you may seek of His bounty; and perhaps you will be grateful" – An-Nahl 14.

In order to avoid misinterpretation regarding the role of humans as the noblest creature, it is clear that human power has also limitations. The authority given to the humans is not an absolute power over the whole creation. It is important to perceive, that in Islam, the only One who has the absolute power is Allah. Allah in Oneness (*Tauhid*) has certain attributive names, which are for instance known as *Al-Qadir* (Most Wanted), *Al-Muqtadir* (Most Powerful), *Malik-al-Mulk* (Supreme Ruler of the Kingdom (Universe)), and *Al-Khaliq* (The Creator).

In Islamic teachings, the human power is granted by God, in order to rule over the earth. Therefore, this human power is not considered as a dictatorial or abusive power, but the divine authority to preserve and care for the whole nature (*Rahmatan lil' Alamin*). The earth and other species are the creations of Allah, and humans are mandated by God to preserve and maintain the creation in full responsibility.

Necessity for Joint Action among the Global Religious Communities

According to the Islamic traditions, humans are mandated by God not only to rule over the earth in absolute authority but most importantly to rule as a caring mother. I remember, both Islam and Christianity share the perspective for caring for the Human Earth. Therefore, efforts to form mutual dialogues and joint actions among the religious adherents to preserve God´s whole creation are a form of obedience to God as the Creator (*Al-Khaliq*).

It is a fact that climate change becomes a real problem for human beings. In this situation, the religious leaders who have influence on millions of religious communities have strong responsibility and role to take initiative for the minimization of global climate change through promoting awareness that their belief and religion can play an important role with regard to this issue. One thing that we can do for minimizing climate change is to formulate constructive interreligious theologies for an eco-friendly environment. This presents an invitation to take seriously the role of religions and also to encourage their adherents to talk with each other and to have a dialogue because the environmental crisis is is a shared and global problem. Dialogue is highly needed because it is one fundamental religious mission in the world to show a positive impact of religion and belief in dealing with the environmental challenges in order to sustain and maintain our life and the life of future generations.

So far, the role of mission and *dakwah* are not yet effective for the mitigation of climate change, but this task actually still can become a unifying and interesting issue to enter into a collaborative agenda and process among religious leaders. A dialogue on climate change can become an effective gate-way for entering into dialogue for wider, more strategic and comprehensive issues about the role of *dakwah* and mission.

For the further process, I believe that mutual dialogue should be deepened in order to develop and collect ideas on the role of religious leaders in facing the problem of climate change. The output of a living and trustworthy dialogue will enable the religious communities to reflect on the future of their respective religious mission particularly as related to the issues of climate change and to the critical issues of a positive relation among human beings. At the end of a dialogical conversation, religious communities should be able to find best knowledge and practice examples and a common implementation strategy for placing the role of religious mission in the context of the reduction of climate change in the framework of Diapraxis.

As a concrete step for ensuring a thematic religious dialogue on climate justice, I would recommend certain targeted and measured joint actions and refer this for a kind attention:

– To develop a religious communiqué on the importance of taking speed action on climate change;
– To enhance collected lessons and joint learning between religious believers in Europe, Africa and Asia in advancing and improving the role of religions in the program of climate change;
– To plan for a roadmap of shared action of believers in planning, implementing and evaluating the role of religious mission and dakwah in the reduction of climate change impacts;
– To develop a set of recommendations on policy, knowledge, strategy and action which are submitted to states, religion-based organizations, civil society organizations, politicians, academics, and journalists for the prioritization of climate change program.

SHORTCOMINGS IN TEACHING ECO-THEOLOGICAL AWARENESS IN THE HISTORY AND LIFE OF THE BATAK CHURCH (HKBP)[1]

Victor Tinambunan

INTRODUCTION

Indonesia faces four major threats nowadays namely the ecological crisis, the negative impact of social media (which contains hoax and hate speech), radicalism, and drugs. The threats I mentioned are severe and eventually will affect Indonesia now and in the future. But at this moment, I will be presenting only about ecological crisis.

In the world, Indonesia ranks in the following ecological world crisis:
- Indonesia ranks first as the fastest massive deforestation.
- Second in producing plastic waste.
- Third in contributing emission
- Fourth in destroying the mother earth
- Some cities in Indonesia are the most polluted cities in the world like Jakarta.

One of the root causes of Indonesia's ecological crisis is the widening palm plantation. In 2018, there had been 11 million acres of palm plantation in Indonesia that resulted in tremendous andmassive clearing of forest campaigns such as cutting trees and burning the forests in order to plant palm trees.

THE HKBP IN THE CONTEXT OF ECOLOGICAL CRISIS

The HKBP (*Huria Kristen Batak Protestant* – Batak Christian Protestant Church) can be called the Batak Church and is one of the largest Lutheran Churches in Indonesia with approximate 3 million members.

Since the autonomy of the HKBP in 1930,[2] there has been no significant change in its theological understanding, liturgy, teaching curriculum, mission and program, particularly those in relation to ecology. The calling of the church in the field of *koinonia, marturia*, and *diakonia* has become a common tradition.[3] These three callings are now embodied in three departments in the HKBP, Department of Koinonia of the HKBP, Department of Marturia of the HKBP, and Department of Diakonia of the HKBP. This applies in the synod level as well as in the congrega-

---

1 HKBP (*Huria Kristen Batak Protestant* – Batak Christian Protestant Church) is one of the largest Lutheran Church in Indonesia with approximate 3 million members.
2 The autonomy of the HKBP marked by the transition of leadership of the HKBP from German missionaries to the Batak pastors because of the arrest of the German missionaries by the Dutch colonial power.
3 Lothar Schreiner, *Telah Kudengar dari Ayahku. Perjumpaan Adat dengan Iman Kristen di Tanah Batak*, Jakarta: BPK Gunung Mulia, 1987,16.

tions level. The task for caring for creation is a part of the task of the Department of Diakonia of the HKBP.

This arrangement happens in all congregations of the HKBP that currently consist of 3582 congregations around the world, both those in the countryside of Sumatra as well as those in the towns or cities of Indonesia and overseas.[4] Unfortunately the establishment of the HKBP congregations in various towns and cities in Indonesia and in other countries such as United States, Singapore and Malaysia where the congregations have directly experienced the impact of ecological crisis, does not seem to make any significant impact in the understanding and attention of the HKBP congregations with regards to these ecological problems. The church life is still relatively akin to those which were in the Batakland. This is clearly expressed by C.G. Schmidt:

> It is widely recognized that urban communities have their collective specific problems, of which pollution and environmental destruction are but two. The Christians find themselves as part of this urban community. Their lifestyle and their health, and the health of their children may be affected by the problems of the community in which they live. Very often the church will respond and do nothing in this realm, mainly because it has been a rural church, the majority of its members still live in the village, and in the rural areas these problems have not yet become acute.[5]

There is an indifferent attitude of the HKBP congregations toward the care for God's creation influenced by the current theological understanding and church life tradition that has not changed significantly. From the past until now, the HKBP still does not consider ecology as one of the very essential parts of its responsibility and ministry.

However, HKBP has documents pertaining to the ecological problem. They are the *Confession of Faith of the HKBP* and *Garis-garis Besar Kebijaksanaan Pembinaan dan Pengembangan HKBP* (The Outline of Policy and Development of the HKBP[6]). Even with these documents, the problem is that on the one hand, that these documents contain only a very brief description on ecology and they are not widely known at the ordinary congregational levels. On the other hand, the formulation of its eco-theology message is still anthropocentric.

In the subsequent section, the primary documents including the Liturgy, Hymn Book, Confession of Faith, Church Order, teaching curriculum, mission statements and programs of the HKBP will be reviewed to present a clearer picture of its theological understandings, especially with regards to its anthropocentric, heavenism, and dualism frameworks[7] in addition to the attitudes and the concrete actions of the HKBP pertaining to God's creation.

---

4 HKBP, *Almanak HKBP 2009,* Tarutung: Kantor Pusat HKBP, 2019, 502.
5 C.G. Schmidt, "How Can a Church of Rural Origins Meet the Challenge of a Developing Urban Society", in Sitompul and Sovik, eds., *Horas HKBP,* 41.
6 Hereafter referred as *GBKPP HKBP.*
7 Norman Habel defines "heavenism" as a term which refers to the fact that so many of us, certainly in the Christian tradition, have been conditioned to believe that heaven is our home, the place where we are going eventually, and so we keep our eyes on that goal and it does not really matter too much what happens to earth, because we are going to leave it, we are pilgrims here. 'Dualism' puts humans over against nature, humans against animals. Humans have got mind, intellect, and a voice, whereas earth is mute and dumb, and so on.
http://www.abc.net.au/rn/relig/spirit/stories/s471562.htm, accessed on 05 July 2017. Also, Norman Habel, "Earth", 127-128.

Victor Tinambunan

1. The Liturgy and Hymns of the HKBP

The HKBP makes use of the same Liturgy Book and Hymn Book in all congregations whether in the countryside or in the city congregations, and even in the HKBP congregation in foreign countries such as in Singapore and in New York. The Liturgy Book and the Hymn Book of the HKBP are the legacy of the missionaries. They have never been revised which is not helpful at a time of ecological crisis which we are now facing.

As a matter of fact, the Liturgy and the Hymn Book of the HKBP could become more influential in forming the mind-set and attitude of the congregation members toward ecological issues compared with other documents such as the Confession of Faith, Church Order, Synod Assembly decisions and teaching curriculum. The reason for this is the fact that the Liturgy and the Hymn Book are used every Sunday, while the other documents are rarely used or studied by the congregation members. The problem, however, is that the Liturgy and the Hymn Book of the HKBP do not speak about Christian responsibility to respect and to care for God's creation.

The current Liturgy and the Hymn Book of the HKBP emphasize more on the salvation of the human soul through the death and the resurrection of Jesus Christ. Nevertheless, there are at least three typical understandings of God's creation in the Liturgy and the Hymn Book. First, there is an understanding of the world as a only a temporary existence . Importance instead is given to heaven or eternal life. Second, this world and other creatures exist merely for the benefit of humankind. Third, the language and symbols of the Liturgy and the Hymn Book are closely related to an agricultural setting and totally unfamiliar with industrial and technological matters.

The emphases on these three characteristic aspects may be traced to the strong influence and teaching of the missionaries and their pietistic backgrounds. These were the missionaries who lived among the Bataks in an agricultural context in the 17th century. Thus, the Liturgy and the Hymn Book of the HKBP which are currently in use can reinforce an indifferent attitude toward God's creation as its emphasis is on the heavenly realm.

The liturgy and the Hymn Book of the HKBP therefore needs to be revised in order to help the congregation to be more sensitive to nature which is facing extensive challenges and crisis being brought about by wide industrialization and pressures of consumerism today. We will develop this further in Chapter V.

For now, the Liturgy and the Hymn Book of the HKBP which are related to ecology are reviewed below.

1.1 The Liturgy of the HKBP

A more anthropocentric theological framework is very dominant in the whole practice of worship of the HKBP. The harvest liturgy, for example, contains thanksgiving to God, for it was God who gave the earth 'to' the human race. Consequently, the harvest festival is a time for the members of the congregations to give a special offering, designated for the needs of the congregation.[8]

In the liturgy there is also a prayer associated with climate conditions. For example, one part of the Sunday prayer says, "Pour out the rain and sunshine on their time .... Our rice fields would not be damaged due to floods or hail and the threat of natural disasters".[9] Associated with it is the 'prayer for a good day' which is recited as, "Oh Lord God, Our Father in heaven. You are the

---

8   HKBP, *Agenda HKBP*, 116. To meet these needs, increasing production becomes very important because every person should work hard to meet his or her own needs and the needs of the church.
9   HKBP, *Agenda HKBP*, 106-107.

owner of heaven and earth and all that is on it. Your hands that created them, and you give life to every living thing ..... Give rain and sunshine in their proper time, which makes fertility and produces a good harvest for our daily food." [10]

The two prayers demonstrate that rain and flood are totally in the hands of God. Nevertheless, the fact that changes in weather pattern can be affected by the destruction of nature because of human factor is not reflected in the liturgy book of the HKBP. It is a fact that many incidents of floods and natural disasters in Indonesia, including in Sumatra, happened precisely because of forest destruction. Sadly, the prayer also states that the harvest is simply for human interests.

Likewise, in every prayer of confession of sin in the order of worship there is no explicit statement about the sin of humankind in destroying God's creation. However, the current prayers are not necessarily unhelpful and therefore need not be abolished. There is still a place for such prayers in the Liturgy of the HKBP. What it needs is a balanced concern which will be developed as a proposal to the HKBP later.

Moreover, in terms of vocation or mission, the liturgy emphasizes the task for 'Christianising' but does not include the task of proclaiming the gospel to all living creatures. One part of the prayer of mission celebration reads as follows:

O Lord Jesus Christ...... send evangelists to other nations, who have never known thee..... Encourage and call them into the church. God would soften their hearts which are still against you. Call and bring mankind from over the world, so they pour into the church: those who are from the North and the South, which from the East and the West, all come into one God's holy Church, which claimed the Lord Jesus Christ as King and God to be God's glory and greatness forever.[11]

Taking notice of the fact that the Liturgy of the HKBP does not include the calling for the caring of God's creation, on 23 February 2007 a letter was sent to the Ephorus (a term used for Bishop) of the HKBP, proposing to observe a particular Sunday as the "Integrity of Creation Sunday" in the HKBP calendar.[12] Although the HKBP has not come up with an "Integrity of Creation Sunday" as it was proposed, the HKBP did set a theme for Sunday, July 12, 2009 as "Environmental preservation". That can be perceived as a momentous first step in the history of the HKBP. The Bible text for the sermon on the "Jubilee year" was based on Lev. 25:1-7[13] and fits well in encouraging the preservation of nature.

1.2 Hymns

The Hymn Book of the HKBP contains 556 songs that are all inherited from the era of old missionaries. The compilation of songs in the Hymn Book is in accordance with the understanding that the Lord Jesus is the Saviour of human beings. Just like the Liturgy Book, all songs related to nature and the harvest is for the benefit of humankind, not for the care of creation. In line with this, the mission objective is conversion.

These songs include the theme of God's omnipotence and his battle against the devil, the salvation of humankind from sin and death, and a calling to look for things that are in heaven.

---

10 HKBP, *Agenda HKBP*, 101.
11 HKBP, *Agenda HKBP*, 119.
12 Some local churches have begun to observe the Ecology Sunday. The CCA has also encouraged its church members to celebrate the Ecology Sunday every June.
13 HKBP, *Almanak HKBP 2009*, Tarutung: HKBP, 2009, 154.

Victor Tinambunan

In fact, some of the songs even hold the understanding of the world as evil, low, and the valley of lamentation.[14]

There is the word "tree" in hymn 373 which is said to be created by God and given to humans. The song contains no message on human responsibility to care for the forest. This is understandable as the hymn was not composed for that purpose.

Those parts of the Liturgy and Hymn Book that can support the preservation of nature refer to the requirement of the use of possession for the glory of God and the warning of the dangers of greed and love of money. There are also some lyrics of the chorus that contain the message not to be occupied by worldly possession. Among them is a chorus that is well-known to almost all of the HKBP congregations saying, "Unang lalap di arta portibi on ... . ai arta na di portibi on lao salpu do sasude" (Do not be preoccupied by the worldly things.....because all material possessions will perish).

However, such warnings have done little to prevent members of HKBP from accumulating earthly treasures. This happens on the one hand due to the strong influence of materialism and consumerism and, on the other hand, to a lack of consistency between what the church proclaims and what it pursues.

These hymns and chorus should be maintained but more songs with the ecological theme should be added. At the same time, the HKBP needs to provide consistent teaching to its members about the direct impact of consumerist lifestyles to the destruction of nature and Christian doctrine that is ecologically friendly.

2. The Confession of Faith of the HKBP

The first Confession of Faith of the HKBP was affirmed and formulated in 1951. That Confession of Faith is silent on the issue of ecology. The confession emphasizes apologetics on true teachings to be followed and false doctrines that must be rejected or resisted, for example, those coming from the traditional Batak culture and other religions.

However, in the second Confession of Faith of the HKBP (1996), which is still valid, there is one chapter on the subject of the environment. The inclusion of this article may be understood as a sign of growing concern of the HKBP regarding the problems of the destruction of nature. The article, among others, stresses the ownership of God over all creation; God gave a mandate to people to care for creation and Christ has come to save humanity and all creation.

Article 5 of the HKBP confession reads as follows:
We believe and confess:
God created human beings with a place for them to live and work in this world (Gen. 2:5-15). All things belong to him and he gives life to all he has created. The place where people work is on the land, sea and in the sky and outer space. God gives authority to human beings to care for the world responsibly. He has given language, musical instruments, art and knowledge as instruments, as well as rules with which to praise God and as a means to maintain and enhance good relations among people so that their culture through the kingdom of God will flourish. However, culture that is corrupted by veneration-of-Ances-

---

14   For example, hymns 295 and 520 *Partangisan do hape anggo hasiangan on* (This earth is a valley of tears). Translation is mine.

tral-spirits beliefs and practices and which is in conflict with the word of God ought to be rejected.

The work of Jesus Christ saves human beings, all creation as well as this world (Col 1:15-20; Rom 8:19-33).

By means of this doctrine:

We confess that human beings have the responsibility to preserve all of God's creation so that they can work, remain healthy and prosper (Ps 8:3-9).

We oppose all activities which destroy the environment such as burning and cutting down trees in forest and jungle areas (Deut 20:19-20). We oppose activities which pollute water and air and also uncontrolled poisonous waste water and water pollution from factories which contaminate drinking water and cause breathing problems (Ps 104:1-23; Rev. 22:1-2).[15]

In addition, the 1996 Confession of Faith addresses the patterns of proper and healthy consumption. Chapter 14 of the Confession states that a life controlled by food, alcohol and cigarettes should be resisted. This warning is implicitly associated with the responsibility of caring for creation.

Three points support the conclusion that the Confession of Faith of the HKBP has had little impact on the life of the congregations. First, a description of ecological matters is minimal. For example, there is no explicit statement that the land is anything more than a commodity, with theological significance as property under the power of God. Second, its content is still dominated by anthropocentric understanding. For example, in the explanation of Sunday (art. 11), 'rest' is only for humans, not for all God's creation. Third, the Confession of Faith is not widely known by the officers and the members of the HKBP.

3. The Church Order of the HKBP

The present Church Order of the HKBP (2002) is the twelfth Church Order of the HKBP. A review of the eleven former Church Orders indicates that ecological problems were not mentioned at all.[16] Likewise, environmental issues are not referenced in the ministry guidelines of three departments of the HKBP. The three departments of the HKBP, Koinonia, Marturia and Diakonia, situate human beings at the center of creation and at the center of Church mission as well. The main task of the Department of Koinonia is to maintain fellowship around the congregation and ecumenical relations. The main task of Marturia Department is to design and carry out evangelism with an emphasis on conversion. The main task of the Diakonia Department is to administer charity and to oversee the schools of the HKBP.[17]

The 2002 Church Order does not consider the content of the 1996 Confession of Faith of the HKBP and the GBKPP of the HKBP regarding the church responsibility to preserve nature.[18] In fact, the 1996 Confession of Faith and GBKPP existed six years and fourteen years respectively before the 2002 Church Order applied. The committee members who prepared the draft of the 2002 Church Order, and Synod Assembly that decided it, did not refer to the 1996 Confession of Faith and the GBKPP HKBP in their discussions.

---

15   HKBP, *Konfessi HKBP 1996*, Tarutung: HKBP, 1996, p. 88. Translation is mine.

16   The summary, see Tinambunan, *Bergereja*, pp. 46-67.

17   HKBP, *Aturan dohot Paraturan Huria Kristen Batak Protestant*, Tarutung: HKBP, 2002, pp. 46-49.

18   This shows that HKBP is more attached to certain people or leaders, and not the result of an existing decision.

The 2002 Church Order of the HKBP focuses on the importance of productivity without any consideration to the needs of all living creatures. The economic growth and the rise of the assets of the church become extremely important.[19]

Such practices are still held in various HKBP churches today. In fact, tithing and other form of givings have increased from time to time. Currently, the HKBP requires all congregations to collect offerings three times during every Sunday worship, one or two times in the weekly Bible study group, monthly pledges from each family or full church member, plus special collections for the construction of church buildings.

4. Teaching Curriculum

One of the oldest teaching materials of the HKBP, which is still in use today is Martin Luther's Small Catechism. The sections of the Catechism that should specifically be reference for the task of caring for the creation are the first article of the Apostle's Creed, the fourth commandment, the Lord's Prayer, and the meal prayer. However, the responsibility of caring for creation is not included in these parts.

The explanation of the first part of the Apostles' Creed says:
"I believe in God, the Father almighty, creator of heaven and earth" means: I believe that God has created me and all that exists; that he has given me and still sustains my body and soul, all my limbs and senses, my reason and all the faculties of my mind, together with food and clothing, house and home, family and property; that he provides me daily and abundantly with all the necessities of life, protects me from all danger, and preserves me from all evil.[20]

The explanation primarily highlights the importance of God as "creator" and his character as "omnipotent". Furthermore, the using of the words "me" and "my" indicates an anthropocentric and individualistic view. Moreover the word "powerful" is also related to the power of God to protect people rather than sustaining the whole of creation.

There is another example of anthropocentric emphasis. The very essence of the Sabbath is seen as a moment of resting solely for humans without direct links to the necessity of the rest of the creatures and nature itself. The explanation of the fourth commandment states, "Remember the Sabbath day, to keep it holy" means "we should fear and love God, and so we should not despise his Word and the preaching God's word, but deem it holy and gladly hear and learn it".[21]

In addition, when commenting on the petition "Give us today our daily bread", the Small Catechism notes, "To be sure, God provides daily bread, even to the wicked, without our prayer, but we pray in this petition that God may make us aware of his gifts and enable us to receive our daily bread with thanksgiving." Furthermore, the meaning of "daily bread" is "everything required to satisfy our bodily needs, such as food and clothing, house and home, fields and flocks, money and property".[22]

---

19 Pedersen, *Batak,* p. 82.
20 Theodore G. Tappert, ed., *The Book of Concord,* Philadelphia: Fortress Press, 1959, p. 345; Translated into the Batak language in HKBP, *Katekhismus Dr. Martin Luther,* Tarutung: HKBP, 2009, p. 27.
21 Tappert, *The Book of Concord,* p. 342.
22 Tappert, *The Book Concord,* p. 347.

In fact, there is a relevant statement of the Small Catechism in relation with ecological responsibility in the section "grace at the table" which states:

> When children and the whole household gather at the table, they should reverently fold their hands and say: "The eyes of all look to Thee, O Lord, and Thou givest them their food in due season… Thou openest thy hand; Thou satisfies the desire of every living thing".
> (It is to be observed that "satisfying the desire of every living thing" means that all creatures receive enough to eat to make them joyful and of good cheer. Greed and anxiety about food prevent such satisfaction).[23]

Regrettably, for no apparent reason, this statement was not translated into the Batak and Indonesian versions of the Small Catechism. Instead, we now have seven short anthropocentric prayers which replaced that statement.[24] Clearly, one thing that needs to be done is to revise the Batak and Indonesian translations by referring to the original Small Catechism, including the details which were omitted. Otherwise, the Small Catechism as one of teaching materials in the HKBP cannot become a robust means to develop an awareness to preserve God's creation.

From what we have shown, there is enough documentary evidence to conclude that the HKBP has made some attempts to develop the basic theological concepts of ecology. However, the formula is ineffective because of its anthropocentric focus. The anthropocentric barrier has not been broken down. Furthermore, it has not been adequately explained to the larger congregations and it has never become part of concrete action taken by the three departments of the HKBP (*koinonia, marturia, diakonia*). The HKBP still needs to develop and disseminate in a more detailed and synchronous manner, all the documents of the HKBP –liturgy, hymn, confession of faith, church order, GBKPP, teaching modules-- accompanied with substantial efforts in the daily life of every congregation member and all congregations.

5. Towards a HKBP Eco-Theology

Educational and religious institutions in Indonesia are expected to play a vital role in shifting the mind sets of every person. The urgent call for repentance from toxic theology to eco-theology must also be highlighted as one of the vital teachings, and surely should never be ignored.

Moral teachings on greediness and overconsumption to a simple lifestyle must be encouraged to every person regardless of the economic status. Hoarding and too much buying of needless and unnecessary things always result in financial mismanagement and later in debt.

The following are believed to be beneficial in solving toxic theology. First, Christian churches in Indonesia must establish strong biblical ground especially on the area of stewardship. Just as written in Psalm 24:1,"The earth is of the Lord and everything in it". Second, Christian churches must have a Bible reinterpretation, including a shift from anthropocentric to cosmocentric perspectives. Third, Ecological Ethics Subjects at Seminaries must be taught. (STT HKBP is the only seminary in Southeast Asia that offers Ecological Ethics). Fourth, Dialogue with other faiths in building a common understanding in eco-theology must not be undermined as Indonesia is composed of many different religions and they influence man's act of moral. Lastly, the Respect for Local Wisdom is a very crucial issue. Indonesia is the house of many local wisdom traditions in respecting and caring nature.

---

23   Tappert, *The Book*, p. 353.
24   HKBP, *Katekhismus*, pp. 65-66.

THEMATIC
CONTRIBUTIONS

WORSHIP AS PLACE-BASED ECOLOGICAL FORMATION

Chad Rimmer

I thank you the invitation to contribute to this panel on Priorities for Ecumenical Eco-ethics, specifically practical dimensions related to liturgy and worship. As an ordained pastor by vocation and a theological ethicist who focuses on eco-ethics by training, I want to first observe that when talking about eco-ethics, or ethics of any sort, we are talking about ethos, or the formation of character. Automatically the concept of ethics as a theological discipline may make some protestant theologians in an ecumenical setting a bit uneasy. But as a Lutheran ethicist, I want to affirm liturgy and worship as a location for eco-ethics, with all practical and pedagogical dimensions.

I approach eco-theological ethics from an eco-feminist point of view. By that I follow Celia Deanne-Drummond's fundamental assertion that eco-theology, properly speaking is not simply to reflect theologically about the status or agency of non-human nature, but more fundamentally about restoring just relationships in every aspect of life.[1] It is a relational look at being and community among all creatures, non-living ecology included. Relationality is the starting point of every eco-feminist, eco-womanist, and even indigenous approach to eco-theology. This relational methodology of eco-theology as a theological discipline also serves as the direct link to eco-theological ethics. In other words, beginning with the Trinity as a relationship of Love (perichoresis), then creation, redemption and sanctification are part of the one economy of the Trinity – one movement of being and act that grounds the inherent goodness and dignity of creatures. Defining creature's self-hood (theological anthropology) as a relational, interdependent subject already implies the mutuality, responsibility to the other creature as neighbour and your culture within an integral ecology.

Because relationship is both the object of theology and the means of forming the ethical creature, the epistemological link between eco-theology and eco-theological ethics. Creation is a subject that communicates knowledge of the Creator, and the object of our moral relationship. For that reason, the disconnect between human and non-human creatures, and between the non-human environment and the built environment or culture (including economic, social and political systems) is part of our brokenness. If the fall is a story of ecological disintegration, redemption is the story of cosmic reconciliation, and ecological re-integration is part of our sanctification.

The focus on the immediate integral ecology as the location for moral discernment, and faith formation has an immediate application of this concept to ecologically rooted placed based Christian education and worship. This notion has been outlined in my own forthcoming book, Greening the Children of God,[2] and recently in the work of other eco-theological ethicists such as Michael Northcott in Place, Ecology and the Sacred the Moral Geography of Sustainable Com-

---

1 "Overall, eco-theology seeks to uncover the theological basis for a proper relationship between God, humanity and the cosmos", Celia Deanne-Drummond, Ecotheology (St. Mary's) 2008. p. xii.
2 Chad Rimmer, Greening the Children of God :Thomas Traherne and Nature's Role in the Moral Formation of Children (Wipf & Stock) 2019.

munities[3], and of course, the works of eco-feminists such as Rosemary Radford Reuther. While it is important in an ecumenical setting to allow for non-occidental and indigenous notions of time and history, we can affirm across the ecumenical that our ecological location is just as important as our cultural and social location in understanding how we participate in the reconciliation of all creation that was begun in Christ Jesus. A primary location, strictly speaking for that formation is the Eucharist, where the God encounters us through the Spirit, recreating, nurturing and sanctifying us where the body of Christ is met in Word and sacraments. Of course, here we find another opportunity for our confessions to revisit the atonement theories that operate in our proclamation and in our liturgical theologies. Nevertheless, the spirituality of worship engages all five senses, bodies, voices, fruits of the earth and creation itself in an ecological place. This gracious eschatological encounter is the primary place where we can ritualize the justice that results from justification, and include creation in our worship. If we are looking for a vehicle of Christian education or formation that can engender the truth that redemptive justice and the common good for all creation is inextricable to the good news of salvation that Christ has come to proclaim, then worship is perhaps the primary place where we can integrate the local ecology into our worship. To conceive of it in the other direction, the Eucharist is an eschatological event that breaks into a local community, in time and space. Therefore, it is logical that we see that worship as a chance to highlight the ecological place in which the good news of cosmic reconciliation breaks in. The happy exchange that occurs in this Eucharistic moment involves the place in which we are located, and extends to every creature, and the geography that make up the local Eucharistic community. In this way, worship can promote an eco-theological hermeneutic and be a vehicle of eco-ethical formation.

Liturgy as eco-spirituality

George McLeod, the founder of the Iona Community, has called Iona a "thin place". This is a way of referring to the particular spirituality that is afforded by attention to the unique nature of the ecology and geography in which the Holy Spirit is met in worship. In his book, Stripping of the Altars: Traditional Religion in England 1400-1580, Eamon Duffy has pointed out the fact that this attention to the symbolic and realistic importance of the participation of the local ecology was one of the losses of the reformation's liturgical iconoclasm.[4] Our ecumenical age (particularly on the 20th anniversary of the Joint Declaration on the Doctrine of Justification) allows churches of various reformation traditions to re-incorporate certain liturgical and devotional practices without risk of re-litigating old liturgical controversies. However, Duffy and many eco-theological historians[5] that the ecological destruction that was the logical consequence of the demystification that resulted from the reformation and scientific and social revolutions is a much more difficult disruption to overcome. However, worship can help us in this regard, too.

---

3   Michael Northcott, Place, Ecology and the Sacred the Moral Geography of Sustainable Communities (Bloomsbury) 2015.
4   Eamon Duffy, The Stripping of the Altars: Traditional Religion in England, C.1400-c.1580 (Yale University) 2005.
5   Ellen Davis, Scripture, Culture and Agriculture : An agrarian reading of the Bible (Cambridge University) 2009. Also, multiple works of Norman Wirzba and Lynn White for example.

Chad Rimmer

For instance, Luther always viewed creation as mystical. The created order, in all of its human and non-human aspects were masks of God (larvae dei), which communicated something of the creator. His sacramental understanding of the real presence of Christ in the elements was predicated on a belief that the finite can contain the infinite (finitum capax infinitii). Against the radical reformers, who promoted a disenchanted, symbolic view of liturgy, Luther wrote a treatise on The Sacrament of the Body and Blood of Christ Against the Fanatics. In it, he confessed "God is present in all creatures, and I might find God in stone, in fire, in water, or even in a rope, for God is there."[6] The aim of this treatise is to affirm Christ's real presence in the Eucharist. However, this claim is logically based on the fact that God is present and active in, with and under all of creation. To deny this, he says, would be to deny the incarnation itself. Luther himself provides the basis for Lutherans to overcome the demystification of the reformation and scientific revolution. The Liturgy of Word and sacrament becomes THE primary thin place to perceive the presence of God's Spirit.

This is morally significant, because for Lutherans (as in many of our traditions), worship plays a primary catechetical and pedagogical role in addition to being the location for our formation and sanctification. Gordon Lathrop has explored the liturgical and soteriological implications of this confession in Holy Ground: a Liturgical Cosmology[7], and in A Watered Garden: Christian Worship and Earth's Ecology[8], Benjamin Stewart has written about the very practical and pedagogical possibilities of seeing worship as a primary location for theological formation.

Worship: theology of the Spirit and as spiritual theology

Luther's liturgical reforms were rooted in the fundamental historic understanding that in a generally illiterate, pre-literate, or auditory society, worship was the most important pedagogue for Christian formation. It was second only, perhaps to catechism in the home. But again, this was not an innovation. Rather, as I demonstrated above, this affirmation was rooted in a basic Trinitarian confession. The church and the whole of the Christian life are part of the work of the Holy Spirit, as professed in the ecumenical creeds. Luther's treatise on The Sacrament of the Body and Blood of Christ demonstrates the direct link between the Spirit's continual creative and transformative work in creation, and the revelation of that spiritual activity as gift and promise in worship. The only concern for Luther is that God's immanence not be terrifying or burdensome. Rather, that the revelation is received as good news. Luther states that while the Holy Spirit is everywhere (in a stone, fire, water, and a rope), so that you do not stumble on the rope, burn yourself in the fire, drown in the water, or hang yourself with the rope blindly groping to find God, the Spirit of God reveals itself where Christ promised – namely where the Word is proclaimed and the sacraments administered. For Luther, the proper definition of the communion of saints is that community in which Christ promises to meet us, to reveal the activity of the Spirit as gift and promise, so that we can learn to see that activity in our daily interaction with creation as gracious.

And therein lies the link between the theology of the Spirit in worship, and the pedagogical impact of worship as spiritual theology. The Eucharist is the place where we experience the happy

---

6 "The Sacrament of the Body and Blood", WA 19, 492, 5; LW 36: 342.
7 Gordon Lathrop, Holy Ground: a Liturgical Cosmology (Fortress) 2009.
8 Benjamin Steward, A Watered Garden: Christian Worship and Earth's Ecology (Fortress) 2014.

exchange among the members of the community where the Spirit meets us. Word and Sacrament are made efficacious by this community, or communion of the Spirit, an element as a vehicle (spoken word, water, wine, bread), and someone to receive it. It is the very real and present communion between actual beings that renders the Spirits work perceivable or efficacious. 17th century Anglican priest and poet Thomas Traherne referred to this kind of communion as a "theatre of love". The local assembly of creatures in a places constitutes the theatre in which the Spirit moves and resonates. In this way, the spirituality of worship is communicative. While even Luther does not disagree with other faiths who speak philosophically about the immanence of God's Spirit in nature, the relationality of Christian worship provides a particular location in which that revelation can be perceived as a gracious exchange. And here we see the practical pedagogical possibilities of non-human creatures participating in that communion and the local ecology itself as the theatre in which that communication resonates.

The purpose of corporate prayers, public reading of scripture and the mutual conversation and consolation of faith is to realize the presence, needs and voices of various members of the body. By standing in the public assembly and naming a person who is ill, in need of employment, or suffering a particular injustice is to embody them as an important participants in this community. This re-membering in the body is a vehicle for participation, but also a recognition and normalization of their voice, whether it is for thanksgiving or lamentation. If the parish does not exclude its non-human members from this worshipping community, but rather embraces[9] the non-human species and the local ecology in worship and prayers then worship becomes an opportunity to amplify the cries of creation, and normalize the voices of non-human creatures in the Christian assembly.

When one stands in the physical presence of the suffering neighbour, the perceived enemy, the estranged one, prays for them publicly, hears their voice honoured and spoken into the community, and then takes a place shoulder to shoulder or hand in hand at the meal of reconciliation, the formational impact of worship is obvious. This physical embrace of non-human creatures in worship, and physically linking worship to the local ecology has the same pedagogical, theological and ethical impact.

Allow an example. During my doctoral studies in Edinburgh, I was welcomed via ecumenical hospitality to serve on the clergy team of St. Columba's by the Castle, Scottish Episcopal church. In this urban congregation, there were several members who were transitioning from homelessness through a partnership with a local ministry. One man in particular was named Matthew. He was a shepherd in the Highlands before coming to Edinburgh, and becoming homeless. Since his days shepherding in the fields, Matthew was always accompanied by his sheepdog named Patch, who was his companion in the fields, on the streets, and every Sunday in the back row of the sanctuary. Matthew was slow to integrate into the life of the congregation despite the adamant welcome and the community's profound embrace of Matthew, and his dog. Eventually, Matthew was convinced to usher and then to serve communion, including the practice that communion assistants stood around the table during the Eucharistic prayer and words of institution. The first Sunday that Matthew served was Easter Sunday. And there, as I set the table with bread and wine, the fruits of the earth, the community assembled represented by the assistants...there came Patch. Walking beside Matthew who carried the bread, Patch followed his friend and sat among

---

9   Miroslav Volf, Exclusion and Embrace:A theological exploration of identity, otherness and reconciliation (Abingdon) 1996.

Chad Rimmer

our circle. And there, as I prayed the Eucharistic Prayer, there sat our Canine friend, participating in a very real way, in the central Feast of Reconciliation between the Creator and all Creation.

But that is not even the end of the story. Months later, the congregation was in the process of writing a profile for calling their next priest. The congregation lovingly decided to ask its children to respond to each question, so that their voice would inform the parish's self-understanding. One of the questions was, "Who are we?" To that question, the children knowingly and perceptively replied, "We are lots of loving people and one dog." The pedagogical and ethical implications of including non-human creatures and the local ecology in worship is profound for those who experience communion as rooted in a local place.

Liturgy as resistance

But, in addition the pedagogical and moral implications for the inclusion of all creation in the local assembly, a place-based sense understanding of worship has public and prophetic implications as well. In his book Torture and Eucharist: Theology Politics and the Body of Christ[10], William Kavanaugh documented the way that worship was a form of resistance to the political injustice exercised during the Pinochet regime in Chile. Under Pinochet, the state's main tactic for shrinking democratic space and oppressing dissent was to disappear bodies altogether. In this context, (and in the context of a theological exploration of ex-communication versus communion) Kavanaugh brilliantly demonstrates that the public act of Eucharistic worship is a political act of embodiment. Not only does it incarnate the body of Christ, in the sacrament of word and Sacrament, but it incarnates the body of Christ as a political body in the world. Those who are re-presented by their bodies' membership in the body have their agency and dignity as political beings publicly recognized. In the face of a political body who utilizes its power to dis-appear bodies, Christian liturgy is an act of resistance insofar as it appears, embodies, realizes those bodies in the public space as creatures with inherent dignity. Kavanaugh is a Roman Catholic theologian, but this theme of the political nature of worship has been followed by many protestant theologians, including Lutheran Bernd Wannenwetsch in Political Worship[11], and Mennonite theologians such as John Howard Yoder, who emphasize the non-violent power of liturgical resistance.

The point I am making here is that we live in an increasingly nihilistic age, where every creature is commodified. While disappearances are still a political tactic, particularly with respect to human rights defenders, journalists and women, the valuation and disintegration of local ecology and non-human creatures from public moral and political discourse is a form of disappearance that requires resistance. Advocacy, protests and conservation campaigns are well known methods for "appearing" non-human species and the land, or giving them voice in public discourse and political debate about ecology and climate justice. But Christians must realize how public worship is a powerful from of resistance against the commodifying will-to-power of the dominant political and economic systems.

By including all of creation in the assembly and integrating worship into the local ecology as a place based, public act, Christian liturgy offers a chance to publicly re-member the whole of creation in a way that cannot be denied. Standing Rock provides us with a clear example. The

---

10 William Kavanaugh, Torture and Eucharist : Theology, Politics and the Body of Christ (Wiley) 1988.
11 Bernd Wannenwetsch, Political Worship : Ethics for Christian Citizens (Oxford) 2004.

land, the non-human species who lived on the land, and the Native American culture that was formed by the land had been commodified by the political and economic leaders of the energy sector. The land around Standing Rock was calculated to provide the most economically expedient corridor to between the Canadian tar-sand fields and the port at the Gulf of Mexico. Because economic narrative ignored the cultural and ecological significance of the land, the land and its people were disappeared from political and economic deliberation. In light of this disappearance, Native American Lutherans were among those who stood on the land itself, and protested the annexation of this thin place. The very fact of their prayers for the land and its inhabitants being located in the land itself was an act of resistance, in the fact that it embodied a land and creatures that had been disappeared from public debate and discourse in the halls of power.

Public liturgy can be what eco-womanist Emilie Townes calls a "counter-memory".[12] From her womanist perspective, part of the resistance to dominant economic narratives about utility, and the dualistic, rationalist anthropologies that underwrite narratives about the demystification of bodies, non-human creatures and the land, is to provide a counter-memory to who and what we are. This notion of counter-memory as resistance is similar to the Biblical command to "remember". When faced with the temptation to suffer the injustices of powers and principalities in exile and otherwise, God's people were called to liturgical remembrance. When faced with ethical questions about how to relate to widows, orphans and the refugee in their midst, God's people were pedagogically reminded to "remember" that they, too were once strangers in a strange land, oppressed and now liberated. Just as the liturgical remembrance of Passover provides the fundamental counter-memory of liberation to dominant narratives of political oppression or economic commodification, for Christians the Eucharist (including the proclamation of the Gospel and the acramental re-membering of the body) provides the fundamental counter-memory to today's narrative that commodify and objectify creatures as means to an economic end. In the Eucharist, every human, non-human creature and the land in which our worship is cultivated are in themselves ends of the Creator's love.

Creation is part of God's story about love, being and becoming, so it must be part of our story, too. The land plays such a role in the story of God's people and the formation of their identity and liberation, and it plays a tremendous role in our story of the formation of our identity and liberation. This ecological countermemory is part of our resistance to domination narratives. Our public, liturgical counter-remembering is an act of resistance that strengthens our Christian witness to God as Creator, and our faith in what God is doing in Christ to reconcile all of creation, and re-form us as moral agents of this transformation.

Liturgy in the public space and as public space

I am trying to suggest that including non-human creatures and the local ecology as members of the worshipping community has pedagogical and morally formative implications for those who take their place among that communion, but it is also important to the public sphere in which that liturgy takes place. This is another way of saying that the church, as a worshipping community has a role to play in the public space, and it must see itself as a public space that can be open to embracing all creatures of the Creator.

---

12   Emilie Townes, Womanist Ethics and the Cultural Production of Evil (Palgrave McMillan) 2006.

Chad Rimmer

The LWF's study document The Church in the Public Space emphasizes this two-fold aspect of the church's public witness. This approach is rooted in a Lutheran understanding of our baptismal vocation to participate in the reformation and transformation of creation, and in our commitment to engage the world through Luther's theological framework of the Two-regiments or three estates (economic, political and ecclesial spheres). One effect of this engagement in the public space is to highlight the importance of public worship. Liturgy is a vehicle for practically forming the community as a moral body that re-presents, embodies and embraces the young, vulnerable and other creatures marginalized or excluded by shrinking democratic and public spaces. Liturgy is also an opportunity to give voice to the cries of the young, vulnerable and creation itself, as a public space. The experience of worship becomes a vehicle for informing the ethical judgements, and therefore public witness, of everyone formed by the experience of resonating with the prayers, proclamation and communion with creatures excluded in other public spaces. The ethical implications, and even eco-ethical implications of our liturgy has been a significant part of the LWF's public witness since the LWF's 8th Assembly in Curitiba. In 1990, the Brazilian context was an opportunity to amplify the voices of the poor and linked to the cries of creation itself. The importance of giving space to the cries of creation has continued to be a factor in our public worship and assemblies as a communion throughout the decades. Fast-forwarding to today, Brazil is once again the location of a coalition of ethno-nationalism and economic neo-liberalism that threatens to disappear and silence the cries of creatures and the land itself. Public liturgical witness and remembering continue to be an important counter-memory, as an act of resistance on behalf of creation, and as location for the eco-theological and ethical formation of every member of the body of Christ.

Some final practical dimensions of our eco-theological, place based liturgy

That Lutheran witness is an important tributary to a great stream of ecumenical theological consensus about the significance of liturgy in Christian education and formation, and ecumenical worship as public witness on behalf of creation and the climate vulnerable. This river is joined in content and form by liberation theologians, eco-feminists, Protestant communions, the Holy See most recently through Pope Francis' promulgation of Laudato Si, and of course the Orthodox witness embodied particularly in the ministry of His All Holiness Ecumenical Patriarch Bartholomew I of Constantinople. In the content of our ecumenical dialogue and in the form of our ecumenical diapraxis, our commitment to care for creation provides us with a location for differentiated consensus, and visible unity of the body of Christ through public, ecumenical liturgy.

In 1989, the Orthodox instituted 1 September as a Day of Prayer for the Care of Creation, in which many protestant and reformed churches began to participate by 2001. In 2015, Pope Francis instituted the day, and in the intervening years, our ommunions began to celebrate the period between 1 September and St. Francis's feast day on 4 October as a liturgical Season of Creation. This ecumenical celebration is being promoted as a liturgical season, which is appropriately observed during the "green time" of Pentecost, dedicated to ecumenical prayer, action, education and solidarity. As a point of fact, the LWF is a member of the Ecumenical Season of Creation, along with the Global Catholic Climate Movement, World Council of Churches, World Communion of Reformed Churches, World Evangelical Alliance, Conference of European Churches, A Rocha and others. Very practically, Season of Creation annually publishes a resource that includes an ecumenical prayer service based on the theme of the year, and points to resources for parishes to engage in joint action, place-based environmental education, and campaigns for ecological mitigation.

In addition to the Season of Creation, a myriad of online platforms are devoted to helping pastors, liturgists and preachers engage in ecologically themed worship planning throughout the year. Websites such as Sustainable Preaching, Lutherans Restoring Creation, Green Anglicans (and inter-religious platforms such as Interfaith Power and Light and Green Faith among others) offer lectionary based resources and resources for planning ecologically centred worship throughout the liturgical years. Online resources are also a critical tool for ongoing education and research regarding the natural roots of the liturgical cycle itself. For instance, Easter is related to Passover, which is a lunar date related to the Spring solstice in the northern hemisphere, and consequently new life and revival. Pentecost is a season of growth and renewal, and Christmas is close to the winter solstice in the northern hemisphere, which offers new symbolic interpretation of light in the darkness. While it must be contextualized to other hemispheres and bioregions, simply renewing our awareness of the ecological rhythms that inform our liturgical calendar help us to incorporate the rhythms of our local ecology into our liturgical seasons and worship. The seasons and rhythms of the earth have always informed the theological reflection and liturgical patterns of God's people, and it is still a way for us to incorporate the voices and counter-memories of female, indigenous, young and marginalized voices into the liturgical life cycles of our communities.

Liturgical rites and rituals that mark the life cycles of individuals also offer another practical opportunity to incorporate local ecologies and non-human creatures. Every eucharist involves bread and wine, which can be locally sourced and every baptism involves water. But we can also link every rite and ritual to our local ecology. For instance Bishop Shoo of the Evangelical Lutheran Church of Tanzania established the practice of planting trees for every baptism and wedding that happens within the ELCT. In this way, every member of the church knows and practices the fact that their local ecology shares in the life giving, renewing and transforming hope that is embodied in these liturgical acts of thanksgiving. This is one practical example, but the opportunities are endless.

Conclusion – a hermeneutic of hope

In conclusion, Christian worship and liturgy are particularly suited to provide profound opportunities for practically promoting eco-theological ethical formation. Rooted in our ecumenical theology of the Spirit, and our diverse traditions of spiritual theology, worship provides us with a location for Christian education and formation. Worship can easily and profoundly incorporate local ecology and non-human members of our earth community. Such communions provide an ecological hermeneutic that can shape and form our theological anthropology, and our moral identity as creatures, in communion with all of the Creator's creation.

In our age of climate change, there is enough fear and trembling that can sometimes cause a certain paralysis from eco-anxiety.[13] By promoting worship and liturgy as the location for parish-

---

13   Panu Pihkala explores this topic in several writings, including Early Ecotheology and Joseph Sittler (LIT Verlag) 2017.

ioners to encounter the Holy Spirit in communion with the other non-human members of their local ecology, churches can provide an ecologically shaped and rooted context in which our ecological vocation can be received as gift and promise. When we gather in the context of our local ecology to proclaim the good news to all creation, and administer the sacraments in a theatre of love with every creature, we are offering a hermeneutic of hope.

In our contemporary age, moral motivation comes from many different quarters, some of which are driven by economic or political ends. In this ethical milieu, the church has a particular calling to proclaim hope. The Holy Trinity is love, the source of our faith and the horizon of our hope. Faith, hope, and love, remain the theological virtues that motivate Christian vocation, shape our public engagement in ecological and environmental ethics, and form our theological anthropology about who, what and where we are made into creatures who bear the image of our Creator.

ECONOMY OF LIFE INDEX AND GREED LINE AS ALTERNATIVE CONCEPTS OF SUSTAINABILITY

Louk Andrianos[1]

Abstract
Multidimensional greed or "pleonasma" is the greatest threat against justice, peace and sustainability. The society of 21th century relies on unrestricted structural greed and promotes it through unlimited growth, overconsumption and individualistic competitive behavior.

This paper aims at analyzing greed and defining the notion of Economy of Life index. By promoting greed line as an alternative concept for growth and sustainability, the findings give answers to critical questions such as "What is greed and what are the limits of greed (greed lines); "Is it possible to measure them and –if yes- how?; How greedy are we as an individual or as a community; Why should we worry more about controlling greed in order to promote sustainable economy of Life?"

We developed a new model called "GLIMS" which stands for Greed Lines and Life Indexes Measurement System. It uses fuzzy logic reasoning and inputs from statistical indicators of natural resources consumption, financial realities, economic performances, social welfare, ethical and political facts. The outputs are concrete measures of three primary indexes of ecological, economic and socio-political greed (ENV-GI, MON-GI, POW-GI) and one overall multidimensional Economy of Life index (EcoLI) or a Multidimensional Structural Greed index (MSGI). The results are Economy of life index scores or greed indexes that are expressed in a scale of zero to one hundred. Greed index score of 100 corresponds to Economy of life score equal to zero, which is the maximum level of greed for the subject of analysis.

Starting as a pilot project of the World Council of Churches in linking poverty, wealth and ecology, it is the first time that crisp measurements of Economy of Life index is proposed using a set of nine greed indicators for selected economies and individuals. The vision is to promote greed line as an alternative concept of growth and sustainability by offering practical tools for sustainable policy making in corporations, churches and institutions.

1. INTRODUCTION

As a follow-up to the Alternative Globalization Addressing People and Earth (AGAPE) process which concluded with the AGAPE Call presented at the 9th General Assembly of the World Council of Churches[2] (WCC) in Porto Alegre in 2006, the WCC initiated a program focused on eradicating poverty, challenging wealth accumulation, and safeguarding ecological integrity based on the understanding that Poverty, Wealth, and Ecology (PWE) are integrally related. After

---

1 World Council of Churches, consultant for the Care for Creation, Climate justice and Sustainability.
2 http://www.oikoumene.org/en/resources/documents/wcc-programmes/public-witness-addressing-power-affirming-peace/poverty-wealth-and-ecology/neoliberal-paradigm/agape-background-document.html?print=1%22%20onfocus%3D%22blurlink%28.

the 10th Assembly of the World Council of Churches which took place in Busan, Republic of Korea, from 30 October to 8 November 2013, the diverse initiatives for promoting sustainability are referred to Ecological and Economic Justice (EEJ) works of the WCC programmes on Public Witness and Diakonia.

In this work, we analyze the mechanism of structural greed which is based on the analysis of its root causes and its consequence to global crisis and poverty. The root cause of greed is examined from the perception of Christianity belief and theological conception of the Trinitarian human needs and the overall creation as a whole. The conceptual description of structural greed is presented in correlation to the findings of the WCC greed line group study on poverty, wealth and ecology.

The Lord Jesus Christ warned us to *"take care to guard against all greed, for though one may be rich, one's life does not consist of possessions"* (Luke 12:15)" and *Einstein* once said *"Three forces move the world"*: *"Stupidity, fear and greed"*. "The earth produces enough to satisfy human needs but not greed," he said once, very well, *Gandhi*. Because the healthy mind (logic) regulates the measure, so with a sound spirit (wisdom) it is possible to get the optimal measure (index). What is the "optimal measure"? It is the mean between two opposite, avoiding extremes[3] .

In Ancient Greek philosophical terms, there are many lessons which refer to greed and the necessity of its measurement to preserve human happiness and to avoid mass destruction. *Plato*, (427-347 B.C.), urged about the need for determining wealth line and said: *"The form of law which I propose would be as follows: In a state which is desirous of being saved from the greatest of all plagues (GREED)—not faction, but rather distraction—there should exist among the citizens neither extreme poverty nor, again, excessive wealth, for both are productive of great evil . . . Now the legislator should determine what is to be the limit of poverty or of wealth."* Democritus, (470 - 370 BC) said, in reference to greed line: *"If someone exceeds the measure – average-, the most enjoyable things could become the most unpleasant"* .

The *"cup of justice"* which was invented centuries ago by the wise *Pythagoras*, is also called *greedy cup*. The message it conveys is as crystal clear as is the water that we can drink from it: "You may drink little or more, even a little more, if you like. You may share with others and satisfy your needs. But do not wish to fill the cup to the rim (greed line), in order to drink more than the others. Because then you will lose it all![4] . The respect of the "greed line" should be the rule in all dimensions of systemic decision-making on all levels; otherwise the consequence is catastrophic for human being and for the Earth.

In this paper, the first two chapters will give a brief description on the concept of structural greed and economy of Life. The chapter 3 deals with the methodology of assessing economy of Life Index with the "GLIMS" model. The following chapter 4 will present empirical results, sensitivity analysis and recommendations from sampling results using MATLAB/GLIMS on national levels. This last chapter 5 will conclude by answering the critical questions such as "how greedy is a country or a person?", and to raise discussions. The aim is to present a new alternative concept of sustainability and the possibility to measure Economy of Life index on global, communal, institutional and individual level.

---

3   Dictionary Tegopoulos Smith.
4   http://greedline.webs.com/.

2. THE CONCEPT OF STRUCTURAL GREED and ECONOMY OF LIFE

2.1 Descriptions of greed

There are many descriptions of greed according to subject: individual, institutional, national, corporal and global. One of the hallmarks of human behavior is greed. In Greek the word "greedy" is 'a-plistos'. "Aplistos" is derived from the privative "a" and "plistos" which means "complete" or "full". Therefore "greedy" is having more, insatiable, by the unfulfilled desire. The opposite of greed is the "plistos" which means "full-integrated" or theoretically defined as a standard value, because supposedly doing well with his or her situation.

The wholeness of human being consists in the fulfillment of a balanced threefold need: material, mental and ethical or spiritual. Jesus Christ said, "It is written: 'Man shall not live on bread alone, but on every word that comes from the mouth of God' (Mathew 4:4; Deuteronomy 8:3). According to Ancient Greek philosophers, happiness could be reached if all needs are satisfied in moderation, avoiding extremes[5], one of the seven sage of ancient Hellas, stated "everything is best in moderation or average" [*ΜΕΤΡΟΝ ΑΡΙΣΤΟΝ*]).

2.2 What is greed?

(Raiser, 2011) Greed could be defined as the *desire to have more than one's legitimate share of material goods and power* (mental and psychological). In contrast to poverty which deals with needs that can be objectively defined and even quantified, greed is about desires which are *"difficult to contain"* and involve an *"emotional energy that seeks to transgress or disregard limitations"* and which are consequently difficult to circumscribe and measure.

2.3 The concept of structural greed and its measurement

"In today's complex economy where people often fail to recognize the structural connections between their desire to improve their living standards (status) and the poverty suffered by others (Raiser, 2011), Christian churches and ecumenical organizations have the task of making visible – and lifting up the voices of – those people who are in the socio-economic margins." The systematic approach of greed focusing on the holistic interconnections between its potential causes and its effects to the global society or its manifestation in the Trinitarian nature of human being is attributed to structural greed (Andrianos, 2011).

The development of *Multidimensional Greed Indicators (MGI)* in counterpart to the multi-dimensional poverty indicators first developed by Oxford University was proposed by Michael (Taylor, 2011). The indicators could focus on categories of health, education, empowerment, relationships, environment and security and, in each case, would refer to the potential greed (status) of an individual and its consequences for others (desire/trends). The MGI basically would address the questions: *Am I greedy? How am I greedy?*. In summarising approaches to developing a greed line, a distinction between static and *dynamic approaches* has been made, with the latter showing changes – growing enrichment versus growing impoverishment – *over a period of time* (Goudzwaard, 2011). Moreover, choosing a particular approach would depend on *"whom we like to address"* and the availability of data. Ideally, racial, gender and other forms of discrimination should be captured. Also it is recommended to develop a social ethical consumption function that factors in inequitable socio-economic conditions and ecological limits, and in deriving the

---

5   Cleobulus of Rhodes (6th cent. BC).

greed line from said function (Larrea, 2012). Finally, it is suggested that defining greed line using fuzzy logic approach by computation using "linguistic values" and developing a multidimensional structural greed index by "fuzzy combination" (simulation with uncertainty) of the three pillars of the society (ecological sustainability, economic-financial performance and socio-political justice) could give a solution for a practical monitoring of structural greed (Andrianos, 2012).

Bible study pointed out the Pauline teachings revealing that *human greed is a sin that has adverse consequences not only on our neighbors (natural ecosystem and human kind), but also on Creation as a whole*[6]. On individual aspect, structural greed ought to take into account the effects of greed into the balance of threefold human need: *material, mental and spiritual (Andrianos, 2012)*. And on national level, it must include the effects of greed onto the three basic pillars of the society: *ecological sustainability (Material overconsumption), monetary accumulation (economic-financial) and power inequality (socio-political)*.

2.4 Concept of Greed lines

If greed is "having too much" money, resources and power (in contrast to describing poverty as "having too little"), when does one "have too much"? (Peralta, 2011) It was proposed that the point or level when individuals or societies "*have too much*" is approached or describes a situation *(status)*, first of all, *when other individuals and societies have too little resources to live by and, second of all, and when the accumulation of wealth and power undermines the common good or threatens (desire/ trends) the global commons.*

While the poverty line is drawn at the point of personal consumption allowing for the satisfaction of basic needs, the *greed line could be drawn at "the highest point of personal consumption which can be obtained without negatively affecting the integrity of nature, the welfare of society and that of future generations (Larrea, 2011)."*

Greed lines are the levels of resource consumption, money accumulation or power seizure over which societal or individual behaviors may harm human well being and the Creation integrity. These negative effects of behaviors beyond greed lines could be expressed in term of relative poverty or socio-economic injustice or sentimental offenses and environmental destructions.

Concept of the Economy of Life index (EcoLI).

The WCC ecological and economic justice group (WCC-EEJ) began to explore the possibility of identifying *multi-dimensional indicators of greed at the structural level which could be further developed into a structural greed index which is the opposite of the Economy of Life index.* The indicators could have as its basis people's economic, social and cultural rights enshrined in the United Nations human rights conventions, which essentially define the protective limits for maintaining human life and promoting human development[7]. As with the MGI proposed by Michael (Taylor, 2011), the indicators ought to be simple and manageable enough *(amounting perhaps to not more than 15)* so as to be able to effectively communicate a message to a targeted audience of churches, policymakers, business establishments and citizens. Aside from *raising awareness* among the general public, the indicators are envisioned to eventually lead to the development and implementation of policies and measures *(decision-making)* to promote an economy of life by averting structural greed.

An economy of life is by definition an economy where greed lines and poverty lines are carefully respected. An economy of life is optimal when greed indicators' values are in moderation

---

6 [Rom. 8:20].
7 UNDP, Human Development Report, 2011. http://hdr.undp.org/en/.

with respect to the currently maximum achievable (greedy human performance) and the minimum (poverty human status) statistically available.

3. ASSESSING ECONOMY OF LIFE INDEX (EcoLI) WITH THE "GLIMS" MODEL

Our assessment of greed is based on Christian teaching, which sheds light on the Trinitarian nature of human being (Andrianos, 2011). Greed is the desire for the fulfillment of the threefold needs of human being: material (ecology), mental (economy) and spiritual (socio-political) needs. Therefore, the Economy or life assessment should have three simultaneous targets:
- **Ecological sustainability/integrity**: Measure of natural resources consumption in supporting human needs and economical growth;
- **Economic sustainability/performance**: Quantification of money accumulation which is an assessment of mental achievement of human being to secure standards of living; and
- **Socio-political sustainability/justice**: Evaluation of power inequality and ethical implications for the improvement human happiness and survival now and for the generations to come.

The Economy of life index (EcoLI) is the inverse of the Multidimensional Structural Greed index (MSGI) in percentage:

EcoLI = 100 – MSGI %

The MSGI of the system whose greed level we are asked to appraise has three major dimensions: environmental or ENV-GI (ecological sustainability), monetary or MON-GI (economic financial) and socio-political or POW-GI (power inequality) [Fig.1]. These three indexes will be referred to as the primary components of the MSGI. The overall Multi-dimensional Structural Greed index is then a function of the individual subsystem's integrity, which will be devised logically via fuzzy logic in an equal weight. This function consists of combinations of IF-THEN rules operating on rule bases derived from expert knowledge. By their nature, such functions are highly non-linear. The term integrity is defined as the degree to which each greed variable fulfills criteria of greed lines. Criteria of greed lines are recommended critical target that each greed indicator should pass to become in a greedy status.

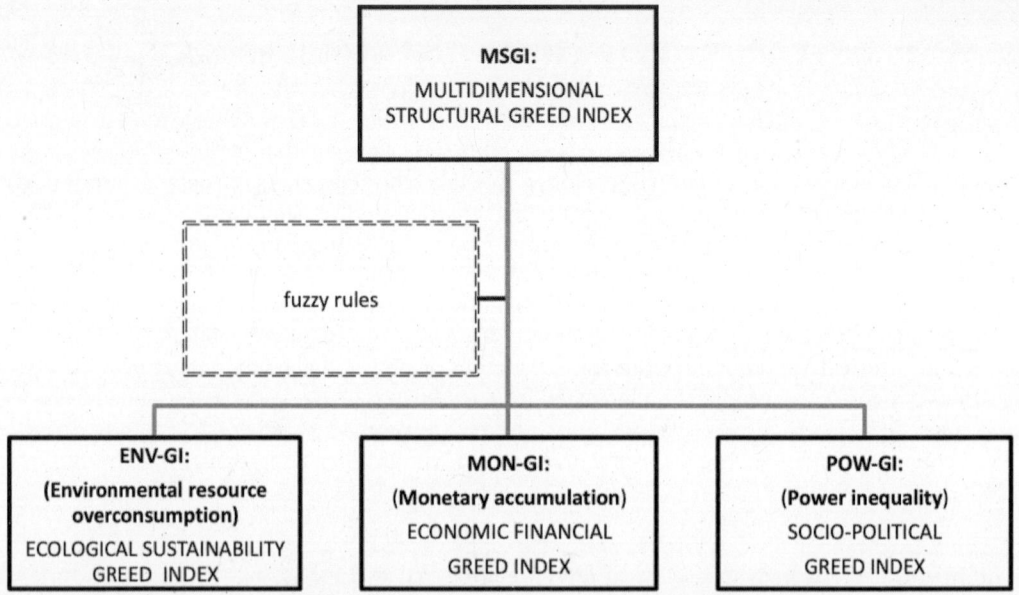

Figure 1: Linguistic variables for the multidimensional structural greed index measurement

3.1 Measurement methodology and selection of greed indicators

The methodology of the measurement of greed indexes, as well as the concept for the selection of greed indicators are depicted in the following figure 2 [Fig 2, see next page].

Analytically, the multidimensional structural greed index (MSGI) of a country/individual is a combination of three primary component of structural greed:
– **Environmental component (ENV-GI)**, referred as the ecological sustainability greed index,
– **Monetary component (MON-GI)**, measured as the economic financial greed index, and
– **Power greed component (POW-GI)** that is the socio-political greed index.

The Physical dimensions of the three primary greed indexes comprise five secondary structural greed indexes, which are:
– Ecological sustainability greed index (ESUS-GI),
– Financial greed index (FINA-GI),
– Economic greed index (ECON-GI),
– Social greed index (SOCI-GI), and
– Political greed index (POLI-GI).

Louk Andrianos

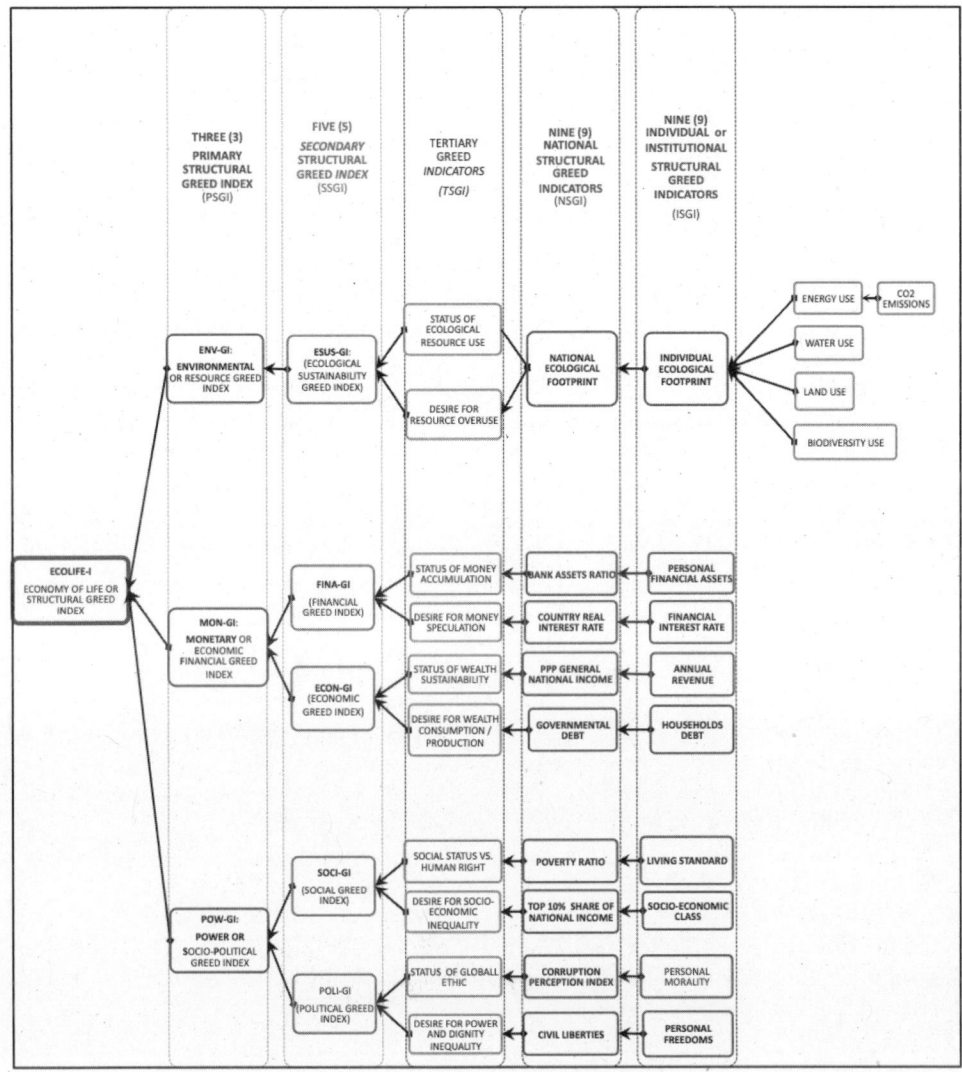

Figure 2: Methodology of the greed indexes measurement and selection of indicators

Each secondary greed index is then assessed using the "Status-Desire/Trends" approach, which assumes that greed is computed by the assessment of the current achievement (status) of accumulation or consumption of goods, money or power and the "desire" to increase or to reinforce that situation (desire/trends).

Therefore the five secondary greed indexes are the result of the combination of nine (9) *variables* of structural greed, called "*greed indicators*" as represented in the figure 2.

- **Ecological sustainability greed index (ESUS-GI)** comprises only one greed indicator:
  (1) The *global ecological footprint (on national or individual level)*, because it is an evaluation of both status and desire aspects of resource use including "land use", "biodiversity use", "water use", "energy use" and CO2 emissions;
- **Financial greed index (FINA-GI)** comprises two tertiary components or financial greed indicators, which are:
  (2) The bank assets ratio (national level of financial assets share) or personal financial assets (on institutional or individual level) as status indicator for money accumulation;
  (3) The *country real interest rate* (national level) or *fiancial interests rates* (on institutional or individual level) as desire/trends indicator for money speculation greed;
- **Economic greed index (ECON-GI)** comprises also two tertiary components or economic greed indicators, which are:
  (4) The *PPP GNI* (purchase per parity gross national income) or *annual revenue* (on institutional or individual level) as status indicator for wealth sustainability;
  (5) The *governmental debt as percentage of GDP* (national level) or *households debts* (on institutional or individual level) as desire/trends indicator for wealth production vs. consumption;
- **Social greed index (SOCI-GI)** comprises three tertiary components or social greed indicators, which are:
  (6) The *poverty ratio* (national headcount percentage) or *living standard* (on institutional or individual level) as status indicator for social greed with respect to human right;
  (7) The *top 10% of national income* (national level) or *social class* (on institutional or individual level) as desire/trends indicator for socio-economic inequality;
- **Political greed index (POLI-GI)** comprises two tertiary components or political greed indicators, which are:
  (8) The *corruption perception index* (national level) or *morality standard* (on institutional or individual level) as status indicator for global ethic;
  (9) The *civil liberties indicator* (national level) or *personal freedoms* (on institutional or individual level) as desire/trends indicator for power seizure and dignity inequality;

To build the fuzzy rules within the GLIMS model, membership functions, greed line functions and greed index function should also be attributed to all greed variables of primary, secondary and tertiary greed indexes.

3.2 Membership functions and greed line functions

The final MSGI and the three primary linguistic variables (Environmental, Monetary and Power) of greed indexes take the linguistic values: *"very poor"* (VP), *"poor"* (P), *"sufficient"* (S), *"greedy"* (G), and *"very greedy"* (VG).

The linguistic variables for the five secondary greed variables (Ecological, Financial, Economic, Social and Political) are: *"very low"* (VL), *"low"* (L), *"intermediate"* (I), *"high"* (H), and *"very high"* (VH).

For the nine basic greed indicators, we use three linguistic values, which are: *"poor"* (P), *"sufficient"* (S), and *"greedy"* (G).

Illustrations of membership functions of the linguistic values are shown graphically in Figure 3.

Louk Andrianos

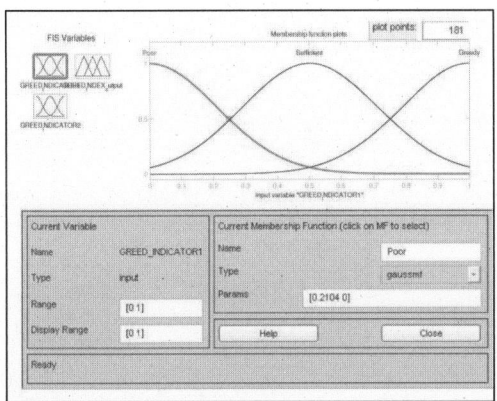

Figure 3: Examples of membership functions for linguistic values of greed

Greed line functions could be a decreasing or increasing function of the values of indicators. It would be a decreasing function of environmental protection, incidence of democracy and morality and would be an increasing function of the ecological footprint, resource consumption, income per capita, poverty, inequalities and disrespects of human rights.

3.3 Fuzzy rules and Economy of Life index (EcoLI) measurement

The knowledge ruling the computation of EcoLi or MSGI of any system is represented by fuzzy rules whose general form is:

"IF (PREMISE) THEN (CONCLUSION)"

The rules are expressions of the role of inter dependencies among various dimensions of greed. These rules are the results of multidisciplinary analysis about greed and its polymorphous effects. Economists, ecologists, theologians and other experts agree that the three components of greed should be given identical weight in an overall measurement[8]. Knowledge acquisition methodologies, such as interviews or questionnaires, can also be used to build the rules[9].

Examples of fuzzy inference rules used in the GLIMS model are shown in the following figure 4 (see next page).

3.4 Data processing and greed indicators manipulations

To measure the multidimensional structural greed on national and individual level, a Simulink model, named GLIMS, was built with the aid of fuzzy logic within MATLAB toolbox. The model comprises four steps of data processing which correspond to four orders of knowledge as follows:

- *First order knowledge bases:* Collection of greed indicators' data and normalization of statistical vales in a scale of [0, 1]. That step comprises exponential smoothing and imputation of missing data imputation.
- *Second order knowledge bases:* "Fuzzification" of the normalized value of the nine greed indicators and assessment of the five secondary structural greed indexes (ESUS-GI, FINA-GI, ECON-GI, SOCI-GI, and POLI-GI).

---

8 (IUCN / IDRC, 1995).
9 (Zadeh, 1973; Ericsson and Simon, 1984).

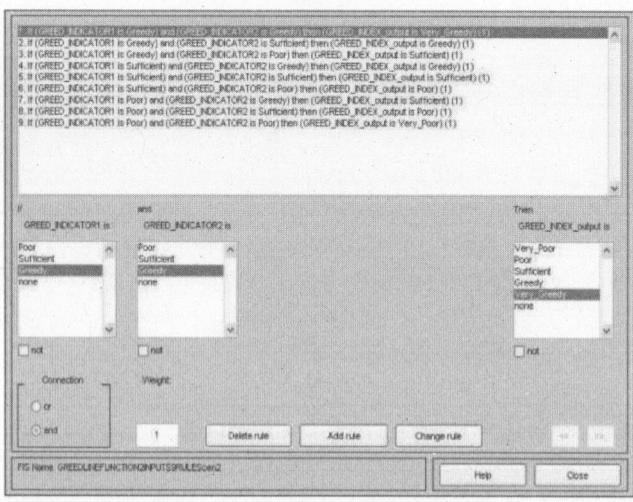

Figure 4: Examples of fuzzy rules for greed index assesment

- *Third order knowledge bases:* "Fuzzification" of the normalized value of the five secondary structural greed indexes and assessment of the three primary structural greed indexes (ENV-GI, MON-GI, and POW-GI).
- *Forth order knowledge bases:* "Fuzzification" of the normalized value of the three primary structural greed indexes and computation of the overall multidimensional structural greed index (MSGI).

Each step includes a "defuzzification" of linguistic values into crisp scores and it could be an object for sensitivity analysis, which constitutes a practical tool for decision making (awareness and recommendations).

Quantitative values of greed indicators, whose statistical data can be obtained from many sources such as, United Nations University (WIDER)[10] and related organizations, World Bank[11], World Resources Institute[12], International Federations, governmental and nongovernmental organizations, etc., constitute the physical domains of greed variables.

Data for each basic greed indicator are normalized on a scale between zero and one to allow aggregations and to facilitate fuzzy computations. This is done as follows. To each basic indicator c we assign a *target* that we refer as the "*greed line target*", a *minimum* $\underline{c}$, and a *maximum* value $\bar{c}$ The greed line target can be a single value or, in general, any interval on the real line of the form $[t_c, T^c]$ representing a range of desirable values for the greed indicator. The maximum and minimum values are taken over the set of available measurements of the indicator from various countries or ecosystems. Detailed explanations of the selected nine greed indicators with their respective greed line assignment are given in the Annex 1.

---

10   www.wider.unu.edu.
11   http://data.worldbank.org/data-catalog/world-development-indicators/wdi-2012.
12   http://www.wri.org.

Louk Andrianos

4. EMPIRICAL RESULTS, SENSITIVITY ANALYSIS AND RECOMMENDATIONS

We apply the GLIMS model to six economies (Greece, USA, Madagascar, Ecuador, Malaysia, Canada), which are representative of major trends, in order to evaluate their EcoLI and greed indexes. The results are compiled in the following table (Table 1):

Table 1: EXAMPLES of EcoLI and greed indexes measurements for selected economies (2013-2016)

National economies EcoLI/GREED INDEXES	Greece	USA	Madagascar	Ecuador	Canada	Malaysia
ESUS-GI	41.31	63.99	25.90	31.26	55.89	33.68
ENV-GI	**41.58 (E)**	**64.17 (VG)**	**30.60 (F)**	**32.45 (F)**	**55.60 (G)**	**33.95 (F)**
FINA-GI	39.23	45.33	54.54	44.20	32.11	40.92
ECON-GI	50.20	49.87	36.12	24.70	42.96	36.48
MON-GI	**47.10 (E)**	**48.95 (E)**	**47.22 (E)**	**39.59 (F)**	**42.32 (E)**	**43.29 (E)**
SOCI-GI	29.36	28.77	51.07	37.99	22.83	34.19
POLI-GI	47.60	29.09	54.05	57.43	31.12	57.62
POW-GI	**45.46 (E)**	**36.12 (F)**	**51.88 (G)**	**48.71 (E)**	**33.39 (F)**	**47.39 (E)**
Overall MSGI score	**46.88 (E)**	**49.93 (E)**	**48.91 (E)**	**44.87 (E)**	**46.42 (E)**	**46.96 (E)**
ECONOMY OF LIFE INDEX (EcoLI=100-MSGI%)	53.12%	50,07%	51,09%	55,13%	53,58%	53,04%
Linguistic values for greed indexes: L = Low; F = Fair; E = Enough; G = Greedy; VG = Very Greedy; EG = Excessively greedy						

In a scale of 0 to 100, the discrete values corresponding to linguistic scores for "EcoLI" and "Greed indexes" are as follows:

- L = LOW for $0 < MSGI < 20$
- F = FAIR for $20 \leq MSGI < 40$
- E = ENOUGH for $40 \leq MSGI < 50$
- G = GREEDY for $50 \leq MSGI < 60$
- VG = VERY GREEDY for $60 \leq MSGI < 80$
- EG = EXCESSIVELY GREEDY for $80 \leq MSGI \leq 100$
  One economy is considered as greedy with respect to specific aspect of greed when its greed index score is greater than 50. The greed line for MSGI measurements is then [50-60] and the red light is 40 (enough level). The data for the whole set of greed indicators for each country were extracted from various statistical websites [6, 17, 19, 20, 21, 22].

National governments, institutions, churches and individuals using the Economy of Life index (EcoLI) or the multidimensional structural greed index –MSGI- measurements would be able to:
- Assess the value of their greed indexes in various sections of their functionality and activities,
- Monitor and manage their performance with respect to justice and sustainability,
- Identify their risks associated with ecological, monetary and socio-political greed,

- Set policy that is informed by behavioral realities and makes safeguarding greed lines a top priority,
- Measure progress toward their goals in overcoming greed and promoting justice.
- Perform sensitivity analysis in order to improve or design sustainable policy priorities.

We now provide some examples illustrating the application of sensitivity analysis to support structural decision-making. Sensitivity analysis pinpoints those parameters that affect the overall EcoLI or greed index MSGI critically. Policy makers then should take proper corrective actions in these critical directions. We examine the Greek economy as case study. We compute the primary components of sustainability and their sensitivities to each input greed indicators. We make the following remarks:

1. If the *derivative* with respect to a greed indicator is *negative*, then we classify this indicator as *anti-greed indicator* because an increase of its value will reduce the degree of greed index.
2. If the derivative is *positive*, then the indicator is classified as *pro-greed indicator* because an increase in its value will lead to higher greed index. Anti-greed and pro-greed indicators are crucial in establishing the best practices overcoming structural greed.
3. When the derivative is zero, the indicator is classified as *neutral greed indicator* and policy makers could ignore it when recommending short-term policies.

According to the results of sensitivity analysis and the target for each greed indicator, we may design policies to advance environmental, economic, financial, socio-political and overall greed management by

- proposing mechanisms and projects to improve *anti-greed* indicators,
- taking precautionary measures to correct *pro-greed* indicators, and
- adopting conservative actions for neutral indicators.

As the flexibility of the model permits the use of any set of indicators (in quantity and in quality), we can perform various sensitivity analysis of different greed indicators in order to evaluate strategies for overcoming greed. For technical and time based constraints, we restricted our attention to five economies, one country per continent, which could represent the prevailing political and social conditions in most countries (Mshana, 2007-2009-2012). The latter is very important because the GLIMS model takes into account subjective evaluations concerning human rights, democracy, law enforcement, etc.

To achieve the reduction of overall greed index, a balanced and continuing improvement of the three components of EcoLI is needed. Thus, a prerequisite for controlling overall structural greed is the detection of critical greed indicators that affect the value of ENV-GI, MON-GI, POW-GI and MSGI, or influence the value of ESUS-GI, FINA-GI, ECON-GI, SOCI-GI and POLI-GI.

In general, policy makers or managers should be able to identify the factors that promote or impede progress towards structural greed and obtain quantitative information about them. Each greed index is a function of a couple of basic greed indicators. Thus, for a given country or institution, just decisions should be based on assessments concerning the contribution of each indicator to the final value of ENV-GI, MON-GI, and POW-GI. Using these assessments one could set priorities for critical *anti-greed* or *pro-greed indicators* on which future policies should focus.

On national level, GLIMS sensitivity results show that more just policies for Greece should focus on enhancing the following two (2) *anti-greed indicators* and five (5) **pro-greed** indicators (ranked in order of importance in Table 2):

Louk Andrianos

Table 2: Critical greed indicators for the Greek society	
Pro-greed factors	*Anti-greed factors*
1. Central government debt,	1. Corruption index,
2. Poverty ratio at national poverty line,	2. PPP GNI
3. Ecological footprint,	
4. Income share held by highest 10%,	
5. Bank assets ratio,	

Practically, the Greek governance needs restructuring of debts and fair redistribution of wealth. Also a purification of the political system and an improvement of the ecological footprint of the Greek society are imperative.

In addition to sensitivity analysis, a further development of the Economy of Life index measurement with the GLIMS model could be very promising in raising awareness and exhorting immediate actions to control the destructive effects of greed in various levels. Among others, we recommend the followings:

- *A ranking of all countries depending on their annual EcoLi and MSGi index scores (awareness) and time series monitoring of greed indicators (database) for policy-making purpose;*
- *The promotion of online Economy of Life index measurements on individual and corporal level for self-reflection and decision making (repentance and spiritual guidance).*
- *The constitution of training centers on Economy of Life and structural greed (capacity building) on local and global level; Further researches on greed science (academic exchanges and inter-faith dialogues); and*
- *The publications of findings and actions against ECONOMY OF LIFE and structural greed problems (workshops, campaigns, websites, newsletters, and books ...).*

5. CONCLUSIONS

Church leaders, policy makers and any believers would need a scientific tool to clarify the meaning of economy of Life and quantify the effects of greed in order to establish policies for more justice and sustainability. In a scale of zero to 100, the discrete values corresponding to linguistic scores for the Economy of Life index are described as "low" ($0 < EcoLi < 20\%$); "fair" ($20\% < EcoLi < 40\%$); "satisfactory/enough" ($40\% < EcoLi < 50\%$); "good" ($50\% < EcoLi < 60\%$); "very good" ($60\% < EcoLi < 80\%$); or "excellent" ($80\% < EcoLi < 100\%$).

Similarly, one individual can be described as "excessively greedy" if the score of his/her Economy of Life index is low ($0 < EcoLi < 20\%$); or as "very greedy" if EcoLi is "fair" ($20\% < EcoLi < 40\%$); or as "greedy" if EcoLi is "satisfactory" ($40\% < EcoLi < 50\%$); or as "just" if EcoLi is "good" ($50\% < EcoLi < 60\%$); or as "very just" if EcoLi is "very good" ($60\% < EcoLi < 80\%$); or as "fully just" if EcoLi is "excellent" ($80\% < EcoLi < 100\%$).

One economy or an individual is considered as "greedy" with respect to a specific aspect of greed when its Economy of Life index score is smaller than 50%. The greed line interval for EcoLI measurements is then [40%-50%] and the red light is 40% (satisfactory level).

We present a new model, called "Greed Lines and Life Indexes Measurements System" or GLIMS, in an attempt to provide an explicit and comprehensive description of the concept of economy of Life versus structural greed. Using linguistic variables and fuzzy linguistic rules, the model gives quantitative measures of several greed indexes, which are then combined into a multidimensional structural greed index (MSGI) and finally into the Economy of Life index assessment of the system. The model allows the measurement of greed indexes in national, corporal and individual level. Therefore it is helpful for sustainable policy-making and ethical behaviors reflections.

A sensitivity analysis of the model permits to determine the evolution of greed variables subject to perturbations in the values of greed indicators. Then, the problem of overcoming greed in policy-making becomes one of specifying priorities among critical greed indicators and designing appropriate policies that will guarantee more justice and sustainability.

To achieve an economy of Life and preserve sustainability, recommendations differ from economy to economy and corrections from individual to individual. More developed countries need to focus mostly on the effect of their environmental greed whereas less developed countries should strive to correct both the monetary and socio-political system.

The Economy of Life index approach using fuzzy evaluation provides new insights of sustainability concept by tackling greed at its roots. It may serve as a practical tool for decision-making and policy design on national, corporal, communal and individual levels. Such approaches need to be prioritized and urgently implemented if we want to solve the problems of climate justice, peace and sustainability systematically.

6. REFERENCES

Andrianos, L. (2012), "Setting the greed line using biblical insights and sustainability ethics in order to avert ecological crisis". In «Ecological Theology and Environmental Ethics Vol. 2 (ECO-THEE-11) book, (editors), publications OAC, 2012. ISBN 978-960-86383-7-2.

Andrianos, L. (2011), Environmental ethics and sustainable development: a fuzzy approach. Latvian Christian Academy publication.

Andrianos, L. (2011), Structural Greed and Creation: A Theological Reflection. The Ecumenical Review, 63: 312–329.

Andriantiatsaholiniaina L. A., Kouikoglou V. S., and Phillis Y. A., (2004). "Evaluating strategies for sustainable development: Fuzzy logic reasoning and sensitivity analysis," Ecological Economics, 48(2), 149-172.

Atkinson, G., Dubourg, R., Hamilton K., Munashinge, M., Pearce, D. and Young C., (Editors), 1999. Measuring Sustainable Development: Macroeconomics and the Environment. 2nd ed., Edward Elgar, Northampton.

Global Footprint Network (http://www.footprintnetwork.org/en/index.php/GFN/page/footprint_for_nations)

Goudzwaard, Bob (2011, unpublished), "Problems and Possibilities of Indicating Poverty, Wealth and Greed," paper presented at the 2nd meeting of the Greed Line Study Group, March 2011, Crete

Larrea, Carlos (2011), "Inequality, Sustainability and the Greed Line: A Conceptual and Empirical Approach," Ecumenical Review Vol. 63, Issue 3.

Mshana, Rogate (2007), Poverty, Wealth and Ecology: The Impact of Economic Globalisation, WCC: Geneva, retrieved from http://www.oikoumene.org/fileadmin/files/wcc-main/documents/p3/poverty_24p.pdf

Mshana, Rogate, ed. (2009), Poverty, Wealth and Ecology: Ecumenical Perspectives from Latin America and Caribbean, WCC: Geneva.

Mshana, Rogate, ed. (2012), Linking Poverty, Wealth and Ecology in Africa, WCC: Geneva.

Peralta, Athena, ed. (2010), Poverty, Wealth and Ecology in Asia and the Pacific: Ecumenical Perspectives, WCC, CCA and PCC: Geneva, Chiang Mai and Suva, retrieved from http://www.cca.org.hk/resource/books/olbooks/poverty_wealth_and_ecology_in_ap.pdf.

Phillis, Y.A. and Andriantiatsaholiniaina, L.A., 2001. Sustainability: an ill-defined concept and its assessment using fuzzy logic. Ecol. Econ., 37: 435-456.

Raiser, Konrad (2011), "Theological and Ethical Considerations regarding Wealth and the Call for Establishing a Greed Line," Ecumenical Review Vol. 63, Issue 3.

Taylor, Michael (2011), "On Greed: Toward Concrete and Contemporary Guidance for Christians," Ecumenical Review Vol. 63, Issue 3

The MathWorks Inc., 2012b. http://www.mathworks.com.

UNDP, Human Development Report, 2011. http://hdr.undp.org/en/

World Council of Churches, http://www.oikoumene.org

http://www.sustainability.tuc.gr/index.html

http://www.moralityindex.com/

http://www.footprintnetwork.org/en/

www.wider.unu.edu

ANNEX 1: Explanations of the nine selected greed indicators on national level

The GLIMS model uses nine (9) structural greed indicators that could be related to different levels (world, national, institutional, communal or individual) and permits to assess three (3) primary greed indexes (ENV-GI, MON-GI, POW-GI) in addition to the overall Economy of Life index (EcoLI).

The following tables explain the physical domain and greed lines values for each greed indicator on national level:

1ST greed indicator: ENVIRONMENTAL RESOURCE USE

Basic indicator denomination	**National Ecological Footprint**
Primary component:	Environmental greed index(ENV-GI)
Secondary component:	Ecological sustainability greed index (ESUS-GI)
Tertiary component:	Sustainability index which includes both STATUS and DESIRE aspects of ecological greed
Explanation and link to greed:	The ecological footprint is the amount of biologically productive land and sea area necessary to supply the resources a human population consumes, and to assimilate associated waste. We use the global ecological footprint which is related to the biocapacity of the Earth. Lower "ecological footprint" means less greedy behavior.
Data Sources:	Global Footprint Network[13]
Units	Planet Earth or hectares per person per year
Legitimate target	The optimum value should not exceed one planet capacity. Real values are between min=0.4 planet and max=10.7 planets; the world average is 3.1 hectares per person for 2011.
Greed line interval	**[0.9 -1 planet].** Higher values mean greedier behavior.
Red light	**When national ecological footprint average is > 1 planet Earth**

2nd greed indicator: MONEY ACCUMULATION

Basic indicator denomination	**Bank capital to assets ratio (%)**
Primary component:	Monetary greed index (MON-GI)
Secondary component:	Financial greed index(FINA-GI)
Tertiary component:	Money accumulation (STATUS)

---

13 (http://www.footprintnetwork.org/en/index.php/GFN/page/footprint_for_nations)

Louk Andrianos

Explanation and link to greed:	Bank capital to assets is the ratio of bank capital and reserves to total assets. Capital and reserves include funds contributed by owners, retained earnings, general and special reserves, provisions, and valuation adjustments. Capital includes tier 1 capital (paid-up shares and common stock), which is a common feature in all countries' banking systems, and total regulatory capital, which includes several specified types of subordinated debt instruments that need not be repaid if the funds are required to maintain minimum capital levels (these comprise tier 2 and tier 3 capital). Total assets include all nonfinancial and financial assets. Higher bank assets ratio reflects higher greed for money accumulation.
Data Sources:	International Monetary Fund, Global Financial Stability Report, World Development Indicators, World data bank[14]:
Units	Percentage (Financial assets divided to total assets)
Legitimate target	The optimum level should be in moderation between min=4,5% and max=21% . The World mean bank assets ratio for most recent data 2008-2012 is 9,35 %.
Greed line interval	**[0- 4,5%]. Higher values mean greedier behavior.**
Red light	**When bank assets ratio > minimum positive value=4,5 %**

3rd greed indicator: MONEY SPECULATION

Basic indicator denomination	**Country real interest rate (%)**
Primary component:	Monetary greed index (MON-GI)
Secondary component:	Financial greed index(FINA-GI)
Tertiary component:	Money speculation (RESPONSE)
Explanation and link to greed:	Real interest rate (RIR) is the lending interest rate adjusted for inflation as measured by the GDP deflator. Higher values express high level of greed for money speculation.
Data Sources:	International Monetary Fund, International Financial Statistics and data files[15]:
Units	Percentage
Legitimate target	The optimum level should be in moderation between min = minus 28,2% and max=41,7% . Any positive interest rate is a form of greed. The World average for all economies in 2011 is 4,5 %.
Greed line interval	**[0% – 5%].** Higher values mean higher level of greed.
Red light	**Red light when RIR value is > 5%**

4th greed indicator: WEALTH SUSTAINABILITY

Basic indicator denomination	**Purchasing power parity general national income (PPP GNI) per capita**
Primary component:	Monetary greed (MON-GI)
Secondary component:	Economic greed (ECON-GI)
Tertiary component:	Wealth sustainability and accumulation (STATUS)

---

14 (http://data.worldbank.org/indicator/FB.BNK.CAPA.ZS/countries?display=default)
15 (http://data.worldbank.org/indicator/FR.INR.RINR/countries?display=default)

Explanation and link to greed:	GNI per capita based on purchasing power parity (PPP). PPP GNI is gross national income (GNI) converted to international dollars using purchasing power parity rates. An international dollar has the same purchasing power over GNI as a U.S. dollar has in the United States. GNI is the sum of value added by all resident producers plus any product taxes (less subsidies) not included in the valuation of output plus net receipts of primary income (compensation of employees and property income) from abroad. Data are in current international dollars. This indicator is commonly used to evaluate the status of wealth sustainability at the national level. Higher values express higher level of greediness for wealth accumulation (between min=530$ and max=37910$ for 2011)
Data Sources:	World bank indicators16
Units	Current U.S.$ based on PPP, purchasing power parity / capita
Legitimate target	29453 U.S.$ (95 percentile of accumulated data, over which the structural economy could be considered as greedy). Moderation between the min=340 U.S.$] and max=86440 U.S.$ for 2011]
Greed line interval	**[30000 U.S.$ – 40000 U.S.$] / capita.** Higher values mean greedier economy.
Red light	**Red light when ratio is > 40000 U.S.$/ capita**

5th greed indicator: WEALTH CONSUMPTION VS. PRODUCTION

Basic indicator denomination	**Central government debt, total (% of GDP)**
Primary component:	Monetary greed (MON-GI)
Secondary component:	Economic greed index (ECON-GI)
Tertiary component:	Wealth consumption vs. production (DESIRE)
Explanation and link to greed:	CGD is the entire stock of direct government fixed-term contractual obligations to others outstanding on a particular date. It includes domestic and foreign liabilities such as currency and money deposits, securities other than shares, and loans. It is the gross amount of government liabilities reduced by the amount of equity and financial derivatives held by the government. Because debt is a stock rather than a flow, it is measured as of a given date, usually the last day of the fiscal year. Lower values mean less greedy government (between min=0 and max=483,84%)
Data Sources:	World Bank[17]
Units	Percentage of Gross Domestic Product (GDP)
Legitimate target	100%: limit over which the nation is considered as over-indebted and suffer socio-economic crisis because of greedy governmental behavior
Greed line interval	**[80% – 100%].** Higher values mean greedier economy.
Red light	**Red light when ratio is > 100%**

---

16 http://data.worldbank.org/indicator/NY.GNP.PCAP.PP.CD/countries
17 http://data.worldbank.org/indicator/GC.DOD.TOTL.GD.ZS?display=graph

Louk Andrianos

6th greed indicator: SOCIO-ECONOMIC STANDARD

Basic indicator denomination	Poverty headcount ratio at national poverty line (% of population)
Primary component:	Greed for power (POW-GI)
Secondary component:	Social greed (SOCI-GI)
Tertiary component:	Socio-economic situation (STATUS)
Explanation and link to greed:	National poverty rate is the percentage of the population living below the national poverty line. National estimates are based on population-weighted subgroup estimates from household surveys. In any case, poverty is an indicator of greed insofar as it gives an unjust picture of income distribution.
Data Sources:	Global Poverty Working Group. Data are based on World Bank's country poverty assessments and country Poverty Reduction Strategies. Catalog Sources World Development Indicators18 or "Population below poverty line by country", CIA World Factbooks 18 December 2003 to 28 March 201119.
Units	Percentage of population living under the poverty line.
Legitimate target	The legitimate target is zero poverty. Any positive poverty ratio can be translated as greed for inequality and social injustice. Values range between min=1,1% and max=86%.
Greed line interval	**[0% - 10%]**. Higher values mean greedier economy.
Red light	**Red light when ratio is > 10%**

7th greed indicator: WEALTH INEQUALITY

Basic indicator denomination	Income share held by highest 10% (top 10% income share)
Primary component:	Greed for power (POW-GI)
Secondary component:	Social greed (SOCI-GI)
Tertiary component:	Wealth redistribution (DESIRE/TRENDS)
Explanation and link to greed:	Percentage share of income or consumption is the share that accrues to subgroups of population indicated by deciles or quintiles. This indicator is known as the Top 10% or Top 1% share of national income depending on the deciles used. Income inequality refers to the extent to which income is distributed in an uneven manner among a population. In the United States, income inequality, or the gap between rich and poor, has been growing markedly for some 30 years. In 2007, the top 1% share of national income peaked at 23.5%. The only other year since 1913 that the wealthy had claimed such a large share: 1928, when the top 1% share was 23.9%. The following year, the stock market crashed, and the 'Great Depression' began. After peaking again in 2007, the U.S. stock market crashed in 2008, leading to the so-called 'Great Recession.' In any case, whether or not inequality is linked to market crashes, it is an indicator of greed insofar as it gives an unjust picture of income distribution.

18   http://data.worldbank.org/indicator/SI.POV.NAHC/countries
19   Retrieved from http://www.NationMaster.com/red/graph/eco_pop_bel_pov_lin-economy-population-below-poverty-line&b_printable=1

Data Sources:	World Bank, Development Research Group. Data are based on primary household survey data obtained from government statistical agencies and World Bank country departments. Data for high-income economies are from the Luxembourg Income Study database. For more information and methodology, please see PovcalNet [20] .
Units	Percentage: Income inequality distribution share held by highest 10%
Legitimate target	The legitimate target for top 10% share of income can be set at the smallest value that current economies may achieve. Analyses have shown that the share of top income earners should not exceed 20% otherwise economic crisis might be inevitable[21] . Values range between min=25.8% and max=44.4% and an average of 35,8%
Greed line interval	[0% - 20%]. Higher values mean greedier economy.
Red light	**Red light when Top 10% share ratio is > 20%**

8th greed indicator: ETHIC AND MORALITY

Basic indicator denomination	**Corruption perception index (CPI)**
Primary component:	Power greed (POW-GI)
Secondary component:	Political greed (POLI-GI)
Tertiary component:	Global ethic (STATUS)
Explanation and link to greed:	International Transparency, the coalition against corruption, gathers data for all countries to compute the Corruption Perceptions Index (CPI). CPI expresses a degree of misuse of power by public officials and politicians for private gain such as bribes, favoritism, embezzlement of money, etc. Corruption is an obvious expression of greed in that decisions of public or institutional interest are distorted for private gain.
Data Sources:	Transparency International[22]
Units	The CPI ranks countries on a scale from 10 (very clean) to 1 (highly corrupt). As of 2012, the CPI ranks 176 countries "on a scale from 100 (very clean) to 0 (highly corrupt).
Legitimate target	10: We should have zero tolerance for corruption as it is an obvious sign of greed. Lower values reflect a corrupted and obviously a greedy society. Real values range between min=1.7 and max=9.6.
Greed line interval	[6– 8]. Higher value is for less greedy society.
Red light	**Red light when ratio is < 6 which means that we need zero tolerance to greed in corruption**

---

20   (http://iresearch.worldbank.org/PovcalNet/index.htm).http://data.worldbank.org/indicator/   SI.DST.10TH.10/ countries

21   (http://inequality.org/income-inequality/).

22   http://www.transparency.org/policy_research/surveys_indices/cpi;   http://en.wikipedia.org/wiki/Corruption_Perceptions_Index

Louk Andrianos

9th greed indicator: PROTECTION OF HUMAN DIGNITY

Basic indicator denomination	Civil liberties (CL)
Primary component:	Power greed (POW-GI)
Secondary component:	Political greed (POLI-SGI)
Tertiary component:	Human right (TRENDS)
Explanation and link to greed:	Freedom is a basic human right need. Less freedom results from greedy behavior of the powerful ones. The Freedom House Annual Survey employs a Civil Liberties checklist to help monitor the progress and decline of human rights worldwide.
Data Sources:	World Audit[23]
Units	Each country is rated on a seven-category scale, 1 representing the least free and 7 the most free.
Legitimate target	1: One should not tolerate any violation of freedom as it is an obvious sign of greed. Higher values reflect high level of liberty and low values imply violation of human right in a greedy society. Values range between min=1 and max=7.
Greed line interval	**[5 - 6].** Higher value is for less greedy society.
Red light	**Red light when ratio is < 5** which means that we strive for zero tolerance with respect to greed in freedom violation

---

23 (http://www.worldaudit.org/civillibs.htm)

THE THIRD PARTY IN THE COVENANT

A Theology of Animals

Bernd Kappes

This contribution is about the input of Theological Zoology[1] on Ecological Theology. Ecological theology strives for a theological redefinition of the relationship between humans and nature. What is the place of humans in creation? Theological zoology strives for a theological redefinition of the human-animal relationship. What are human beings – In relation to animals?

The relationship between humans and animals is a prominent case of ecological theology. "Nowhere does nature ... meet us more vividly and directly than in animals."[2] In the human-animal relationship, the individual and social relationship to nature becomes particularly clear, tangible and evident. At the same time, our interaction with animals is an outstanding field of learning, which enables us to put into practice a new relationship with nature as a whole.

Theological zoology takes up the findings of evolutionary biology (1) and behavioural biology (2). It aims to rediscover the biblical culture of respect towards animals (3). Thus a theology of animals can finally redefine the human-animal relationship (4) and plead for a culture and spirituality of creature and fellow-creature (5).

1. Close and Distant Relatives – Evolutionary Biology

A friend of mine underwent neck surgery last year. At first she didn't want to tell me what exactly had to be done. Later she told me: It was the gills that caused the problems. The gills? My friend – a fish?

Yes, the fish in us.[3] The reptile in us. The monkey in us. But only the evolutionary kinship with the monkeys has made it into our consciousness. The tailbone, on which once a tail hung, reminds us sometimes painfully of it. But fish and reptiles also belong to our family tree. And LUCA can explain to us why.

LUCA is our all "Last Universal Common Ancestor". This is the famous first unicellular organism that was formed in water about 3.5 billion years ago. All life on Earth comes from this grandmother-grandfather-cell: animals, plants, human beings. The unicellular organisms became multicellular organisms, from which sea animals and aquatic plants eventually developed.

Much later, about 370 million years ago, the marine animals went ashore. Fins became legs. In the history of evolution, the gill arches developed into our lower jaw, the bones of the middle ear

---

1 Concerning the approach of Theological Zoology see the work of the Institute for Theological Zoology in Münster, which celebrates its 10th anniversary in 2019: https://www.theologische-zoologie.de/ .
2 Simone Horstmann/Thomas Ruster/Gregor Taxacher: Alles, was atmet. Eine Theologie der Tiere, Regensburg 2018, 17. [All quotes from German texts are translated into English by the author.]
3 Cf. Neil Shubin: Der Fisch in uns. Eine Reise durch die 3,5 Milliarden Jahre alte Geschichte unseres Körpers, Frankfurt/M 62015.

and the vocal apparatus (larynx). We usually don't take any notice of that. But with some people the heritage of the gill arches becomes suddenly noticeable at the neck, or can always be seen as a tiny hole at the edge of the ear.

And as far as the reptile in us is concerned: in the first weeks of pregnancy it becomes apparent that our ancestors laid eggs. At the beginning of the embryonic stage, a yolk sac is visible with ultrasound. However, yolks no longer exist and the corresponding genes are no longer active. Likewise, the protective skin of dead cells on the upper side of our epidermis is an evolutionary remnant that reminds us of our relationship to the reptiles.

"Kinship" is the decisive keyword: As human beings we are not only related to other human beings. As humans, we are not only descendants of Adam and Eve, but also of LUCA, the first cell from which all life on earth developed. That's why we're related to everything that lives. Also plants, animals, fungi and bacteria belong to our – close or distant – relatives.

While we are not descended from the turtles that come to the beach on the Pacific coast in El Salvador to lay their eggs, we are related to them, because "Tiktaalik"[4] is our common ancestor – the transitional animal between fish and land creature, which Darwin did not know in his time, but which he called "the primeval creature" that had long ago crawled out of the water and onto the land.

In his concluding sentence in the "Origin of Species", Darwin already expressed his admiration for the connection between the common origin of all life, and yet the wonderful diversity of life on earth: "There is grandeur in this view of life, with its several powers, having been originally breathed into a few forms or into one; and that ... from so simple a beginning, endless forms most beautiful and most wonderful have been, and are being, evolved."[5]

Who are we humans? Who are we – from an evolutionary point of view – in relation to the animals? In the Tree of Life we humans are not the crown, but only a small branch. We are not separated from the animals by a large ditch – humans and animals are only two (or more) branches of the same tree.

Animals (and plants) are our relatives. Humans are not only social beings, but "biosocial"[6] beings. Humans are one (very special) species amongst other (very special) species.

Principally, we know all that. "But where has the memory of man's animal origin remained in cultural history? Have humans lost their evolutionary memory? Have they repressed their animal past?"[7] Although we actually "know" about the closeness and kinship of all species, we seem to be culturally more concerned with opposing this and making distinctions between the two categories "human" and "animal" (or "nature"). One must understand that. It's all about our identity.

2. Human and Other Animals – Behavioural Biology

The scientific image of animals has undergone fundamental change in recent decades. Speaking of a "paradigm shift" is appropriate here. The gap between humans and animals has narrowed further and further. There is not only the "animal in man", but also much more "man in animal".[8]

---

4   Neil Shubin a.a.O., 47ff. reports about his discovery of the transitional animal "fish with fingers".
5   Charles Darwin: On the Origin of Species, 1859.
6   Larry Rasmussen: Earth-Honoring Faith. Religious Ethics in a New Key, New York 2015, 12.
7   Horstmann/Ruster/Taxacher, loc. cit., 119.
8   With regard to the following insights of modern behavioural biology cf. Norbert Sachser: Der Mensch im Tier. Warum Tiere uns im Denken, Fühlen und Verhalten oft so ähnlich sind, Reinbek [2]2018.

Three decisive dogmas of the scientific animal image have collapsed:
1. Dogma: No statements can be made about the emotions of animals.
2. Dogma: Animals can't think.
3. Dogma: Animals behave for the good of their species.

2.1. Emotions

Animals have feelings. Scientific statements made by behavioural biologists about the feelings of animals are based on the one hand on the measurement of stress hormones, and on the other hand on observations of behaviour.

Behavioural indicators of animal discomfort are lack of food intake, apathy, neglect of personal hygiene, idle movements, and movement stereotypes. In threatening situations, different species of mammals even show identical fear reactions: A racing heart, deep breathing, stress hormones, a face of fear.

Mutual licking, crawling and cuddling can be observed as indicators of well-being. But even sounds emitted by animals are signs of their well-being. Rats, for example, "laugh" or whistle when they are tickled, and they like to be tickled. All mammals like to play, also many bird species, even some fish, and even some invertebrates, e.g. field wasps.

The observations of behavioural biology are confirmed by the findings of evolutionary biology: emotions are generated in the limbic system, one of the oldest brain structures present in all mammals. Whether a child or a piglet is happy: the same nerve pathways, the same messenger substances and the same genes are activated.

2.2. Thinking

Already Aristotle was of the opinion: Animals lack reason. Aristotle regarded the assumption that only man had logos/reason as the essential distinguishing factor between humans and other living beings. Modern cognitive biology, on the other hand, assumes that all animals learn, many think, and some have ego-consciousness:

All animals learn, i.e. they change their behaviour based on their own experiences or they learn from others: Macaques were observed learning the "culture" of potato washing from each other. The building of sunroofs for orang-utans or the use of leaves as gloves is also "culturally" conditioned.

Many animals think, i.e. they solve problems not only by trial and error, but also by insight, knowledge and plan: Not only apes use tools, but also sea otters and dolphins, ravens and parrots.

Some animals have a consciousness of themselves, i.e. they can recognize themselves in the mirror: Apes, elephants, dolphins and magpies.

2.3. Animal Personalities

Descartes regarded animals as automatons whose behaviour is determined by fixed stimulus-reaction reflexes. In the same 17th century and on the basis of the same assumptions, dogs were dissected alive. Behavioural biology today speaks of animal personalities whose behaviour is shaped by genes, environment, socialization and social experience.

As with humans, the prenatal phase, childhood (animal children need a social environment, the satisfaction of material needs is not enough) and adolescence (with the hormonal changes and social experiences of adolescents taking place here) are decisive for the formation of the respective animal personalities.

So in scientific research: the individuality of the different animals moves into the centre of attention. Animals have their own specific personalities and their individual characters. They show permanently distinguishable behaviour – and this applies not only to chimpanzees, elephants and dolphins, but also to songbirds, fish, reptiles and insects. Leaf beetles, for example, show courage or are hesitant when it comes to exploring a new environment.

2.4 Conclusion

Animals have many characteristics and abilities which until recently were regarded as typically human. This applies, as illustrated, to feelings, thoughts and behaviour. But it also applies to the egoism of animals: there is also violence, rape, infanticide (lions) and wars (chimpanzees) among animals. Man in the animal – that also means: animals are not the better human beings.

Common features of all mammals can be recorded: The same genes (the correspondence between humans and chimpanzees is 98.5%, i.e. we are as closely related as horses and donkeys are[9]), the same brain structure (similarities down to the smallest detail, e.g. identical neuronal processes, e.g. in anxiety) and the same hormones (sexual hormones and stress hormones occur in the same form in humans, bats, rhinos and dolphins).

But then, what is the difference between humans and animals? "There is no doubt that man possesses the highest cognitive abilities of all living creatures."[10] But is it a gradual or categorical difference between humans and animals? "On the one hand, no animal composes a symphony, writes a novel, builds a cathedral or formulates an action programme against climate change. On the other hand, animals are capable of cognitive performance to which two, three or four year-old children of our own species are incapable."[11]

Do humans have a special position and role among all living beings? We will come back to that question later.

3. The Third Party in the Covenant – Biblical Theology

Is it appropriate to speak of a "biblical culture of respect towards the animals", as I did at the beginning of this article? Cultures exist only in the plural, and it is not without reason that a basic anthology on animals in ancient Israel bears the title "Companions and Enemies of Man"[12].

In fact, it would be inappropriate "to argue against the ignorance of animals in the Christian tradition with the assumption of a generally animal-friendly attitude of the Bible".[13] Just think of the words from Gen 9,2: "The fear and dread of you shall rest on every animal of the earth, and on every bird of the air, on everything that creeps on the ground, and on all the fish of the sea; into your hand they are delivered."

Nevertheless, the declared aim and interest here is to pay attention to some central biblical

9   Richard David Precht: Tiere denken. Vom Recht der Tiere und den Grenzen des Menschen, München 2018, 101.
10   Sachser, loc. cit., 243.
11   Sachser, loc. cit., 244.
12   Bernd Janowski/Ute Neumann-Gorsolke/Uwe Gleßmer (Ed.): Gefährten und Feinde des Menschen. Das Tier in der Lebenswelt des alten Israel, Neukirchen-Vluyn 1993.
13   Horstmann/Ruster/Taxacher, loc. cit., 148. Special challenges for an animal theology arise, for example, through the biblically testified practice of ritual animal sacrifice or through the distinction between pure and impure animals. Cf. Horstmann/Ruster/Taxacher, loc. cit., 241ff and 273ff.

traditions which express the connectedness and community of humans and animals as well as of God and animals.

3.1. Balaam's Donkey

For a biblical theology of animals, the story of Balaam's donkey (Numbers 22, 21-34) can be the portal through which we enter the space of biblical traditions of the human-animal relationship. Animal ethics, partnership of human beings and animals, as well as the relationship of animals to God come into view here.[14]

"What have I done to you that you have struck me these three times?" Balaam beats his donkey, he beats her again, finally beating her with the riding crop. Here the ethical question is raised: Do humans have the right to apply direct and structural violence against animals? Are we allowed to "beat" animals?

"Am I not your donkey?" The possessive pronoun here seems to be less an expression of ownership than of trust and relationship. Animal and man, Balaam and his donkey are on the way together, "from long time ago until this day". Here the partnership between humans and animals is concerned, the common history and community of the fellows and their mutual interdependence. Humans need the animals, are carried by the animals, live a life "on the back of the animals"[15]. The story emphasizes closeness, connectedness and togetherness between humans and animals.

"The donkey saw the angel of God standing in the road." The donkey saw the angel of God – the prophet did not see him. The animal obviously has its own relationship to the divine, obviously also its own senses and ways of knowledge, which are not accessible to man. What's more, the animal even helps the prophet to perceive the divine in the context of everyday life.

3.2. Creation

Jürgen Moltmann distinguishes between two ways of reading the biblical narratives of creation (Gen 1-3):

> "According to the modern interpretation, man is the 'crown of creation'. Humans alone are created in the image of God and destined for dominion over the earth and all earth's creatures. ... According to the second account of creation they should 'cultivate and preserve' God's Garden of Eden more like a gardener. This sounds milder and more mindful, but in both creation narratives man is the subject and the earth together with all its other inhabitants are the objects. ...

According to the new ecological reading of the same creation stories of the Bible, man is the last creature of God and thus the most dependent creature. Man depends on the existence of animals and plants, on the air and the water, on the light and the times of day and night, on the sun and the moon and the stars and cannot live without them. Man only exists because there are all these other creatures. They can all exist without man, but man cannot exist without them. ... man is first of all a creature in the great community of creation and 'a part of nature'. ... According to biblical traditions, God breathed his divine spirit not only into man, but into all his creatures."[16]

---

14   Cf. Rainer Hagencord: Diesseits von Eden. Verhaltensbiologische und theologische Argumente für eine neue Sicht der Tiere, Regensburg ⁴2009, 185ff.
15   Hagencord, loc. cit., 185.
16   Jürgen Moltmann: Die Hoffnung der Erde. Die ökologische Wende der christlichen Theologie und der christlichen Spiritualität, EvTh 74 (2014), 217ff.

I follow the ecological reading and add: God's blessing of the creation is not only for humans, but also for animals. Animals are even "the first who are blessed"[17]. The land animals are created like humans on the sixth day of creation and are closest to humans. Humans and animals appear here as creatures and fellow creatures in the greater community of creation.

3.3. Covenant

Humans and animals perish together in the flood and are saved together in the ark. It is remarkable that in the story of the flood not only the "cute and the useful"[18] are rescued in the ark, i.e. not only the domestic animals and the farm animals, but all animals. Here the criterion for the preservation of the species is apparently not the benefit for humans, but the will to live and the right to live of all living beings.

After the Flood, God makes a covenant – not only with humans, but also with animals. "As for me, I am establishing my covenant with you and your descendants after you, and with every living creature that is with you, the birds, the domestic animals, and every animal of the earth with you, as many as came out of the ark." (Genesis 9:9 f.) Also the animals are God's partners in the covenant – the third party in the covenant!

3.4. Wisdom

The words of God in the Book of Job (Job 38-41) express that humans are not alone in the centre of divine attention: "Do you know when the mountain goats give birth? (Job 39:1) "Who has let the wild ass go free?" (Job 39:5) In this divine invitation to integration and humility, humans are not at the centre of creation, but rather part of a larger life context. The animals have their own habitats, needs and rhythms.

"All eyes await thee, O Lord, and thou givest them their food in their time. You open your gentle hand and satisfy everything that lives there with pleasure." Are we aware that these words from Psalm 104, set to music by Heinrich Schütz, do not only refer to human beings, but to "everything that lives there", that is to say also to animals and plants? In this psalm, man is a part of creation and is nourished like "others": "You cause the grass to grow for the cattle...". (Ps 104,14) "The trees of the Lord are watered abundantly." (Ps 104:16) In this psalm there is no expression of a special position of humans in creation. It is not about human dominion, not even about humans as stewards of creation.

In these texts the animals have their own right to life, independent of humans and human interests. God's attention and care is also for the animals, not only for human beings. It is not without reason that the "intrinsic value of every creature" is one of Laudato Si's central motifs.[19]

4. Man – Crown of Creation?

What is the place of man in creation? What is the human being – in contrast to the animal? Is man the crown of creation?

The findings of evolutionary biology show that humans are not the aim of evolution. Human life is, in evolutionary perspective, one form of life among others. Modern behavioural

---

17   Rainer Hagencord: Die Würde der Tiere. Eine religiöse Wertschätzung, Gütersloh 2011, 123.
18   Rainer Hagencord: „Sein Tierreich komme", Greenpeace Magazin 2/2019, 44.
19   Pope Francis: Laudato Si. On Care for our Common Home, 2015, No. 16.

Bernd Kappes

biology describes the proximity of humans and animals in terms of feelings, thinking and behaviour. And also in biblical perspective a human being is not the crown of creation, but rather the Sabbath.

But what is then the explanation of the de facto special position of human beings? How has it come about that one species de facto dominates all other species – in forms of domestication, extinction or allocation in reserves?

"Humanity has indeed subdued the earth,"[20] Yuval Noah Harari soberly states. "70,000 years ago, Homo Sapiens was an insignificant animal living in a remote corner of Africa. In the following millennia, it became the ruler of the entire planet and the terror of the ecosystem. ... Again and again the massive increases in human power meant no improvement for the individual human being and immense suffering for other living beings."[21]

Is language the secret of human success? Was it language that gave the human species almost absolute power over all other species? But what is new and special about human language? Many animals have languages, even if we as humans cannot perceive or understand them. What do humans see, hear and understand with their limited senses at all? The laughter of the rats and the song of the whales – even trees communicate with each other![22]

Harari sees the decisive difference in man's ability to "fictitious language"[23]: We can talk about things that don't exist. What's more, we can even imagine fictitious things *together*. This is how collective imaginary worlds emerge, which Harari calls "invented orders": nations, money, human rights, laws, companies, and gods – things on which we have intersubjectively agreed.[24]

"Invented orders" enable effective cooperation between people who have never met before. People in Puebla and Baunatal believe in the existence of the same company and follow the same rules – in the end a VW Golf rolls off the production line. Only man can do that. The invented, but very powerful orders thus ensure man's ability to work together flexibly and in large groups. Some of these invented orders function for a certain time without any problem due to generally shared convictions, e.g. the idea of private property. Other orders are enforced and maintained by coercion and violence, e.g. the invention of borders.

Harari illustrates just how powerful ideas, narratives and myths can be with the example of the French Revolution: Yesterday people still believed in the rule of the king, today they believe in the rule of the people and sweep away the monarchy.

Harari concludes: "As individuals and even as small groups, we are so similar to chimpanzees that it is almost embarrassing. Clear differences are visible only when we cross the magic line of 150 individuals."[25] And: "Humans are relatively weak animals, whose strength lies above all in their ability to communicate and cooperate in large groups."[26]

This is no good news for all the other species that are not capable of this kind of communication and cooperation and suffer from dominion and power of the human species.

The good news, however, is that invented orders can be questioned and changed or replaced by new invented orders. Only people can replace the idea of monarchy with the idea of democ-

---

20   Yuval Noah Harari: Eine kurze Geschichte der Menschheit, München [23]2015, 428.
21   Harari, loc. cit., 507.
22   See Peter Wohlleben: Das geheime Leben der Bäume. Was sie fühlen, wie sie kommunizieren – die Entdeckung einer verborgenen Welt, Kiel 2015.
23   Harari, loc. cit., 37.
24   For the distinction between objective, subjective and intersubjective see Harari, loc. cit., 148ff.
25   Harari, loc. cit., 54.
26   Harari, loc. cit., 197.

racy. Yes, only people write novels and build cathedrals, but also only people found and set up women's movements (after having followed patriarchal concepts for centuries).

No collective idea of order has fallen from the sky: apartheid, caste system, colonialism, slavery, patriarchy, the hierarchy of rich and poor – everything is contingent, changeable, object of struggles for power, interests and liberation.

Of course, this also applies to our concepts of the human-animal relationship. Also the categorization "human vs. animal" is an invented order. It is "absurd to divide the world of animals into two categories – human and non-human. This gap is first of all – like everything else – a conceptual distinction made by man and not predetermined by nature".[27] We humans are animals too: human animals.

What does this mean in terms of animal rights? "Homo sapiens has as few natural rights as spiders, hyenas and chimpanzees."[28] In other words: The codification of human rights is the result of the struggle for human rights. In the same way we can intersubjectively agree on rights for spiders, hyenas and chimpanzees. Which rights are to apply to whom is always being fought over, negotiated, finally regarded as normal and regulated by law.

In addition to race, gender and class, the question of species must also be added to our analyses of power and domination if we want to overcome our basic assumption of the fundamental preference of the human species over other species). Our collective ideas of order should in future also include the rights of nature and the rights of animals, with whom we inhabit and share the earth as the house of life.

It is also clear: "To grant rights to animals does not mean to treat them like humans."[29] A right to vote for bats wouldn't make much sense. "These rights can only be formulated through the most appropriate human assessment of the needs of animals."[30] We will therefore have to reach an intersubjective agreement on which rights should apply to which species. Every demarcation and hierarchy will be also an "invented order". The minimal goal should be to overcome an instrumental and objectifying understanding that regards animals only from the perspective of human benefit as things and raw material for so-called "meat production".

But even these new worlds of imagination do not fall from the sky, but must be fought for. Theological zoology is a (discursive) contribution to this, as it describes the human-animal relationship as a relationship between creature and fellow creature and promotes a culture and spirituality of creature and fellow creature. Or to express it with the theological idea of God's covenant with humans and animals: "From this covenant 'with us' follow the fundamental human rights. ... From this covenant 'with ... all living beings' follow the rights of nature."[31]

5. House of Life – Ecumenism and Ecology

The encyclical "Laudato Si" bears the subtitle "On care for our common home". The image of the earth as a common home of life is a familiar metaphor within the ecumenical movement. This metaphor easily connects with social and ecological dimensions: As human beings we are connected

---

27 Precht, loc. cit., 51f.
28 Harari, loc. cit., 141.
29 Precht, loc. cit., 235.
30 Horstmann/Ruster/Taxacher, loc. cit., 35.
31 Jürgen Moltmann: Wiederentdeckung der Erde – Neue Spiritualität, DPfBl 2/1995, 53.

Bernd Kappes

with people from other continents, other cultures, other denominations, other religions. We live together in the common "house" (oikos), we share the "inhabited earth" (oikoumene) with each other.

But we share the earth as the house of life not only with other people, but also with animals (and plants). The chamois and wild donkeys also belong to our co-inhabitants in this house of life. Obviously conflicts are part of life and part of the dynamics of living together.

In such an ecumenical-ecological vision our socially based models experience an ecological expansion:[32] community not only as human community, but as community of all life; justice also as ecological justice; overcoming violence also as overcoming violence against animals (and nature); peace as peace with the animals (and with the earth); love also as love for the animals. Within this vision of a "peaceful and friendly coexistence"[33], the basic rule for animal ethics should be "where there is no direct obligation to kill, to treat animals as non-violently as possible."[34]

But how does this vision relate to the fact that only in Germany 600 million chickens, 60 million pigs, 40 million turkeys and 25 million ducks are slaughtered every year?[35] For Jonathan Safran Foer, "war is just the right word" to describe our relationship with animals: "We are fighting a war against all the animals we eat."[36] Why do we have different standards of empathy, ethics and treatment for pigs and dogs? Would we lock a dog in a wardrobe for life?[37]

And how does the vision of community and connectedness of all life relate to the dramatic extinction of species that we are currently experiencing? One million animal and plant species are threatened with extinction in the coming decades. The main reasons for this are agriculture, fishery, climate change and pollution – the ecological consequences of our industrialised way of life. In Africa, half of all mammal and bird species could have disappeared by 2100. In Europe, the number of insects has already fallen dramatically. The report of the World Biodiversity Council IPBES, which was presented to the world public in Paris at the beginning of May 2019, makes it clear that the loss of biodiversity poses just as great a threat to the future of life as climate change.

In our present we are witnesses of the disappearance of animals – through the anthropogenic extinction of species as well as through so-called "modern" forms of animal farming, which largely hide the short life and slaughter of a gigantic number of animals from our eyes. At the same time the animals come closer to us again – through new ways of thinking in behavioural biology, in (sub)cultures and cultural studies and increasingly also in theology and spirituality.

Talking about animals means talking about us as human beings: What is the place of man in creation? What is man – in relation to the animals? Friedrich Schorlemmer puts it in a nutshell: "Humanism means living as humans and fellow humans – and as creatures and fellow creatures."[38] In other words: Until recently the idea of humanism has referred to not treating human beings like things. Today we have to extend this idea to not treating animals like things either.

---

32   About 100 years ago Albert Schweitzer demanded the overcoming of an anthropocentric ethics for the first time: "The big mistake of all previous ethics is that they thought they only had to do with the behaviour of man towards man. In reality, however, it is about how he relates to the world and all life that enters his realm. He is ethical only if life as such, that of the plant and the animal as well as that of man, is holy to him." Quoted after Harald Steffahn (Ed.): Albert Schweitzer. Lesebuch, München 1984, 173.
33   Horstmann/Ruster/Taxacher, loc. cit., 16.
34   Precht, loc. cit., 304.
35   Figures for 2012 cited by Böll Foundation (ed.): Fleischatlas. Daten und Fakten über Tiere als Nahrungsmittel, Berlin 2014.
36   Jonathan Safran Foer: Tiere essen, Köln 2009, 45.
37   See Foer, op. cit., 225.
38   Friedrich Schorlemmer: Unsere Erde ist zu retten. Haltungen, die wir jetzt brauchen, Freiburg 2016, 156.

NOKEN: AN ECO-ETHIC METAPHOR FOR A CREATION-BASED MISSION MODEL

From "Soul Evangelism" to "Life-Flourishing Evangelism"

Maraike Bangun

My Socio-ecclesial Location as a Theological Source: A Brief Introduction I would like to express my gratitude to the committee for inviting me to contribute to the conversation in this important meeting, which aims to find an inter-contextual theological perspective in responding to the complex challenges of the ecological crisis today. Describing briefly my social location in this setting is important to reveal ways in which my social-ecclesial location not only shapes but reorients my theological view on the intertwining of missiology, theology of creation, eco-theology, ecumenism and the theological understanding of sustainability. I am Maraike Joanna Belle Bangun, an Indonesian born in the Philippines when my missionary parents were working in cooperation with the Wesleyan Church of the Philippines. In 1987, my parents returned back to Indonesia and remained active as member of the Indonesian Wesleyan Church. Following my parents' footsteps, for my first fifteen years, I am a member of the Indonesian Wesleyan Church. But when I started senior high school, with the permission from my parents and blessing from my Wesleyan pastor, I joined a local charismatic[1] church, Gereja Kristen Kemah Daud (GKKD/David Camp Church), in Jakarta, Indonesia.

Remain a fervent charismatic follower of Christ, two years after high school, however, I chose to pursue my theological education at Jakarta Theological Seminary (JTS), the oldest Protestant (ecumenical) seminary in Indonesia. The choice is considered unusual for JTS has been considered by many as "liberal" – meaning "unevangelical" and "uncharismatics." My then pastor at GKKD did not suggest me to pursue my theological education at JTS but at the same time gave me the freedom to choose by saying, in 2003, "If you are convinced that it is the voice of the Holy Spirit that leads you to study there, then go." I took her suggestion seriously. I was praying ceaselessly and, along with my spiritual mentor, took a day fast during the discernment time. My conviction to pursue my study at JTS was only becoming stronger.

While maintaining my membership in my charismatic local church, I finished my Bachelor of Theology and Master of Theology studies at JTS. In between the periods of doing the undergraduate and graduate studies, I rejoined (after high school I spent two years helping my parents with the youth ministry) my parents who already assumed their missionary work in Sabah, Malaysia under the auspices of a local charismatic church, Covenant Sanctuary. The members of this church are mainly migrant workers and their families from Indonesia and the Philippines.

---

1   Charismatic in the sense emphasizing more on the work of the Holy Spirit with various signs such as speaking in tongue, laying in the spirit, holy laughter, and many more. Having an intimate relationship with the Holy Spirit through prayer and singing (worshipping) is very important in order to be able to hear God's voice and to discern many aspects in live.

My total five years experience in Malaysia exposed me to the reality of migration. Their narratives of survival, resilience, and their audacity to hope for a better future regardless of the daily discrimination, fear, and uncertainty challenge me to rethink about a concept of mission and evangelism that is relevant for their daily reality. I later channelled their stories through my thesis research that offered a theological perspective on shifting from soul-evangelism to compassionate presence. This work has shaped my understanding, as it is indicated in this presentation, of the need to rethink of mission and evangelism from within the reality of migration. This background has also influenced my interest in focusing on the intertwining of mission, women, migration, and postcolonialism in my doctoral study at Hamburg University.

My church background does not necessarily direct me to focus in the question of eco-care in my spiritual and ecclesial formation. However, my experience as a woman coming from Indonesia, a country with one of the world's largest natural resources (forests, ocean, gold, oil, coal, etc) and with one of the biggest ecological problem, and my theological studies and ecumenical formation at JTS have extended my horizon on the importance of integrating the challenges of ecological crisis into my theological perspective.

In this presentation I offer a missiological perspective on the complex interconnection of theology of creation and ethics of sustainability by sharing the story of West Papuan women of Indonesia. The wider context of their story is the complex interconnection of the history of military violence, deforestation, women's resilience for life, and the role of the church with the women's local and national networks to build a model of sustainable way of life that offers a perspective on eco-ethics of life that based on justice and peace for the earth and its implication on the lives of the most marginalized group in the society: women, children, and the indigenous people.

I call the story of the local West Papuan women a story of noken. Noken is a head-held knotted net or woven bag handmade from wood fibre or leaves made by the Mamas (the nickname for Papuan women). Using noken as a missional metaphor, I argue that the story of local Papuan women, which is shaped by history of violence, ecological crisis, and the resilience for building a sustainable life for all, illustrates the need to construct a creation-based mission model. It is a model that shifts the traditional understanding of evangelism as a soul-centered practice to a life-flourishing practice. Furthermore, it is a model that perceives evangelism as a way of life that sustains and nourishes a just relationship between humanity and the whole creation, including other human being.

A Theology of Creation

It is not a secret that somehow it is difficult to get Christians to care about the environment. What kind of theology of creation do many Christians understand that shapes their understanding of their relationship with God's whole creation? For me, and many of my evangelical-charismatic friends, what is written in Genesis 1 and 2 is the foundation of theology of creation. It explains how the world and humanities came into existence. Some even believe that this narration is "scientific," thus any other explanation that is not in align with this narration would be considered wrong. It is believed that the process of creation stopped on the sixth day. What we are having and living is the effect of creation, the fall of man and God's working of salvation through Jesus Christ. The word evolution is seen as a way of thinking that conforms to the rejection to the "thus God says and it becomes." Even though we learn about the theory of evolution, about how the universe, the earth, plantation, animal and human being came into existence scientifically, we are already used to compartmentalize science from faith. And in this case, faith is the ultimate of our life and the whole creation, especially nature, is secondary or not important at all.

These ways of thinking affect the way we understand salvation. We emphasize more on the importance of saving soul so that one day we can be one with God in the heaven. I still remember a question that triggered me to surrender my life to Christ, "If one day you go out of this place and were hit by a car and died, where you will go? Heaven or hell?" At those times, these questions were very compelling and somehow have changed my priorities in life. The idea that one day God will bring new heaven and earth is understood as something that will happen in "the life after death." We perceive that the world is just a passing ground before we could reach the heaven. Hence, things related to environmental crisis is something strange for our language of faith. In the Indonesian Wesleyan Church and GKKD, I never once in my life time heard of any sermon that is related to the ecological crisis, never.

Another reason that shape our belittling attitude towards nature is the notion that positioned Christianity as superior than the nature because it is believed to be "home" of evil spirits.[2] For instance, Dana L. Robert recorded that German people was "won" into Christianity after Bishop Boniface have felled the Sacred Oak of Thor in northern Hesse in 732 and used the wood from the Oak tree in order to build a church.[3] Another similar story also took place in a village, now a part of Jakarta, Indonesia, where a protestant missionary by the name of Frederik Lodewijk Anthing was able to win many locals in 1870s after he was able to fish in a lake that is considered as "sacred."[4] According to the oral narration, Anthing would normally recite the Trinity formulation, the Lord's Prayer, and the Ten Commandments in the local language in order to beat any "power" before fishing.[5] Based on at least these two examples, though Robert also showed "a diversity of missionary attitudes towards traditional nature-based practices"[6], we can see how Christianity is somehow positioned as greater, powerful and thus superior than any other religions, and particularly over nature.

It is important to note that there are also other practical reasons on why Christians do not see ecological crisis as something urgent. Daniel Gilbert, quoted by Kanan Kitani, argues that human being lack the ability to response to on the ecological crisis because there is no PAIN (Personal, Abrupt, Immoral, and Now). In terms of ecological crisis, it is not clear how it impacts people personally (P) and presently (Now) because it seen as something that will threat us in the future

2   Dana L. Robert stated wrote: "Drawing an analogy with Elijah and the priests of Baal, Boniface challenged the pagan gods to strike him down as he cut down the tree. According to Boniface's first biographer, a wind blew down the oak while he was chopping it. After Thor did not strike Boniface dead, the people began converting to Christianity." In "Historical Trends in Missions and Earth Care" in Creation Care in Christian Mission, ed. Kapya J. Kaoma (Oxford: Regnum Books International, 2015), 72.
3   Ibid.
4   Koernia Atje Soejana, Berakar, Tumbuh, Berkembang dan Berbuah: Mengupas Kisah Perjalanan Injil di GKP Jemaat Kampung Sawah (Jakarta: Majelis GKP Kampung Sawah, 2008), 15-19.
5   Ibid. The Trinity formulation is "Bopo Allah, Putro Allah, Roh Suci Allah, telu-telune dadi siji upas racun dadi towo, lemah sangar, kayu angker dadi towo, isti Gusti, Tuhan Yesus Kristus Juruselamet kami salami-lamina (God the Father, God the Son, God the Holy Spirit, the three in one, poison becomes ineffective, haunted place and woods are not dangerous anymore and lost its power, by the will of God: Jesus Christ is forever more savior)." According to the Dewi Agustina, the pastor at Gereja Kristen Pasundan Kampung Sawah, this method is proven to be effective because until now, most of the older members are very faithful in their faith to Jesus Christ despite of the many obstacle and persecution they experienced when they were young.
6   Robert, ibid., 71.

(Abrupt) and, at the same time, it does not make us feel disgusted (Immoral).[7] Lacking of PAIN is experienced more by those who comes from a middle class society and those who experience PAIN are the mostly affected and impoverished by the ecological crisis like the indigenous people, people living in slum areas, women who have to fetch water for more than 2 km everyday, and those whose living provision is dependent immediately on nature.

Soul-Evangelism as the Core of Christian Mission

In this section I purposely want to deepen our discussion on soul-evangelism as the main reason, apart from the are other reasons, for the many evangelical-charismatic Christians, particularly those who are at the grass-root level, to pay very little oncern, or in my church case not at all, on the issue of ecological crisis. Soul evangelism is a term coined by Bryan P. Stone by explaining "a popular consensus among Christian as to what evangelism is and is not."[8] Out of six, here are the fundamental features of soul evangelism:

- "The dualism between an immortal soul and a perishable body that houses this soul during its relatively short journey on the earth."[9] This dualistic thinking that is inherited from the Greek thought emphasizes that "the world is an inferior and imperfect shadow of something more real, unchanging, and perfect" and salvation in envisioned in terms of "the soul's escape from its earthly prison."[10] Thus, its implication for evangelism is to save souls.
- The implication of saving souls is "its clear preference for personal salvation over corporate salvation."[11] "Salvation is strictly a matter between the individual and God."[12] Hence "emphasis is placed on what has come to be called 'personal evangelism' – the effort to lead individuals to a personal relationship with Jesus."[13]
- "Human existence as a test rather than a constructive project."[14] "Evangelism, in this view, is envisioned and carried out as an effort to get people pass the test, enter the lifeboat, get their ticket, or the like."[15] No wonder, when I asked, through WhattsApp groups, if someone ever heard any sermon about ecological crisis and Christian faith in GKKD, the answer is never. One even answered that we are the citizen of the heaven and not the earth. This is in align with Stone's comment, "If the soul of a person is all that finally matters, any form of evangelism that spends even the slightest bit of energy on anything not directly related to the ripening and harvesting of souls for eternity is doing nothing more than putting a new coat of paint on the Hindenburg."[16]

---

7   Kanan Kitani, a Japanese theologian who is teaching at Doshisha University, presented her paper in Green Reformation: Ecology, Religion, Education and the Future of the Ecumenical Movement conducted by Ecumenical Theological Education (ETE) of World Council of Churches (WCC) on 12th – 15th of May, 2019, in Bossey, Swiss.
8   Bryan P. Stone, Compassionate Ministry: Theological Foundation, 9th ed. (Maryknoll: Orbis Books, 2006), 147.
9   Ibid., 144.
10   Ibid.
11   Ibid., 145.
12   Ibid.
13   Ibid.
14   Ibid.
15   Ibid.
16   Ibid.

Maraike Bangun

Stone concluded that this consensus theology of evangelism "fits in so well with the maintenance of patterns of domination and subordination, racism and segregation, sexism and oppression in our society, not to mention the destruction of our planet's natural biosphere."[17]

"Soul Evangelism" to "Life-Nourishing Evangelism"

It is no doubt that soul evangelism has become an important part of my life and many other Christians. This idea shapes our understanding and the way we relate to others and other creation up to the point where the salvation of human being is the centre of Christian faith thus affecting our understanding of mission. Thus, in this part, I argue that there should be a shift from "soul evangelism" to a "life-flourishing evangelism." Life-flourishing evangelism is a way to testify to the life that is inherent in the whole creation from the site of repentance and vulnerability. It is compelled by a realization, quoting Amos Yong, that:

> "while 'the earth was a formless void and darkness covered the face of the deep,' the author of the creation account notes that 'a wind from God [ruach Elohim] swept over the face of the waters' (Gen. 1:2). So while traditional creation theologies have highlighted the creation of the world through the word of God, the word of God is uttered through the divine breath and the 'history' of the world is 'blown' or swept along by the presence and activity of the ruach Elohim. The partitioning of the waters from land, the emergence of vegetation, the evolution of life itself each of these can be understood from this pneumatological vantage point as being propelled by the breath of God that transcendentally hovered over the primordial creation. But the divine breath is not only transcendent over the creation but also immanent within it. This is because all living creatures have been constituted by Elohim's 'breath of life' (Gen. 1:30)."[18]

This way of testifying is embedded in the hope of the resurrection of the seed of life that is inherent in whole creation. God has the power to resurrect and as human being our testimony is embodied in our participation as steward by watering the seed, making sure that the soil is good, and protecting it. We are called provide a congenial environment so that that seed of life can grow in a healthy or vigorous way – then it will flourish.

Evangelism in this sense is birthed out of metanoia with "a broken spirit and a contrite heart" (Ps. 51:7), a position of repentance from all the greediness[19] that human being possess due to the exploitation of the environment. It is accepting that we are the main cause of environmental de-

---

17   Ibid., 148. This is in align with Kenneth Ross' critique on Christian mission: "It has to be conceded that Christian mission has usually been conceived in terms of the spiritual transformation of individuals and the new inter-human relationships effected through the salvation offered by Jesus Christ. It has been preoccupied almost exclusively with God's interaction with humanity. Concern for the natural environment has been secondary or absent." See Kenneth Ross, Edinburgh 2010: Fresh Perspectives on Christian Mission. (Pasadena: William Carey International University Press, 2010) 69.

18   Amos Yong, "The Mission Spiritus: Towards A Pneumatological Missiology of Creation" in Creation Care in Christian Mission, ed. Kapya J. Kaoma (Oxford: Regnum Books International, 2015), 124.

19   "Human greed is the source of source of most the ills of the world. But human greed is what is needed in the industrial society if you want to make it according to the law of the market." Margot Kässmann, "Covenant, Praise and Justice in Creation: Five Bible Studies" in Ecotheology: Voices from South and North, ed: David G. Hallman, 2nd ed. (Maryknoll: Orbis Books, 1995), 42.

struction. The practice of soul evangelism has failed to transform the sin of greediness because it "allows white middle and upper classes to retain their social privileges and comfort and still consider themselves Christian" and at the same time "allows minorities and the poor in our society to adjust psychologically to their exclusion and dehumanization, to put up with it."[20] In regards to the environment, we can say that the environment has become "the least among us" and the practice of soul evangelism has failed to serve the environment. The claim that people whose souls are saved authentically, by accepting Jesus as their personal saviour, will begin to transform society and work to overcome poverty and justice, is proven wrong! This human-centeredness of salvation, on the other hand, has become the basis of turning our eyes from the exploitation of the environment, and to some extent the exploiter.

Life-nourishing evangelism is practiced with from the site of vulnerability, knowing that we as human being are completely nothing without the whole creation. It is oes not come from the site of abundance and power that claims to have the truth thus should be translated to others. Hence, the sustainability of life should be the guiding principle of evangelism. The question that has to be raised intentionally is "Does our evangelism nourishes life for all?" There should be no more binary compartmentalization between human and the rest of creation or between body and soul or between gospel and social activities. We are interrelated to one another. From a Trinitarian perspective, it is impossible to detach God the Creator from Jesus the Word, Jesus the Word from Holy Spirit the Breath of God and Holy Spirit the Breath of God from God the Creator. This interrelatedness and interconnectedness is no stranger for many indigenous worldview regarding themselves and the nature.[21]

Not until the church pay less attention on life after death and the crowns/rewards "to be accepted" in "heaven," the church will never lay its eyes on the earth. All effort, money, resources and life will be centred on "saving souls" through various programs and targets. There should be a paradigm shift in understanding the theology of salvation that is not limited to ones soul but to the whole being of creation, in which human being is in it.

Noken: Life-Nourishing Mission and its Implication for Ecumenical Eco-ethics

"We women of Papua have been bruised, cornered, besieged from all directions. We are not safe at home, and even less so outside the home. The burden we bear to feed our children is too heavy. The history of the Papuan people is covered in blood, and women are no exception as victims of the violence of blind military actions. We have experienced rape and sexual abuse in detention, in the grasslands, while seeking refuge, no matter where we were when the army and police conducted operations in the name of security."[22]

---

20   Ibid., 147-148.
21   Upolu L. Vaai, a Fijian theologian who is now the rector of Pacific Theological College (PCT), employing the local wisdom of the people in Fiji, suggested that there should be a shift from Eco-Theology (ET) to Eco-Relatedness-Theology (ERT). He presented his thoughts at Green Reformation: Ecology, Religion, Education and the Future of the Ecumenical Movement conducted by Ecumenical Theological Education (ETE) of World Council of Churches (WCC) on 12th – 15th of May, 2019, in Bossey, Swiss.
22   https://www.ictj.org/publication/enough-enough-testimonies-papuan-women-victims-violence-and-human-rights-violations accessed on 17th of June 2019. This is report "'Enough is Enough!': Testimonies of Papuan

In this last section of this paper, I would like to draw our attention to the Papuan women in Papua and West Papua Provinces in order to borrow their spirit of resiliency in facing a massive violence that destroys their body as women and also the nature where they live in. The quotation above is a testimony of a survivor of systematic gender-based violence from the military of Indonesia and also domestic violence in their own household that is reported by International Center for Transitional Justice (ICTJ), the Women Commission, and the Women Working Group of Papuan People Assembly. The report is a collection of stories of violence and abuse that occurred in 1963-2009 that was done over three months, interviewing 261 people (243 women and 18 men).[23] "This documentation effort aims to understand different patterns of violence, including abuses committed by security forces and resulting from efforts to seize natural resources in Papua, as well as violence women have experienced in their own households since the army took control of the region in 1963."[24]

In this context, noken plays an important role in the daily lives of the Papuan women. I would like to suggest that the way we relate and understand each other in the sphere of ecumenism, and also in the interreligious relationship sphere, can be symbolized by a noken. Noken is a head-held knotted net or woven bag handmade from wood fibre or leaves by communities in Papua and West Papua Provinces of Indonesia. The materials being used is mostly tree roots or tree barks. The mamas (the nickname for Papuans women) will knit the fibres into a bag. Noken symbolizes the birth of life and fertility that is represented from the way noken can accommodate many objects and how it resembles the female's womb which contains a baby. According to Rev. Dr. Fransina Yoteni, when a baby is born, people will ask, "Is it a noken (female) or an arrow (male)?"[25]

By using noken the Papuan women carries their children, food resources (Lebensmittel), seeds for farming, or earth productions to be sold at the traditional market.[26] Noken also functions as cloth or blanket that warms the body; it accompanies the Papuan women wherever they are – from birth to death.[27] In the context of political suppression from the military, Papuan women are prohibited from knitting the cultural symbol of Bintang Kejora[28] (the rising star) on their noken because this symbol is considered as subversive – a symbol of the desire to be separated from Indonesia. Though prohibited, Bintang Kejora, that is also a symbol of dignity for the Papuan, is inherent in the pattern of the knitting.[29] The cultural-philosophical of noken births new lives through the coming of the raising star.[30]

The ability to knit noken is handed from generation to generation by the Mamas. This is a testimony of the flourishing life in the the lives of the Papuan women who are survivor of vio-

---

Women Victims of Violence and Human Rights Violations 1963-2009" is prepared in cooperation of the National Commission on Violence Against Women (Women Commission), Women Working Group of Papuan People's Assembly and the International Center for Transitional Justice (ICTJ) Indonesia with support from HIVOS and the Swiss Embassy. The report can be downloaded through the link above.

23   Ibid.
24   Ibid.
25   Interview with Rev. Dr. Fransina Yoteni, a lecturer at I.S. Kijne Theological Seminary in West Papua and member of the Central Committee of World Council of Churches (WCC), on 17th of June 2019. I wrote some questions and she replied in a hand-written note.
26   Ibid.
27   Ibid.
28   Ibid. Fransina wrote: "According to the law, UU No. 21/2001, Bintang Kejora/Bintang Fajar is a cultural symbol. Thus the Indonesian government should not fear us. For us to be able to live on a daily basis is a grace of God."
29   Ibid.
30   Ibid.

lence, but also survivor of the exploitation of their natural resources. It is no secret that Papuan mountains are being destroyed for the greedy American corporation and Indonesian government. Fransina wrote:

"When the management of Freeport McMoran met the local Papuan people, Mama Yo-sepha Alomang carried her noken and spoke, "We had carried you in this noken but now we throw you out because you have destroyed my breast, that is: Ersberg and Grasberg mountains.""[31]

In the sphere of ecumenical eco-ethics, we can borrow noken as a symbol of life-flourishing evangelism in order to emphasize the importance of offering the good news from the site of vulnerability – without other creation we are doomed – with a realization that life itself is inherent in the

---

31 Ibid. Translation from "Satu contoh lagi ketika terjadi pertemuan antara Management Freeport McMoran dengan masyarakat adat, Mama Yosepha Alomang pikul dia punya noken lalu bicara dan bilang, 'Kami sudah mau kamu, dulu kami taruh dalam noken in tetapi sekarang kami buang, sebab ko bikin rusak mama punya dada, yaitu gunung-gunung Ersberg dan Grasberg.'" Mama Yosepha Alomang is a Papuan women activist who advocates the issue of human rights against Papuan women.

Maraike Bangun

whole of God's creation through God's breath. We should not see others merely as object of soul evangelism, but the spirit is how can we work together to regenerate and nourish a flourishing life for all. The Papuan women, whose body is destroyed through the military and domestic violence is again destroyed when their mountains, forests, water, and lands is exploited for the benefit of a little people.[32] The knitting of Noken is a symbol of resiliency and hope. Ecumenically, in the face of the ecological crisis worldwide, we invited to knit and carry Noken together at this present time and pass this spirit to the next generation.

In the end, "we are reminded that evangelism is ultimately an activity of the Holy Spirit and is not subject to our own calculus of effectiveness and 'return on investment.'"[33] The Mamas who are knitting Noken can never calculate what will happen next, but as the rising star is knitted in the Noken, there is always dignity and hope for the flourishing of the whole creation. Noken can accommodate so many things, so should our ecumenical relationship be able to accommodate one with another in testifying to the life that is inherent in the whole creation.

Agreeing with Yong's thesis – that "the dynamism of the Spirit or the ruach (breath) of God helps us think about the dynamic and unfinished character of the world"[34] – a creation based

---

32 More information in order to understand deeper the experiences of women victims of violence in the provinces of Papua and West Papua can be accessed through a film "Sa Ada di Sini: Suara Perempuan Papua Menghadapi Kekerasan yang Tak Kunjung Usai" (I Am Here: Voices of Papuan Women in the Face of Unrelenting Violence). It can be accessed through https://youtu.be/5HHE5lfuNOA. Subtitle in English is available.

33 Bryan P. Stone, Evangelism after Christendom: The Theology and Practice of Christian Witness (Grand Rapids: Brazos Press, 2006), 21.

34 Amos Yong, "The Mission Spiritus: Towards A Pneumatological Missiology of Creation" in Creation Care in Christian Mission, ed. Kapya J. Kaoma (Oxford: Regnum Books International, 2015), 124.

model mission gives us an assurance that God is still in the creative process of bringing and at the same time resurrecting life to and in the whole creation. As one of God's creation, we are given invited and also given the responsibility to take part in the partnership with the Spirit to support the flourishing of all life. We are invited, in our vulnerability, like Mamas in Papua, to knit life through the Spirit in the community of God's creation ecumenically. Let us continue to knit and carry Noken with us.

THE CREATED LIVED AND VULNERABLE BODY RESONATING WITH THE WORLD

Perspectives for a non-anthropocentric anthropology and a body-sensitive eco-theology

Claudia Jahnel

1. Introduction: The Spirit of God poured out on all flesh and the breath of God giving life

When, in Acts 2, on the day of Pentecost the apostle Peter explains to the crowd the "strange signs" they see – enthusiastic people speaking in different languages but yet understanding each other – he recalls God's incredible promise prophesied by the prophet Joel (2, 28): "*I will pour out my Spirit on all flesh.*" This promise still awaits its complete fulfilment. Nevertheless, it has also already come true. Because, when God created the world the "Spirit of God was hovering over the waters" (Gen 1,2), and when God created "man". God breathed the "breath of life into his nostrils so that they became *living beings*" (Gen 2,7).[1] Therefore, Elihu, the friend of Job, witnesses: "The *Spirit of God* has made me; the *breath of the Almighty* gives me life" (Job 33,4).

The Biblical tradition understands human beings as *lived bodies*, in being and becoming. They consist of both: flesh and spirit. Like the whole of creation human beings are en-fleshed *and* lived creation, as the theologian of the Pietistic movement in Württemberg, Friedrich Christoph Oetinger declared: "the lived body is the final point and goal of God´s deeds."[2] The church father Tertullian says it more provocatively by using the word "flesh" and thereby bringing flesh and lived body together: "caro salutis est cardo" – the *flesh* is the cardinal point of salvation.[3]

My thesis that orients this proposal for a non-anthropocentric anthropology and a body-sensitive eco-theology is twofold:

1. Keeping flesh and lived body together is an essential point in a *theological anthropology*. The Biblical tradition neither follows the *naturalistic reductionism* that perceives the body only as object, which is susceptible to manipulation and subject to consumption. With their witness to the living Spirit of God embodied in the body of human beings as in all lived creation the stories of creation as well as of Pentecost contrast the assumption that the body is only matter and material. According to the Biblical tradition the body is not only an object that we *have* but also a body that we *are*. Nor does the Biblical tradition follow the line of a *transcendental*

---

1 Pentecostal theologians like Amos Yong or Lyle Dabney remind us that the Spirit is – together with God's word – co-actor in creation, see e.g.: Amos Yong, The Spirit of Creation: Modern Science and Divine Action in the Pentecostal-Charismatic Imagination, Grand Rapids 2011; D. Lyle Dabney, The Nature of the Spirit: Creation as a Premonition of God, in: Michael Welker (ed.), The Work of the Spirit: Pneumatology and Pentecostalism, Grand Rapids 2006, 71–86.
2 Friedrich Christoph Oetinger, Biblisches und Emblematisches Wörterbuch, Heilbronn 1776, 407: "Leiblichkeit ist das Ende der Werke Gottes".
3 Tertullian, De carnis resurrectione, VIII (2), in: Tertullian's Treatise on the Resurrection. The text edited with an Introduction, Translation and Commentary by Ernest Evans, Eugene 1960, 24.

relativism that ignores the pain, violence and injustices that material and lived bodies are exposed to, the cry of the people, the affects and emotions.

2. Building on this body-oriented Biblical anthropology I argue that keeping flesh and lived body together is crucial for an *eco-theology* because the *vulnerable and lived body* is existentially exposed to the environment with which it interconnects. The Biblical tradition reveals this resonance between the human body and creation as a whole, e.g. in the promise of the life supporting shalom that embraces the political, judicial, religious, social and creatural context.[4] Other disciplines, too, have developed schools of thought that call for a revaluation of the material and lived body. Sociologists like Hartmut Rosa e.g. state, that already in the womb the body is in touch and in deep communion with "the world." The lived body resonates with the world[5] and exposes and opens us to the other. It is, as Judith Butler claims, this interdependence between bodies that constitutes the body as starting point of ethical connections and as source for an ethical attitude towards the other.[6] My claim is, that just as the resonance between bodies can further moral sentience and ethical commitment towards other human beings[7] the resonance between body and the broader environment – the lived world – can further an ecological commitment.

The thesis might convey the impression that bodily resonance is "naturally" given as if the body autonomously follows "natural" rules of an individual interior and disregards social discourses on the body. This is not the case. Marcel Mauss has convincingly shown that physical and psychological behavior rests on learnt body-techniques and are marked by the moral codes of a society. Even emotions like weeping are not free, "spontaneous" reactions but social facts.[8] Certainly, not all, if any, bodily reactions and resonances can be understood exclusively as socially "learnt" reactions and attitudes. As Susan Brison has shown in her illuminating study on trauma, bodily resonances and reactions cannot be explained monocausally. They rather reflect the complexity of the self that contains various interlinked aspects: "the accounts of the embodied self, the self as narrative, and the autonomous self are compatible and complementary."[9]

For the purpose of developing a body-sensitive and body-oriented eco-theology this means: the resonance of the lived body toward the lived world – that I hold to be a crucial element in the development of an ecological commitment and an eco-ethical attitude – is not "naturally" given. The resonance is rather largely an informed resonance molded by various experiences and knowledge. In dependence on Brison I claim that this resonance is compatibly and complementarily shaped by embodied social discourses, by narratives of the self and by the autonomous self which consists of mind and body.

In the following I will first continue to ponder on the resonance of the body with the "world" and on how changes in the environment impact this resonance. Trends in the contemporary discourse on the body and cultural body practices and expectations are of heuristic value with

---

4 Odil Hannes Steck, Friedensvorstellungen im alten Jerusalem. Psalmen, Jesaja, Deuterojesaja (ThSt 111), Zürich 1972, 29.

5 Hartmut Rosa, Resonanz. Eine Soziologie der Weltbeziehung, Berlin 2018.

6 Judith Butler, Frames of War. When is Life Grievable? London 2010.

7 See Moya Lloyd, Towards a Cultural Politics of Vulnerability: Precarious Lives and Ungrievable Deaths, in: Terell Carver/Samuel A. Chambers (eds.), Judith Butlers Precarious Politics. Critical Encounters, London, New York 2008, 93f.

8 Marcel Mauss, L'expression obligatoire des sentiments [1921], in: Essais de sociologie, Paris 1968; id., Les techniques du corps [1936], in: Sociologie et anthropologie, Paris 1950.

9 Susan J. Brison, Aftermath. Violence and the Remaking of a Self, Princeton 2002, 41.

Claudia Jahnel

regard to this resonance because they reveal core attitudes as to how human beings experience themselves in the world and in relation to non-human creation. In a second step I will highlight apparent parallels between the contemporary body-logic disclosed by these body practices and the rhetoric of the "Anthropocene." The Anthropocene paradigmatically represents a wide-spread logic of the relation between human beings and nature. Based on critiques of the Anthropocene as well as on philosophical traditions that challenge dominant utilitarian conceptions of the body and of nature I will develop alternative perspectives for a non-anthropcentric anthropology and a sustainable body-sensitive and body-oriented eco-theology.

2. The body as indicator of environmental and social changes: between new appreciation and degradation of body and nature

Starting eco-theology with the body means to start with our socially constructed, yet fundamentally experienced way of being in the world, perceiving the world, the self and others and of being affected by the world and the other. Language witnesses this interrelatedness of the body and being in the world in a plentitude of body metaphors: "To keep one's feet on the ground" means to be sensible, well oriented and rooted in the world, physically and emotionally. We normally don't worry about the ground we stand or walk on. Our body has learned to trust that the ground will not suddenly disappear. It is an ontological certainty. Yet, in situations of crisis it can feel as if someone has "pulled the rug from under my feet."

Due to this interconnectedness of body and world, changes in the environment immediately affect the body, its orientation in the world, and the way human beings relate to the world and to nature. The extent to which alterations in climate and nature leave marks on the body is enormous up to critical. Some changes like the increase of air pollution or temperature are immediate and, likewise, leave immediate imprints on the body. Besides well-known impositions on health and emotional well-being these changes force transformations of the life-style up to the severe necessity to migrate.

Yet, climate-change is also accompanied by indirect dynamics which are highly co-responsible for the destruction of the ecological balance, e.g.: the constant acceleration of time, the escalation in which our society produces and consumes goods or the tendency to regard a certain prosperous and autonomous lifestyle as guarantor for "good life." These socio-ecological dynamics, too, leave clear marks on the body.

We can therefore state that the body is an indicator of environmental and social alterations: It embodies the sentiments, emotions, norms, and narratives that accompany socio-ecological changes, and resonates with the world, others, and nature according to this knowledge. This knowledge is by no means only cognitive knowledge but to far extent "knowledge" in the bones acquired through informed and learned experience. In order to gain more insight into the contemporary resonance between the body and its environment and into its guiding narratives I propose a closer look at dominant body practice and explore their heuristic value.

A prevalent term that comprises the current dynamic of body practices and discourse is the term "body turn."[10] Body turn indicates that after a period of disregard the body today gains crucial attention in various areas of social life. Yet, this revaluation of the body is paradoxically

---

10   Robert Gugutzer, body turn. Perspektiven der Soziologie des Körpers und des Sports, Bielefeld 2006.

accompanied by a simultaneous devaluation and suppression of the body up to the point that the body is almost disappearing. Technical and media developments make the physical presence of the body less important. Artificial intelligence and robotics replace the body and the internet creates space for fleshless avatars and "second lives." This process has its roots in the transit from modern to postmodern times. One of the characteristics of this transit are the changes in the working environment from predominantly physically hard labor to forms of work which involve mainly the brain and the "sitting capacity" of the body.[11] At the same time the process of civilizing, disciplining, regulating, and normalizing the body altered: articulations like sweating, blowing or eating without proper cutlery fell under the regime of shame over the body.[12]

On the other side, and as said above, today the body has come to the fore and is revalued, in various ways. There is e.g. an obvious increase of practices of "body enhancement" that can be observed in the fitness and sports-boom as well as in aesthetic surgery or tattooing. The more spare time we have due to technical developments, the more forms of body culture are developed for every age. The tourism branch offers a plentitude of body-experience-events, for younger as well as for "elder" people who due to the enhanced living conditions today are still in "good shape." It seems that in a time of increasing mobility, fluidity and virtuality the physical body becomes the last instance and authority of one's identity. Jean Starobinski interprets this cultivation of bodily sensations and body-narcissism as a form of regression from a world that is dominated by technical innovations.[13] New body rituals promise compensation for a rationalized world and serve as bulwark against modernity and its achievements.[14]

More critically, Terry Eagleton perceives this body-hype as "fetishisation" of the body in North-American culture, which has its roots in the American dream of self-creation – as individual beings as well as a nation. What this body cult hides and suppresses is the reality of being vulnerable as well as the idea of political resistance and solidarity. The body, Eagleton states, has a strange dual status. It is something universal and something very individual. It is the naked body which can be the base for universal connectivity of humanity because it is the conditio humana. Nakedness and its vulnerability can lead to a universal, connecting ethic of global solidarity and interdependence.[15] Eagleton's argument must not be confused with a naturalistic reductionism that conceives of the body only as manipulable material. His emphasis on nakedness and vulnerability rather stresses relationality as basic dimension of the lived body and contradicts the "making of the body" that has become normative in today's culture.

In summary, the current dominating body practices reveal the desire to shape the body according to "one's own" taste. This taste is influenced by social norms and aesthetic regimes.[16] They govern the sensations and the resonance of the body to other bodies, and shape our way of being in and perceiving us in the world. The ambition to enhance the body up to the transhumanistic appetite to expand the lifetime of the body tends to claim the superiority of "man" over the "rest" of creation, culture over nature, and emphasizes the difference between the human and the non-human. At the same time, it masks the finiteness and vulnerability of the body. It conceals the

---

11 Robert Gugutzer, Soziologie des Körpers, Bielefeld 2015, 39–42.
12 See Norbert Elias, The Civilizing Process. Sociogenetic and Psychogenetic Investigations. Revised edition. Oxford 2000; Michel Foucault, Discipline and Punish: the Birth of the Prison, New York 1977.
13 Jean Starobinski, A Short history of body consciousness, in: Humanities in Review 1 (1982), 22–39, 38.
14 Gideon Stiening, Aufklärung widerlegt! Philipp Sarasin schreibt Körpergeschichte, in: Merkur 57 (646), 2003, 164–168.
15 Terry Eagleton, The Idea of Culture, Chapter 4: Culture and Nature, 87–111, Malden 2000.
16 Jacques Rancière, The Politics of Aesthetics: The Distribution of the Sensible, London 2006.

Claudia Jahnel

fact that our earthly and compostable bodies are aging and dying, and marginalizes "other," not streamlined – precarious – bodies.

Nevertheless, the body practices today also disclose the desire to experience, sense, and feel meaning. Body practices are marked by a search for identity and – as e.g. practices of tattooing – a desire for firm relationships and connectedness to others and even to nature in a rapidly changing world.[17]

The current body practices are, therefore, not only paradoxical in the sense that they simultaneously devalue and revalue the body. They also implicitly disclose a clear ambiguity with regard to the relation and resonance between the human being and human body on the one side and the non-human world and nature on the other side. How is this relation reflected in explicit narratives and their authoritative dogmas?

3. The devaluation and revaluation of nature: The Anthropocene and its postcolonial critique

One dominant narrative in the field of the relation between the human and the non-human is the so called "Anthropocene." It represents the climax of a very anthropocentric and utilitarian view on nature. The word "Anthropocene" refers to the nobel prize winner in the field of chemistry, Paul J. Crutzen, who in 2002 wrote the essay "Die Geologie der Menschheit."[18] Crutzen claims, that the interventions of human beings in nature have had such tremendous impact on nature – especially through the CO_2 emissions – that we need to perceive our time as a new geological epoch. Since then the notion "Anthropocene" has developed from a rather descriptive term to an ideology and a "global ethos," which constructs human beings as avant-garde and masters of evolution, and hominizes the word – making it more human and more ready to serve human beings.[19]

The idea of the Anthropocene reflects, as Jürgen Manemann critically states, the American "dream of the unlimited access to resources and the individual's self-entitlement to extravagance".[20] It is the "dream to live on an unlimited earth and to live life in a constant flow of short-term rewards."[21] Human beings become the cultivators of the world, but in a radical way, using genetics and technical options.

The narrative of the Anthropocene reveals striking similarities to the current body hype. In its striving for the enhancement of the living conditions for human beings – at least for those who can afford it – it can be even viewed as an enlarged version of the contemporary body discourse. Both hold the tendency to manipulate the body and nature, and to be in control of its improvement.

---

17   This is, of course, a very generalized statement representing a Western view. Comparisons of body-identity-practices in the Global North and in the Global South reveal far more differentiated insights and issues of agency and resistance. During the last two decades the amount of studies in this field has increased too much to name them, reaching from hair-politics over mixed-race-studies to the body-politics in African Pentecostal churches.
18   Paul J. Crutzen, Die Geologie der Menschheit, in: Paul J. Crutzen, Das Raumschiff Erde hat keinen Notausgang. Energie und Politik im Anthropozän, Frankfurt a.M.: 2011, 7–10. See Jürgen Manemann, Kritik des Anthropozäns. Plädoyer für eine neue Humanökologie, Bielefeld 2014, 15.
19   Christian Schwägerl, Menschenzeit. Zerstören oder gestalten? Wie wir heute die Welt von morgen erschaffen, München 2012, 17.
20   Manemann (2014), 20.
21   Maneman (2014), 49.

In light of the fact that various aspects of the Anthropocene are not a future scenario or utopia but are, rather to the contrary, already realized critiques of the Anthropocene like Manemann call for counter-narratives: not the hominization of the world but the humanization of human beings should guide the political decision making as well as the daily life. The megalomania of the ideology of the Anthropocene should be unmasked and confronted with the vulnerability of human beings and the earth.

A radical counter-narrative is suggested by Donna Haraway. In her article "Anthropocene, Capitalocene, Plantationocene, Chthulucene: Making Kin"[22] Haraway provokes the anthropocentricism in the Anthropocene by elaborating a compost-ist perspective. "We are all compost not posthuman", she claims.[23] Instead of seeing human beings as different "kind" of species and of searching for the survival of "our kind" we should perceive ourselves as "kin" to every living being on earth and develop a multispecies eco-justice. "Bacteria and funghi abound to give us metaphors; but metaphors aside [...] we have a mammalian job to do, with our biotic and abiotic sym-poietic collaborators, co-laborers [...] we need to make-with – become-with, compose-with – the earth-bound."[24] Haraway's anthropology radically questions the underpinnings not only of the narrative of the Anthropocene but also of the assumption that has for centuries dominated the interpretation of the narrative of creation in the Old-Testament: that "man" is the "crown" of creation, the peak-point of evolution. Haraway de-mythologizes this narrative by assessing the Anthropocene as "more a boundary event than epoch" and by demanding: "our job is to make the Anthropocene as short/thin as possible."[25]

Questioning the Western roots of the ideology of the Anthropocene Haraway points to less anthropocentric "more-than-human, other-than-human, inhuman, and human-ashumus" traditions in non-Western cultures: "with names like Naga, Gaia, Tangaroa (burst from water-full Papa), Terra, Haniyasu-hime, Spider Woman, Pachamama, Oya, Gorgo, Raven, A'akuluujjusi."[26] Without mentioning it Haraway's critique thereby reveals clear parallels to post-colonial critiques of Western anthropocentrism. Gayatri Spivak e.g., calling for non-euro-centric ecological justice,[27] claims that subaltern people still reveal traces of a different, non-dichotomous – animistic – understanding of nature: in animistic thinking "nature is also super-nature in this way of thinking and knowing. (Please be sure that I am not positing some generalized 'tribal mind.') Even 'super' as in 'supernatural' is out-of-the-way. For Nature, the sacred other of the human community, is, in this thinking, also bound by the structure of ethical responsibility."[28] "Animism," therefore, for Spivak does not represent an alternative theology, as Catherine Keller states in a thought provoking article that elaborates Spivak's reference to theologies of liberation.[29] Animism rather delineates a certain form of sensitivity towards the non-human.

---

22 Donna Haraway, "Anthropocene, Capitalocene, Plantationocene, Chthulucene: Making Kin", in: Environmental Humanities, vol. 6 (2015), 159–165.
23 Haraway (2015), 161.
24 Haraway (2015), 161.
25 Haraway (2015), 160.
26 Haraway (2015), 160.
27 Gayatri Chakravorty Spivak, Critique of Postcolonial Reason. Toward a History of the vanishing Present, Cambridge 1990, 380.
28 Spivak (1990), 382.
29 Catherine Keller, The Love of Postcolonialism. Theology in the Intristices of Empire, in: Catherine Keller/Michael Nausner/Mayra Rivera (eds.), Postcolonial Theologies. Divinity and Empire, St. Louis 2004, 221–242, 296.

Claudia Jahnel

Spivak is – in her commentary in brackets – keen to avoid any "othering" of the animistic concept of nature in its relation to human beings. She even sidesteps the term "alternative" when talking about indigenous understandings of nature. Rather, she draws a fine line between these concepts and concepts of ethical responsibility that are familiar to Western thought. She thereby challenges the exotic essentialisms that some concepts of "indigenous nature-spirituality" or the "Western" concept of the "dark green religion"[30] reveal. This exoticism – be it imposed on these concepts by others or a self-identification – is a trap because a seemingly exotic point of view and critique tends not to be taken seriously but loses its power.[31]

Both, Haraway and Spivak, propose not only an alternative view on the way of being in the world, of the resonance toward the earth and nature, and of perceiving the world, the self and others. To a further or lesser extent, they also include the human body, bodily resonance to the world, and the body's interrelatedness to nature. Haraway's concept of kinship depicts the human body as "biotic" and "sym-poietic" and thereby as, for my understanding, "nature" – alike all nature including flowers or bacteria – and as "culture" (poietic) – alike the whole "rest" of nature who are cultural collaborators. In both, the natural and the cultural aspect, the resonance between human and non-human as well as their interdependency and co-dependency is apparent.

Spivak's concept does not go so far as to eliminate the difference between the human and the non-human body. Claiming that Nature (Spivak writes it with a capital N) is the "sacred other of the human community" she rather holds on to the difference. Yet, the non-dichotomous – animistic – understanding of nature reveals a desired yet often lost resonance between human and non-human, human community and sacred Nature.

There are several points of contact between the critique of Haraway and Spivak and those concepts of philosophers that have taken their starting point at the lived and enfleshed body.

4. The lived body as foundation for a non-anthropocentric anthropology

One of the core-body-concepts is the so called body-phenomenological approach or lived-body approach (Leib-Phänomenologie). To my knowledge it has not yet been regarded to high extent in the eco-theological debate.[32] The body-phenomenology leads back to the philosopher Maurice

---

30. See Bron Taylor, From the Ground Up: Dark Green Religion and the Environmental Future, in: Donald K. Swearer (ed.), Ecology and the Environment: Perspectives from the Humanities, Cambridge 2008, 89–107, 89. For a critical review of this concept see: Jens Koehrsen, Eco-Spirituality in Environmental Action: Studying Dark Green Religion in the German Energy Transition, in: JSRNC 12.1 (2018), 34–54.

31   Evidence of this dynamic is paradigmatically given in contemporary public political debates on environmental challenges in Germany as portrayed by Jan Grossarth, Die anti-ökologische Hysterie. Liberale spotten im Gleichklang mit Populisten über "grüne Religion", Klimaleugner outen sich im Rotary-Club. Welcher Teufel ist eigentlich in die bürgerliche Intelligenz gefahren? SZ Nr. 125 (Friday, 31.5.2019), 9.: Alice Weidel, a politician of the right-wing-party AfD wrote: "One cannot speak about the hegemonic hyper-morality without taking into account that the *green ideology* has a dominating influence on the political discourse in the German republic." And the "liberal party" states, from a completely different perspective, that the "*green ideology*" in environmental and climate politics threatens the basis of economy and trade – freedom. When the engagement for nature and the care for the victims of climate change are defined as ideology or even as religion it tends to be perceived as private affair, irrelevant opinion or even irrational belief. Thereby the critical arguments are undermined and the critical challenges lose their political power.

32   An exception is the article of Gregor Etzelmüller, Risiken einer verkörperten Schöpfung, in: Heike Springhart, Günter Thomas (eds.), Risiko und Vertrauen. Risk and Trust. Festschrift für Michael Welker zum 70. Geburtstag, Leipzig 2017, 87–110.

Merleau-Ponty (1908–1961) whose thoughts were further elaborated by various contemporary scholars – mainly from the field of philosophy but also in sociology and theology –, like Hermann Schmitz, Bernhard Waldenfels, Käte Meyer-Drawe, or Thomas Csordas. Body-phenomenology offers a thoroughly elaborated base for a non-anthropocentric anthropology. This anthropology is, I claim both necessary in face of the ecological challenges today and theologically sound. It confronts the anthropocentric underpinnings of the Anthropocene and reflects the Biblical anthropological witness. Non-anthropocentric anthropology, as revealed in the lived-body approach, emphasizes a relational ontology and the interconnectedness and resonance of human beings with nature as a whole. Thereby it is also open for different relational and holistic narratives like the ones Donna Haraway has portrayed, and offers points for the dialogue with eco-theologies especially from the Global South. The lived-body approach therefore might contribute to a planetary eco-theology – a term used by Gayatri Spivak and Leonardo Boff – which is less Euro-centric, less anthropocentric, and more committed to interdependence.

Body-phenomenology derives from a "Western" philosophical tradition that challenges those "Western" concepts of the body that, influenced by the natural sciences and philosophy, reduce the body to materiality. Also, this Western tradition perceives consciousness and ratio as conditions that originate from a place outside of the body. Two of the characteristics of the Leib-Phänomenologie are the *inalienability of the body* and the *intercorporeality, interspatiality, and interdependence of the body*.

4.1 Inalienability of the body

According to Maurice Merleau-Ponty human awareness and thought does not exist apart from the body but is always intertwined with the "lived body" and its relationship to the world. Objects as representations are perceived specifically through our bodies as they interact with the world.

Sandra and Matthew Blakeslee illustrate this idea with the following example:

"If you were to carry around a young mammal such as a kitten during its critical early months of brain development, allowing it to see everything in its environment but never permitting it to move around on its own, the unlucky creature would turn out to be effectively blind for life. While it would still be able to perceive levels of light, color, and shadow – the most basic, hardwired abilities of the visual system – its depth perception and object recognition would be abysmal. Its eyes and optic nerves would be perfectly normal and intact, yet its higher visual system would be next to useless."[33]

"Without embodied access to the environment," Alessandro Colarossi concludes, "the cat cannot develop its nervous system with regard to proper responses to external stimuli."[34]

This discovery is underlined today by cognitive science[35] and discloses the inescapable dependence of awareness, consciousness, and (body)knowledge on the lived body and bodily experience made in its environment. At the same time, it challenges the duality of body and mind, intuition and intelligence, nature and technology.

---

33 Sandra Blakeslee, Matthew Blakeslee, The Body has a Mind of its Own. How Body Maps in Your Brain Help You Do (Almost) Everything Better, New York 2008, 12f.
34 Alessandro Colarossi, Focusing On The Brain, Ignoring the Body, in: Philosophy Now 2013 (https://philosophynow.org/issues/97/Focusing_On_The_Brain_Ignoring_the_Body, accessed July 2019).
35 See e.g. Shaun Gallagher, How the Body Shapes The Mind, Oxford 2006.

Claudia Jahnel

4.2 Intercorporeality, interspatiality, and interdependence of the body.

Another crucial point in the body-phenomenology following Merleau-Ponty is the intercorporeality, interspatiality, and interdependence of the body. We get an idea of what Merleau-Ponty means when we think of phenomena like yawning or smiling. If we see someone yawn or smile we often start to yawn or smile too. Social and behavioral studies call this mechanism the perception-action loop between self and other. Perceiving the other's action prompts the same action in the self.

Merleau-Ponty comments on this phenomenon as follows:

> "In perceiving the other, my body and his are coupled, resulting in a sort of action which pairs them. This conduct which I am able only to see, I live somehow from a distance. I make it mine; I recover it or comprehend it. Reciprocally I know that the gestures I make myself can be the objects of another's intention."[36]

Another field where this intercorporeality is experienced is art. When painting we try to get to the essence of the painted object. This encounter of my gaze with the object that catches my attention takes place in the context of intercorporeality. The intercorporeality between the painter and the object is the precondition for the genesis – the birth – of something new: the painted picture.[37]

The purpose of the examples given and many other examples Merleau-Ponty uses to illustrate his thesis is to demonstrate the bodily and even fleshly interconnectedness not only between human beings but also between human beings and nature and the world. There are no limits between body and body and body and nature and world. The I, the other, and the world mix in every sensation and in senso-motoric dynamic so that it is not possible to discern whether the body is in the world or whether that which is seen and perceived, is in the body. It is only one texture. There is no duality, yet, also, there is no complete oneness. There is difference but interdependence. The resonance takes place in an interspace that interconnects – via empathy (Einfühlung) – seeing and being seen, subject and object, activity and passivity. There is no complete freedom of self and will. These insights resonate with Biblical tradition of the interconnectedness between the whole of creation and emphasize empathy as key to resolving the dichotomy.

4.3 The body is not mine, "because I am bound to the other" (Emanuel Levinas)

Other philosophers have further developed these and other ideas on the interconnectedness. One provocative concept that can only be mentioned without going into detail is Levinas' idea of the I as completely depending on "the other." This idea radically questions the "Western" idea of an autonomous ethical subject. The ethical embodied subject is not self-sufficient but, passively, depends on the intervention of the other's fragile bodily life. Its identity is mediated by passive exposure of the body to the other.

Levinas also calls for respecting the radical alterity of "the other" – a thought that leads to respecting the alterity of nature, as Spivak claims, without falling into dichotomous pitfalls.

4.4 Vulnerability, solidarity and political action (Judith Butler)

In Butler's works the body becomes *the* instance of vulnerability. Its vulnerability derives from its openness and exposure to the other. Butler claims: "it cannot be that the other is destructible while I am not; nor vice versa." To claim not to be as vulnerable as "the other" derives from the

---

36 Maurice Merleau-Ponty, The Child's Relations with Others [1951], in: id., The Primacy of Perception and Other Essays, Evanston 1964, 118.
37 Maurice Merleau-Ponty, Das Auge und der Geist, Hamburg 1984, 87.

intention to present oneself – or one's nation – as superior.[38] Vulnerability and being aware of the own vulnerability leads to moral affection and responsibility for the vulnerable life. An important goal then is to learn to accept the own vulnerability because this is the "source of an ethical connection."[39]

5. Toward a non-anthropocentric anthropology and a body-sensitive eco-theology: Learning with the body to become lived, vulnerable and solidary bodies

My understanding of a non-anthropocentric anthropology resonates with some reflections of Jürgen Moltmann in one of his recent publications.[40] A non-anthropocentric anthropology must be shaped, Moltmann states, not only by the theocentric turn that had marked the eco-theological approach in the 1970ies and 1980ies and that perceived "man" as steward and co-creator – rather than as holding dominion over creation. Yet, what needs to be emphasized today in face of the fact that "man" still desires to hold dominion over and utilizes the world, is, Moltmann claims, a non-anthropocentric anthropology. This anthropology does not only de-center human beings. It is also characterized by a moment of passivity.

Moltmann's final chapters "Sabbath – the feast of creation" recalls the insights of the Leib-Phänomenologie that I have just sketched as well as "the other side" of Hannah Arendt's "vita activa": the "*vita passiva*." Yet, what is meant here is not a passivity that originates in disillusion but rather a passivity that in humbleness perceives human beings not primarily as actors but as recipients. This notion contradicts the idea of the autonomy of the social subject that is so prevalent in the Anthropocene. It challenges the ego because it reveals that "man" or "woman" are not in control but that nature can take over control. It even might include, as Donna Haraway states, "mourning irreversible losses"[41] – which I interpret as dying to anthropocentric concepts –, so that other life-giving relations toward the whole earth become stronger. This view takes seriously what Scheler calls the "excentric positionality" of "man" – that human beings are exposed, open and vulnerable beings. And it offers a point of contact to a crucial Christian dogma: the passive justification that we receive through Christ and that transforms us.

A non-anthropocentric anthropology must not be confused with a romantic hope in the self-healing powers of nature – as if nature, earth and world would be saved if human beings just kept out of it. Rather, Moltmann's ethic is – in an interesting coincidence with the topic of the last World mission conference in Arusha, Tanzania, in 2018 – an "*ethic of discipleship*" motivated by a transformative eschatology (the promise of a new earth) and the call to participate in the transformation of the world. The special human responsibility for the earth is not delimited. Rather, according to Moltmann's interpretation of the Biblical narrative human beings hold a central position: to be transforming and transformed disciples for life supporting transformations.

---

38   Judith Butler, Frames of War: When is life grievable?, London 2000.
39   Moya Lloyd, Towards a cultural politics of vulnerability: Precarious lives and ungrievable deaths, in: Terell Carver/Samuel A. Chambers (eds.), Judith Butler's Precarious Politics Critical Encounters, London, New York 2008, 93.
40   Jürgen Moltmann, Ethik der Hoffnung, Gütersloh 2010, 159.
41   Haraway (2015), 160.

Claudia Jahnel

There are obvious differences between Moltmann and e.g. Donna Haraway with regard to the position and ontology of human beings. Yet, what they both call for – together with authors of the Leib-Phänomenologie, Levinas or Butler –, is that an alternative, less dichotomous narrative needs to shape the social discourse and has to be embodied. I have tried to delineate traditions that focus on the body as resonating with the world and therefore as starting point for the revaluation of this resonance. Yet, as said, this resonance is not naturally given but socially informed. This means that the question whether resonance is furthered or not depends on the cultural aesthetic regimes. The Biblical tradition understands human beings as en-fleshed and lived bodies – in being and in still becoming. Philosophers like Brison and sociologists like Reckwitz[42] convincingly argue, that bodies are not completely pre-determined, fixed by social norms and unable to change. Rather, the body is an intelligent agent of learning. It learns by imitating in mimicry, and every imitation creates something new. It learns via dissonances as well as by letting oneself be affected by the other, passively. It learns by actively using the body as an instrument of learning.

Informed resonance with the world demands to overcome the animosity toward the body and the flesh and requires to learn to become lived, vulnerable, finite and solidary bodies. This is by no means an easy task. It neither offers security nor does it please the ego, but calls for creative uncertainty and for the involvement of the whole body, the senses and especially imagination. Yet, this learning is possible and continues to be on the way – as we see in the powerful movement Fridays for Future.

---

42 Andreas Reckwitz, Kreativität und soziale Praxis. Studien zur Sozial- und Gesellschaftstheorie, Bielefeld 2016.

ECOFEMINISM AND ECOFEMINIST THEOLOGY

Reclaiming Earth-based Spirituality

Muriel Orevillo-Montenegro

1. Introduction

When I began thinking about writing this paper, I was struggling with flu and allergy from cigarette smoke, and with high and humid temperature. My room was like an oven. I could not imagine a world with temperature going beyond 40 degrees Celsius. Then, as I was convulsing with fever, images of an old movie I saw as a teenager flashed back: "Soylent Green" It prophesied the horrors of a dystopian future set in the year 2022 in New York City: population explodes, basic resources were depleted, especially water and food. The greenhouse effect brought about an all year-round very humidity, pollution, poverty, looting, and legal euthanasia clinics ("going home clinics").

Upon recovery, I checked out the movie. I was shocked that the flats for rent came with girls as "furniture." To make the story short, a detective found out that Soylent Green, supposedly "a high energy vegetable concentrate" from the ocean are human beings. He shouted:

> Soylent Green is people! Ocean's dying, plankton's dying... it's people. Soylent Green is made out of people. They're making our food out of people. Next thing they'll be breeding us like cattle for food. You've gotta tell them. You've gotta tell them![1]

I already forgot about this movie, but it surfaced from my subconscious when I was sick. The film showed the interconnected effect of climate change on the bodies of people, and of woman's body as an object. It showed sheer commodification of human bodies – recycled as food and as "furniture." In the film, the priest is catatonic, symbolic of the church's inability to denounce the evils of the time. It was gruesome to think of people being processed into food. So far, at present, I have not heard yet of human bodies being processed into luncheon meat literally. But who knows?

Metaphorically, human bodies are processed and fed into the machinery of capitalism. Vulnerable women continue to be treated as objects in new forms of slavery. In the past fifty years, the response to the challenge of climate change and patriarchy had been very slow. While conferences, seminars, and summit meetings of scientists, theologians, and government leaders had been held, yet, the destruction seems unabated. We hear of whales weighed down with tons of plastic garbage in their bellies. Big consumers of fossil fuel refuse to reduce their carbon dioxide emissions. Consistently, these countries are also the biggest producer of plastic garbage.[2]

---

1 Produced in 1973 MGM-UA, starring Charlton Heston and Leigh Young, from a story "Make Room! Make Room!" by Harry Harrison.
2 Samada Dorger, "These Countries Produce the Most Plastic Waste," in https://www.thestreet.com/world/countries-most-plastic-waste-14878534. Cf. "Largest producers of territorial fossil fuel CO2 emissions worldwide in 2017, based on their share of global CO2 emissions", in https://www.statista.com/statistics/271748/the-largest-emitters-of-co2-in-the-world/

In this paper, I will say that ecofeminism and ecofeminist theology have something to offer to the efforts to make theology and ethics responsive to the present ecological degradation and destruction. I affirm that in a patriarchal, androcentric, and phallocratic contexts, there is a need to reclaim women's earth-based spirituality and wisdom on matters that affect the day-to-day Earth life.

2. Embracing Feminism as a Basic Principle

Feminism became the impetus that brought about the awakening and rising of women in doing theology. Feminism came a long way. Basically, it argues that "the systematic mistreatment and devaluation of females cross-culturally is a paradigmatic human harm with grave and pervasive consequences."[3] Feminism took as central issues meanings of privilege and oppression, sex, gender, sexuality, race, nation, some of the core areas of philosophy, ethics, epistemology, politics, and ontology.[4] Feminism shows how knowledge and structures of social institutions are deeply gendered. It critiques and deconstructs[5] androcentric structures, concepts, symbols, and language, among others. Feminism seeks to analyze conditions of violence and subjection, of specific social norm and practices, and inquiries into the deep relations of embodiment, power and identity. Feminism debunks the patriarchal assumption that men are presumed superior and have authority over women. It is both a political movement and a theoretical field that seeks to bring down the inequalities between men and women,[6] and is committed to changes that "women desire for themselves and for the world."[7] As such, feminism functions as a corrective to patriarchal and androcentric constructs about things that matter in this world.

Feminism has provided a very significant change in society, albeit slowly in other parts of the world. The women and young girls of this generation have gained more freedom in constructing their identities, thanks to the trailblazing work of the feminists. Gender justice is now mainstreamed in the social discourse and had generally influenced in all dimensions of society practice, in general. Then and now, feminism continues to challenge the hard-core patriarchal culture of societies. It continues to envision practical implications of things, as it is concerned with ethics and practice in the realm of the human being's existence. Yet, a lacuna of human existence is left unattended in the feminist discourse and practice. Some feminists have seen that human beings could not become apart from their communities of accountabilities. And these communities are not just composed of human. There are non-human citizens and of elements of these communi-

---

3   Alison Bailey and Chris Coumo, "The Feminist Turn in Philosophy," in *The Feminist Philosophy Reader* (New York: McGraw Hill, 2008), 2-3.

4   Bailey and Coumo, "Preface", in *The Feminist Philosophy Reader* (New York: McGraw Hill, 2008), viii.

5   Deconstruction is a form of philosophical and literary analysis introduced in the 1960's by Jacques Derrida that questions the basic conceptual distinctions or "oppositions" in Western philosophy through a close scrutiny of the language and logic of philosophical and literary texts. It seeks to destabilize the "grand narratives" that are universalizing. The term has become a designation of a range of radical theoretical enterprise in diverse areas of humanities and social sciences, including law, psychoanalysis, architecture, anthropology, theology, feminism, LGBT studies, and political theory, historiography, and film theory. It is popularly used to mean a critical dismantling of tradition and traditional modes of thought.

6   Linda McDowell, "Feminism" in *A Feminist Glossary of Human Geography*, edited by Linda McDowell and Joanne P. Sharp (New York: Arnold/Oxford University Press, 1999), 88-89. Its beginnings go back to the early 19th century.

7   Griselda Pollock, cited in McDowell, "Feminism", 88.

ties and without them, life will not exist. Thus, they began to see not just communities of people, but they see Earth communities.

3. Ecofeminism: Rising and Moving towards a Higher Plane

Serious attention on the destruction of ecology in the academic circle emerged in response to the work of a physicist, Rachel Carson. Carson did not claim to be a feminist or an ecofeminist, but she pointed to the lethal effect of chemicals to the "integrity of the natural world that supports all life."[8] Critical theological thoughts about the situation of the ecology came with the work of the church historian, Lynn White, Jr. In his 1967 essay, "The Historical Roots of our Ecologic Crisis," argued that orthodox Christian theology, with its "arrogance" has blessed science and technology that led towards the ecological crisis.[9] While it took some time for the vies of Carson and White, Jr. to catch the attention of many, some women took their vision of feminism to a higher plane of understanding the suffering of women in relation with the suffering of the Earth. In 1974, a French writer Françoise d'Eaubonne coined the word *ecofeminisme* to represent the potential of women in bringing about an "ecological revolution to ensure human survival."[10] This revolution demands not just a new gender relation between women and men, but also between human beings and the earth. Several strands of ecofeminist strands emerged. Liberal ecofeminists were concerned with passing laws and regulations to reform environmentalism. The radical ecofeminists situate the ecological problems within its critique of patriarchy and offer alternatives to liberate women and nature. On their part, the socialist ecofeminists see the ecological problem as an effect of capitalist patriarchy that regards women and nature as resources of its market economy. Thus, a socialist revolution would dismantle the domination of women and nature. Among the ecofeminist movements, the socialist ecofeminism puts in the center the matter of reproduction and production. It seeks to "develop sustainable, non-dominating relations with nature and supplying all peoples with a high quality of life."[11] Although these strands of ecofeminism differ in their analysis, they are all concerned with improving the relationship between the human beings and the earth. Their ultimate goals of political action and short-term objectives overlap, and there is more unity among women in their "common goal of restoring the natural environment and quality of life for people and other living and non-living inhabitants of the planet."[12]

---

8   Rachel L. Carson, "The Obligation to Endure," in *Readings in Ecology and Feminist Theology*, Mary Heather MacKinnon and Moni McIntyre, eds. (Kansas: Sheed and Ward, 1995), 19-24. This chapter is part of Carson's work that came out in 1962, *The Silent Spring*.
9   Lynn White, Jr. "The Historical Roots of our Ecologic Crisis," in Mary Heather MacKinnon and Moni McIntyre, eds., *Readings in Ecology and Feminist Theology*, (Kansas: Sheed and Ward, 1995), 25-35. This work first appeared in the journal *Science*, 1 Report, Vol. 155, 1967, pp.1203-07.
10   Carolyn Merchant, "Ecofeminism and Feminist Theory," in Irene Diamond and Gloria Feman Orenstein, eds., *Reweaving the World: The Emergence of Ecofeminism*. (San Francisco: Sierra Club Books, 1990), 100.
11   Merchant, "Ecofeminism and Feminist Theory," 100-105.
12   Ibid.

4. Feminist Theology Rising

Since time immemorial, the God-talk that dominated the Christian world was male-talk. Consequently, the language and discourse in the male-talk God-talk is androcentric. God was imaged as a strong old man sitting on the throne up in the clouds, if not marching unto war. Women's voices were muffled, even if there were stories of audacious women in the pages of the Bible. Women were considered dumb, incapable of discerning spiritual matters, and are good only for the house, raising children and chickens. Church fathers and theologians posit that women are incapable of discerning spiritual matters, that woman is the cause of Christ being hanged on the tree, that women are misbegotten males, etcetera.

From the inspiration that feminism has spurred, feminist theologians have uncovered and deconstructed the patriarchal, androcentric, sexist, and misogynistic biblical texts. They rejected the misogynistic discourse of the church fathers and theologians. They struggled to move away from the patriarchal mould. They examined theological constructs that are hazardous to women's health and being. They challenged the androcentric discourses and patriarchal language in addressing God. Feminist theologians contested church doctrines that perpetuate patriarchy, and constructed new theological paradigms that are liberating to women. They also had to face the reality of gender blindness in churches and seminaries, and the reality that Christians have difficulty shedding of the old mind-sets and habits. The clergy, including the well-meaning ones who work for social justice, have difficulty re-imagining God, and are stuck with the image of God as Father Almighty.

Yet, like their sisters, the feminist theologians also realized that their theologies must address the prevailing situation of the Earth. Thus, a good number of feminist theologians have incorporated the ecofeminist agenda in their theological constructs.

5. Ecofeminist Theology: A Call to Reclaiming the Earth-based Spirituality

Ecofeminists do no romanticize the past, and argue for the return towards the past. We know that cannot be done. But the challenge at hand is to think of philosophical, theological and ethical foundation for human beings to stop destroying the Earth and avoid an omnicide to happen.

A contribution of ecofeminism to this call to mitigate the Earth's destruction is a theology that is intertwined with Earth-based spirituality. Spirituality is about one's lifestyle in living out one's faith. It involves "one's deepest moral values and most profound experience."[13] So an Earth-based spirituality is "about one's felt connections with, embeddedness in, and belonging to, this living and sacred earth."[14] Earth-based spirituality is grounded in the belief that the Earth is the center, and that human beings are earthlings, being part of this Earth ecosystem.

5.1 Reclaiming Native Wisdom and Spirituality
The first time I heard of the word "ecofeminism," I immediately understood it somehow. Yet, such understanding goes back to my experience of growing up in the village. I understood this connection of the natural world, the ecosystem, with the world of human beings, other creatures and even the unseen ones. This comes from native wisdom, from an Earth-based spirituality.

---

13   Bron Taylor, "Earth and Nature-Based Spirituality (Part I): From Deep Ecology to Radical Environmentalism." Available in https://pdfs.semanticscholar.org/9939/8acc90aaaf8f80cea51c6c503cbc65539ffe.pdf.
14   Ibid.

In the village, the children were taught by the elders to be respectful to nature and the spirits that live there. So, we have to say "*tabi*" or "excuse me" when we go to a forest patch to gather wild fruits called *pahauli*,[15] or when we cross a stream, or pass by a big tree. It is an expression of respect for the beings – the trees, animals and the spirits. This concept of nature as the one that gives birth to all life on Earth comes from the indigenous peoples' wisdom. Yet, with the process of Westernization through the education system and of evicting the indigenous peoples from their ancestral domain, the rich indigenous culture that is anchored on the nature is gradually waning. The indigenous meaning of "community" is gone.

In school, we were taught that a "community" means a group of people living together in one place, having common interest and character. Unfortunately, this definition points only to the human community. It is only in recent years that in community mapping, the rivers and parks are included in community mapping. Having spent half of my childhood in the rural area, I understood "community" as human beings living in relationship with their wells, springs, rivers, forest patches, cows, dogs, cats, pigs, the rice paddies, the mud ponds where carabaos (water buffalos) wallow and mudfish grow, the trees, the birds, etcetera. Without these non-human members, the word "community" is meaningless. This also points to the loss of native wisdom and Earth-based spiritualities.

I had a personal experience of unconsciously disrespecting the spirits that resided on the *madre de cacao* tree. Consequently, every time I touch water, I would have these painful and itchy rashes. My laboratory test results were fine. The doctors could not find any problem. Desperate, my father brought a shaman to our house. The shaman noted that a child spirit wanted to play with me but I did not pay respect, as I hurried to the spring to bathe. She whipped me with the flowers of the tree that created that curse of rashes. Rituals were done to appease the spirit, and I was healed after a month.

Perhaps, you too, who are here will say that what I went through was superstitious and pagan. But nobody can take that experience away from me. Certainly, this experience is not acceptable in the Christian tradition. In Sunday School, we sing that there are no spirits in the trees, rocks, and fields. Yet, at an early age, I heard the words of Jesus saying that if human beings will remain silent, even the "stones would shout out" (Luke 19:40). The Psalmist declared that the mountains and the hills will "burst into song, and all the trees of the field shall clap their hands." (Isa. 55:12) The Earth-based spirituality has been buried from our memories, and even if snippets of such memory are found in the Bible, these were not highlighted. Surely, the teachings that separated us from nature have certainly taken away from us the Earth-based spirituality of respecting and regarding nature with mystery. These teachings surely became the strong underpinnings for huge projects of scouring the bowels and depths of the Earth, of plundering and raping the body of the Mother Earth.

5.2 Spirituality of Interconnectedness

An ecofeminist theology comes from an ecofeminist women's experience. Everything on this planet is part of the web of life. When one thread of the web is destroyed, the whole web is affected. When the forest is gone, the lung of the Earth is gone. They absorb the carbon dioxide in the atmosphere, and produce the oxygen that we need to live. Biblically, the metaphor used is the human body that has many parts (I Cor. 12:17-27).

---

15   This is a kind of wild tropical vine that bears fruits, some are round, others are oblong, and in cluster. The fruits come in yellow, red or orange when ripe. The pulp inside is white with small black seeds. The fruit, according to the village people, relieves hunger and restores energy, which is why they are called pahauli, which means relief.

An ecofeminist theology also holds on to the indigenous people's concept of the Earth as a Mother. This mother sustains the creatures that she gives birth. Women can relate to the concept of the pain of birthing and the joy of nurturing the new life she has given birth. This is where one finds the connection: in nurturing life. One has to nurture the soil because all life springs from it. This concept helps us understand the cycle of birth and death, of springing from the Earth and of going back to womb of the Earth.

An ecofeminist theology examines and rejects traditional spirituality that equates woman and body with sin. It rejects the traditional theology's assent to Plato's dualism that separated the body from the spirit. It debunks the discourses that regarded women's bodies and sexuality as the source of sin and temptation. Thus, ecofeminist theology explores the interconnection of sexuality and spirituality, the issues of power, the ethical dimension of desire and pleasure with issues of power. It seeks the interconnection of the violation of women's bodies with the body of the Mother Earth. Women's bodies are violated not only through rape, but also with the medicalization of pregnancy, childbirth, gestational surrogacy (womb for rent), prostitution (as "furniture") and through cosmetic surgeries.

5.3 Openness to a Cosmocentric View of Creation

An ecofeminist theology opens itself up to a cosmocentric view. The recognition that we are children of the Earth calls for a broadening of our Earth-stories towards the cosmos, of the entire universe as a unified whole. The planet Earth is only a part of the universe. Yet, our life on Earth is affected by the movements of the cosmic system. Life cannot survive without the sun. The skies will not be bright at night without the stars in the galaxy. An ecofeminist theology has no difficulty moving beyond the privileged creation stories of religions. We can look at these stories as part of the "the cosmic creation story."[16] In doing so, cultures that focus on human beings as the center and ruler will hopefully be diminished or simply come to an end. From a cosmocentric view, ecofeminist theology advocates for a simple, subsistence kind of lifestyle. It interrogates the notion of "sustainable" living as part of the anthropocentric paradigm.

5.4 Rejecting the Sin of Anthropocentrism

Theologians say that sin is hubris, the excessive sense of pride that leads one to defy or turn away from God. Men played God, women did not. The women, being regarded as inferior and told to be subservient to man, do not resonate with this male notion of men. Valerie Saving, in her essay on the human condition, argued that the sin of women is triviality.[17] Women have internalized the socialization that they are worthless and insignificant. Responding to the challenge of claiming their worth, women began to rise. Then they discovered men's sin of patriarchy, androcentrism, and sexism. But there was one more that had implications on the life of all life – of the Earth, and that is the sin of anthropocentrism. I imagine anthropocentrism as worst, because it has led and continues to lead not just towards biocide or ecocide, but also towards omnicide, the danger of the extinction of life through a global anthropogenic ecological catastrophe.

---

16   Brian Swimme, "The Cosmic Creation Story," in Readings in Ecology and Feminist Theology, Mary Heather McKinnon and Moni McIntyre, eds. Mary Heather MacKinnon and Moni McIntyre, eds., Readings in Ecology and Feminist Theology, (Kansas: Sheed and Ward, 1995), 249-258.

17   Valerie Saiving, "The Human Situation: A Feminine View," in Readings in Ecology and Feminist Theology, Mary Heather McKinnon and Moni McIntyre, eds. Mary Heather MacKinnon and Moni McIntyre, eds., Readings in Ecology and Feminist Theology, (Kansas: Sheed and Ward, 1995), 3-18.

The Christian tradition as practiced is not only patriarchal and androcentric; it is deeply anthropocentric. Like White, Jr., ecofeminists have pointed out that anthropocentrism is a crucial impetus for human being's destructive behaviour towards the nature. Human beings, particularly male human beings, are viewed as the center of creation, and everything around him are subject to his control. Preachers and biblical interpreters have highlighted this notion for years. The concept of stewardship is inextricably intertwined with dominion. The concept could veer away from the greed line. When the ecological crisis began to awaken some people, biblical interpreters and theologians tried to revisit the biblical texts and tried to redeem the creation stories by reinterpreting the notion of domination and stewardship. Yet, they could not fully remove the androcentric and anthropocentric nuances of the texts, along with the explicitly patriarchal and sexist ones. One has to have the ecofeminist consciousness to be able to re-read and interrogate the texts.

5.5 Ecofeminist Theology is a Theology of Struggle for Peace
An ecofeminist theologian does not shy away from the issues affecting the life in its wholeness. As such, it is a struggle for genuine, positive peace. It is a struggle because from experience, the process is a long haul, and so the process must be given emphasis. Moreover, it is a struggle because there are various expressions sin and evil that must be faced. These are manifest in social, political, cultural, economic and ecological injustices. One has to face and counter the reality of capitalist patriarchy that creates the system of globalization, of war, of scarcity of food and water. Issues such as disability, single parenthood, widowhood, illnesses, caregiving, and many more are issues that ecofeminist theology must reflect and address because women and children are the ones who suffer the most in the face of these realities.

5.6 Ecofeminist Theology as Interfaith Theology and Spirituality
The concern for the predicament of our Earth and the cosmos is not a monopoly of the Christians. An ecofeminist theology from the context of Asia must consider the plurality of religions. There are religions and faith traditions in Asia teach about respect and value life in its wholeness. For example, *ahimsa* is a concept of nonviolence, which is inclusive of humans and non-humans. In Asia, the academic framework for theology is useful, but it is challenged to move beyond it towards the contexts of survival of the Earth, as the Earth and cosmos is our context.

An ecofeminist interfaith theology calls on people to explore the need to recover the value of living together with adherents of other Asian religions, rather than using religions for personal or political interests. This is crucial in the Asian context today. An ecofeminist interfaith theology also needs to examine religious symbols, rituals and language that can create conflict or that promote one's political or personal agenda. Moreover, it also needs to explore the function of religion as "boundary-setting."

6. Conclusion

In theologizing and peacebuilding, all the things mentioned above must be taken into consideration. Ecofeminist theology does not call one to be a superwoman or superman. Foremost, it calls upon everyone to cultivate and practice compassion for life. Such posture will open the heart towards a new way of understanding the web of life in the cosmos, and in approaching God as a Divine Mystery.

TOWARDS ECOLOGICAL SENSITIZATION AND ECOLOGICAL JUSTICE

A Call for A Joint (Women's) Inter-religious Peace-building

Nadja Furlan Štante

Introduction

For ecofeminists, ecological crisis is a reality, a threat and a warning to contemporary humanity. Climate changes, global warming and the reduction of biodiversity and other processes, which are supposed to be the result of environmental pollution and long-term excessive use and consumption of natural resources are certainly a reflection and consequence of the globalized consciousness of consumer imperialist relationship of human vs. nature. This hypothesis can also be heard in the Pope's words: »I do not know whether this is all merely a human error, but mostly it is. Man is constantly slapping nature,« which the Holy Father said before journalists on the plane, somewhere halfway between the area where, ten years ago, the tsunami killed more than 35,000 people and the area in which the Haiyan typhoon killed 6,000 people in November 2013.[1]

Although, the claim about global warming is one of the most controversial scientific issues of our time, also because some scientists claim that the anthropogenic threat of global warming is not real[2], the ecological crisis and global warming are not just scientific questions, but questions relating to economics, sociology, ethics, values, religion, (geo) politics and individual lifestyle choices. All these require a careful consideration both on the personal level, as well as on the religious and social levels.

The purpose of this article is to put forward the ecofeminist paradigm of the ecological ethics of interdependence of all human and nonhuman living beings, of human and nature in the web of life. The centrepiece here is an analysis of the power of feminine within the phenomenon of Christian ecofeminism, and its ethics of peace and ecological sensibility in terms of inter-faith theology of oikos and eco-justice. From this pesrpective, the paper is premised on the question of human vs. nature relationship, which is still deeply marked by the collective memory of domination of human beings over nature, especially in the western, consumerist societies and (christian)

---

1   Baković, Zorana. 2015. Papež Frančišek na Filipinih: človek je naravi prisolil klofuto. Delo, 17. januar. Http://www.delo.si/svet/globalno/ papez-francisek-na-filipinih-clovek-je-naravi-prisolil-klofuto.html (the Delo newspaper) (retrieved 22. 5. 2016).
2   The reason for climate changes are seen in the events in Earth's atmosphere as a result of certain major events, such as the impact of a comet on the Earth's surface, in natural climate variability (minor ice age in the 17th and 18th centuries, the natural development of the atmosphere) or in variable Sun activities. However, only a small part of the professional public concludes that global warming represents a serious global problem. American geologist James Lawrence Powell has done an analysis of scientific papers recorded in the network of Web of Science. Of the 13,950 reviewed scientific researches on global warming, written between 1991 and 2012, only 23 (0.16 %) deny global warming. Of the 33,690 authors of these studies, only 34 (0.1 %) deny global warming. James Lawrence Powell argued the in-depth findings of these studies in his monograph, *Revolutions in Earth Sciences, From Heresy to Truth* (2014).

religious communities and Churches. The negative stereotype of human superiority in relation to nature remains deeply rooted in the collective consciousness, which is reflected even in the current agreements on environmental protection, which put at the forefront the reduction of environmental change and its harmful effects for humans but not as much the harmful effects for other living beings and nature as such. However, as a number of environmental ethicists highlight, among them also Arne Naess, the founder of deep ecology, it is unlikely that such a such grave utilitarian approach should be able to overcome the current environmental crisis, which is essentially still based on the old ethics pattern of human domination over nature and human rights of its exploitation.

Nobel Prize winner (2007) Al Gore at the reception at the award ceremony said: »We face a true planetary emergency. The climate crisis is not a political issue, it is a moral and spiritual challenge to all of humanity. It is also our greatest opportunity to lift global consciousness to a higher level.«[3] Albert Einstein argued that humanity can not solve problems if it remains at the same level of consciousness on which it has been created.[4]

To create a new ecologically sensitive society, we will need men and women with new mental paradigms, and ecologically sensitized heart attitudes and empathy. Or as Rosemary Radford Ruether has stated: »A heald relation to each other and to the earth than calls for a new consciousness, a new symbolic culture and spirituality. We need to transform our inner psyches and the way we symbolize the interrelations of men and women, humans and earth, humans and the divine and divine and the earth. Ecological healing is a theological and psychic-spiritual process.«[5] And we must strat by recognizing that metanoia, or change of consciousness, begins with us. In this segment, the positive contribution of christian eco-feminism is of the utmost importance. With the help of hermeneutic key of Christian eco-feminist theology, the paper thus draws attention to the urge of cultivating ecological sensibility of postmodern humanity in relation to nature.

Ecological transformation, metanoia and the role of Churches

It is important to take into account, the notion that our understanding of nature and our attitude towards it, is constructed and percieved by various socio-philospohical and cultural processes and through different living practices this conceptualization is created, recreated and transformed. The conceptualization of nature is such a dynamic cultural process that all the time fluctuates between everyday placement on the one hand and social impact on the other.

Therefore, the ecological restoration begins with personal restoration and transformation of prejudices and negative stereotypes and metanarratives. At that point the instutionized religion plays an important role, as a meaningful system for producing the meaning is (so)responsable for (non)ethical behaveour of society and vice-versa. The culture and religion are not just the area of passive influences but also a meaningful system for producing the meaning. The culture and religion give the notions, the beliefs which become unnoticed and non-rectified patterns by which the people live by. That is why in the sphere of cultural society beside the positive life phenomena also negative stereotypes and prejudices are formed and we absorb them non critically. Stereotypical conceptions which are linked mostly to gender stereotypes and prejudices regards

3   Al Gore, Nobel Peace Prize acceptance speech: http://www.abc.net.au/news/stories/2007/10/12/2058573.htm
4   Albert Einstein: http://www.green-agenda.com/globalconsciousness.html
5   Rosemary Radford Ruether, *Gaia and God*, New York: HarperOne, 1992, 4.

Nadja Furlan Štante

the nature have a very important role here. These stereotypes have a destroying influence on the comprehension and notion of oneself, of the other gender and nature and consecutively of all relations. They are creating a distance between a man and a woman, human beings and nature and the ideal of symbiosis of gender differences and respectful-harmonious relation between sexes and the comprehension of nature. Negative stereotypes and prejudices encourage, preserve and tolerate patriarchal hierarchical marks of human and human-nature relations and spread hierarchy of power on every field of life. Innocent patriarchy's parasites live and transfer through the language, images and thoughts. Negative stereotypes and prejudices paraliyse and prevent healthy mutual relations. These are heart and health of a person, of partner and family relations and also of the whole net of relations and society. Healthy relations mean healthy society and vice versa.[6]

In the context of environmental discourse, eco-feminism is placed among the so-called radical (revolutionary) green theories, alongside deep ecology and social ecology. As for all other radical green theories, it applies also for eco-feminism to stand for fundamental social, political and economic changes, for the changes within the entire mental paradigm. Eco-feminists thus mostly highlight the moral critique of modern industrial societies and the exploitative nature of neo-liberal capitalism and consumer society. Eco-feminisms require deeper values, which in turn bring radical social, political and economic changes. In contrast to the softer approaches[7] in solving environmental problems, which speak in favour of »management and technological« solutions and focus merely on treating the symptoms of environmental crisis, trying to mitigate the effects of excessive interference to nature, ecofeminism treats the environmental or ecological crisis as a result of unethical and improper relationship that humans have toward nature and environment, the relationship that is partly the result of the impact of mental paradigm conceived by hierarchical Cartesian binaristic dualisms ... In light of the discrimination and subordination of women and nature by the patriarchal system, ecofeminism critically points out the hierarchical evaluation and construction of certain negative stigmatized binaristic dualities: culture/nature; male/female; me/other; reason/emotion; human/animal. In line with ecofeminist theory, nature is dominated by culture, woman by man, emotion by reason, and animals by man. This hierarchical structure of relationships is, according to ecofeminist theory, ordered and created by the patriarchal system.

Considering the huge variety of forms and orientations of ecofeminism[8] it would perhaps be better for us to speak about a plurality of ecofeminisms. Today, there are several dimensions of ecofeminism, including liberal ecofeminism, spiritual/cultural ecofeminism, and social/socialist

---

6 Nadja Furlan Štante, *Viskanju Boginje: Kozmologija senzibilnosti in gostoljubja*, Koper: Univerzitetna založba Annales, 2014, 27
7 In the context of environmental discourse or the so-called green discourse, we roughly distinguish two approaches: a reformist approach, which is marked as a light green (for example: the theory of sustainable development), and the radical or revolutionary (ecofeminist, social ecology, deep ecology ...). The reformist measures of environmental protection only see to repair the existing situation, whereas the radical approach aims for a change in mental paradigm, a change in values ... It is therefore not necessary to emphasize that the latter requires an integrated approach that embraces and offers a comprehensive, structural and in-depth solutions. Instead of partial, sectoral, multi-surface solution advocated by the reformist approach and followed by practically all the existing green policy, the radical green theories deal with society (and religion) in its foundations. They strive for new metaphysics, epistemology and the new cosmology and the nature of the new ethics of the relationship of human vs. nature (the planet). However, it should be noted that a revolutionary ecological flows also support the majority of reformists' goals and, besides that, want to intervene even more deeply.
8 Heather Eaton divides the different forms of ecofeminism into four models: the ecofeminist model of activism and social movements, the academic ecofeminism model, religious ecofeminism model and global ecofeminism model (Heather Eaton, Introducing Ecofeminist Theologies, New York: T&T Clark International, 2005, 23).

ecofeminism (or materialist ecofeminism). There are also many interpretations of ecofeminism and how it might be applied to social thought, including ecofeminist art, social justice and political philosophy, religion, contemporary feminism, and poetry.

Heather Eaton compares this wide diversity of ecofeminisms to »an intersection point of multiple pathways« for »[P]eople come to ecofeminism from many directions and have taken it to other places, disciplines and actions«.[9] But regardless of the wide variety of individual types and forms of ecofeminism, which result from the many disciplines and approaches to it (from humanities, social and natural sciences, environmental studies and technology to political activism …), they all have in common the awareness of the fact that it is impossible to solve the ecological issue without at the same time including the feminist question and vice versa. The common element of feminism and ecology is therefore the battle for liberation from the shackles of cultural and economic oppression and exploitation. The connection between the abuse of the natural world and the oppression of women is thus the key and common point of all types of ecofeminisms.[10]

Given the ramification or the extension of various women's religious eco-feminist movements and efforts it is possible to speak about eco-feminist theology as of a special philosophy of religions[11] and eco-theology of religions[12].

Ecological feminism or ecofeminism is a feminist perspective based on the premise that the oppression of women and the exploitation of nature are two interconnected phenomena and two categories that are subjugated and discriminated against by the patriarchal system. Essentially, ecofeminism is based on the premise that what leads to the oppression of women and to the exploitation of nature is one and the same thing: the patriarchal system, dualistic thinking, the system of dominance, global capitalism. The common denominator of all forms of violence is the patriarchal system, understood as a source of violence. Ecofeminism thus experiences the patriarchal system as a conflictual system building on an exploitative hierarchical relationship, unaware of the equality, unity and connectedness of all living beings in the space of life. This is the reason why the patriarchal system is ruining the harmonic connection of man and woman, man and nature ... It is a pest with a destructive effect on nature, as well as people.

Ecofeminism thus sees the basic interconnection between the domination of women and the domination of nature. This connection is displayed in two levels: the ideological-cultural and socioeconomic. The ideological-cultural level is based on the premise or prejudice that women are closer to nature than men, more in tune with their own bodies, the emotional and animal worlds. The socioeconomic level, on the other hand, confines women to the field of reproduction, education and care of children, cooking, cleaning, tidying up – in short, the woman is here confined

---

9   Heather Eaton, Introducing Ecofeminist Theologies, New York: T&T Clark International, 2005, 12.
10   A. Baugh, Gender. In: Bauman, A. W. et al. (eds): Grounding Religion, London, New York: Routledge, 2011, 131.
11   The possibility of *feminist theology as a philosophy of religion* was noted by Pamela Sue Anderson, who saw feminist theology as a new form of philosophy of religions. For details see: Pamela Sue Anderson, *Feminist Theology as Philosophy of Religions*, in: Susan Frank Parsons, *The Cambridge Companion to Feminist Theology*, Cambridge: Cambridge University Press, 2002, 40-57.
·12   *Feminist theology as a theology of religions* is a relatively new expression, which in the opinion of Rita Gross denotes the awareness that in the background of religious plurality and diversity there exists a key common to all religions. In the case of feminist theology it is thus about the common key of women's experience of patriarchal subordination and discrimination of women by all religions. Gross appeals to all feminist theologians to try to develop the right approach for women's participation in interreligious dialogue to truly come alive. See: Rita M. Gross, *Feminist Theology as Theology of Religions*, in: Susan Frank Parsons, *The Cambridge Companion to Feminist Theology*, ibid., 61.

and limited to the mere household, and her chores are devalued in comparison with the public tasks falling into the domain of men and with the power of modern culture. Rosemary Radford Ruether, a pioneer in Christian theological ecofeminism assumes that the first level acts as an ideological basis to the second.[13]

The question of power and negative power-relations is of crucial importance for ecofeminism. Spiritual ecofeminism (Starhawk) differentiates between three kinds of power: »power over«, »power within«, and »power with«. Power over is the basic mode of power of patriarchal societies. It expresses the logic of domination by which some, mostly elite males, dominated women and subjugated classes and races, as well as the nonhuman world. This kind of power is fundamentally competitive. The more power one side has, the less the other side has. Power within, by contrast, is a process by which dominated people shake off the control of others and their own realization of the powerlessness and inferiority projected on to them, laying hold of their own innate power and goodness. Power with is the development of ways to share power that do not negate others in order to affirm oneself, but can mutually affirm one another, while being able to acknowledge the special talents of particular people. In this relation of mutual empowerment each person flourishes by also promoting the flourishing of others.

Ecofeminist theory asserts that a feminist perspective of ecology does not place women in the dominant position of power, but rather calls for an egalitarian society in which there is no one dominant group.

All types of theological ecofeminism thus strive for a deconstruction of the patriarchal paradigm, its hierarchical structure, methodology and thought. They try to deconstruct the entire paradigm of man's supremacy over woman, of mind over body, Heaven over Earth, of the transcendent over the immanent, of the male God, alienated and ruling over all Creation, and replace all this with new alternatives. All major world religions are in this sense challenged to self-questioning and self-criticism in their judgement of the possible negative patterns that contribute to the destruction of the environment, and to restoring environmentally-friendly traditions. From an ecofeminist and environmentally fair perspective, it is essential that religions do away with the negative stereotyped prejudices which strengthen the domination over nature and social domination.[14] The Christian tradition, for instance, has (from an ecofeminist point of view) contributed several problematic images and symbols that have consolidated and survived in form of stereotypes and prejudices and taken root in the legacy of the western philosophical-religious thought. Ecofeminist Christian theologies thus seek to revive the lost images and the symbol of understanding the universe as the body of God (Rosemary Radford Ruether, Sallie McFague). This used to be a typical metaphor (albeit present in various forms) and the focal image of the sensibility of the western (Mediterranean) world, but was replaced by a mechanistic worldview model in the 17th century (Carol Merchant and Vandana Shiva). In 1974, the radical feminist theologian Mary Daly drew a link between the ecological crisis, social domination and the Christian doctrine. As an antithesis to the Christian ethics of missionary work in the sense of uncompromising Christianising (converting at any cost all pagans, who were considered barbarians) she offered a vision of a cosmic commitment to sisterhood that envelops our sister Earth and all its human and nonhuman inhabitants and elements. That would, in Daly's opinion, enable a potentially positive change in the ecological awareness and environmental ethics and lead us from the culture of

---

13   Rosemary Radford Ruether, *Integrating Ecofeminism Globalization and World Religions*, New York: Rowman & Littlefield Publishers, 2005, 91.
14   Radford Ruether, 2005, XI.

predators and desecrators into a culture of reciprocity, where we would look upon the earth and other planets as individual parts of a whole, as being with us, not for us.[15]

Ecological interconnectedness, interdependence and the Enacting[16] of the divine

Being in relation, according to much of eco-feminist theology, is in the first place an ethical activity. Here the core of (eco)feminist ethics of relationality – interconnectedness of all beings in the web of life, plays a part. The web of life is a quite widespread metaphor originating in ecofeminism and poetically denoting the dynamics of the collective feminine view of a world of interconnected subjectivity. Rosemary Radford Reuther understands ecological interdependence in the sense of a life-giving web as a pantheistic or transcendentally immanent web of life. This common source in her opinion fuels and maintains a continual renewal of the natural life cycle and at the same time allows and binds us to fight the exploitative forms of hierarchical relationships and strive for the establishment of renewed relations of mutual acknowledgement.[17]

Ecocentric egalitarianism includes all humans as well as nonhumans. Ecofeminists, insist on the intimate connections between the domination of women, people of colour, and others with the domination of nature. The awareness of this fundamental interconnectedness, and of the consequent interdependence and joint responsibility in the ethical-moral sense, therefore, represents the next step in the evolution of interpersonal relationships and all relations within the web of life.

From this standpoint, Christian (eco)feminist theology wishes to rethink the idea of immanence and place it centrally in the weaving of theology. It understands God as a part of the evolutionary process of the created order, and as its Creator, God would not stand apart from it. This has direct consequences for many areas of theology. For example, Christology can be reimaged from seeing the Christ descending to viewing the Christ growing up the divinizing process of communities and the individuals within them. Ethics can no longer be seen as »sent down« but once again have to be experienced as growing out of the creative immanence that exists between people. Here the importance of the relationality is emphasized. Relationality emerges as a key concept in (eco)feminist theology, and particularly in (eco)feminist ethics. It includes the concepts of interdependence and mutuality. In some schools of feminist discourse it also suggests a special relationship between women and nature. It also implies a call for the reconceptualization of sacred symbols to take account of immanence and to forge new relationships between the deity, human beings and the earth. Carol Gilligan (1982) argues that women have a distinctive modus operandi in ethics. This has become the classic statement of relationality. She shows that women display different perspective on the self, relationships and morality that described by traditional theories of moral development. This discussion is brought a stage further by (eco)feminists. Mary Grey (1989) proposes a »metaphysics of connection«, which will begin with an understanding of

---

15   A. Primavesi, Ecofeminism, In: Isherwood, L. et al. (eds): An A to Z of Feminist Theology, Sheffield: Sheffield Academic Press, 1996, 46
16   »Enact« can mean, first of all »to legislate«, which carries a creative, active sense. But »enact« can also mean »to put on a play«, in which case the persons who »act« are not acting as autonomous ego but are the vehicles for something else, namely, the identities that they are representing on the stage. Similarly, to enact the divine is to actualize the self's creative powers at the same time that the self is formed by something beyond itself.
17   Rosemary Radford Ruether, *Gaia and God*, 1992, 260.

Nadja Furlan Štante

redemption as self-affirmation and right-relation and which will empower ecological healing and growth. A feminist vision which stresses the importance of relationality recognizes the need for the reformulation of the metanarratives of Western culture. Rosemary Radford Ruether (1992) argues that, in the quest for earth healing, we need to create new narratives which will evoke eco-justice and will endorse the metaphysic of connection. This leads naturally to the reconceptualization of primary sacred symbols, so that human talk about divine will inspire relationality. Carter Heyward suggests conceiving of the Christian God as power-in-relation model which ought then to be mirrored in egalitarian and just relationships in society. In this light, placing the emphasis on divine immanence consequently requires the construction of a new relationship between humanity and the rest of the created order; since the later conveys the divine as much as the former.[18]

The shift from anthropocentric theological paradigm to so called a »life-centred theological paradigm« in which God's entire creation including women and nature become the subject of theologising occurs. Eco-feminist theologians presuppose that this dialogical paradigm will mutually enrich each other and critically correct each other and thus contribute to the life of God's whole creation. The indwelling presence of God in human and nature is understood in terms of the model of world as the body of God. Because of that Christian (eco)feminism considers land as a sacrament of God. Richard Grigg has highlighted another important characteristic of (eco)feminist theology in terms of understanding divine, saying that »there is an implicit motif in much of current feminist theology according to which God is a relation that human being chooses to enact«.[19] As he elaborates further on, this does not entail reducing the divine in Feuerbachian fashion to an unconscious, alienating projection or dismissing it as a mere imaginary entity. On the contrary, essential constituent elements of the divine may genuinely transcend the human – both nature and the »power of being« are familiar candidates in feminist thought – and one actualizes a relation to them consciously and in a way that is productive not of alienation but of positive transformation. But neither is God conceived in this current of feminist theology as an independent reality. Human beings do not simply enact a relation to the divine, they enact the divine itself, insofar as God is a particular transformative relationship between the self and nature, or the self and the power of being, or perhaps the self and other selves. The pattern seems much closer to Martin Buber's observation that the »I« is formed by the relations in which it is engaged: the »I« of the »I – IT« relation is a different »I« from the »I« of the »I-Thou« relation (Buber's position obviously has influenced a large number of feminist religious thinkers: Carol Christ, Rosemary, Judith Plaskow, Mary Daly…). Human beings choose to enact the divine, but they are to a large degree creatures of this relation and not just its creators. Or as Richard Grigg has put it: »traditional Western theism understands the divine as a transcendent Supreme Being. Modernity negates theism by reducing it to a projection of human subjectivity. The feminist position negates this negation by conceiving of the divine as neither an independent supernatural being nor a product of misplaced human imagination, but as a way of existence, a particular kind of relation that human beings can enact between themselves and others and between themselves and nonhuman beings and forces. /… / The divine is a relation that human beings decide to enact. Theology's task, then, is not to gain access to and make claims about some objective entity that it naively supposes is ›out there‹, but to actualize the divine.«[20]

---

18   Carter Heyward, *The Redemption of God: A Theology of Mutual Relation*. Lanham, Maryland: University Press of America, 1982.
19   R. Grigg, Feminist Theology and the Being of God. *Journal for the Study of Religion* 74 no.4: 1994, 507.
20   R. Grigg, 1994, 508.

This claim follows naturally on the feminist inclination to pursue a theology that is, in the fullest sense of the phrase a theology »from below«, a theology that is openly a function of women's experiences and goals. All of this implies a rejection of the traditional image of the divine as a supernatural individual who can stand outside the finite. At the same time, there is a type of transcendence that can be combined with the emphasis on immanence so essential to feminist theology, at least according to thinkers such as Radford Ruether. She rejects the transcendent imperial God of patriarchal Christianity in favour of the root human image of the divine as the primal matrix, the great womb within which all things, Gods and humans, sky and earth, human and non-human beings are generated... Here the divine is not up there as abstracted ego, but beneath and around us as encompassing source of life and renewal of life.[21] In this image of what Radford Ruether would have us call »God/ess«, the divine is clearly immanent, but also all-encompassing, also transcendent to some degree. The term »primal matrix« suggests an embracing framework or ground, something beyond us that we are nonetheless a part of. Or as Cartear Heyward claims that, God is the power of relation.[22] Similarly Radford Ruether's claim that God/ess is experienced »in and through relationships, healing our broken relations with our bodies, with other people, with nature«. It is when we overcome the destructive mind-set of man versus woman, rich versus poor, and spirit versus matter – dualisms that separate us from nature and from other human beings – that we find ourselves in relation to divinity: »Community with God/ess exists precisely in and through this renewed community of creation«.[23]

Conclusion

The basic integration of all people is reflected in the dignity of every person and in the intrinsic value of nature. This awareness is a call to *metanoia*, a change in consciousness and heart, it is awareness of a common solidarity in the pursuit of »experienced holistic ecology,« which consequently leads to social conversion from the culture of consumerism to cultural ecology.

Within the context of theological ecofeminism the individual's identity is faced with the model of fundamental interconnection of all beings in the web of life. The awareness of the fundamental interconnectedness, of the consequent interdependence and joint responsibility in the ethical-moral sense therefore represents the next step in the evolution of interpersonal relationships and all relations within the web of life.

In this context, the understanding of religion as an announcer of ethics and morality in the sense of responsibility taken on by religious communities for the common good, is necessarily subject to the principle of equal recognition of the female principle as a *sine qua non* condition for moral dialogue. For only a spirituality or religion which is built on the basis of equivalent recognition of male and female principle and intrinsic values of both sexes and nature is (or can be) the basis for a peaceful, dialogical, inclusive, intercultural and inter-religious dialogue and harmony. In this context, the hermeneutic key of equivalent recognition of femininity in the field of religious and spiritual, and the care for nature and the recognition of its intrinsic ethical maxim which needs to remain a *sine qua non* condition of moral code of accepting others and nature, and the key to human sensitization of an individual for better harmony in cultural and religious diversity.

---

21   Rosemary Radford Ruether, *Sexism and God-talk*. Boston: Beacon Press, 1983, 48-49.
22   Carter Heyward, 1982, 299.
23   Radford Ruether 1983, 163.

Ecumenical Patriarch Bartholomew, who is also known as the Green Patriarch and the Eco-Pope, as Pope Francis has repeatedly been named, warn the Christians that the »crime against nature is a crime against ourselves and a sin against God.«[24] The more people respect their neighbours, the more sense of respect for nature and the environment we will have and vice versa. In this context, the concern for the environment is always the concern for people. An ecological conversion, already urged by John Paul II., is necessary to create a lasting change and is consequently also a social conversion. In doing so, what is relevant are moderation and modesty, but above all, the harmony of the heart, which justifies the belief that »less is more«. And last, but not least, the word ecology does come from the Greek word *oikos* meaning home. This means that the very etymology of the word ecology calls for care for our common home.

---

24   Pope Francis 2015, 8.

PRACTICAL
CASE STUDIES

CHANGES IN ECO-THEOLOGICAL ATTITUDES IN GERMANY

Anja Vollendorf

The Anthropocene is the name of the era we are living in today. The Neocene lasted 13,000 years and is over, has passed. We are human beings. As Christians we say that we are a creation of God, but it is a creation which has successfully managed to exercise supremacy, some say white supremacy, in every sphere of creation everywhere on our planet. Mankind has already succeeded in omitting the next ice age, which should have come in about 7,000 years time.

I think nobody is here from Kennedy airport? But keeping that distance in mind, you are responsible for 32 square meters of ice disappearing in the Antarctic. Did anyone cancel their participation in this conference because of the damage he or she would do to our planet traveling to Wuppertal? Did anybody show a desire "to protect what he loves" due to apocalyptic fear? We care and worry and fear hurt being done to the people and places we love. Why should this be a contradiction? We need to incorporate the knowledge of earth systems researchers into our theologies, and to think about the consequences. We need to be worried. Earth Overshoot Day comes closer and closer each year. World population grows each year. Change is necessary. There are people willing to change theologies, ethics, minds, behavior, attitudes.

I know young people who refuse to travel by plane. Most people, though, don't want to change their life style. And they see their living standard threatened when we dare to talk about also being abstinent in our use of resources. Structurally Germany depends on car production and we talk about e-cars, because it's a new innovative idea for selling new cars, but we need to promote other mobility solutions instead of using the car, too.

We need ecology within our economic structures. We need to get out of our comfort zones as Christians! We need a "critical turn" now! We need eco-theology, not only as additional theology in our education system, but as mainline theology which reads the texts of the Bible the right way, with a new hermeneutic support in the background which strengthens this re-lecture of the Bible.

This re-lecture finishes with stressing the dominium terrae of Gen 1, 26 and stresses 1,30 that God gives so much life and plants for food and that all this was very good (Brigitte Kahl). We don't need just a few "'greening' church practices and engagements" in the church, we need a systematic approach. There is no use in having a worship service in nature if you throw meat on a grill after the service and if you go by car to that rural worship service. In that case, please stay at home in the city and have a vegetarian lunch!

Paul says:

"We know that the whole creation has been groaning in labor pains until now; and not only the creation, but we ourselves, who have the first fruits of the spirit, groan inwardly while we wait for adoption, the redemption of our bodies." (Rom 8, 22+23)

Even if you try to separate creation and humankind, as Paul seems to do, the groaning for redemption is not different between us and the animals and plants and the earth. We live together on this planet. We need a convivial theology, a cosmological theology and spirituality (Leonardo

Boff), a life style of togetherness with all that lives. What has happened to the reverence of life ("Ehrfurcht vor dem Leben") of Albert Schweitzer as a theological ethical approach? What has happened to the humility in the ethics of Jesus? And what has happened to the prophetic tradition of the church – which is left out all the time when it comes to the threat of losing our church members in Germany.

Yes, we need to rediscover that there is holiness on earth and we need a non-anthropocentric anthropology (Jürgen Moltmann), for anthropological and theological reasons. Creation – humankind groans and needs God to redeem us from a passive attitude, so that we come to an active and proactive life style and work for social structures which enable us to live in peace with the earth, as the Busan document of the WCC Assembly in 2013 invites us to.

We Germans always fear a "brown / nationalist esoteric movement" and the re-sacralising of German Earth and Soil", but this was a concept of greed to conquer the earth of other nationalities, to dominate and rule over them. It was not a concept of love and compassion, protection, responsibility, dignity, rights, and democratic commitment with respect for everybody on earth. No, on the contrary, it was based on racism, war, and the murder of 6 million Jews and others. We need to develop an understanding of a "good life" (buen vivir) and an ethics of enough together, which is possible through using fewer resources for the transformation of a greedy economic system and life style.

Churches do problematise a traditional Christian understanding of the world and the nature/ spirit, man/woman, world/mankind and other dichotomies, but they don't succeed in adapting human behaviour and attitudes sufficiently and they fail to adapt structures. The power of hegemonial economic structures and all that they have to offer is very seductive not only in our societies but also in the churches. We have church declarations on protecting bees from dying and on solidarity with the young people's movement "Fridays for Future". But how can churches become more reliable, more accountable to their declarations?

We became involved in the Pilgrimage of Justice and Peace "to work together in a common quest, renewing the true vocation of the church through collaborative engagement with the most important issues of justice and peace, healing a world filled with conflict, injustice and pain."[1] We need a follow-up to that in Karlsruhe in 2021.

It should avoid an understanding of the movement which seems to allow us to avoid the theological aspect of this movement. It's not a movement of people who like to peregrinate around in some beautiful landscape. It is a theological issue. The three dimensions (via activa, via passiva, and via transformativa) enable us to do a theological context analysis.

The via positiva celebrates God's mercy and love, places and spaces of spiritual resources. The via negativa means experiencing the places of pain, mourning, threats, and violence. And the transformative way of life is about being together with the disciples on the Road to Emmaus, talking, reflecting, finding new ideas for life, so that people can be agents of change for life.

Let's change attitudes. More and more German cities are declaring a climate state of emergency (Klimanotstand). This makes it possible to prioritise financial measures to fight climate change. Let's advocate for that in our government. And let`s declare the climate emergency in our churches!

---

1   https://www.oikoumene.org/en/what-we-do/pilgrimage-of-justice-and-peace.

Grüne Reformation. Ökologische Theologie, hg.v. Michael Biehl, Bernd Kappes, Bärbel Warten-
    berg–Potter, Hamburg 2017
Schöpfung. Miteinander leben im gemeinsamen Haus, hg.v. Klaus Krämer / Klaus Vellguth, ThEW
    11 Theologie in der Einen Welt,Freiburg 2017

RECENT ECO-THEOLOGICAL INITIATIVES AS PROMOTED BY THE LUTHERAN WORLD FEDERATION

Chad Rimmer

The Lutheran World Federation has been engaged in initiatives related to creation or climate change for over three decades. The first statement on creation issued by LWF governance was in 1977 at the 6th Assembly in Dar es Salaam, Tanzania. In 1984, one of the sub-themes of the 7th LWF Assembly was *In Christ: Hope for Creation*. At the 8th Assembly in 1990 in Curitiba, Brazil, the theme *The Cry of the Poor* became a platform to highlight the disproportional effects of climate change on the poor, relating the cries of creation to those of the climate vulnerable. That nexus also related the theological concept of justification and justice. LWF Council increasingly released statements on climate justice[1], and the Department of Theology (*in different forms*) produced many eco-theological studies on creation and climate change. The most recent evolution of the LWF's environmental engagement focuses on the intergenerational injustices of climate change (which we see in the Kids Climate Court Case, global strike-out for the climate demonstrations inspired by Greta Thunberg). The Youth led LWF COP Delegations are a vehicle for many of our joint ecumenical engagements in the UNFCCC Processes, and youth implemented climate projects across the communion. So, in mapping recent initiatives in eco-theology, I wish to characterize them as the most recent incarnations of the LWF's historical initiative.

In 2017, the 12th LWF Assembly met under the theme, *Liberated by God's Grace*, which included a sub-theme, *Creation Not For Sale*. The Assembly passed two resolutions regarding climate justice, care for creation and the need for education and diakonia. These resolutions led to a process of outlining strategic directions for engaging climate justice, and greatly influenced the LWF Strategy for 2019 -2024. Rooted in the Assembly's mandate, the new strategy prioritizes a commitment to build the capacity of LWF member churches to advocate, educate (including theological education), and to engage in adaptation, mitigation and youth led climate initiatives. In other words, our vocation to minister to creation and the climate vulnerable are playing an increasing role in forming the LWF's self-understanding of what it means to be "a communion in Christ, living and working together for a just, peaceful and reconciled world."

By explicitly prioritizing climate justice in the new strategy, the LWF is realizing Celia Deanne-Drummond's concept of eco-theology as a discipline concerned with recovering the bases of just relationships in a holistic sense. As I speak, the LWF Council is still in session. I left early to attend this conference, but not before the Council passed a new structure to implement the new strategy. This new structure gives an important signal about the LWF's desire to expand a programmatic commitment to eco-theology. One must first remember that the LWF is a communion of

---

1 The theme of 2008 LWF Council in Tanzania was titled, "The Melting Snow on Mount Kilamanjaro – a witness to the Suffering of Creation". In total, 18 LWF Assemblies and Council meetings have produced statements on creation or climate justice. A summary can be found at https://www.lutheranworld.org/climate-justice/resolutions-statements-climate

churches. So, in a very real sense, everything that is done by any member church, represented even on this panel by the Church of Sweden, EKD churches and others, are part of the LWF's public witness. Obviously the initiatives are too numerous to begin listing here. However, our global programs, projects and advocacy commitments represent an additional layer of initiatives as a communion of churches. That is why the new structure is significant.

Within the new structure, the LWF will establish an Action for Justice Unit. This unit will use a local to global methodology to coordinate advocacy and resource projects. I can say more about that methodology if you are interested. But the important point is that within this unit, the LWF has recruited a new Climate Justice Officer. This person will lead the Communion Office in advocacy issues related to UNFCCC and other climate related processes in civil society, and coordinate work with LWF World Service Country Programs to resource adaptation and mitigation projects. In addition to coordinating humanitarian responses to disaster relief, our diaconal interventions will build the resilience of member churches needing to adapt to loss and damage and their capacity to engage in national advocacy. These capacities will be increasingly significant as we strive to secure NDCs during the implementation phase of the Paris rulebook.

There is one other structural development that signals the LWF's initiative related to eco-theology. The diaconal, humanitarian and advocacy engagements that I mentioned above embody important parts of the LWF's public witness to climate justice. However, all of our diapraxis and advocacy related to climate justice needs to be continually reformed by ongoing theological reflection and education. This critical, transformative task is the domain of eco-theology as a trans-contextual, theologico-ethical discipline and as a spirituality.

For this reason, the new Department of Theology, Mission and Justice will dedicate a program within the Theological Studies Unit specifically to the area of eco-theology. A programmatic focus on eco-theology will integrate the ecological implications of gender studies and economics, or integrate human rights discourse and public theology with the eco-theological narratives of children, youth and indigenous communities. Integrating diverse theological enquiries is necessary to a proper understanding of eco-theology. It will also help us explore Lutheran theological commitments related to creation, anthropology, and vocation. It will help us explore our Trinitarian theology of the Spirit and spiritual theology related to our liturgical seasons and place-based worship (*which I will speak more directly to in tomorrow's session*). Securing this programmatic commitment to study eco-theology as a communion can also coordinate our member churches' and theological institutions efforts to develop and share educational resources dedicated to creation care, and promoting ecological and placed based education in Christian education curricula.

Practically, these strategic commitments will open up a few new initiatives. First, a global Network for Theological Education and Formation will be a platform for convening seminars and facilitating education partnerships related to eco-theology between member churches and theological institutions. For example, an upcoming seminar on teaching eco-theology will be led by the Church of Norway. Second, we can highlight the eco-theological implications of gender justice, and the gender implications of climate justice. Third, we will be in a good position to strengthen our commitment to intergenerational climate justice. Youth will continue to inform our rights based approach through theological research and fostering a local to global approach that connects the theological reflection of member churches to the global initiatives. Finally, we will strengthen our Lutheran commitment to joint ecumenical witness, particularly in close collaboration with the World Council of Churches, ACT Alliance, and our interfaith partnerships at the level of the COP. Eco-theology has provided another entry point for new partnerships

Chad Rimmer

through the Season of Creation. The Season of Creation brings us into a new ecumenical constellation with the Global Catholic Climate Movement, Green Anglicans, WCRC, A Rocha, World Evangelical Alliance, et. al. Our collaboration a way to demonstrate ecumenical solidarity with creation prayer, worship and joint action. For 2020, the Season of Creation prayers, parish resource and youth statement will focus on the theme of Biodiversity.

So the LWF can add new initiatives to the map in the area of eco-theology. But all of these initiatives grow out of our communion's historic commitment to justice and reconciliation. Particularly in an era of ethno-nationalism and forces of disintegration, these programmatic initiatives witness to our belief in the hope of communion for the healing of the whole inhabited earth. To that end, eco-theology is not just about non-human creation. An ecological hermeneutic looks to the holistic dimensions of restoring right relationships among creation, which must necessarily integrate economic, political, social and anthropological commitments under one Trinitarian theological ecology.

ECO-THEOLOGY AND CLIMATE JUSTICE IN RWANDA

Gloriose Umuziranenge

Introduction

Nowadays, one of the greatest problems over the world is climate change and Global climate is warming at an unprecedented rate[1]. According to the Fourth Assessment Report of the Intergovernmental Panel on Climate Change, developing countries are expected to suffer the most from the negative impacts of climate change[2]. Indeed, poor developing nations who have done little to cause the emissions of greenhouse gas are also affected by the impact of climate change at the same level as developed countries who have emitted much of the pollution and who have a strong capacity of dealing with the consequences through mitigation and adaptation measures.

Rwanda is located in the central-eastern part of Africa. It shares boarders with Uganda in the North, Tanzania in the East and South East, Burundi in the South and Democratic Republic of Congo in the West. Rwanda is a small landlocked country of 26,338 Km². It is one of the highest population densities in Africa (1,060/sq mi) and its population is estimated at 12.79 million in 2019[3]. Therefore Rwanda's future socio-economic development is uncertain as its population grows and the climate changes, causing pressure on land, water, food and energy resources. Rwanda is experiencing severe consequences of climate change where especially in rural parts of Rwanda heavy rains caused widespread, flooding, severe soil erosion, landslides, crop and livestock loss, and destruction of road infrastructure and property countrywide and in some parts, the highest cost of human life[4]. In addition it threatens agricultural production. Climate change associated impacts found to be a main challenge for rural poor farmers dominating the agriculture sector because of their limited adaptive capacity to cope with these impacts[5]. Therefore in rural areas where people depend on agriculture, farmers face substantial risk of crop failure and famine when drought hit.

The Ministry of Disaster Management and Refugees (MIDIMAR) from January to end April, 2018 recorded 95 people dead and 195 injured. Disasters damaged 4,560 Ha of crops and de-

1   IPCC. Summary for Policymakers. In: Stocker TF, Qin D, Plattner G-K, et al., eds. *Climate Change 2013: The Physical Science Basis. Contribution of Working Group I to the Fifth Assessment Report of the Intergovernmental Panel on Climate Change.* Cambridge, United Kingdom and New York, NY, USA.
2   IPCC, 2007: Summary for Policymakers. In: Climate Change 2007: Impacts, Adaptation and Vulnerability. Contribution of Working Group II to the Fourth Assessment Report of the Intergovernmental Panel on Climate Change, M.L. Parry, O.F. Canziani, J.P. Palutikof, P.J. van der Linden and C.E. Hanson, Eds., Cambridge University Press, Cambridge, UK, 7-22.
3   National Institute of Statistics of Rwanda (NISR, 2012), Fourth Rwanda Population and Housing Census. Thematic Report: Population Projections.
4   REMA. (2013). "The Assessment of Economic Impacts of the 2012 Wet Season Flooding in Rwanda." Kigali, Rwanda
5   MINAGRI. (2013). "Plan for the Transformation of Agriculture in Rwanda – Phase III." Ministry of Agriculture and Animal Resources. Kigali, Rwanda.

stroyed 370 houses. They destroyed 12 roads, 7 churches, 18 bridges and killed 700 livestock[6]. According to the study conducted to assess the effects climate change on food security in Rwanda (case of Bugesera District), decline in the food crop productivity has been found to be the main effects caused by extreme climatic events[7].

To address the adverse impacts of climate change especially on agricultural productivity in Rwanda several adaptation measures have been discussed and put in place by the government in order to intensify agriculture sector and further improve economic growth such as the promotion of non rain-fed agriculture, increased use of modern agricultural techniques, cultivation of drought-tolerant crops in arid and semiarid zones, introduction of precocious (early-maturing) varieties in arid and semiarid zones, promotion of value addition and other postharvest techniques for agricultural products and reinforcing early-warning and rapid intervention systems.

In its vision 2050, Rwanda envisages to be a developed country, with a strong services sector, low unemployment and low levels of poverty. It is a country where agriculture and industry have a minimal negative impact on the environment, operating in a sustainable way, and enabling Rwanda to be self-sufficient regarding basic necessities. By 2050, development will be achieved with low carbon domestic energy resources and practices, reducing Rwanda's contribution to climate change while allowing it to be independent of imported oil for power generation. Finally, Rwanda will have the robust local and regional knowledge to be able to respond and adapt to changes in the climate and the resulting impacts, supporting other African countries as a regional services hub to do the same[8].

The National Green Growth and Climate Resilience Strategy 2011-2050: 14 programmes of action

In Rwanda, 14 programmes of actions for green growth and climate resilience were put in place by the Government as follows:
– Sustainable intensification of small scale farming
– Agricultural diversity for local and export markets
– Integrated Water Resource Management and Planning
– Sustainable Land Use Management and Planning
– Low carbon mix of power generation for national grid
– Sustainable small-scale energy installations in rural areas
– Green industry and private sector investment
– Climate compatible mining.
– Efficient resilient transport systems.
– Low carbon urban settlements.
– Ecotourism, Conservation.
– Sustainable forestry, agroforestry and biomass energy.
– Disaster Management and Disease Prevention
– Climate data and projections

---

6   https://reliefweb.int/report/rwanda/midimar-supported-and-comforted-population-affected-disasters.
7   Rwanyirizi and Rugema. (2013). "Climate Change Effects on Food Security in Rwanda: Case Study of Wetland Rice Production in Bugesera." *Rwanda Journal 1 (1): 35–51.*
8   Gov of Rwanda. (2011). Green Growth and Climate Resilience National Strategy for Climate Change and Low Carbon Development. Kigali-Rwanda.

Among the successful green economy in Rwanda, we can highlight the Rehabilitation of degraded ecosystems (Lands, forests, National Parks, Wetlands), CIP: Crop Intensification Program[9], Tourism revenue sharing to benefit local communities around national Parks shifted from 5% to 10 % since 2017, Ban on plastic bags use[10], successful Green village pilots has demonstrated poverty reduction benefits: Ease access to electricity and other infrastructures and community empowerment and awareness increased, green demonstration villages.

What the Bible says on Creation and stewardship?

The issue of environment deterioration and its consequences has ethical and spiritual dimensions, among others. The biblical concept on Creation and stewardship by human being teaches clear that "Human beings" are responsible for taking care of God's creation. (Genesis 2:15). Theologically, this means that salvation brought by Jesus Christ do not only send us to be witness to others but rather and more importantly to take care of God's creation in its wholeness. Hence, the Church of God is called and sent to sensitize the community for the change of attitudes and practices towards environment.

In Rwanda the majority of the populations are believers in one of the existing religions. The dominant religious group is the Catholics, who represent 44% of the resident population of the country. The second most prevalent religious group are the Protestants (38%), while other religion groups are made up of Adventists (12%), Muslims (2%) and Jehovah's Witnesses (1%). While those with no religious affiliation represent 2.5%, adherents of the traditionalist/animists and of other religions each represent less than 1% of the population. Thus, Christian religious groups represent 95% of the population of Rwanda[11]. In addition, religion is cultural language which people in Rwanda understand well because they are deeply imbedded into religion systems and rationalities. Christianity being a majority, a better understanding on (Holy writings), can help the sensitization. However in this paper let me confine myself in Christianity responsibility on environmental conservation.

Christians believe that God created the universe, everything created belongs to God, not us, God gave human beings the responsibility to care for it and they believe that a good Christian is the one who protect the environment. He created the male and female, blessed them, and said, "Have many children, so that your descendents will live all over the earth and bring it under their control. I am putting you in charge of the fish, the birds, and all the wild animals. I have provided all kinds of grain and all kinds of fruit for you to eat; but for all the wild animals and birds I have provided grass and leafy plants for food" (Genesis, 1). The Lord God placed the man in the Garden of Eden to cultivate it and guard it. Unfortunately, in proudness of wanting to be like God, human beings rebelled, one of the consequences of human rebellion is the rejection of being God's stewards. Human have destroyed the Creation of God to the extent that even human beings

---

9   The policy about crop intensification program is aimed at boosting agricultural productivity through an improvement of productive inputs use, irrigation coverage and soil quality. Under CIP, the government procures improved seed and fertilizer, which distributes to farmers in selected zones chosen for their food crop production potential.
10   Danielsson, M. (2017). The plastic bag ban in Rwanda: local procedures and successful outcomes.
11   National Institute of Statistics of Rwanda (NISR, 2012), Fourth Population and Housing Census. Thematic Report: Socio-cultural characteristics of the population.

Eco-Theology and Climate Justice ...

are in turn destroying themselves. Indeed, in so much as it has neglected the socio-ecological implications of its teachings; Christianity has a certain responsibility in helping to bring about the ecological crisis despite also holding within itself the potential to provide a robust foundation for socio-ecological actions linking social justice and ecological health as the essence of environmental justice[12]. Therefore environmental justice seeks for better conservation outcomes by involving all people and treats them fairly in all activities regarding the environment[13]. It refers to the process by which environmental actors and the community work together by identifying needs, shared values and challenges and setting up measures and goals to address them as well as implementing together different activities and projects. This concept is linked to the principles of eco-theology in connecting the pain of people to degraded ecosystems, seeking to alleviate both human pain and ecological degradation[14]. Therefore religious philosophy ought to have the option to address current emergencies and crisis for offering progressively natural and socially sustainable initiatives and choices.

In Rwandan context, there is a sense of responsibility for creation care in the community. However, the Church has never, and should not be an observer when it comes to her responsibility as an institution called by God to be steward of God's creation. Moreover, there is a change, role and the understanding of what the church should do the local community. Furthermore, the Church called to give spiritual hope or Christian education but also much more education related to environment education. By having the church as an actor Christians can bridge scientific arguments on climate change that can be translated into Christian's understanding and culture. The church is important in translating climate data and climate change information into cultural practices and behaviors of the people in the community. Thus, it is easy for Christian to believe that respect for God can be connected to the respect of creation.

Protestant Churches green initiatives in Rwanda

In Rwanda there are strategies and processes which try to strengthen the role done by churches in environmental education. Since Churches have the advantage that they talk the language which God commanded to Christians on creation care. Reminding Christian values, the church can take as a point of departure when addressing the problem of environmental destruction and major actions of conserving the environment. Churches are much easily in contact with the local people (Christians) and they could embed climate change effects and climate justice into Christian language and rationality. This is even what the states can learn and do properly.

On the track of dealing with climate change effects in Rwanda, Protestants churches were not left behind. Protestant University of Rwanda, in a partnership with United Evangelical Mission, stated an environmental awareness program to help underserved communities shape their knowledge with regards to environmental protection, especially climate change mitigation and adaptation measures as a matter of environmental justice, as well as a biblical perspective with

---

12   Dawson, N., Grogan, K., Martin, A., Mertz, O., Pasgaard, M., & Rasmussen, L. V. (2017). Environmental justice research shows the importance of social feedbacks in ecosystem service trade-offs. *Ecology and Society, 22*(3).
13   Leciejewski, M., & Perkins, H. A. (2015). Environmental justice in Appalachia: Procedural inequities in the mine permitting process in Southeast Ohio. *Environmental Justice, 8*(4), 111-116.
14   Hrynkow, C. W. (2017). Greening God? Christian Ecotheology, Environmental Justice, and Socio-Ecological Flourishing. *Environmental Justice, 10*(3), 81-87.

regard to environmental care. In fact, 80 participants from Protestant churches received trainings to help address local environmental, health, and economic challenges thanks to UEM to the support provided in the implementation of this activity. The training has been held at PIASS since January 2017 in consecutive phases. It is aimed at improving knowledge and skills of church members, most from the Anglican Church, the Presbyterian Church and others, about mitigating and adapting the effects of climate and its consequences on human welfare, especially on food security in Rwanda, waste management and sustainable development goals, as well as learning from what other practitioners have done in environmental protection related matters. Participants were Church Leaders, Mother's Unions associations, Protestants Schools' directors, and churches development officers. The partnership between PUR and UEM created a working group with the emphasis on the connections between environmental justice and the role of Protestant churches and how they can integrate environmental justice and trainings in their strategic planning. The training facilitates collaboration between churches and environmental justice stakeholders and it strengthens the capacity of communities and church-based organizations to engage in environment advocacy and awareness in planning. Trainings offer knowledge to the participants and make them able to respond to nature conservation in their communities. It is expected that, at the end of each training, the trainees are be able to explain the consequences of human actions on the deterioration of the integrity of creation, articulate theological and biblical insights on the place of human beings in the created world and their responsibility as stewards of God in taking care of creation and argue the role of Christians in sensitization, advocacy and practices for the integrity of the created order.

Implemented activities by EAR[15] in Rwanda
Implemented activities by churches in Rwanda are community mobilization on environmental conservation, training and sensitization on energy saving stoves (EAR Diocese Shyogwe), training on soil management and soil erosion prevention, trees plantation and distribution of seedlings in local community, distribution of ceramic water filters in local community. Initiatives carried out by EAR are community improvement initiatives and are operated as a joint activity between Butare, Cyangugu, Kigeme and Shyogwe dioceses of the Anglican Church of Rwanda. The 4 dioceses agree with that the church has a critical position to play inside the socio-economic development of the human beings. They recognition on selling harmony and participating in the healing technique of the human beings inside the 4 dioceses via social transformation introduced approximately through non secular change and participation of the community in identifying and enforcing applicable tasks to overcoming their each day issues. The church has a role as a restoration ministry in reconciliation, restoration, and rehabilitation. The church has also been concerned with rural improvement, vocational education, schooling, and in the war against HIV/AIDS. The agricultural improvement Inter-Diocesan carrier (RDIS) is a community development undertaking operated as a joint movement via Butare, Cyangugu, Kigeme and Shyogwe dioceses of the Anglican Church in Rwanda. The enterprise has very deep involvement in the groups it works with, no longer only because of the presence of the Anglican Church inside the vicinity, but additionally on the basis of the numerous initiatives and programmes that it is undertaking, together with threat reduction and environmental protection, tree nursery were prepared, improved cooking stoves, land terracing, Swamp control, Saving and credit score, Mobilization of

---

15   Eglise Anglicane au Rwanda

saving groups, promotion of profits-producing sports, nutrition safety interventions, Irish potato developing - rice developing, Pineapple growing and processing, fish farming, animal herding, goats, pigs, hens, water and sanitation, water conservation, water tanks, Biogas (very few trials, mainly in schools), go-phase/ability building, own family making plans, financial savings and credit attain and animal husbandry. Moreover, the Dioceses run various colleges and fitness facilities. With reference to climate change mitigation and adaptation huge achievements of the church are highlighted under: advanced cook Stoves undertaking: From 2007 to 2013, RDIS distributed approximately 3000 improved Stoves (ICS), constructed from locally available substances (bricks, clay, cement). And given that since 2012, RDIS is effectively implementing a Carbon project for improved cooking Stoves and Water Ceramic Filters in Rwanda. The reason of this project (Carbon Emission reduction for Self Sustainable Environmental Care) is particularly to lessen the use of firewood, which is extremely scarce in Rwanda. RDIS is likewise concerned with reforestation through the establishment of tree nurseries and capacity building activities. RDIS therefore, participate in the distribution and mobilization on the use of power-saving stoves as a very important activity as a way to reduce the use of charcoal and firewood[16]. This project has facilitated beneficiaries in the cooking process which seems to be easy compared with the use of firewood, the process which is very quick, reduced smokes in the Kitchen, and the cleanness of the kitchen. Water ceramic filters have reduced the time spent on drinking water boiling and water born diseases were reduced according to beneficiaries, the project generated employment in the local community. Even though Churches are committed to address some of the effects of climate change, they still face the challenge of low community awareness about the risks of climate change which constitutes an obstacle to ownership of protection measures, lack of knowledge and skills among community and church members in relation to climate protection, difficult collaboration between environmental actors (churches, civil society, foreign agencies and government services and Lack of enough resources to implement projects to address climate change.

Conclusion and recommendations

Environmental justice as a new paradigm in conservation and protection of environment could be linked to community empowerment due to the fact that when the community is socially and economically empowered, threats which they cause to the environment are reduced. Raising awareness of the community on environmental justice related matters and promoting equality in using natural resource impact promote a holistic for sustainable development. For a country to advance in sustainable development and enhance environmental justice there is a need to strengthen community participation in different projects and domains so that they can feel comfortable with what is happening in their living environment. Environmental Justice links human rights and development to achieve a human-centred approach, safeguarding the rights of the most vulnerable and sharing the burdens and benefits of climate change and its resolution equitably and fairly. Therefore citizens of the developed world should intervene to minimize the impacts of climate change on the most vulnerable by supporting developing countries and communities to adapt their livelihoods, protect their resources and embrace low carbon development (climate justice). Better environmental conservation actions require active participation and in-

---

16 2nd Assessment of Environmental Protection Activities in UEM member churches in the African Region 2011-2015

volvement of all including women, children, vulnerable people, and very poor people as they are the ones who firstly affected by the consequences of climate change. Churches should actively participate as they have advantage of translating climate change and climate justice information at local community scale through gospel that Christians can understand easily. And as God's people, Christians have a responsibility to work for climate justice by reducing climate crisis. Churches should be involved in carbon emissions reduction strategies. For instance, churches should be involved in promoting ecological agriculture using organic fertilizers. Churches may also include teachings related to protecting our planet as a God given treasure, especially in Sunday schools so that people feel concerned with this matter from a very young age.

RECENT LATIN AMERICAN AND CARIBBEAN ECO-THEOLOGICAL INITIATIVES

A reading guide

Guillermo Kerber

In this presentation I will focus on recent developments on eco-theology in Latin America and the Caribbean. Two criteria have guided this focus: the international perspective and the ecumenical commitment. Though rooted in Latin America, the initiatives presented below have had an international scope as well as an ecumenical matrix.

It would be misleading to think that eco-theology and related topics have only become a preoccupation recently in Latin American and the Caribbean. Although Pope Francis' Laudato Si' (LS) encyclical published in 2015 has brought ecological concerns to a wide audience, one of its key messages, to listen at the same time to "the cry of the earth and the cry of the poor" (LS 49), picked up the title of a book and the perspective of Brazilian liberation theologian Leonardo Boff. "Cry of the earth, cry of the poor"[1], originally published in 1995, already catalysed years of reflection by him and other Latin American thinkers on ecological topics from a liberationist perspective. In Boff as well as in other theologians, though Catholic rooted, the reference to other Christian denominations and theologians, notably Jürgen Moltmann[2], was key.

Taking into consideration the two criteria mentioned earlier: the international and ecumenical perspectives, it is also worth mentioning that in 2019 we commemorate thirty years of a process that started in 1989 with the Encounters on Culture, Ethics and Religion (CER) facing the challenge of Ecology, with three editions in Montevideo (1989), Buenos Aires (1990), Porto Alegre (1992).[3]

The themes of these Encounters which gathered not only Latin American but also theologians and philosophers from other regions, show the interest of the time: the social ecology, the ecological and social crisis, the justice dimension of the crisis. While the first CER was part of a larger initiative organized by the Franciscan Centre in Montevideo (the *Centro de Investigación y Promoción Franciscano y Ecológico* – CIPFE), the First Latin American Congress on Ecology[4] which brought over a thousand participants from all over the world, the other two, held in Buenos Aires and Porto Alegre in the following years, were activities on their own and were organized with a long list of counterparts, among them the Latin American Council of Churches – CLAI, ISEDET (the Theological Protestant Faculty in Buenos Aires) and the *Escola Superior de Teologia e Espiritualidade Franciscanas* (ESTEF), represented at that time by Fr Luiz Carlos Susin O.F.M., which later became the Executive Secretary of the World Forum on Theology and Liberation.

---

1 Leonardo Boff, *Cry of the earth, cry of the poor*, New York, Orbis 1997.
2 See Jürgen Moltmann, *God in creation*, London, SCM 1985.
3 2019 is also thirty years after the European Ecumenical Assembly in Basel which adopted the document "Peace and Justice for the whole creation". Both the European Assembly and the Latin American CER had the Justice, Peace and Integrity of Creation (JPIC) conciliar process, led by the World Council of Churches as key reference.
4 See (in Spanish), Eduardo Gudynas, Ricardo Xalambrí (eds.) *Actas del Primer Congreso Latino Americano de Ecología*, Montevideo, CIPFE 1989.

Thirty years after these initiatives, we can see that what were somehow "exotic" adventures in the context of the churches and the ecumenical movement in the region, have become a strong component of the regional theological reflection.

In fact, two regional initiatives have included and even mainstreamed eco-theology in their production. I am referring to the Latin American chapter of the Ecumenical Association of Third World Theologians (EATWOT) and its publication "Voices"[5] and the World Forum on Theology and Liberation (WFTL).

The Latin American section of EATWOT and the theological journal Voices

Several issues of Voices have focussed over the last decade on eco-theology with a strong contribution and coordination by the Latin American section of EATWOT. The choice to develop an electronic theological journal [6] has not prevented the publication from being able to convince several printed theological journals in the region to include all or some of the articles being published in Voices in their printed versions. [7] While most of the articles are written in Spanish or Portuguese, the electronic version of the Journal includes sometimes English or French versions of the articles.

In 2009 the journal had as theme: "Eco-crisis. Theological visions" and included regional perspectives from Asia, Africa, Latin America, North America indigenous peoples, feminist ecotheology.[8]

The first issue of 2011 focussed on "Ecology and Religion in this hour of planetary emergency" with three articles written by Leonardo Boff and others by theologians from different Latin American countries.[9]

In 2013, the theme of the issue was "Liberation theology, 40 years old". In the introduction José María Vigil, the editor, expressed that " the EATWOT Theological Commission and the Latin American Coordination show that the theological production of liberation theology today tries to respond to the challenges of the current times with new contextual theologies (pluralist theology of liberation, indigenous, feminist and ecological theologies).[10]

The theme of 2014's double issue was "Deep Ecology, Spirituality and Liberation", with twenty articles which developed a wide understanding of deep ecology (and not only the perspective of philosopher Arne Naess who developed the concept), many of them translated into English.[11]

---

5   http://eatwot.net/VOICES/
6   The different issues of Voices are available free online at: http://eatwot.net/VOICES/
7   These are some of journals that included some of the articles of Voices in their printed editions: Christus, Mexico DF, Mexico; Caminos, La Habana, Cuba; Senderos, San José, Costa Rica; Alternativas, Managua, Nicaragua; La Antigua, Panamá, Panamá; Franciscanum, Bogotá, Colombia; Vinculum, Bogotá, Colombia; Spiritus, Quito, Ecuador; Páginas, Lima, Perú; Revista Eclesiastica Brasileira, Petrópolis, RJ, Brasil; Horizonte, PUC-Minas, Belo Horizonte, MG, Brasil; Ensayos Teológicos, Asunción, Paraguay; Soleriana, Montevideo, Uruguay; Obsur, Montevideo, Uruguay; Vida Pastoral, Buenos Aires, Argentina.
8   http://eatwot.net/VOICES/VOICES-2009-June.pdf.
9   http://eatwot.net/VOICES/VOICES-2011-1.pdf.
10   Voices 2013, *Liberation theology 40 years old*, Introduction, p. 19. ; see: http://eatwot.net/VOICES/VOIC-ES-2013-4.pdf.
11   http://eatwot.net/VOICES/VOICES-2014-2&3.pdf.

Guillermo Kerber

In 2016 the second volume of the year was dedicated to "Laudato si' and ecology" with articles also translated into English.[12]

The World Forum on Theology and Liberation[13]

Although the name refers to the global perspective of the initiative, the World Forum on Theology and Liberation (WFTL) has had a strong Latin American and Caribbean component, on the one hand because of its genesis as part of the World Social Forum (WSF) whose first editions took place in Brazil and on the other hand because of its secretariat hosted in Porto Alegre, Brazil[14]. Since its inception the WFTL has had eco-theological concerns at its core. Its Chart of Principles expresses: "Each WFTL has taken place in the context of the World Social Forum. It has, therefore, as framework "Another world is possible". It takes over and reformulates WSF principles in order to bring together and articulate people interested in theological mediations, being aware of the complexity and diversity of ethical, aesthetic and spiritual experiences and is committed to just alternatives for cultures and societies, genders, religions, in favour of ecological and planetary spiritualities. " [15]

At the first WFTL held in Porto Alegre in January 2005, Leonardo Boff said: "Liberation theology was born when it heard the cry of the poor...But not only the poor cry. Waters, woods, animals, ecosystems, the whole Earth cry. All of them are victims of the same logic that create impoverishment. In the preferential option for the poor and against poverty – the trademark of liberation theology – the Earth, who is the Big Poor, must be included. The Earth is the only common home we have to live in. Liberation theology will be integral if it includes in its reflection and practice the liberation of the Earth as system of systems, as superorganism in which we all live as sons and daughters with all other living beings, our brothers and sisters, produced and fed by Mother Earth". [16]

The third WFTL took place in 2009 at the heart of the Amazon region, in the city of Belém, Brazil, and focussed explicitly on care for creation. The theological reflection showed that beliefs, spirituality and sacred values are a double-edged sword: they can potentiate the destruction or redemption of Mother Earth. A sacralization of domination, appropriation, unlimited growth makes the change we need today for the continuity of life on earth impossible. Spiritual traditions, however, have also the potential to focus on the sacredness that surrounds every form of life, including, of course, the fragile form of human flesh. In the Amazon forest, the planet is more water than land, and the marriage of water and land is so intense that the Amazonians insisted that the motto of the WFTL should be "Water and Earth for another possible world."[17]

---

12   http://eatwot.net/VOICES/VOICES-2016-2.pdf
13   See http://wftlofficial.org/
14   Fr Luiz Carlos Susin OFM, who, as we mentioned earlier, was already one of the organizers of the Third Encounter on Culture, Ethics and Religion facing the challenge of ecology (CER) in 1992 in Porto Alegre, has been the Executive Secretary of the WFTL for almost two decades.
15   http://wftlofficial.org/wp-content/uploads/2017/03/cartadeprincipios_portugues.pdf
16   See Leonardo Boff, Dos urgentes utopías para el siglo XXI, in Juan José Tamayo, Luiz Carlos Susin (eds.) Teología para otro mundo posible, Madrid PPC 2006, p. 220-221. There is an English edition: Marcella Althaus-Reid, Ivan Petrella Luis Carlos Susin (eds.), Another Possible World. Reclaiming Liberation Theology, London SCM Press 2007.
17   See (in Portuguese) http://wftlofficial.org/historico/. The publication which collected the presentations at this edition of the WFTL is: Luiz Carlos Susin, Joe Marcal Dos Santos (eds.) Nosso planeta, nossa vida. Ecologia e teologia, São Paulo, Paulinas 2011.

When the WFTL were held in Tunisia (2013 and 2015) the role of religion in society was a crucial issue. Ecology, and especially climate change challenges, was part of the discussions of these editions of the WFTL, in dialogue with the Climate Space held at the World Social Forum.[18]

Conclusion

A crucial topic in today's theology, eco-theology has a history of more than thirty years in Latin America and the Caribbean. What could be seen as an eccentric concern for a bunch of theologians in the 1980s has become an important aspect of theological reflection. As shown in previous pages, the process has been ecumenical, both in the sense of bringing together different Christian traditions, especially Catholic, Orthodox and Protestant and of addressing the "whole inhabited world". As mentioned in this chapter and developed in many books, the Justice, Peace and Integrity of Creation Conciliar Process, led by the World Council of Churches but implemented far beyond WCC's constituency was a benchmark which inspired theologians and Christians in various parts of the world to include ecological concerns in their reflections and actions.

---

18   See the publication of the presentations at: Gerald M. Boodoo (ed.), *Religion, human dignity and liberation*, WFTL, São Leopoldo, Oikos 2016.

Guillermo Kerber

PASTORAL ACTION PROGRAM FOR THE PROMOTION OF THE CARE OF CREATION OF THE EVANGELICAL CHURCH OF THE RIVER PLATE

Context, approach, balance and projection

Daniel Beros

1. Introduction

The Evangelical Church of the Rio de la Plata (known as the IERP for its abbreviation in Spanish) is a church of the River Plate region with a united tradition (Lutheran and Reformed).

In the course of its young history as an autonomous church, the IERP /ECRP has progressively developed a marked ecumenical and diaconal profile. This has been achieved in various ways in the struggles that have occurred in the societies of the three countries in which it is present, among which should highlighted its active participation in the defense of human rights, the accompaniment and promotion of the poorest, and the protection of the environment.

The "Pastoral Action Program for the Promotion of the Care of Creation" (PAPPCC) — an initiative that the IERP carries out through its diaconal arm, the Protestant Foundation for Diacony "Time to Work" (PFDTW) – is part of that line of commitment, proposing to promote an active awareness in and from the faith communities about the Christian responsibility in the care of creation, with particular emphasis on the economic, environmental and health problems that derive from the extractivist model of "agribusiness" prevailing in the entire region of the Southern Cone of America.

2. Context

2.1 The dominant regime of exploitation

The fundamental framework of PAPPCC is based on the premise that the present stage of the world system, governed by the dominant forces of transnational financial capitalism, continues to determine, for the subaltern countries and regions, a deep -and increasingly asymmetric- insertion in the relations of production and exchange.

As is well known, the role assigned to peripheral societies in this framework is essentially that of the production of raw materials (such as soy bean) or of goods with scarce industrial processing (such as soybean oil). The conditions of this exchange have been and continue to be imposed by the actors that control the (badly) so-called "free market." They fundamentally benefit a few circles of international concentrated capital and its regional partners. And in exchange, these conditions not only bring great human and environmental damage to the peoples of the periphery of the global south, but also a meager and poorly distributed revenue, which specifically adopts the form of exploitation and permanent mass alienation of its resources in favor of the central countries and the local elites associated with them.

It is, therefore, a deeply unjust regime, sustained in various forms of dispossession, damage and violence.

2.2 The role of monocultures and transgenic soybeans

For our region, what characterizes the scheme of global assymetric exchange has been and continues to be the imposition of a (neo) colonial model of extractivist exploitation of natural resources, within which framework some monocultures have played a prominent role, such as soy, tobacco, eucalyptus or pine, among others. These crops under conditions of the prevailing political-economic rationality are often produced on the basis of "technological packages" that include, among other factors, the use of genetically modified seeds and the intensive application of agrotoxins.

In the particular case of transgenic soybeans, their cultivation was introduced from Argentina, starting in the mid-1990s. Since then, the "RR" (Roundup Ready) soy started its triumphal march incorporating millions of hectares year after year to its cultivation, not only in Argentina, but – crossing its border, first illegally – in all the neighboring countries of the region. Exports of soybeans and some of their derivatives, in a few years removed from the podium other traditional crops (such as wheat or corn), becoming the main source of currency income of the country.

Over the course of recent years, public opinion has gradually become aware of the serious consequences of the practices that sustain this production model for the living and health conditions of the population and for the environment. This has been due mainly to public demonstrations of protest and resistance by the directly affected population (peasants, indigenous peoples, neighbors, etc.), as well as by people and organizations that have expressed solidarity with their struggles (environmentalists, trade unionists, academic, etc.).

These actors have been denouncing, on the one hand, the causal relationship given between the massive application of agrotoxins, that such crops demand, and the exponential increase in the suffering of diseases such as cancer, anatomical malformations in newborns or miscarriages by pregnant women; they have denounced repeated fumigations over towns or rural schools and the poisoning of water tables or other water courses with various agrotoxins.

In turn, the movement of social resistance has put on the table the causal relationship given between the destruction of entire ecosystems on the altar of soybeans, produced by the massive deforestation demanded by the uncontrolled advance of the agricultural frontier, with diverse and dramatic manifestations of climate change, which threaten to further deepen the deterioration of living conditions: devastating floods and diluvial storms alternating with periods of pronounced drought in areas that traditionally did not know this type of extreme events.

2.3 The place of the church and its membership

Conditions such as those described, naturally do not escape the reality experienced in one way or another by the people and groups that make up the churches of the region in general and the ecclesial communities of the IERP in particular. In their daily existence, church members share the crossroads and dilemmas of the social sectors of which they are a part, often debating each other, as do those who are not in the churches, between fascination, guilt, fears, contained anger and resignation. If we also take into account the imbrication of the church and its ministers in their relationships of economic and labor dependency, which ultimately refer to the prevailing production regime as a basis for support, the enormous complexity and tension that qualify the place of the church and its membership in that situation become clear.

Daniel Beros

3. Pastoral approach

The theological approach that offers guidance to the pastoral project (which will be set out separately), leads, in the first instance, to maintain a healthy critical reserve with respect to those assessments that tend to evaluate the problem posed, focusing predominantly on its ideological and moral aspects. As this approach knows that such a modus operandi gives rise to discursive and practical interventions that -as a result of the empire of the speculative logic of self-justification- too often promote the aggressive foundations of impasse and mutual disqualifications. Thus they do nothing but contribute to deepening the "crack" between a "they" and a "we", between "progressives" and "conservatives", between "good" and "bad", between "saved" and "condemned".

The PAPPCC has developed its own outlook from texts such as Luke 24, 13-35 ("The disciples of Emmaus"), which describes a process of transformation that starts from the facilitation of the word, goes through a critical rereading of Scripture and gives rise to a renewed experience of reality. From this perspective, the PAPPCC conceives its approach to the problem as a perspective that – by suspending the general ideological and abstract moral proposals – aims to promote in and from the sphere of the church the formation of *spaces that facilitate the word and respectful mutual listening*, protagonized by the various people and groups involved. Through the PAPPCC we seek to promote *a critical review of reality in the light of faith*, from which a *transforming commitment to this reality* is assumed.

Therefore, from the PAPPCC there has been an effort to draw out the methodological and practical consequences of the biblical narrative. Through the precise form of dialogue and critical reflection that qualifies it as "pastoral", it seeks to promote a process of awareness of the concrete implications of Christian responsibility in the care of creation. And it does so by dedicating particular focus and attention to the socio-economic, ecological and health issues generated by the "agribusiness" model that dominates agrarian production throughout the region, in order to promote various alternative practices, which surpass it, such as, for example, those proposed by the agro-ecological agriculture movement.

This approach involves working from a broad ecumenism, which does not take into account only the ecclesial sphere, but goes to, invites, involves and gets involved with popular organizations, academia, political and trade union forces, etc.

4. Preliminary Balance and Projection

4.1 – Balance

The various indicators that the team and the evaluators have been collecting after the first three years of implementation of the program (2016-2018), underscore the importance and significance attributed to the fact that the church has assumed the challenge of carrying out a plan of pastoral action in order to promote a transformative awareness in relation to the problems derived from the extractivist model of agribusiness based on transgenic monocultures and the massive use of agrotoxics. For the vast majority of voices that have expressed themselves in this regard, both the membership of the IERP, and people from other institutional and social spaces, this is a crucial and relevant initiative, which should be continued, expanded and deepened.

Another noteworthy aspect is that, in general terms, the PAPPCC has contributed to the securing and concretizing, both in the institutional agenda and in the conscience of a part of the leadership and the membership of the church, an outstanding place for the question of the "care of creation" and for the active search for transformative alternatives in various orders (productive, legislative, educational, etc.). In this regard, it is worth highlighting the significance of the theological approach developed by PAPPCC, which promoted the recognition of the essential nexus of the issue of the care of creation in relation to the faith it professes and the spirituality that moves the church and the men and women that conform its membership.

Likewise, one way in which the experience undertaken in this project has shown success is the methodology of respectful facilitation of the word and mutual listening, which consciously avoids the issuance of generic moral judgments in advance in order to favor a process of expression, exchange and critical review of the reality among the participants, whatever their previous position in relation to the problem. Although the concrete experience in the spaces of dialogue and reflection was not linear by any means, nor was it free of certain tensions, a general balance of the same allows us to highlight as very positive this approach that, associated with the theological focus in the background, characterize it essentially as "pastoral".

Training spaces (such as workshops and international consultations) and – above all – the most direct and existencial experiences, be they in the celebratory and liturgical aspect (in devotionals and worship services) or in the aspect of productive activity (especially through visits to alternative agroecological establishments) have been evaluated as highly significant. In such instances the participants have been able to play an active and protagonistic role, which permitted many of them to be able to experiment a series of lived activities, achieve perceptions and acquire knowledge that were evaluated as very relevant, and that were aligned to a great extent with the goals that were proposed in the PAPPCC.

Finally, it is worth highlighting the articulation process carried out by the PAPPCC with various institutional and personal instances in the areas of science, academia, social militancy, politics and trade unions, etc., which the project counts as a very important assets at the time of thinking about its projection. This process allowed us to become aware of the true charisma that an ecclesial initiative like the PAPPCC can have when dealing with complex problems of society such as those proposed by the agribusiness extractive model. It consists precisely in the "connector" role that can be played by bringing and facilitating dialogue and cooperation between agencies that often develop their activity in a dissociated and disconnected manner. The active, generous and conscious exercise of that role – which should be able to be extended to other issues of heated debate and conflict, such as those posed by, for example, questions of gender – should be a valuable contribution of the churches to society as a whole.

Of course, beyond the positive aspects indicated here, there are a number of questions that demonstrate the flaws and limitations in the development of the program. A quick review of its results makes it possible to verify that a project with the characteristics of the PAPPCC finds clear limitations in terms of its capacity for real impact, not only in certain areas and sectors of the church, but above all in its broader social environment. This has been due in part to the serious difficulties that the pastoral team has had at times to develop an adequate interaction in certain areas and milieux, inside and outside the church, characterized by very particular social relations and mentalities, highly impermeable to the type of action that the program proposed to sustain in them.

4.2 Projection

The experience gathered over the course of the three years in which this ministry has been carried out, allows us to point out a series of aspects that invite its leadership to dream of the development of a new stage, which would allow for the consolidation of the acquired knowledge, for the working out the shortcomings and for the deepening of the successes, by extending the scope of the project towards horizons of greater depth, richness and breadth.

At the time of tentatively specifying its description, it is worth mentioning in the first place what seems a truism, but carefully analyzed is not so: having first focused on the problems associated with the production model has led to the recognition of the importance of addressing, at the same time, the problems linked to the chains of commercialization and consumption – as "faces" of what constitutes the same "currency-model". For that reason, a new phase of PAPPCC should consider expanding its objectives and intervention strategies in order to include such aspects. Here, the promotion and facilitation of the establishment of relations of direct exchange between producers and consumers of agro-ecological foods could play a significant role, both within the scope of the church itself, as well as in that of civil society and the State.

Another fundamental challenge for a new stage should be to intensify the articulation with other allied actors of civil society in order to promote and maximize change, from extractive production forms, to forms of agro-ecological production. Here we should look for forms of association that enable the establishment of relationships accompaniment and technical advice in agroecology and alternative production. Although the ministry has already made significant contacts and some specific experiences in this regard, it is important to expand them, in order to facilitate the decision-making processes of those producers who wish to bet on a progressive reconversion from one model to the other.

In turn, the PAPPCC should intensify the catechetical action linked to the question of the care of creation in general and the problems related to the production, marketing and consumption of foods in particular. This would have to give rise to an action of accompaniment of the men and women who serve as catechists and youth leaders, women's and men's groups, etc., in order to facilitate a relevant articulation of the various relevant aspects of the problem in the light of Faith. In this same line, the proposal should include, in addition to the continuation of spaces such as workshops and consultations, the realization of camps and practical experiences in agro-ecological establishments, intervention actions in the public sphere, etc.

Finally, a prominent aspect of the projection of decisively taking up again the question of how an experience like that of the MPCC can contribute to rethinking the curriculum in the field of theological and pastoral formation. In this sense, the recent creation of the Ecumenical Network of Theological Education (ENTE), sponsored by the IERP together with four other churches of ecumenical Protestantism in the River Plate region, offers a good opportunity for presenting the mentioned challenge in a very concrete way. Also, to provide a platform for critical eco-theological and agroecological formation that surpasses the dominant model of production and consumption, both for its membership in general, and for its younger, new leaderships in particular.[1]

5. Concluding

The Evangelical Church of the River Plate has, as we said, a long and rich experience of commitment to the defense of human and environmental rights, which far exceeds the initiative that we have been trying to describe – the Ministry of the Promotion and Care of Creation. In turn,

---

1   More information about this new ecumenical space of theological education in the River Plate area, a successor for the I.U.ISEDET, at: www.reet.org.ar and www.facebook.com/RedEcumenicaREET

this experience of the IERP, is part of a very wide ecumenical journey, of which it is a part and to which the church is indebted.

Within this framework, the PAPPCC understands itself to be a particular and contextual effort to incarnate the search for the "justice, peace and integrity of creation" initiated by the conciliar process promoted several decades ago by the World Council of Churches. Inspired by this greater pilgrimage, it will continue to seek to incarnate, in the face of the problems derived from the extractivist model of "agribusiness", a committed and transforming response in the region of the River Plate, as part of the public witness to what is called the One-Church of Jesus Christ.

PRIORITIES FOR ECUMENICAL ECO-ETHICS IN THE 21ST CENTURY

Thoughts and lessons from SAFCEI, a multi-faith eco-justice organisation in Southern Africa

Geoff Davies and Kate Davies

1. Setting the scene

The global climate crisis and ecological collapse is too enormous to be dealt with by individuals, politicians, technocrats and business leaders with vested power and financial interests. It requires a new level of mobilisation that is underpinned by values and ethical principles and led by trusted, visionary and co-operative leadership. It requires a transforming tipping point.

A ray of hope is emerging from mass and interconnected global movements. Extinction Rebellion[1], Rise for the Climate[2], the Fossil Free Divestment Campaign[3] and the youth led Fridays for Future[4], initiated by Swedish teenager Greta Thunberg, are some of the campaigns that are demanding a different kind of world.

Where is the voice of faith communities? For more than two decades, statements and declarations calling for a new way of living and valuing the world have been issued by the world's living faiths and its leaders.[5] Pope Francis' 2015 Encyclical, *Laudato si'*, makes a plea to all humanity to

---

1 Extinction Rebellion: https://rebellion.earth/ (Accessed 11 September 2019).
2 Rise for the Climate: https://riseforclimate.org/ (Accessed 11 September 2019).
3 Fossil Free: https://gofossilfree.org/ (Accessed 11 September 2019).
4 Fridays for Future: https://www.fridaysforfuture.org/ (Accessed 11 September 2019).
5 Faith Statements:
The Assisi Declarations, 1986. http://www.arcworld.org/downloads/THE%20ASSISI%20DECLARATIONS.pdf (Accessed 11 September 2019).
World Council of Churches 1991. *Giver of life – Sustain your Creation*. http://oikoumene.net/eng.home/eng.global/eng.canberra91/eng.canber.2.5/index.html (Accessed 11 September 2019).
The Earth Charter, 2000. http://www.unesco.org/education/tlsf/mods/theme_a/img/02_earthcharter.pdf (Accessed 11 September 2019).
Declaration by Pope John Paul II and the Ecumenical Patriarch Bartholomew I, 2002. http://w2.vatican.va/content/john-paul-ii/en/speeches/2002/june/documents/hf_jp-ii_spe_20020610_venice-declaration.html (Accessed 6 September 2019).
World Alliance of Reformed Churches 2004. *The Accra Confession: Covenanting for justice in the economy and the earth*. http://www.oikotree.org/wp-content/uploads/accra-confession.pdf (accessed 18 August 2014).
Evangelical Lutheran Church in America 2006. *Awakening God's call to earthkeeping*. www.ecla.org/stewardship/teaching (accessed 11 August 2014).
South African Council of Churches Climate Change Committee 2009. *Climate Change: A challenge to the churches in South Africa*. Marshalltown: SACC.
World Council of Churches 2013. *EC 12 The Earth community groans: A call to ecological justice and peace in the face of climate change*. file:///C:/Users/Kate/Downloads/Ecumenical_Conversations.pdf (Accessed 6 September 2019).

---

cherish our only home.[6] The Pope continues to champion the earth, but this has not been enough to mobilise an ecological uprising amongst the world's one billion Catholics.[7] The Ecumenical Patriarch, Dimitrios I of the Orthodox Church declared a Day of Prayer for Creation in 1989.[8] A number of mainline Christian denominations now include a six-week Season of Creation from the 1st of September in their liturgical calendars.[9] In 2006, eighty-six evangelical church leaders in the United States of America issued a strong call to action entitled Climate Change: An Evangelical Call to Action.[10] In spite of these and many other calls from other faith constituencies, there is scant evidence of the moral voice and mass transforming eco-justice action that communities of faith could be spearheading in an unfair world that is fractured by violence, poverty, climate disruption and ecosystem collapse.

We are mindful of the decades of theorizing work that has been done by theologians and Christian leaders. They have explored and written about eco-theology and the ethics of sustainability and have created an important and helpful foundation.[11] In this paper, we share our concern that an initiative to establish 'eco-friendly churches' is a good start, but is not nearly radical enough. There is a much bigger task ahead. We share our thoughts on work from a multi-faith perspective. We recount our experiences and reflections on the establishment of SAFCEI, a multi-faith eco-justice institute in southern Africa, discussing its rationale and vision for the future. Finally, we highlight the Christian imperative to become earth keepers.

2. Kairos moments, ecumenism and eco-justice

2.1 Kairos moments

Some critical moments of our time have been marked by bold moral statements that have been crafted by courageous religious leaders. The prophetic significance of Kairos documents may only become apparent retrospectively, but they help clarify the thinking and rationale that underpin calls for action and resistance.

The historic 1934 Barmen declaration,[12] which challenged Nazi Germany's authority over the Church, provided a symbolic backdrop, eighty-five years later, for the 2019 Wuppertal *Kairos for Creation* statement. This declaration, drafted in the same city by a gathering of Christians from

Islamic Declaration on Global Climate Change, 2015. http://www.ifees.org.uk/declaration/; (Accessed 2 September 2019).

National Religious Coalition on Creation Care, 2019. *Religious declaration of unprecedented human emergency.* http://nrccc.org/PDF/Human-Climate-Emergency.pdf (Accessed 6 September 2019).

6   *Laudato si',* 2015. https://w2.vatican.va/content/dam/francesco/pdf/encyclicals/documents/papa-francesco_20150524_enciclica-laudato-si_en.pdf (Accessed 2 September 2019).

7   Global Catholic population. https://www.google.com/search?q=global+catholic+population&rlz=1C1OK WM_enZA784ZA801&oq=Global+catholic&aqs=chrome.2.69i57j0l5.8713j0j8&sourceid=chrome&ie=UTF-8 (Accessed 14 September 2019).

8   Day of Prayer for Creation, 1989. https://www.patriarchate.org/-/message-by-h-a-h-ecumenical-patriarch-dimitrios-upon-the-day-of-prayer-for-the-protection-of-creation-01-09-1989- (Accessed 2 September 2019).

9   Season of Creation www.seasonofcreation.org (Accessed 2 September 2019).

10   The Evangelical Climate Initiative, 2006. Climate Change: *An evangelical call to action.* https://www.npr.org/documents/2006/feb/evangelical/calltoaction.pdf (Accessed 15 September 2019).

11   Conradie, E 2006. *Christianity and Ecological Theology.* Stellenbosch: Sun Press. Rasmussen, L. 2013. *Earth-Honoring Faith: Religious Ethics in a New Key.* New York: Oxford University Press. And many others.

12   The Barmen Declaration, 1934. http://www.westpresa2.org/docs/adulted/Barmen.pdf (Accessed 14 September).

around the world, draws attention to the mushrooming ecological crisis. This is a global crisis that is not restricted to Western Europe.

Kairos moments are not new to South Africa. The 1982 *Belhar Confession*[13] was drawn up by the Dutch Reformed Mission Church in its resistance struggle against Apartheid. This was followed soon afterwards, in 1985,[14] by *The Kairos Document*, drafted and signed by a group of Christian leaders and their churches. It challenged the Apartheid regime for its viscous clamp-down of freedoms following the declaration of a state of emergency. In 2006, *The Oikos Journey, a reflection on the economic crisis in South Africa,*[15] completed a South African Kairos trilogy. The *Oikos* statement opened up a new issue, connecting economic injustice and the commodification of the earth with growing poverty and environmental degradation.[16]

The final paragraph of the 1985 Kairos Document states, "We pray that God will help all of us to translate the challenge of our times into action." This call to action applies as much to our contemporary global *Kairos for Creation* as it did to the Kairos appeal during the dark days of Apartheid. How soon will we hear and respond to this cry?

2.2 Ecumenism

The Wuppertal call, articulated in the *Kairos for Creation*, addresses the global ecumenical movement, Christian world communions and the World Council of Churches. The modern interpretation of ecumenical, as espoused by the World Council of Churches, refers to members of the worldwide fellowship of Christian Churches.[17] We believe our understanding of ecumenical should be broadened. We need to rediscover the original Greek meaning of *oikoemene*, as 'the whole inhabited earth'.[18] Christendom, representing roughly a third of the world's population,[19] is too small a faith constituency to act alone to confront the impending global ecological collapse.

It is easier to work with the intricacies of Christian theology than trying to grapple with the complexities of other religions. Furthermore, it is less complicated to communicate with members of one faith, even one denomination. However, in terms of justice and peace, and the seriousness and urgency of the crisis, it is imperative that the world faiths collaborate, co-operate and work together. We also need to respectfully listen to and learn from the wisdom of indigenous communities. Religious leaders will need to surrender self-seeking power and control in order

---

13   The Belhar Confession, 1982. The Dutch Reformed Mission Church https://kerkargief.co.za/doks/bely/CF_Belhar.pdf. (Accessed 16 September 2019).

14   The Kairos Document, 1985. http://oikoumene.net/fix/file/dokumente/The%20South%20Africa%20Kairos%20Document%201985.pdf. (accessed 16 September 2019).

15   The Oikos Journey 2005. Diakonia Council of Churches 2006. *The Oikos Journey.* http://www.diakonia.org.za/attachemnts/39_The%20Oikos%20Journey.pdf (accessed 11 August 2014).

16   Davies, K. 2015. Greening Christian institutions and practices: An emerging ecclesial reform movement. In Conradie, E. and Pillay, M. (eds.): *Ecclesial reform and deform movements in the South African context.* EFSA series, Stellenbosch: SUN.

17   World Council of Churches understanding of ecumenical: https://www.oikoumene.org/en/resources/documents/assembly/2006-porto-alegre/3-preparatory-and-background-documents/ecumenical-conversations/changing-ecclesial-and-ecumenical-context-ecumenical-conversations?searchterm=ecumenism. (Accessed 4 September 2019).

18   Oxford Classical Dictionary definition of *oekomene* https://oxfordre.com/classics/view/10.1093/acrefore/9780199381135.001.0001/acrefore-9780199381135-e-8008.(Accessed 4 September 2019).

19   Global Christian population, 2019. http://worldpopulationreview.com/countries/most-christian-countries/ (Accessed 15 September 2019).

to follow the universal principles of justice and love. These principles, like the Golden Rule,[20] are common to all faiths. Such principles and values will help the human family urgently and collectively to embrace and implement local, regional and global action.

2.3 Eco-justice[21]

Another division, even suspicion, is that which has long existed between faith communities and environmentalists. Many faith communities have disregarded the natural environment and well-being of the planet. A primary function has been seen to be to 'get people to heaven'. Environmentalists have criticised Christians for offering 'pie in the sky' escapism while some Christians are suspicious that environmental care will lead to accusations of Pantheism.

Environmentalists do not worship nature. They are caring for God's creation. Even if creation has taken nearly fourteen billion years to get to where it is today, it has been declared by God to be 'very good' (Genesis 1:30). In Judeo-Christian terms, people have been commissioned by God to take care of it, to 'keep' the earth (Genesis 2:15). Responding to news of the establishment of a multi-faith environment institute, world renowned South African conservationist, Dr Ian Player responded, "Thank God! At last the faith communities are starting to recognise their responsibility." All living faiths, with guidance from their own sacred texts and beliefs, should urgently respond to the call in the 2019 'Kairos for Creation'. They need to become actively involved in eco-justice for the future wellbeing of all the community of life on the planet. This is not exclusive work for Christians.

3. A Southern African faith based eco-justice response

At the turn of this century South Africans were in a state of euphoria, still celebrating their young democracy. Although armed with a new Constitution which enshrined environmental protection, concern for the earth and our life support systems was not high on anyone's agenda. During the Apartheid years, leaders from many Christian denominations and other faith communities had been collectively involved in the resistance struggle. They were accustomed to collaborating on social justice issues. After 1994 the energy of this multi-faith co-operation began to dissipate as faith leaders' refocussed their attention on human rights issues and the escalating social problems, especially those associated with the HIV/AIDS pandemic, unemployment and alleviating poverty. Small pockets of greening actions, led by local faith champions sprung up in the region but nothing was mainstreamed.

After several decades of eco-justice work within the Anglican Church of Southern Africa, and recognising the need for greater collective action, a new initiative began to develop. In 2005, with backing from the South African Council of Churches (SACC), a conference of Christian leaders was planned to discern the interest and support for an ecumenical environment organisation. Encouragement from the UNDP small grants programme persuaded us to invite not only Christians, but leaders from all the major faiths.

South Africa, which had called itself a Christian country in the Apartheid era, had at this time shown little official recognition of the variety of different faiths. Members of other faiths invited

---

20   The Golden Rule. https://philosophyterms.com/golden-rule/. (Accessed 15 September 2019).
21   Eco-justice definition, World Council of Churches. https://www.oikoumene.org/en/what-we-do/eco-justice. (Accessed 15 September 2019).

Geoff Davies and Kate Davies

to the conference expressed deep gratitude and appreciation for their recognition and inclusion. Acknowledging that environmental responsibility is a shared concern, the conference participants enthusiastically endorsed a proposal to establish the Southern African Faith Communities' Environment Institute, SAFCEI.[22] With the twin agenda of promoting eco-justice action (emphasising both economic and ecological justice) and co-operative peace-building, the time was ripe to expand the challenge beyond the Christian community and include all people of all faiths in the region.

Since then, the organisation, which is led by a Board with diverse faith affiliation, has become a significant leader in the faith and eco-justice landscape in South and southern Africa. Members are deeply respectful and appreciative of the different faith perspectives, discovering that earth-keeping is life affirming and a unifying and enriching endeavour that promotes bridge-building and peace-keeping. SAFCEI made a conscious decision to describe itself as a multi-faith rather than an inter-faith organisation. There was no intention to come to any theological synthesis and work is respectful of all faith traditions. SAFCEI's unifying purpose is collectively to protect and care for the planet, our only home.

At the heart of SAFCEI's vision is a call to all faith communities to cherish living earth. Through its mission as 'an institute of people of many faiths that are united in diversity through a common commitment to earth keeping,' SAFCEI strives to increase awareness and understanding, and to encourage faith leaders and their communities throughout southern Africa to take appropriate climate and eco-justice action.

SAFCEI's objectives have guided a multi-pronged approach to support and promote eco-justice action amongst all faith communities.
"Through collaboration, networking, research and action, SAFCEI seeks to:
– Raise environmental awareness
– Engage in formulating policy and ethical guidelines within faith communities
– Facilitate environmental responsibility and action
– Confront environmental and socio-economic injustices
– Support environmental training and learning."

Africa is a region where faith congregations are the most widely networked communities of any civil society organisation and where religious leaders are often better trusted than their political counterparts. With underpinning moral values of justice and equity along with compassion and generosity, faith communities, acting individually and collectively, were seen as fertile ground for growing the emerging earth-keeper movement. With a small passionate team, SAFCEI undertook a two-pronged approach.

The first was to engage with faith leaders and encourage them to bring eco-justice onto their agendas. They were asked to take the lead in faith based earth-care policy-making, to 'walk the talk', to speak publicly and write about eco-injustice. They were urged to encourage their communities to pray, teach and act for the whole earth community, not just for humans. The second approach was to establish a network of eco-congregations. Led by champions, local congregations were encouraged and supported to become centres of sustainability and good practice. SAFCEI believed that faith centres could re-invent themselves as vibrant hubs of transformation by building a groundswell of community eco-agency, recognising that we worship a creator God. SAFCEI envisioned not just community minded 'eco-friendly' churches, but clusters of engaged and active

---

22   SAFCEI, The Southern African Faith Communities' Environment Institute. www.safcei.org.

congregations passionate about eco-justice action, advocacy and agency, springing up in every city and town.

SAFCEI also developed a vibrant eco-justice advocacy component. Environment work has for long been perceived by previously disadvantaged South Africans as an exclusive 'white' conservation issue.[23] Interpreting ecological challenges as issues of justice and human rights has gradually changed this perception. SAFCEI, along with a number of other civil society partners, has taken the lead in confronting a variety of politically and economically charged eco-justice issues.

A recent and significant milestone was the successful high court challenge, in partnership with Earthlife Africa Johannesburg, another small NGO, regarding a corrupt and unconstitutional nuclear energy deal agreed to between the former South African President, Jacob Zuma, and Russia. The implications of this April 2017 court decision for a just energy transition has been is enormous.[24] In a bleak and despondent time in the country's history, civil society was greatly encouraged by the outcome of this David and Goliath struggle. Energy, and food and climate justice programmes are currently two key focus areas of SAFCEI's faith-based civil society and advocacy work, not only in South but all of southern Africa. However, our involvement also embraces biodiversity loss and habitat destruction which is being fuelled by the extractive industries, collective human avarice and corruption, and the needs and expectations of a growing human population.

4. Work amongst faith leaders on the ground

The day to day lived experiences of increasingly frequent catastrophic weather events, prolonged droughts and devastating fires is building concern about climate disruption and human suffering amongst faith based communities in southern and eastern Africa. However, in spite of growing scientific knowledge and consensus, there is a limited understanding of the how humans are fuelling climate change amongst the general population in southern Africa. SAFCEI's plea to the faith sector to become involved in earthkeeping has been slow to gain traction. While senior faith leadership make statements and call for action,[25] the teachers, preachers, imams, rabbis, gurus and spiritual leaders working with communities and congregations on the ground do not always share or act on the information. Social justice, not environmental issues, continues to gain attention and mass protest.

In 2015, SAFCEI launched a new approach to building faith-based action through a Faith Leaders Environmental Advocacy Training (FLEAT) programme.[26] The programme includes

---

23 De Gruchy, S. 2007. An olive agenda: First thoughts on a metaphorical theology of development. *Ecumenical Review* 59 2&3, 333 – 345

24 Corrupt government nuclear deal court challenge by SAFCEI and Earthlife Africa Johannesburg. https://safcei.org/knowledge-base/nuclear-deal-legal-documents-and-media-resources/. (Accessed 15 September 2019).

25   Statements emerging from the African region:

SACC Climate Change Committee 2009. *Climate change – A challenge to the churches in South Africa*. Marshalltown: SACC.

Anglican Eco-Bishop's statement 2015. https://anglicanalliance.org/anglican-alliance-welcomes-statement-from-anglican-eco-bishops/. (Accessed 15 September 2019).

African Bishops call for ecological justice, 2018. https://www.anglicannews.org/news/2018/09/african-bishops-call-for-ecological-justice-to-top-agenda-at-2020-lambeth-conference.aspx. (Accessed 15 September 2019).

26   Faith Leader Environmental advocacy Training SAFCEI: https://safcei.org/project/fleat/. (Accessed 15 September 2019).

Geoff Davies and Kate Davies

training, learning, and follow-up with faith leaders who are selected for their interest and desire to develop an eco-faith approach with their faith communities. It strives to enhance the capacity of faith leaders to engage with their communities and help them respond to the challenges of environmental degradation and climate change, and to develop advocacy tools for eco-justice. It becomes evident that when different faiths come together to address common challenges, they are able, through interaction and partnerships, to work effectively towards co-creating greater climate resilience.

5. Grasping the Kairos moment

A question remains as to why there has been such limited interest in eco-congregations. The variety of geographic, socio-economic, cultural, literacy, linguistic and religious contexts in southern Africa means no one model fits all. While not part of an eco-stewardship programme, and often out of expediency, many individual congregations have long been taking eco-actions like saving water and energy, growing and sharing food, planting trees, upcycling waste, and sharing transport. Many faith leaders are caught up in the day to day socio-economic challenges and demands of their work which makes them reluctant to take on any new responsibilities. Another deterrent is a lack of content knowledge and confidence to integrate earth-care into the life of their communities. Many do not have the mandate or support from their senior religious leadership to do so. They in turn do not encourage experienced and enthusiastic lay eco-champions to take a lead.

The sacred texts of all living faiths are infused with ecological wisdom. Many Christian academics and theologians are now writing about eco-theology. Eco-ethics is being taught in a growing number of institutions. In spite of this, there is a gap between theory and practice. It is a matter of urgency that faith institutions integrate earth care and eco-advocacy into their praxis. SAFCEI provides accessible resource materials and advocacy training to FLEAT participants. It is only a pilot project, but this model could be rolled out in a variety of contexts with immediate benefits.

6. Christian eco-justice foundational principles

All faiths uphold ethical principles and values. For Christians, the Bible abounds with ethical principles that would provide guidance for an ecological reformation and lead us towards a more sustainable future. Christians would do well to be informed by this ancient and sacred wisdom and heed the call to respect the sanctity of life, practice non-violence, seek peace, show kindness, mercy and love, uphold justice and equity, not become servants of wealth and consumerism, nor invest in the power of armaments.

All life is sacred. "God saw everything that he had made, and indeed, it was very good," (Genesis 1:31). It was not only to humankind that God said "Be fruitful and multiply," (Genesis 1:28), but to "every living creature that moves, of every kind. "God blessed them saying 'be fruitful and multiply and fill the waters in the sea, and let the birds multiply on the earth,'" (Genesis 1:21-22).

Christians are called to uphold the sanctity of life with an explicit command: "You shall not kill," (Exodus 20:13). The fundamental principles of love, non-violence and peace-making follow. These are proclaimed and lived by Jesus who tells us to love our enemies, (Luke 6:27, Matthew 5:44), to be peacemakers, (Matthew 5:9), and to heed his radical teaching concerning retaliation, (Matthew 5:38-41).

St Paul affirms this: "Jesus proclaimed peace to you who were far off and peace to those who were near..." (Ephesians 2:17). Peace is dependent on justice and righteousness: "… let justice roll down like waters, and righteousness like an ever-flowing stream," (Amos 5:24).

Equity is built on the foundations of justice. When God fed the Israelites with bread from heaven, they were commanded to "Gather as much of it as each of you needs……. And those who gathered much had nothing over, and those who gathered little had no shortage; they gathered as much as each of them needed," (Exodus 16:16,18). Inequality in the world has reached gross and unacceptable levels. It is an affront to God. St Paul makes a plea "That there may be a fair balance," (II Corinthians 8:14).

Zechariah pronounces on kindness and mercy: "…Render true judgements, show kindness and mercy to one another, do not oppress the widow, the orphan, the alien, or the poor; and do not devise evil in your hearts against one another," (Zechariah 7:9,10).

But we generally don't show kindness and mercy. Our contemporary world maintains inequality and injustice and feeds our greed through the force of armaments. The bible has strong warnings about military expenditure. "A king is not saved by his great army; a warrior is not delivered by his great strength. A war horse is a vain hope for victory, and by its great might it cannot save." (Psalm 33:16,17). Jesus said at the time of his arrest: "Put your sword back into its place; for all who take the sword will perish by the sword," (Matthew 26:51-52).

We are charged to "Depart from evil, and do good; seek peace and pursue it. The eyes of the Lord are on the righteous, and his ears are open to their cry," (Psalm 34:14,15). Global expenditure on so called defence (US$1,822 billion in 2018)[27] is irresponsible, iniquitous and a violation of God's intention for us to live sustainably and in peace. Even half of this global defence expenditure would go a long way in overcoming poverty and environmental destruction and help to establish peace to the world. Current weapon sales encourage conflict and destruction. Central to this are nuclear weapons. People of faith must call for a nuclear free world.

---

27   Tian, N, Fleurant, A, Kuimova, A, Wezeman, P, and Wezeman, S, 2019. *Trends in world military expenditure, 2018*. Stockholm International Peace Research Institute Fact Sheet 2019. https://www.sipri.org/ (Accessed 29 August 2019).

Geoff Davies and Kate Davies

Seeking wealth and endless economic growth on a finite planet defies logic and the possibility of building a peaceful and sustainable world. Jesus is clear that to establish human and planetary well-being, "You cannot serve God and mammon." (Matthew 6:24). He also calls us to "... strive first for the kingdom of God and God's righteousness, and all these things will be given to you as well," (Matthew 6:33).

In all things, we are called to honour God's covenant made with the whole community of life "... with you and your descendants after you and with every living creature ... on Earth," (Genesis 9:9-10). Isaiah warns of the dire consequences of defiance: "The earth dries up and withers, the world languishes and withers; the heavens languish together with the earth. The earth lies polluted under its inhabitants; for they have transgressed the laws, violated the statutes, broken the everlasting covenant" (Isaiah 24:4-5). It is time for us to wake up and heed this warning.

7. Conclusion

The challenge to engage faith communities in eco-justice work is enormous. Because of the dominant anthropocentric approach of Abrahamic faiths, leaders have long believed their primary mandate is to be concerned about social justice, human rights and the wellbeing of people. Growing global inequality, unemployment, hunger, inadequate education, poor health services, corrupt political leadership and vested interests of corporate power, makes eco-justice action ever more urgent, demanding and daunting.

The planetary crisis has reached such serious proportions that the very web of life is unravelling. The whole household of God needs to act together to steer us towards a more sustainable future.

The WCC General Assembly in 2021 will be the last Assembly that can resolve to take the urgent and positive steps that are needed to turn the situation around. If we do not change direction over the next decade, we will be locked into the destruction of life as we now know it on this planet, our only home.

If we are to establish planetary wellbeing, a flourishing web of life and a peaceful earth community, we must heed both the cry of the earth and the cry of the poor.[28] Statements from faith leaders are not enough. Sacred texts from every faith persuasion need to be read and re-viewed through green spectacles. Eco-ethics must be deeply embedded in our value systems and consciousness if actions are to flow from our hearts.

---

28   Boff, L 1997. *Cry of the earth, cry of the poor.* New York: Maryknoll.

ECO-FRIENDLY ACTIVITIES IMPLEMENTED BY SYUNIK-DEVELOPMENT NGO, ARMENIA

Hayarpi Aghankanyan

Syunik Development NGO (www.syunikngo.am) was founded in 1995 in Vayots Dzor Region after the collapse of the Soviet Union. During its 24 years of work the NGO has become one of the largest non-governmental, church-related organizations in Southern Armenia. Syunik Development NGO's mission is to develop communities, where the youth see their future perspectives in their own communities and are integrated into a wider world. Accordingly, the organization's goal is to promote the improvement and development of regional livelihood through cultural-educational, socio-economic projects and create local and international linkages.

Currently Syunik Development NGO has structured its organizational work into the following departments: Social, Agricultural, Youth and Tourism Development. At the same time actions are being taken to establish an environmental department at Syunik Development NGO to enlarge the scope of environmental projects and establish potential environmental impacts associated with solar power and continue overall interventions in the environmental field.

Located on the crossroad between Europe and Asia (Southeastern Europe/Western Asia, East of Turkey, North of Iran and South of the mountainous Caucasus region (Transcaucasia), Armenia does not remain indifferent from the global environmental challenges. Global environmental challenges are effected and linked to the local issues, such as loss of biodiversity, over-use of natural resources and environmental and health issues, poverty and the sustainability of ecosystems. Vayots Dzor region is presently struggling with a number of environmental problems, such as waste disposal, mining and energy and water supply issues. This situation is well known to the local churches, which want to help people to improve the environmental situation and promote awareness building about the ecological challenges among the local population. According to the Theology of Armenian Apostolic Church the human being is created as the owner of creation and co-creator. But this doesn't mean that human being is a supreme ruler, just the opposite: being the owner and co-creator in Christianity means being caring, being the protector and defender of nature according to Jesus Christ's saying: "Even as the Son of man came not to be ministered unto, but to minister, and to give his life a ransom for many" (Math. 20:28). And this understanding of the owner as the protector is also expressed in 10 exhortation/ commandments that have been developed by the Armenian Apostolic Church and aim to recover the lost harmony in Nature:

1. We should confess that we are guilty towards Nature; we should regret and repent to start completely new life.
2. We should be wise enough to restraint our desires in scope of means, which are not indispensible for our livelihood.
3. We should strengthen our souls through fasting, to win the invisible struggle against material and bodily desires.
4. We should try to be satisfied with less and save everything /household appliances, office, manufacturing, industrial and agricultural means, devices and equipment, minerals and everything that is being used by human being/.

5. We should love, respect and take care of flora and fauna by avoiding cutting trees, taking part in tree planting activities, cultivating our gardens and avoiding hunting and fishing as a form of entertainment.
6. We should keep the environment clean avoiding polluting it and organizing cleaning activities.
7. We should try to decrease the usage of weapons and ammunitions.
8. We should avoid unnecessary journeys to save fuel, to minimize the usage of means of transportation, to save time, human resources and minimize polluting the atmosphere.
9. We should take part in the rituals of blessing the creation /blessing the earth, blessing the house, blessing the water/.
10. Not only by our words but mainly by our actions and behavior we should become live sermon for others and exhort them to feel the responsibility of saving and taking care of the creation.

In order to minimize above mentioned issues and taking into consideration the very important point that all of us are accountable before God and we understand ourselves as servants, stewards and trustees of the creation, Syunik Development NGO under the patronage of Armenian Apostolic Church has its modest contribution to reduce environmental challenges in the Southern Armenia. During many years Syunik NGO is trying to find practical solutions to our current issues, shifting from a consumer society to a broader, community-oriented sustainable lifestyle, in harmony with nature. As humankind's survival is dependent on a healthy environment, our NGO is trying to help local people to acknowledge that nature has its own rights to exist and thrive, just as humans do and to realize that nature's limits are inviolable and human action has to be restrained accordingly. This relationship is both science- and ethics-based. When we threaten the planet we undermine our only home- and our future survival. All of us should become the parts of movement for sustainable development.

Keeping this message in mind Syunik NGO has become one of the main initiators in Vayots Dzor region to raise the awareness of the population on ecological issues and the global challenges. Environmental awareness rising has been carried out through many trainings, workshops and Summer Academies on

- Recycling: What do people do and what are the consequences? What alternatives are there?
- Ecological Production: What does it mean and what are the potentials for our development?
- Eco friendly Technologies: Renewable energy and energy conservation.
- Ecological degradation – ecological restoration.

Also a wide range of the practical activities has been taken to involve community members and parishes from different regions with the approach of "learning by doing". Within these initiatives five green zones have been created in the rural and urban communities, almost 5000 trees have already been grown in Noravank gorge and the newly planted 10 Christmas trees by the German priest are come to fill the commitment and our responsibility for the Creation and spread the message of Jesus Christ "We reap what we sow".

Through ecosystem-based disaster risk reduction, we are contributing to the strengthening of resilience and reduction of disaster losses by encouraging communities to minimize actions that result into disasters like landslides and floods. Therefore, in the high areas of the mountains, we are planting trees and in the low laying areas, we have equipped people with skills to dig trenches to reduce the effects of flooding and soil erosion.

Ecological issues are linked with all spheres of life and as long as it goes issues become more and more, especially in the areas where agriculture is a major sector of the economy and the source of people's income. From this point our task is to illustrate most environmentally-friendly

Hayarpi Aghankanyan

possible practices to our local farmers, establish eco-friendly gardens, use organic treatment for pests, how to receive compost instead of burning leaves /people in Armenia have bad custom of burning the leaves in Fall and in Spring/. Many people are skeptical about these possible methods, but demonstration plot founded by Syunik NGO serves the best example for the whole region and promotes the creation of such gardens.

One of our last initiatives was the establishment of solar drying unit for dryfruits offering a promising alternative to produce high quality marketable products, which is chance to minimize Post-Harvest losses and improve the economic situation of the farmers as well as to increase a sustainable way of food processing.

Syunik NGO has been awarded by Energy Globe National Award 2013 for the project of "Agent for Changes". Within this project we have managed to organize garbage collection in the territory of ten cultural monuments and churches, organizing ten worships and awareness raising forum-theatres in isolated communities of Armenia.

Now, as mentioned above, environmental department is in the process of establishment to enlarge the scope of environmental projects. In July 2019 in Syunik Development NGO a two-day environmental-cognitive excursion by three initiative groups was conducted in three community centers of Vayots Dzor region /Yeghegnadzor, Vayk and Jermuk/. The excursion had two main aims: 1. To emphasize the importance of nature as the main source of human existence, to promote eco-friendly activities and 2. To introduce church complexes located in this area and to foster the importance of protection of these monuments. A wide range of activities were planned including:
–   Walking to the historical churches
–   Having talks and discussions on the importance of protection of nature and historical monuments
–   Having film watching and focus discussions on environmental issues and eco friendly activities
–   Cleaning the pathway to their destination
–   Organizing quiz-games to improve gained knowledge and skills
–   Organizing puppet show, to emphasize the importance of waste recycling
–   Organizing brainstorming on "Environmental issues of Vayots Dzor region and the ways of solutions"
Besides this another project called "Environmental Education and awareness Building in Vayots Dzor Region of Armenia and in Zakarpatia Region of Ukraine" has started from April 2019. The project aims to enhance the environmental awareness of the rural population in Vayots Dzor Region of Southern Armenia and in the West of Ukraine to address some of the issues related to waste disposal problems and to growing energy consumption in the region. This will be achieved through the transfer of knowledge during the environmental seminars and secondly, with a number of practical small scale pilot projects, which all aim to raise the awareness for the change of people's habits towards a more sustainable lifestyle. The project wants to encourage people to take responsibility for the wellbeing of their environment as their own quality of life and the whole economic development of the region depends on it.

Thus, Syunik Development NGO as a Church related organization during many years of its activity has addressed and now is continuing to address a wide range of environmental and ecological concerns. Keeping in mind God's message that we are given the responsibility for taking care of all creation we try to find practical solutions to local current issues. For this purpose we organize a range of seminars, workshops and trainings on environmental awareness rising, as well as organizing a wide range of practical activities to involve community members and parishes from different regions with the approach of "learning by doing".

ECO-THEOLOGY AS A PRACTICAL DIMENSION

A view from the Armenia Inter-Church Round Table

Karen Nazaryan

2 Timothy 1:7

"…God gave us a spirit not of fear but of power and love and self-control."

The starting point of this contribution is aligned with materials of WCC Busan Assembly "A Call to Ecological Justice and Peace…"

Herewith we would like to communicate what the Armenian church, civil society and the international community are doing to address climate change and ecological destruction.

Ecological challenges are many in the current life of Armenia. From the Soviet Union we inherited a country with a developed mining system and a strong chemical industry. Development of a small part of it, the mining in particular, creates many ecological problems due to a lack of nature friendly approaches. This, in its turn, has created an active resistance from ecological NGOs and the public in general.

Being an active part of civil society and a Faith Based Organization (FBO), the Armenia Round Table (ART) could not stand aside in this situation. A couple of years ago we initiated discussions on the interrelation between ecology, the protection of nature and theology. The first publication in that field in Armenia, a textbook entitled "Green theology", was an initiative of the ART, where the two authors, a theologian Rev. F. Minas and an ecologist Prof. K. Grigoryan, have made the first attempt to align biological and theological views on ecology and nature protection. The textbook was further used as study material for students of the seminary.

At the same time, we started our collaboration with the global Alliance of Religions and Conservation (ARC). The mutually elaborated idea was the following: practically all religions have their sacral places, that are regularly visited by pilgrims. Mostly, after massive pilgrimages, lots of unwanted ecological consequences are taking place. But…

Colossians 3:14

"And above all these put on love, which binds everything together in perfect harmony. So, together with worship we shall put this in harmony with nature."

We want to combine nature friendly pilgrimage with other ecological activities, like tree planting, greening the sacral territory, availability of organic products, etc. The most important sacral place for Armenians is H. Etchmiadzin, where one of the first Christian churches was erected in 305 and where Christianity was proclaimed as a state religion. Since then, H. Etchmiadzin has been the residence of Armenian Catholicoses. Later, due to the turbulent history of the Armenian nation, the residence moved to several different locations in Armenia, and from 1441 up to the present day it has been re-established in H. Etchmiadzin.

Two words about modern Armenia. After the collapse of the Soviet Union, Armenia became an independent country with a population of only 3 million, though the total number of Armenians worldwide is around 10 million. Thus, thousands of diaspora Armenians arrive in the country as pilgrims, and practically all of them are visiting H. Etchmiadzin. So, undoubtedly, we can assume, that it is the most important sacral place for all Armenians, and, on top of that, many tourists visiting Armenia every year also come to H. Etchmiadzin. For that reason, our program of green pilgrimage at H. Etchmiadin is very important. In cooperation with ARC we elaborated a comprehensive approach, which includes the sections below:

Greening

- About 50.000 seedlings will be planted to expand the existing city parks, comprised of local varieties of plants, as well as drought resistant, endemic, disappearing and other species.
- 16 playgrounds for children and recreation areas with sports equipment will be placed in the parks.
- 1.5 ha of organic garden will be established in the city as a demonstration project.
- Rehabilitation of the historical Nersisyan forest.
Improvement and greening surroundings of churches and other sacred places.

Water and sanitation

- Dripping and shower irrigation schemes have already been established and will cover all green areas of the Monastery, including gardens, lawns and orchards.
- Parks and crowded places to be furnished with 20 bio toilets.
- Public lavatories / biotoilets to be established on pilgrim routes and at the convergence points.

Energy

- The energy saving lighting in the parks/green areas will serve pilgrims and population in the dark time of the day.
- The energy saving lighting will be established in municipal buildings, streets and city parks.
- A1 MW solar plant is under construction in the compound of the Mother See.
- The solar energy harnessing PV modules will be installed in 8 kindergartens, 2 music schools, the sports school, city library, municipality, bus stops, etc.

Transport, walking routes

- Establish electric buses/mini-buses transportation in Etchmiadzin.
- Establish cycle-friendly road network, safe and easy cycle routs.
- Establish walking and walking/cycling networks.
- Construct ramps and pavement inclinations for ensuring mobility of disabled persons.

Karen Nazaryan

B&B-s

- Organize training on basics of hospitality and B&B operations.
- Establish B&Bs and small hotels (via 0 % loans, mini grants), using ARC standards in operations of B&Bs and hotels.
- Study visits to other B&Bs in Armenia and abroad.
- Registration at travel agencies and internet B&B resources.
- Produce and distribute promotional materials.

Food

- Training for the staff of cafes and restaurants for using high ecological standards with the emphasis on the traditional Armenian food.
- Establish cafes/restaurants (support of 0 % loans and mini grants is possible)
- Assist farmers to start organic food production and certification.

Education

- Organize trainings at schools, colleges, universities in Etchmiadzin.
- Develop, publish and distribute handbooks on various aspects of environmental protection and green pilgrimage.
- Organize annual competitions among schools and college/university students.

Research centre

- Building / (re)construction of the Research Centre premises, following all possible concepts of modern architecture and construction to show up to date trends in energy saving, greening, environmental protection, etc.
- Explore environmental issues for pilgrimage centres across the region, and provide information and recommendations on existing developments worldwide.
- Study visits for better understanding of modern developments worldwide.
- "Green pilgrimage"-related publications in several languages.
- Give specific consultancies on various aspects of "green" pilgrimage (e.g. how to install solar panels in your house, etc.).
- Networking with ARC green pilgrimage sites.
- Coordination activities.

Several activities, mentioned in this communication, have already been performed, others are in the planning or implementation process. We are moving forward in that direction, keeping in mind a quotation from Martin Luther King Jr. "If you can't fly, then run, If you can't run, then walk, If you can't walk, then crawl, but whatever you do, you have to keep moving forward."

REGIONAL APPROACHES TO ECO-THEOLOGY IN THE CONTEXT OF ETHIOPIA

Misgana Mathewos Detago

1. Introduction

Climate change and its effects is an existential problem that continues threatening the very existence of many Africans today. This is general truth but also practical realty. I believe that every one of us, as the members of the society and of the body of Christ, can be well and passionately expressive of the effects of climate change in our specific localities. This can be taken as an starting point but we think of the broader role that we play in our ecclesial and academic leadership.

1.1 Personal experience creates a personal conviction that serves as an important rudimentary motivational factor.
This is not to mean that only those who experience the climate change and its effects in their locality can speak or act better than those who have not (the reverse is true in many ways), but we want to affirm, that that African church leaders must have an opportunity to reflect on/feel the pains that ecological crisis has brought forth on their societies.

I personally feel this pain. I was born and grew up in a high land of south central Ethiopia where it was known for proportionate rain, favorable climate for agriculture, foggy weather in the morning and chilly in the evening, indigenous trees, numerous wild animals and birds and even a sizable area of rain forest – to mention some among many of its unique features. However, in the past three decades, the environment scenario of the region has changed to the extent that the above-mentioned ecological signifiers have shown significant decline.

1.2 Our academic engagement informs practical problems of the church and society and can serve as huge motivational factor for our speech and action.
As we interpret the biblical and theological texts, they have power to challenge us (as we read the text, reciprocally the text reads us; Anthony Thiselton). My teaching of the Old Testament (OT), particularly of Genesis and Psalms, and hermeneutics (where ecological hermeneutics is part of it) at Mekane Yesus Seminary[1] (MYS) (prior to 2013) and at the Ethiopian Graduate School of Theology[2] (EGST) (since 2013/14) informed me of interconnectedness within created order and stewardship of creation.

In the past 20 years of my engagement with Old Testament scholarly works, I found that the theme of eco-theology has been addressed inadequately, though some encouraging publications has been seen recently.[3]

---

1   https://www.facebook.com/pages/Mekane-Yesus-Theological-Seminary-Addis-Ababa-Ethiopia/115242
191823214
2   https://egst.edu.et/
3   For example, Terence Fretheim E. *God and World in the Old Testament: A Relational Theology of Creation.*
Nashville: Abingdon, 2005; Richard Bauckham, Bible and Ecology: *Rediscovering the Community of Creation*

2. General Context

In what context does the Church operate? To answer this question, it is important to present a brief note on current Ethiopian ecological situation.

2.1 Regional Context: Horn of Africa
General
Churches in the Horn of Africa exist and operate in a largely volatile situation:
- political instability and recurring conflicts
- A majority of people lives under poverty line though the governments claim they have devised policies and implemented them to reduce poverty
- High level of illiteracy
- Traditional ways of existence
- Persecution

2.2 Ethiopia
Ethiopia is characterized by diverse ethnic groups and cultures, rich natural resources and bio-diversity and diverse geographical settings and climate. It's current population is estimated to be more than 105 million – that makes it the second most populous country in Africa after Nigeria. A large number of this population, more than 80 % (4 in 5 persons), are dependent on agriculture for its subsistence and income[4].

Despite being one of the poorest countries in the world, it has been repeatedly acclaimed by international community for experiencing a fast growing economy in sub-Saharan Africa in the past decade consecutively.

In 2011, the country decided to abandon conventional economic development routes and instead developed the document called *Ethiopia's Climate Resilient Green Economy: Green Economy Strategy*[5] (2011) that aims at achieving sustainable economic growth by following environmental friendly paths and strategies. This document identifies the green economy development action plan based on four pillars:

"1. Improving crop and livestock production practices for higher food security and farmer income while reducing emissions;

2. Protecting and re-establishing forests for their economic and eco-system services, including as carbon stocks;

3. Expanding electricity generation from renewable sources of energy for domestic and regional markets;

4. Leapfrogging to modern and energy-efficient technologies in transport, industrial sectors and buildings" (*Ethiopia's Climate Resilient Green Economy – executive summary)*[6].

(Baylor University Press, 2010); ------, *Living with Other Creatures: Green Exegesis and Theology* (Paternoster, 2012).
4   See: Girma Kebbede, *Environment and Society in Ethiopia*, 2017:1.
5   https://theredddesk.org/countries/plans/climate-resilient-green-economy-crge-strategy;   https://www.undp.org/content/dam/ethiopia/docs/Ethiopia%20CRGE.pdf
6   https://www.undp.org/content/dam/ethiopia/docs/Ethiopia%20CRGE.pdf, page 2ff

Misgana Mathewos Detago

The country's Growth and Transformation Plan (GTP)[7] that foresees the middle-income Ethiopia by 2025 is said to have informed by this green economy strategy.

Eight years after the development of this strategy, despite high level of awareness in the schools and other public sectors and certain gains, Ethiopia is still suffering from the effects of climate change such as loss of biodiversity, deforestation, droughts, lack of drinking water and food security. The documents such as *Ethiopian Environmental Review: Forum for Environment No I & II* (Addis Ababa, 2011, 2012)[8] reflect on this reality and the book authored by Prof. Girma Kebbede (Environment and Society in Ethiopia, Routledge, 2017)[9] recently elucidates how the abovementioned and related environmental problems have still persisted in Ethiopia.

Despite the efforts of the Ethiopian government and other Environmental agencies to mitigate the causes and effects of climate change, why does the problem persist? Prof. Kebedde mentions the following research-oriented, illustrative reasons, though those reasons are not entirely new:

1. Ethiopia owns "a large geographic area, high agricultural potential, and substantial energy and mineral wealth," but it has failed to ensure environmental and economic sustainability because of "prevailing extractive political systems and misguided government policies" (p. 2).
2. The population growth in Ethiopia is quite alarming. The annual growth rate that moved between 2.2 and 2.6 % from 1960-1980 jumps to to 2.8-3.2% from 1980-2000s. The implication of such population growth on environment and natural resources is unambiguous. Soil, water, air, forests, minerals, animals and other natural resources suffer when human beings send their hands largely for consumption rather than for proper use and protection (pp. 5-6). "However, the country's agricultural resources are under increasing pressure from growing rural population, growing urban demands and increasing conversion of land for the production of biofuels and large-scale commercial food production for export" (pp. 42-43).
3. Political instability and insecurity – The focus of successive governments (three in the past four decades) mainly shifts to ensuring security and stabilizing the political structure. When conflict happens between different ethnic groups and when political system of the ruling party is challenged, a talk about environment will become secondary (pp. 8-9).

Prof. Kebbede sums up the current ecological and sustainability situation of Ethiopia in the following words: "Human economies depend on the extraction of natural and environmental resources: soil, water, pasture, forests, wildlife, and minerals. The well-being of a given society depends on the quality and quantity of its natural and environmental resources and how it manages them in the pursuit of achieving sustained economic development and improvements in human welfare. Unsustainable or improper human activities reduce both the quality and quantity of available natural and environmental resources, such as soil, water, forest, pasture, and biodiversity. There is much to worry about Ethiopia's environment and resource base" (p. 183).

---

7   https://www.greengrowthknowledge.org/national-documents/ethiopia-growth-and-transformation-plan-ii-gtp-ii
8   http://www.phe-ethiopia.org/pdf/Ethiopian_Environment_Review.pdf
9   See as e-book: https://www.lehmanns.de/shop/naturwissenschaften/37616490-9781315464282-environment-and-society-in-ethiopia

3. The Response of Ethiopian Protestant Churches: Overview

How are the Ethiopian Churches doing in environmental stewardship and sustainability in afore-stated broader context? Where is the Church "when it hurts?"

3.1 Ethiopia is the home of ancient Christianity (Ethiopian Orthodox Tewahido Church, 4th c., 43.9%), Islam (33.9%), Protestant Churches (18.6%), Catholics (0.7%) and others (3%) (Source: 2007 National Census). The country has immense religious power if rallied around the ecological crisis as it has been happening for peace establishment.

3.2 Continuous Growth of Protestant Christianity
The expansion of the Ethiopian evangelical protestant churches has continued. The national census before 10 years indicated the number of protestant Christianity in Ethiopia was 18% of the whole population but currently it's estimated to be 25%. The Ethiopian Evangelical Mekane Yesus Church (EECMY) and the Ethiopian Kale Heywet Church (EKHC) assume the majority of protestant population, followed by Full Gospel Believers Church and Mesrete Kristos Church, et el.

3.3 The Ethiopian Churches' Response to Environmental Crisis
The Ethiopian Church conducts development activities mainly through their Development Agencies (e.g. EECMY-DASSC; EKHC-DC). Their social engagement emerges from "Serving the Whole Person" motto (e.g. EECMY; others follow suit). In general, the development agencies engage in social and development activities such as food security, water supply, gender equality, health, education, and emergency relief, disaster risk reduction (taken from DASSC; others have similar list with few variations).

3.4 Recently, the EGST researchers (2018) assessed the documents of EECMY-DASSC, EKHC-DC, EFGBC-DC and MKC-DC to see whether these churches have had policies and strategies to tackle the cause and effects of climate change and the outcome is that the churches have lacked these (*Environmental Stewardship*, published in 2019, EGST)[10]. Why does this happen? My assumption is that the churches in general and their development commissions in particular have been heavily burdened by responding to human needs that are quite unprecedented in Ethiopia.

3.5 The motto "serving the whole person" still focuses on persons, not on other natural beings per se. The interconnectedness between humans and other creatures seems to have not deeply rooted in the consciousness the Ethiopian Protestant Churches.
- The public hardly hears the prophetic voice from church leaders in connection to ecological crisis.
- Local congregations (many Christians) do see the issue of environmental stewardship as part of the Bible and so not addressed in church preaching and teaching. Churches mainly focus on what they call "spiritual matters," or "winning souls for Christ" and think that a talk about environment is unspiritual or physical.

---

10   https://egst.edu.et/?p=4323

4. Theological Institutions/ Seminaries

4.1 Recently, two of EGST researchers made an empirical study on the curriculum of six theological institutions to see whether the issue of environment and sustainability was addressed and to write a handbook on this theme. The outcome of the study was that none of those seminaries intentionally created a course or a curriculum on environmental and sustainability education. Therefore, the need to engage theological institutions in this agenda was the utmost recommendation.

4.2 Ethiopian Graduate School of Theology (EGST)
– EGST established a Centre for Environmental Stewardship and Holistic Development (CE-SHoD) in 2012/3 to conduct research, workshops and publications on the theme.[11] The Centre has developed successfully, thanks to Prof. Aklilu Dalelo, Prof. of Geography and Environmental Science at A.A.U. and Regular part-time faculty at EGST.
– The Centre for Environmental Stewardship and Holistic Development (EGST) and Institute for Environmental Education and Communication (INFU, Leuphana University) prepared a joint project and got fund from Alexander von Humboldt Foundation to empower colleges of Teacher Education and theological institutions in Ethiopia. Five teacher training colleges and four seminaries came together in this project; a series of workshops were conducted; research papers were presented; local and international networks have been created. This project is the first of its kind to bring government run colleges and seminaries together to deal with an agenda common to both.
– Besides leading this project, EGST has done two research of its own (Theology and Development Nexus Series I: Development from Biblical, Theological and Practical Perspectives and Environmental Stewardship; both await publication).
– The next step in EGST's programme: continue conducting research and publish; prepare workshops for church leaders and pastors; expand the network to other colleges and seminaries.

5. Challenges and Conclusions

Key priorities for environmental concerns, eco-theology and ethics of sustainability in the Ethiopian context are the following:
– Thinking and working beyond changing and unstable political situations in Africa in order to seriously and continuously pursue the environmental agenda
– Forging collaborative efforts by brining other religions (e.g. Islam) into this common agenda. EGST successfully conducted this with regard to tackling Gender Based Violence (2017)
– Bringing the issues of environment and sustainability down to local congregations
– Engaging theological institutions and Bible Schools as they are the one who train pastors and evangelists for local congregations on eco-theological reflection and ethics of sustainability
– Shaping Post-graduate theological institutions (e.g. EGST) into a major national and global partner in order to reach out to church leaders, other religions, and other educational, civic and political institutions.

---

11   https://egst.edu.et/?page_id=1445

– Equipping Church and/or institutional leaders for advocacy or prophetic voice towards ecological crises.

Further Reading

David Ambrosetti, Jean-Renaud Boisserie, Deresse Ayenachew **und** Thomas Guindeuil (eds): Climatic and Environmental challenges: Learning from the Horn of Africa, French Centre for Ethiopian Studies (CFEE) 2015, in: https://books.openedition.org/cfee/101

CHRISTIAN CONFERENCE OF ASIA'S INITIATIVES IN DEVELOPING ECO-CONSCIOUSNESS AND ECO-THEOLOGY

Mathews George Chunakara

Ecological crisis is the ground reality in many parts of the world and has emerged to be the rampant trend in Asia, with its impacts being manifested in many ways. The effects of climate change on deforestation, destruction of habitat and biodiversity, radioactive and hazardous wastes, water quality and supply, energy exploration and development, pesticides and food security, and environmental health have been escalating despite some attempts to redeem them. The ramifications of these challenges cross national borders and may affect economic, political, and cultural relationships on a vast geographic scale in many parts of Asia. The result of these would cause innumerable Asians to suffer due to the devastating effects of cyclones, floods, earthquakes, drought, acute water shortage, and rise in atmospheric pressure and temperature, which would further result in more heat waves. Many Asians and most Asian countries are victims of environmental destruction. Several studies and surveys in recent years illustrate the magnitude of such devastations in Asia.

The Asian Development Bank studies revealed that:

– Asia occupies 30% of the world's land mass, but 40% of the world's disasters occurred in the region in the past decade, resulting in a disproportionate 80% of the world's disaster deaths. More than 2,200 natural disasters struck Asia in the past 20 years, claiming close to one million lives, with the following six mega-disasters accounting for three-quarters of fatalities: Japan's 2011 earthquake/tsunami (20,000 deaths), the 2004 Indian Ocean tsunami (more than 200,000 deaths), Myanmar's 2008 Cyclone Nargis (140,000 deaths), Bangladesh's Cyclone Gorky in 1991 (140,000 deaths), China's 2008 earthquake (90,000 deaths), and Pakistan's 2005 earthquake (75,000 deaths).

– Asia is home to 75% of the world's population that lives at risk due to the increase in devastating floods every year.

– In 2018, several Asian countries suffered natural disasters due to heavy rain and flood. The most flood affected regions and areas in Asia last year were in Kerala State in India, and Irrawaddy Delta areas in Myanmar. A dam in Lao PDR collapsed on 24 July, 2018; Typhoon *Mangkhut* hit massively in Taiwan on 16 September 2018, and Typhoon *Ompong* struck the Philippines on 17 September, 2018. The ground reality now is that a vast number of people in Asia are the worst hit in natural disasters.

– In 2018 as well as in the immediate past years', earthquakes destroyed the lives and security of people in countries such as in Indonesia, Nepal, Japan, Pakistan, and China, etc.

Ecumenical Responses: early initiatives by CCA

Ecological crisis was not considered a serious problem in many developing countries in the world for a long time. Most of them considered poverty as their most pressing problem and environment related issues were considered only as an issue of the industrialised Western or Asian countries. The interconnection between poverty and environmental degradation was rarely addressed or acknowledged at that time. As early as the 1990s more serious efforts were made to identify and highlight specific instances. A conference on Ecology and Development held in India stated how the poor and impoverished were affected by ecological crisis in the Indian context.

> While all are affected by the ecological crisis, the life of the poor and marginalised is further impoverished by it. Shortage of fuel and water adds particular burdens to the life of women. It is said that the tribals are made environmental prisoners in their own land. Dalits, whose life has been subjected to social and cultural oppression for generations, are facing new threats by the wanton destruction of natural environment.[1]

The Christian Conference of Asia and many of its member churches and councils have been taking ecological concerns seriously for several decades. They have been responding to the ecological crises as a justice issue out of their strong theological and faith convictions. The entry point of CCA's direct involvement in raising eco-consciousness and addressing environmental degradation started as early as the 1970's. CCA identified and advocated, mainly through the programmes of the Development and Service Desk, for the ecological issues as a justice issue.

During the first half of 1970s, several Asian countries started facing serious environmental issues. The newly introduced economic trade and industrial policies of several Asian governments were adding more environmental problems in the respective countries. For example, the Japanese government pursued a 'Project of Reforming the Japanese Islands' that aimed at a drastic change of industrial structure. Heavy chemical industry was encouraged on one hand while the primary industry was deliberately down sized on the other. As a result, environmental pollution started increasing; the sea and the air of Japan became polluted by chemical and nuclear materials. The agricultural policy of the Japanese government since the 1960s encouraged farmers to leave farming and become industrial workers, which resulted in farmers incurring huge amount of debts. Japanese companies were responsible for increasing environmental pollution in several other Asian countries too in those days. Several countries in Asia started experiencing ecological issues such as deforestation, greenhouse effect, acid rain, influx of chlorofluorocarbons, desertification, and natural disasters. CCA's Development and Service Desk and the Urban Rural Mission programme Desk continuously challenged the then existing development models and called for broader interfaith actions and coalitions to promote and protect the environment, and stop the exploitation of natural resources with governmental patronage.

Tropical forests in several Asian countries were destroyed in order to sell timber to affluent countries so as to earn foreign exchange to repay national debts, and provide land for cattle grazing and cash crops which also helped to earn export revenue. In Bangladesh the environmental problems manifested in different forms of natural disasters like flood, cyclone, tornado, drought, river erosion and water pollution. Due to water contamination, the availability of fresh water fish has been drastically reduced. In a country like Bangladesh where 75 % of the total protein supply comes from fish, the overall nutritional supply to a vast number of poor people were hampered.

---

1   Daniel Chetti, ed., Ecology and Development, Madras, BTESSC & Gurukul, 1991, p.96.

Mathews George Chunakara

Starting from the 1970s, the frequency of ecological disasters increased tremendously with widespread devastation due to the global ecological degradation. The CCA started collaborating with the Christian Commission for Development in Bangladesh (CCDB), a social development wing of the National Council of Churches in Bangladesh, which was initiated by the World Council of Churches in early 1970s in raising eco-consciousness in the country.

Indonesia started facing large scale deforestation from the 1970s especially after starting gigantic industrial projects. Indonesian churches and the national ecumenical council, the Communion of Churches in Indonesia (PGI) came forward at that time with a development policy calling churches to participate based on their faith convictions. Since 1980s, Indonesian churches have taken various efforts to raise eco-consciousness among church officials as well as assist people in improving ways of meeting their needs such as providing agricultural skills and sustainable farming. Korean churches, together with other faith based organisations, took the initiatives in the 1980s in addressing the environmental degradation in Korea due to heavy industrialisation and in educating the public about the ecological crises faced in the country. The trend of deforestation supported by the military junta of Myanmar, shifting of cultivation, overexploitation of fish in order to generate foreign exchange, mining and destruction of natural resources were common policies of the Myanmar's military government for many years. It was in such a context that the Myanmar Council of Churches initiated certain programmes to assist the people in rural areas to teach them about reforestation, systematic use of soil and soil conservation, and organic farming. A CCA member church the Myanmar Baptist Convention (MBC) also introduced such programmes in almost all MBC local congregations in 1980s.

During those years, several Asian countries started constructing several new dams. It was also during that time that a large number of Asian governments started easily allowing Multinational Companies to be engaged in search of raw materials through large scale mining, deforestation and clearing of lands for developing agribusiness. Large scale logging industries allowed by the governments resulted in deforestation in many Asian countries in 1970s and 1980s. The CCA initiated, supported and facilitated several studies during those days. Consistent support was extended to the people's movements that emerged in several Asian countries to resist the maldevelopments and their negative impacts. CCA started focusing on ecological and environmental problems in Asia, and took the initiative to address these concerns. CCA's efforts to sensitise the people through its member churches and councils helped facilitate eco-consciousness and assisted in the mobilisation of the affected communities and people.

Regional Consultation on Ecology and Development

CCA articulated its convictions in a more systematic way through various study consultations and seminars with the participation of church leaders and representatives of concerned groups in 1990s. Those programmes were aimed at educating more and more people to be concerned about the relationships between the environment and economic development as the core issue. A regional consultation organised by CCA on Ecology and Development (13-18 July 1992), was held in Chiang Mai, Thailand where the participants adopted a statement in which they called for the need to redefine the concept of "development" and emphasised the need to change the patterns and trends of present development practice.

We met as representatives from churches to consider the impact of human activity and development on the environment following the UN Conference on the Environment and Development (UNCED) Earth Summit...As Christians we have become aware of the damage that is being caused to the earth – God's creation- by humankind. Our meeting recognises the need for reflection on the purpose of God for creation and on our relationship with the natural world.[2]

The Chiang Mai consultation heard stories of the commonalties in terms of the environmental situations in various Asian countries: depletion of the once abundant resources particularly that of forests, commercial demands of natural resources due to the commercial demands for export trading and agricultural products, degradation and destruction of the various related ecological systems –deforestation, loss of biodiversity, and extinction of many animal and plant species due to destruction of their habitat, land/ soil erosion, water and air pollution – which further aggravated rural and urban poverty in each country. The Chiang Mai consultation in 1992 found depletion of rainforests to be a widely discussed issue and ecological consequences and cultural alienation imposed upon the indigenous populations emerged among the most crucial issues in the environmental concerns of Asia. It was also observed by participants who represented various Asian churches that the growing tourism industry was another environmental hazard.

Consultation on 'Churches' Response to Environment in Asia

A second consultation organised by CCA in 1995 on 'Development and Environment: Churches response to Environment in Asia, and held in Jakarta, Indonesia defined people's spirituality and ecology and stated, "it is through creation that God liberated the world from chaos and total disorder. It is the spirit of God that moved over waters and formed the earth that became a systematic and harmonious environment.

The Jakarta consultation further observed:

Faith, which is rooted in Judeo Christian heritage was awakened by the ecological crisis and we have begun to make a connection between faith and the fate of nature. Anchored to our understanding of biblical analysis, theological heritage and our knowledge of the environment and our ecological endeavours a new dimension of faith is fashioned that gives reverence to the creator by caring for the creation".[3]

The Jakarta consultation further observed that in relation to "sustainable development" in Asia, which was undergoing industrialisation and rapid urbanisation, the concept of development must be defined.

---

2   Report of the Consultation on Environment and Development Christian Conference of Asia, CCA: Osaka, Japan, 1993.
3   Nathan and Martha Knoll, ed., Church, Environment, Development in Asia, Christian Conference of Asia: Hong Kong, 1995

Mathews George Chunakara

Inter-religious Consultation on 'Climate Change: A Challenge to Sustainable Development in Asia'

An inter-religious consultation organised by CCA in Kyoto, Japan from November 30 to December 5, 1998 brought together representatives from various religions on a common platform with several ecumenical organisations. The Kyoto consultation analysed and reflected on the responses of religions and society with the perspective of peace with justice and integrity of the creation. The consultation was a breakthrough in building effective interfaith coalition to promote advocacy on climate change and environmental degradation.

The consultation expressed concern on the growing destruction caused to the eco-system through an unsustainable lifestyle promoting aggressive accumulation of wealth, massive consumption and jet speed mobility. A statement adopted by the participants of the Kyoto consultation noted:

> One of the major impacts of this process, euphemistically called economic growth, has been a massive use of fossil fuels with the emission of greenhouse gases that have been disrupting the climate system with a vengeance, a fact that is fairly well documented and affirmed overwhelmingly by scientists all over the world. Although the poor do produce greenhouse gas emissions, they do as a result of emissions from poorly insulated homes. These "survival emissions" are qualitatively different from the "luxury emissions" of the industrialised countries of the North.[4]

Living Together in the Household of God in Asia

The CCA's systematic approach in sensitising the Asian churches with proper theological undergirding was more evident during the 14th General Assembly of CCA held in May 2015. One of the most pertinent foci of the Assembly was on Asian realities with the biblical theological emphasis on household of God and the challenges faced in emerging socio-economic- environmental and political contexts. CCA organised a series of study consultations and seminars in conjunction with the 14th General Assembly based on the main theme of the Assembly 'Living Together in the Household of God'. The theological consultations, seminars and study conferences organised by CCA at the national, sub-regional and the Asia regional levels shared eco-theology and its significance in addressing the challenges in the household of God.

Life Giving Agriculture for Sustainability in God's *Oikos*

Another important area that saw CCA's direct involvement in articulating and facilitating the practical application of ecological concerns was in initiating and organising a series of study consultations on 'Life Giving Agriculture for Sustainability in God's *Oikos*. The CCA organised the first Asian Life Giving Agriculture (LGA) Forum in early 2000s and subsequently CCA, together

---

4   Report of Consultation on Climate Change: A Challenge to Sustainable Development in Asia, Christian Conference of Asia: Hong Kong, 1998.

with Korean Christian Life Giving Agriculture Forum (KCLGAF), organized several consultations of the Life Giving Agricultural Forum in different countries in Asia and tried to develop it as a movement of the people and a way of life that relates to livelihoods; the land, forest and water are gifts of God to all on earth. LGA is a living philosophy based on theology of life. It is a life enhancing process grounded in faith and nurtured in a culture of sharing, caring and loving.

Through LGA, CCA conveys the message that the present dominant development model of agriculture is corporate and market-driven. It is capital intensive, export-oriented, mono-cultural with profit as its motive. It compels farmers to use genetically modified seeds, pesticides including chemical fertilizers. This leads to soil degradation, loss of indigenous seeds, bio-diversity and concentration of lands in the hands of few. It restricts diversity of agriculture based on the food patterns that are dictated by fast-food companies, increases occupational losses, displacement, drought and migration. Decades of these unsustainable agricultural practices have led to erosion of cultures, traditional knowledge and sustainable agricultural systems.

This Ecumenical forum on "Life Giving Agriculture" aims to identify problems and constraints faced by small farmers and consider alternative approaches to agriculture in the Asian context. It also seeks to strengthen existing solidarity networks and establish new ones at the regional, national and congregational levels. Theoretical and practical inputs geared towards supporting ecologically-friendly agricultural activities such as Globalization and its impact on small farmers in Asia, Sustainable Agricultural Technologies and Agro Ecological Practices, Crisis of Agriculture after Fukushima disaster, Pursuit for Alternative Energies and Agriculture, the Cooperative movement, Fair trade, Case studies and sharing of experiences from Asian Communities will be the focus of the forum.

Over the years, CCA facilitated the participation of its member churches and councils from countries such as South Korea, Japan, the Philippines, Indonesia, Malaysia, Thailand, Sri Lanka, Myanmar, Cambodia, Laos, India, Nepal and Bangladesh in the LGA Forum. Now the Korean counterpart KCLGAF has been entrusted with the responsibility of coordinating the Forum on a bi-annual basis on behalf of the Asian ecumenical family.

Response to *Laudato Si*

The CCA and the Federation of the Asian Bishops' Conferences (FABC) jointly organised a study seminar to study Pope Francis' encyclical on the environment and human ecology – *Laudato Si*. The seminar was held in Medan, Indonesia in July 2016 and was hosted by CCA member church HKBP. Several issues and themes related to ecology and environmental concerns were addressed from an Asian theological perspective. Representatives of different traditions of Asian churches including representatives of Asian Evangelical Alliance attended the seminar.

Renewal and Restoration of the Creation: Thematic emphases of CCA's major events

In 2019 and in 2020, CCA has scheduled three major events with the thematic focus on Renewal and Restoration of the Creation.

Mathews George Chunakara

Congress of Asian Theologians (CATS) – IX on 'Reconciliation, Renewal and Restoration of Creation: Divine Initiative and Human Imperative'.

The CATS, a major Asian theologians' summit which is organised on a triennial basis, originally started in 1997. The theme of CATS-IX which was held in Indonesia in August 2019 focused on 'Reconciliation, Renewal and Restoration: Divine Initiative and Human Imperative'. Various issues related to eco-theology, ethics of sustainability and stewardship of the creation were part of the deliberations of CATS –IX. Approximately 120 Asian theologians including Asian theologians in Diaspora attended the summit.

Asian Ecumenical Women's Assembly (AEWA) on 'Arise, Be Awake to reconcile, renew and restore the Creation'.

An Asian Ecumenical Women's Assembly (AEWA), a major ecumenical Asian women's event, will be organised by CCA from 21 to 27 November 2019 in Hsinchu, Taiwan. The theme of AEWA is 'Arise, Be Awake to Reconcile, Renew and Restore the Creation'. The AEWA will be an opportunity for Asian women to articulate theological perspectives with specific feminist emphasis on creation and eco-theology.

General Assembly theme 2020 with focus on 'God, Renew Us in Your Spirit to Restore the Creation'

Asian church delegates meet once every five years as a major representative gathering of CCA for its General Assembly. The 15th General Assembly, to be held in September 2020 in Kerala, India, will focus on the theme 'God, Renew Us in Your Spirit to Restore the Creation'. An assembly is an occasion to initiate several pre-assembly events as part of the preparations. All such initiatives and events will focus on the same theme, which are opportunities to take the message of the Assembly, especially the theme of the General Assembly, to the grassroots. The theological emphases delivered and shared especially through Bible studies, thematic presentations and other discussions will be based on the theme Renewal and Restoration of the creation. The assembly theme focusing on God's creation will be a major impetus for sensitising the members of the Asian churches at the grassroots levels.

Involvements of Asian Churches in local contexts in addressing ecological concerns

In comparison with the recent past, more and more Asian churches are directly involved in responding and articulating their theological convictions on ecology, sustainability of the creation and the need for living together in the household of God in the present day. The churches, including local congregations, are more and more involved in emphasising eco-theology and also involved in the practical application of sustainable ethics of development. Eco-friendly churches/ congregations as well as the idea of encouraging green churches have become a motto of many Asian churches. We receive reports from CCA member churches and related institutions including theological education institutions in countries such as India, Sri Lanka, Bangladesh, Thailand, the Philippines, Indonesia, South Korea, Japan, and Taiwan that are directly involved in promoting eco-friendly churches.

In some Asian countries Christian institutions and organisations have major involvements in promoting ecological and environmental concerns as well as advocating for better stewardships of God's creation. The Climate Technology Park initiated in Bangladesh by the Christian Commission for Development in Bangladesh (CCDB), the social development arm of the Protestant Churches in Bangladesh and a partner of CCA and WCC, is a very creative initiative. Bangladesh is one of the poorest countries in the world where a large number of people are affected for a major part of the year with flood and typhoons. The objective of the initiative is to demonstrate low cost technologies related to climate change adaptation and mitigation that can be replicated at the community level, both in urban and rural setting of Bangladesh. The project is being implemented with the support of the Bread for the World and the Federal Ministry for Economic Cooperation and Development in Germany. Over a period of time, the facility will become a learning centre as well which would facilitate knowledge generation and capacity building to those working on climate change in Bangladesh and beyond. The park will be a space where visitors, especially children, students, teachers, practitioners and policy makers can learn about the technologies from a range of different options including traditional indigenous ones as well as the new technologies.

The National Christian Council of Sri Lanka (NCCSL), a member council of CCA has been trying to sensitise members of NCCSL churches about the concerns for the well-being of their neighbours and a responsibility to care for creation. The NCCSL also promotes the understanding of sustainability in its broadest context and motivates them to educate people to minimise the impacts on the environment in all their activities.

The Malankara Mar Thoma Syrian Church in India, especially the supreme head Joseph Mar Thoma Metropolitan, has been urging for an all-out effort to protect and preserve the environment for the survival of humankind. He has often called upon members of his church to realise how the environment was being destroyed by vested interests, posing danger to society, and asked them to introspect on the devastating situation created by people and take remedial measures. He calls for responsible stewardship in protecting the environment, and encourages people to take the initiative to protect the environment, including rivers and trees.

The Church of South India (CSI) has been involved in a Green Church Campaign which encourages parishes to incorporate ecological concerns in their order of worship and include both advocacy and direct action for eco-justice and the integrity of creation in missional activities. The CSI published Earth Bible Sermons to provide sound theological backing for the Green Church Movement with an aim to teach the members about the faith aspect of the environmental ministry. Member churches of CCA in the Philippines have been engaged in responding to the environmental issues especially participating in people's struggle to protect resources necessary for their subsistence. They have been part of the struggle of the people against the neoliberal policies designed by the Philippine government to encourage nonferrous metals mining by multinational corporations. Mining, an activity with substantial potential for environmental degradation in the Philippines, deprives the poor of their livelihood. The churches in the Philippines have taken a stance opposing mining as an activity that may harm the poor by degrading the environment upon which they depend for their livelihood and further impoverish them.

CCA's Environmental protection guidelines and policy .

The CCA has officially introduced an environmental protection guidelines and policy with an aim to reduce waste by initiating recycling programmes within the office – including the recycling of paper, cardboard, beverage containers, plastic containers, and other materials that are accepted by a recycling provider. As per this policy, CCA purchases environmentally responsible products that have been selected based on criteria including: toxicity, durability, use of recycled or re-furbished materials, reduced energy and/or water consumption, reduced packaging, and ability to be recycled, refilled or re-furbished at the end of its useful life; promote efficient use of resources throughout our facility including water and energy; try to avoid unnecessary use of hazardous materials and seek alternatives whenever feasible. These guidelines and policies are aimed to continually strive to improve environmental performance as well as to educate staff and participants of CCA programmes on relevant environmental issues. CCA also committed to establish a green procurement policy, minimize use of water and energy, and minimize use of hazardous and toxic substances found in the office.

Towards developing a systematic culture of eco-consciousness and eco-theology in Asia

Over the past quarter of a century, there have been many serious attempts and initiatives to create awareness among people to be more environmentally conscious and environmentally friendly. The notion of responding to the ecological crises has been a central concern of churches in different parts of the world especially in the West, and they started reflecting on it from a Christian eco-theological perspective. While there is still a significant part of the population that is not aware of the importance of taking care of the environment in which they live, most people do not know even the buzzwords of "going green," and being "environmentally friendly". Being environmentally conscious can mean something different to each person because it is a broad term that describes many different behaviours, cultural patterns, guidelines that exist to reduce or minimize environmental degradation. There are many different ways people can make changes to safeguard their environment. Being eco-friendly on a personal level can mean changing one's routine, lifestyle and attitude which are not helpful to protecting the environment. Being environmentally conscious is an ever growing and a continuous learning process which could focus on different ways of protecting the environment. Being aware of the problem and helping to educate others are the best ways to be an environmentally friendly person in a congregation or a member of any organisation. The Church can contribute significantly and effectively to mobilise more environmentally friendly people through congregations. The Church in Asia has a responsibility to nurture and inculcate theological values among the members of each congregation. A Church which emphasises upon eco-theology could articulate faith convictions in a more authentic and convincing way.

Eco-theology addresses various forms of environmental issues from theological perspectives. Though it is generally considered to still draw on the authority from the Bible and the Christian tradition, Eco-theology has deeper roots and not just in Christianity. In a multi religious and multi-cultural Asian context, ecological concerns should be taken up as a common concern and cause of adherents of all faiths. In order to protect the household of God and the entire creation, all religions should come forward and contribute their spiritual resources and values. The Christian world often limits their theological perceptions within the orbits of Christian spirituality or theology and interprets it from a common Christian heritage. In this context what Andrew Spencer from the Oklahoma Baptist University observes is relevant. He pointed out in an article on 'Beyond Christian Environmentalism: Eco theology as an Over-Contextualized Theology' that, "still, the relative dearth of focus on central Christian doctrines and the radical revision of the message of Scripture bring into question the trajectory of Eco theology. Based on the current emphases of Eco-theology, it is not clear whether the next generation of disciples of an Eco-theological Christianity can present a coherent witness to the gospel of Christ". [5]

Eco-theology is considered as a contextual theology in Asia, and it is slowly gaining momentum in academic circles. However, more systematic efforts need to be initiated to make people understand the value of eco-consciousness from a theological basis. More concrete steps and actions need to be initiated by Asian churches and the ecumenical movement in the future with more precise practical approaches rather than focusing or repeating certain outdated theological jargons. Norman Habel has expressed his views on theological conjectures of eco-theology and six eco-justice principles developed in the Earth Bible Project[6], an international project that was initiated in Australia. In spite of considerable literature on Eco-theology and Eco-spirituality, it became very apparent that few scholars had undertaken a serious attempt to interpret the biblical tradition from an ecological perspective. No explicit ecological hermeneutic had been developed. While many read the biblical text with a view to understanding ecological topics, few have sought to read the tradition from the perspective of Earth or the Earth community. The principles articulated below are concerned with ecology in general, and ecological concerns linked to the Bible in particular are more meaningful and relevant in developing a new eco consciousness and eco theology in Asia:

The principle of intrinsic worth: the universe, Earth and all its components have intrinsic worth/value.

The principle of interconnectedness: Earth is a community of interconnected living things that are mutually dependent on each other for life and survival.

The principle of voice: Earth is a subject capable of raising its voice in celebration and against injustice.

The principle of purpose: the universe, Earth and all its components are part of a dynamic cosmic design within which each piece has a place in the overall goal of that design.

The principle of mutual custodianship: Earth is a balanced and diverse domain where responsible custodians can function as partners with, rather than rulers over, Earth to sustain its balance and a diverse Earth community.

The principle of resistance: Earth and its components not only suffer from human injustices but actively resist them in the struggle for justice.

---

5   Andrew J. Spencer, "Beyond Christian Environmentalism: Eco theology as an Over-Contextualized Theology", Themeliose, Volume 40 Issue 3 December 2015
6   Norman Habel, "Introduction," in Exploring Ecological Hermeneutics, ed. Norman C. Habel and Peter L. Trudinger (Atlanta: Society of Biblical Literature, 2008), p.2.

APPENDIX

WUPPERTAL CALL IN DIFFERENT LANGUAGES

The Wuppertal Call in German:

Kairos für die Schöpfung – Hoffnungsbekenntnis für die Erde Die Wuppertaler Erklärung

> „Und [wenn] mein Volk, über das mein Name ausgerufen ist, sich demütigt und betet, mich sucht und von seinen schlechten Wegen umkehrt, dann höre ich es im Himmel. Ich verzeihe seine Sünde und bringe seinem Land Heilung." – 2. Chron 7,14.

> "Wenn also jemand in Christus ist, dann ist er eine neue Schöpfung: Das Alte ist vergangen, siehe, Neues ist geworden. Aber das alles kommt von Gott, der uns durch Christus mit sich versöhnt und uns den Dienst der Versöhnung aufgetragen hat" – 2. Kor 5,17-18

Präambel
Vom 16. bis 19. Juni 2019 trafen sich 52 Teilnehmende aus 22 Ländern aus verschiedenen Konfessions- und Glaubenstraditionen in Wuppertal für eine Konferenz mit dem Titel: „Together towards eco-theologies, ethics of sustainability and eco-friendly churches".[1] In Wuppertal haben wir des mutigen Bekenntnisses gedacht, das in der Barmer Theologischen Erklärung (1934) gegen die totalitäre, unmenschliche und rassistische Ideologie der damaligen Zeit formuliert wurde. Barmen ermutigt uns auch heute zu einer "frohe[n] Befreiung aus den gottlosen Bindungen dieser Welt zu freiem, dankbarem Dienst an seinen Geschöpfen." (Barmen 2).

Wir haben Geschichten aus Afrika, Asien, Europa, Lateinamerika, Nordamerika und Ozeanien miteinander geteilt. In ihnen hören wir die Schreie der Erde und die Schreie der Menschen, die von den Folgen des Klimawandels am schmerzlichsten getroffen werden. Dies sind besonders Kinder und ältere Menschen. Wir haben auch die Schreie von jungen Menschen gehört, die intergenerationelle Gerechtigkeit fordern und wir haben die Sorgen von Klimaexperten über aktuelle Klimatrends vernommen.

Wir erkennen die Dringlichkeit der vor uns liegenden Jahre und wollen trotzdem in dieser Situation Mut zur Hoffnung haben. Wir wissen uns verpflichtet, die globale ökumenische Bewegung zu einer umfassenden ökologischen Transformation der Gesellschaften aufzurufen.

Kairos: eine entscheidende Wende auf dem Pilgerweg der Gerechtigkeit und des Friedens
Die ökumenische Bewegung hat sich schon lange zu einem Pilgerweg der Gerechtigkeit und des Friedens und zur Integrität der Schöpfung bekannt. Diese Ziele erfordern dringend neue Schritte auf dem vor uns liegenden Weg der ökologischen Gerechtigkeit. Die Dringlichkeit der Krise verlangt von uns, die Zeichen der Zeit zu lesen, Gottes Ruf zu hören, dem Weg Christi zu folgen, die Bewegung des Heiligen Geistes zu erkennen und die positiven Initiativen der Kirchen weltweit wahrzunehmen, die darauf schon entschieden antworten.

---

1   Die Konferenz wurde vom Evangelischen Missionswerk (EMW), der Evangelischen Kirche in Deutschland (EKD), der Vereinten Evangelischen Mission (UEM), Brot für die Welt und dem Weltkirchenrat gemeinsam verantwortet und organisiert.

Die Symptome der Krise berühren alle Bereiche und Bausteine des Lebens und sind deutlich für alle erkennbar:

- Das Trinkwasser ist verseucht; Gletscher schmelzen; Ozeane sind mit Plastik verschmutzt und Korallenbleiche und Versauerung bedrohen die Meere (das Element Wasser).
- Das Land wird durch nicht nachhaltige Landwirtschaft und ungesunde Ernährungsgewohnheiten zerstört, ein globales Wirtschaftssystem, das Raubbau an Bodenschätzen und Land betreibt, Entwaldung, Desertifikation und Bodenerosion bedrohen die Erde; Tiere ächzen und Kreaturen werden genetisch verändert; Fischpopulationen werden ausgerottet, und der Verlust von natürlichen Habitaten führt zu einem nie dagewesenen Verlust an Biodiversität (das Element Erde). Das Land und die Gesundheit der Menschen werden durch industrielle, landwirtschaftliche, städtische und nukleare Abfälle und durch Pestizide und Chemikalien gefährdet. Immer mehr Menschen werden durch diese Landzerstörungen dazu gezwungen, zu migrieren und werden zu Klimaflüchtlingen.
- Die globalen Kohleemissionen steigen weiter an, Treibhausgase sammeln sich in der Atmosphäre und das Klima wird gestört (das Element Luft).
- Die Nutzung von Energie aus fossilen Brennstoffen treibt diese Veränderungen an (das Element Feuer).

Das empfindliche System der Schöpfung wurde im Anthropozän in einem nie dagewesenen Ausmaß gestört. Wir haben die planetaren Grenzen überschritten. Die Erde scheint nicht länger in der Lage dazu zu sein, sich selbst zu heilen. Die gesamte Schöpfung seufzt. (Röm 8,22). Wir haben es nicht vermocht, unsere ökumenischen Grundanliegen im Auge zu behalten: das Anliegen der Gerechtigkeit angesichts von Armut, von Arbeitslosigkeit und Ungleichheit, das Anliegen einer partizipativen Gesellschaft angesichts von gewalttätigen Konflikten und das Anliegen von Nachhaltigkeit angesichts von ökologischer Zerstörung.

Obwohl Menschen nicht überall auf der Welt in gleichem Maße zu den Ursachen der Klimakrise beigetragen haben, kommen wir als Christ*innen gemeinsam zusammen und bekennen unsere Mitschuld und unsere Gefangenheit in der Sünde:

- Wir waren arrogant darin anzunehmen, dass die ganze Erde sich um uns Menschen und unsere Bedürfnisse dreht (die Sünde des Hochmuts).
- Wir haben uns von unserem katastrophalen Wunsch nach unbegrenztem materiellem Wachstum einfangen lassen und wurden von einer allgegenwärtigen Konsumkultur angetrieben (die Sünde der Gier).
- Wir haben Gottes Geschenke missbraucht, wir haben uns in Gewalt gegen Gottes Kreaturen verstricken lassen und die Menschenwürde verletzt (die Sünde der Gewalt).
- Wir haben uns von dem Land unserer Vorfahren und von indigenen Wissenstraditionen entfernt und die Verbindung zu Tieren als Mitgeschöpfen und zur Erde als unserer von Gott gegebenen Heimat verloren (die Sünde der Selbstsucht).
- Wir wurden von Torheit, Ungerechtigkeit, Verleugnung und Gier überwältigt (die Sünde der Lasterhaftigkeit).
- Wir waren zu langsam darin, unsere Verantwortung anzuerkennen, die entscheidende Krise unserer Zeit zu thematisieren (die Sünde der Trägheit).

Die Authentizität des ökumenischen Zeugnisses wird durch Verzerrungen des Evangeliums, von gefährlichen Narrativen und Theologien unterminiert, die eine totalitäre Logik von Tod und Zerstörung legitimieren. Dies sind Theologien, die Herrschaft, und insbesondere das Patriarchat, unter Vorwänden von "Rasse", Geschlecht, Klasse oder Spezies stützen. In diesen falschen

Perspektiven werden Himmel und Erde, Seele und Körper, Geist und Materie dualistisch und reduktionistisch aufeinander bezogen. Solche Narrative oder Theologien verleugnen anerkannte wissenschaftliche Erkenntnisse oder machen diese lächerlich, mit dem Interesse, die bestehende Ordnung aufrechtzuerhalten. Sie wiederholen den Mythos vom unendlichen Wachstum oder vertrauen allein auf technische Lösungen für ökologische Probleme, statt auf umfassendere kulturelle, moralische und spirituelle Lösungen zu setzen. Solche Narrative und Theologien zeigen sich in Formen eines Pseudo-Evangeliums, in denen die reine Akkumulation von Reichtum als Letztwert erscheint. Sie zeigen sich auch in den Versuchen, sich selbst durch permanente Verschiebung der Verantwortung auf andere zu entlasten oder in Ideologien, die sich mit religiösen Vertröstungen aus der Verantwortung ziehen wollen.

Hoffnung: Mut in Zeiten der Angst und Hoffnungslosigkeit

Inmitten einer Hoffnungslosigkeit, die sich angesichts der Klimakrise verbreitet, verkünden wir – inmitten einer seufzenden Schöpfung – die Hoffnung auf den dreieinigen Gott, „denn auf Hoffnung hin sind wir gerettet." (Röm 8,24). Gott hat die Erde nicht aufgegeben! Wir halten an Gottes Versprechen im Noah-Bund mit der ganzen Schöpfung fest, den er mit „den lebendigen Wesen bei euch für alle kommenden Generationen" (Gen 9,12) geschlossen hat. Wir glauben an Gottes Nähe, wie er sie uns in Jesus Christus inmitten der von den Menschen verursachten Misere offenbart hat. Wir werden von der Kraft des Heiligen Geistes getröstet, der „das Angesicht der Erde erneuert." (Ps 104,30).

Mit Blick auf wirtschaftliche und politische Narrative, die unser Verständnis von gelingenden Beziehungen zwischen Menschen, Schöpfung und Schöpfer verzerren, mag diese Hoffnung kontrafaktisch und widersinnig erscheinen. Die Hoffnung, die wir verkünden, hat aber nicht allein eine kritische Funktion, indem unterdrückende und patriarchale Systeme herausgefordert werden, sondern auch eine ermutigende Funktion, indem sie uns dazu inspiriert, an der Heilung der Erde aktiv Teil zu haben (2. Chron 7,14). Hoffnung ist nicht das gleiche wie blinder Optimismus, der allein auf die Fortschreibung aktueller Trends setzt. Christliche Hoffnung ist nicht billig; sie kostet, sie ist eine teure Hoffnung. Sie hat Bestand trotz überwältigender gegenteiliger evidenter Zeichen des fortschreitenden Klimawandels, weil sie ihren Grund in dem dreieinigen Gott hat und aus ihm selbst hervorgeht. Es ist eine solche Hoffnung, die uns ermutigt und uns zu einer umfassenden ökologischen Transformation unserer Gesellschaften nötigt.

Ein Aufruf an die weltweite ökumenische Bewegung

Im Herzen der ökologischen Transformation steht die Notwendigkeit einer ökologischen Umkehr/Konversion (*metanoia*), eine tiefe Veränderung in den Herzen, Köpfen, Einstellungen, Gewohnheiten und im Handeln (Röm 12,1-2). Diese Veränderung hat Auswirkungen auf alle Aspekte des christlichen Lebens: auf Liturgie und Anbetung, auf das Lesen der Bibel, auf die Verkündigung und auf die Sakramente, auf die Gemeinden und ihr Glaubensleben, auf Beten, Fasten, Spiritualität, Lehre, Ethos, Bildung, Kunst, Musik, Ämter und missionarische Projekte. In dieser ökologischen Reformation des gesamten Christentums wurden und werden wir von unseren Vätern und Müttern im christlichen Glauben, durch Beispiele von unseren Glaubensgeschwistern weltweit und von Kirchenleitenden aus der gesamten Ökumene ermutigt, wie beispielsweise vom Ökumenischen Patriarchen Bartholomäus, von Papst Franziskus, vom ehemaligen Erzbischof Desmond Tutu und vielen weiteren.

Wir rufen die globale ökumenische Bewegung, christliche Weltbünde und alle anderen Kirchen dazu auf, gemeinsam eine 10jährige *Dekade des ökologischen Lernens, Bekennens und*

Handelns angesichts des Klimawandels zu planen, um die folgenden Punkte zu Prioritäten der Kirchen weltweit zu machen:

1. Die ganze Breite der liturgischen und spirituellen Formen und altkirchlichen Traditionen mit Bezug zur Schöpfung im Licht des gegenwärtigen ökologischen Kairos bewusst zu machen und zu erneuern;
2. Die biblischen Texte unter dem Aspekt der ökologischen Sensibilität neu zu lesen und zu interpretieren;
3. Rahmenprogramme zu erstellen, welche das Klimabewusstsein in Kirchengemeinden stärken und ihnen das dafür benötigte Personal, das Knowhow und die finanziellen Ressourcen bieten und die schon existierenden Basisinitiativen unterstützen;
4. Gendergerechtigkeit in Kirchen und Gesellschaften zu fördern, da sie auf vielen Ebenen mit dem Klimawandel verknüpft ist;
5. Junge Menschen zu ermutigen, Führungsrollen in Kirchen und Gesellschaften zu übernehmen und dort für ihre Zukunft einzutreten;
6. Schöpfungstheologische und nachhaltigkeitsbezogene Reflektionen in allen Ebenen der Bildung zu etablieren;
7. Ökologische Werte zu kultivieren und nachhaltige Lebensstile in Haushalten und Gemeinschaften zu fördern;
8. Laien für ihre Berufung so auszustatten, dass sie ökologische Verantwortung übernehmen können, wo auch immer sie leben, arbeiten und beten;
9. Sich in multi-disziplinären Dialogen zu engagieren, die die Erkenntnisse der Naturwissenschaften, der indigenen Traditionen und diverser Theologien zusammenbinden;
10. Für interdisziplinäre Verbindungen, Netzwerke und Partnerschaften mit allen Bereichen der Regierung, mit Wirtschaft und Industrie, mit der Zivilgesellschaft, mit interreligiösen ökologischen Netzwerken, mit anderen Glaubensgemeinschaften und mit allen Menschen einzutreten, die die Verpflichtung mit uns teilen, nachhaltige Alternativen zu den aktuell dominanten Produktions- und Konsumformen zu finden.

Mit Blick auf die anstehende 11. Vollversammlung des Ökumenischen Rates der Kirchen im Jahre 2021 empfehlen wir dem ÖRK insbesondere, dass er eine *Dekade des ökologischen Handelns für die Schöpfung (Decade for the Healing of Creation)* mit den folgenden Zielen ausruft:

- Die Mitgliedskirchen dafür zu mobilisieren, dass sie ihre Prioritäten auf die Verpflichtungen dieser Wuppertaler Erklärung ausrichten;
- Die Agenda der Nachhaltigen Entwicklungsziele (SDGs) der Vereinten Nationen durch verschiedene Allianzen, Netzwerke und Partnerschaften zu unterstützen und gleichzeitig über die SDG-Agenda hinauszugehen, um die Definitionen von Wachstum, Reichtum und Wohlbefinden, die in der SDG-Agenda noch nicht hinreichend geklärt sind, im Hinblick auf die planetaren Grenzen nachhaltig zu bestimmen.
- Globale Entscheidungsträger*innen davon zu überzeugen, dass der Anstieg der globalen Treibhausgas-Emissionen so bald wie möglich gestoppt und drastisch reduziert werden muss, um Netto-Emissionsfreiheit und das Ziel von 1,5 Grad maximaler Temperatursteigerung doch noch zu erreichen.
- Den Prozess der Vereinten Nationen zu unterstützen, einen Rahmen für eine rechtlich verbindliche "Universale Erdrechte-Charta" zu erschaffen ("Universal Charter of the Rights of Mother Earth" (Cochabamba 2010)), ein internationales Rechtssystem für die Umweltrechte („Earth Jurisprudence") zu fixieren und die Möglichkeiten für einen „Rat für die Rechte der

Natur" („UN Council for the Rights of Nature") und für eine Anerkennung von „Ökozid" als Strafrechtstatbestand vor dem internationalen Strafgerichtshof auszuloten.

Diese Selbstverpflichtungen folgen aus dem Verständnis dieses Kairos in der Geschichte, in dem wir uns gerade wiederfinden. Die Aufgabe, die vor uns liegt, ist immens und wird Jahrzehnte größten Engagements fordern. Die Dringlichkeit der Situation lässt eine verspätete Antwort auf diese umfassenden Herausforderungen nicht zu. Das nächste Jahrzehnt wird entscheidend sein, um der Erde eine Zeit der Erholung zu ermöglichen. Die biblischen Motive des Sabbats und des Jobeljahres bieten eine einzigartige Quelle der Hoffnung und Inspiration, auf eine Unterbrechung im Kreislauf von Ausbeutung und Gewalt hinzuarbeiten, ausgedrückt in der Vision, dass: „für das Land ein Jahr der Sabbatruhe sein" soll (Lev 25,5).

Komm, Heiliger Geist, erneuere unsere Schöpfung!

The Wuppertal Call in French:

Kairos pour la création: une confession de l'espérance pour la Terre – L'appel de Wuppertal

«Si alors mon peuple, sur lequel est invoqué mon nom, s'humilie, s'il prie, cherche ma face et revient de ses voies mauvaises, moi, j'écouterai des cieux, je pardonnerai son péché et je guérirai son pays.» – 2 Ch 7,14.

«Aussi, si quelqu'un est en Christ, il est une nouvelle créature. Le monde ancien est passé, voici qu'une réalité nouvelle est là. Tout vient de Dieu, qui nous a réconciliés avec lui par le Christ et nous a confié le ministère de la réconciliation.» – 2 Co 5,17-18

Préambule

Du 16 au 19 juin 2019, 52 personnes de 22 pays et de différentes traditions confessionnelles et religieuses se sont réunies à Wuppertal, en Allemagne, pour une conférence intitulée «Ensemble vers l'éco-théologie, une éthique de la durabilité et des Églises respectueuses de l'environnement»[1]. À Wuppertal, nous nous sommes souvenu-e-s de la profession de foi courageuse de la Déclaration de Barmen (1934) contre l'idéologie totalitaire, inhumaine et raciste de l'époque. Barmen continue à nous encourager aujourd'hui à entreprendre «une joyeuse libération des entraves impies de ce monde pour un service libre et reconnaissant parmi ses créatures» (Barmen 2).

Nous avons partagé des récits d'Afrique, d'Asie, d'Europe, d'Amérique latine, d'Amérique du Nord et d'Océanie. Nous avons entendu les cris de la terre, les cris des peuples vulnérables aux effets des changements climatiques, en particulier des enfants et des personnes âgées, les cris de la jeunesse exigeant une justice intergénérationnelle et les inquiétudes des experts face aux tendances actuelles.

Nous reconnaissons l'urgence pour les années à venir. Néanmoins, nous exprimons le courage de l'espérance et nous nous sentons poussé-e-s à appeler le mouvement œcuménique mondial à entreprendre une transformation écologique globale de la société.

Kairos: un tournant décisif du pèlerinage de justice et de paix

Le mouvement œcuménique s'engage depuis longtemps dans un pèlerinage de justice, de paix et d'intégrité de la création. Ces objectifs exigeront des mesures urgentes qui jalonneront le chemin à parcourir. L'urgence de la crise nous invite à lire les signes de notre époque, à entendre l'appel de Dieu, à suivre la voie du Christ, à discerner le mouvement de l'Esprit et, en réponse, à reconnaître les initiatives positives des Églises du monde entier.

Les symptômes de la crise touchent tous les fondements de la vie et sont visibles de tous et de toutes:

– L'eau douce est polluée, les glaciers fondent, les océans sont souillés par du plastique et deviennent acides, provoquant le blanchissement des coraux (eau).

---

[1] La conférence de Wuppertal était préparée et organisée par l'Association protestante des Églises et de la mission (EMW), l'Église évangélique d'Allemagne (EKD), la Mission évangélique unie (UEM), Pain pour le monde et le Conseil œcuménique des Églises.

– La terre est dégradée par une agriculture non durable et des habitudes alimentaires malsaines, l'industrie extractive dirigée par les puissances financières mondiales, la déforestation, la désertification et l'érosion des sols, les animaux gémissent et les créatures sont modifiées génétiquement, les bancs de poissons sont raréfiés et la perte d'habitats mène à une perte de biodiversité sans précédent (terre). La terre et la santé des populations sont empoisonnées par des déchets industriels, agricoles, municipaux et nucléaires ainsi que par des pesticides et des substances chimiques. De plus en plus de personnes se voient forcées de migrer ou deviennent des réfugiées climatiques.
– Les émissions de carbone ne cessent de croître, les gaz à effet de serre s'accumulent dans l'atmosphère et le climat est déréglé (air).
– La course à l'énergie issue des combustibles fossiles est toujours à la tête de ces changements (feu).

Les systèmes délicats régissant l'équilibre de la création sont perturbés d'une ampleur inédite depuis l'anthropocène. Nous avons transgressé les frontières planétaires. La terre ne semble plus être en mesure de panser ses blessures. Les créatures gémissent dans les douleurs de l'enfantement (cf. Rm 8,22). Nous n'avons pas été capables de faire converger les craintes du mouvement œcuménique concernant la justice dans un contexte de pauvreté, de chômage et d'inégalités, concernant une société participative alors que plusieurs formes de conflits violents font rage et concernant la durabilité en pleine destruction écologique.

Bien que les êtres humains aient contribué à des degrés différents aux causes profondes de cette crise, nous nous rassemblons tous et toutes, en tant que fidèles chrétiens, pour confesser notre complicité et notre esclavage du péché:
– Nous avons été arrogant-e-s en supposant que la planète entière tourne autour de nous, les êtres humains, et de nos besoins (orgueil).
– Nous nous sommes enfermé-e-s dans un désir abyssal de croissance matérielle illimitée, mus par une culture consumériste généralisée (cupidité).
– Nous avons exploité les dons de Dieu, usant de la violence contre les créatures divines et violant la dignité humaine (violence).
– Nous nous sommes aliéné-e-s des terres ancestrales et de la sagesse autochtone, des animaux, nos co-créatures, et de la Terre, la maison que Dieu nous a donnée (privation du bien).
– Nous avons été emporté-e-s par la folie, l'injustice, le déni et l'avarice (vice).
– Nous avons été lent-e-s à assumer notre responsabilité dans la lutte contre la crise la plus déterminante de notre temps (paresse).

Et pour ne rien arranger, l'authenticité du témoignage œcuménique est mise à mal par toutes sortes de distorsions de l'Évangile, de récits toxiques et de théologies qui légitiment une logique totalitaire de la mort et de la destruction. Ces théologies sont notamment celle de la domination au nom des différences de race, de genre, de classe et d'espèce, celle de la légitimation théologique de la domination patriarcale, celle des manières réductrices et dualistes de relier la terre et les cieux, le corps et l'âme, l'esprit et la matière, celle visant à nier et tourner en dérision l'expertise et les données scientifiques au service du maintien de l'ordre actuel, celle du renouvellement du mythe du progrès illimité, plaçant la confiance uniquement dans les solutions technologiques aux problèmes écologiques sans tenir compte de leur nature culturelle, morale et spirituelle, celle du pseudo-Évangile prônant une accumulation de richesse et la prospérité, celle des attitudes égoïstes envers les difficultés en faisant porter le blâme à autrui, et celle des faux-fuyants face aux victimes de l'injustice écologique.

L'espérance: le courage à une époque d'angoisse et de désespoir

En proie à un désespoir sans précédent lié à une crise écologique accablante, nous proclamons l'espérance en un Dieu trinitaire au cœur de la création gémissante, «car nous avons été sauvés, mais c'est en espérance» (Rm 8,24). Dieu n'a pas abandonné la Terre. Nous nous attachons à la promesse divine symbolisée par l'alliance avec «tout être vivant avec vous, pour toutes les générations futures» (Gn 9,12). Nous croyons en la présence de Dieu révélée par Jésus Christ au cœur du chaos qui nous entoure. Nous sommes conforté-e-s par la puissance de l'Esprit qui «renouvelle la surface du sol» (Ps 104,30).

Face aux discours économiques et politiques qui déforment notre compréhension des véritables relations entre les êtres humains, la création et le Créateur, une telle espérance peut sembler contre-intuitive. L'espérance que nous proclamons non seulement critique les systèmes oppressifs et patriarcaux de domination, mais est également une source d'inspiration pour que nous prenions part à la guérison de la création (cf. 2 Ch 7,14). L'espérance ne s'apparente pas à de l'optimisme aveugle qui fait confiance à une simple poursuite des tendances actuelles. Une telle espérance n'est pas donnée, elle a un coût. Elle jaillit en dépit des preuves accablantes du contraire, car elle réside en un Dieu trinitaire. Une telle espérance nous encourage et nous exhorte à entreprendre une transformation écologique globale de la société.

Un appel au mouvement œcuménique mondial

Au cœur de la transformation nécessaire se trouve le besoin de conversion (metanoia) écologique, d'un changement de cœur, d'esprit, d'attitudes, d'habitudes quotidiennes et de formes de pratique (cf. Rm 12,1-2). Cela a des incidences sur tous les aspects de la vie chrétienne: la liturgie et le culte, la lecture de la Bible, la proclamation, les sacrements, la communauté et la pratique paroissiale, la prière, le jeûne, la spiritualité, la doctrine, l'éthos, l'éducation, l'art, la musique, les ministères et les missions. Cette réforme écologique de l'ensemble du christianisme a été encouragée par nos mères et nos pères dans la tradition chrétienne, par l'exemple de nos frères et sœurs du monde entier et par les responsables œcuméniques, à l'instar du patriarche œcuménique Bartholomée, le pape François, l'archevêque émérite Desmond Tutu et bien d'autres voix. 3

Nous appelons le mouvement œcuménique mondial, les communions chrétiennes du monde entier et toutes les autres Églises à lancer une décennie d'apprentissage, de confession et d'action globale écologique afin de réorienter les priorités ecclésiales, en prenant les engagements suivants:

1. Renouveler l'ensemble de la pratique liturgique et spirituelle ainsi que les anciennes traditions ecclésiales relatives à la création à la lumière du présent kairos;
2. Relire les textes bibliques et les étudier en adoptant une sensibilité écologique;
3. Élaborer les cadres favorables aux paroisses écologiques, les dotant du personnel et des ressources financières nécessaires et en appuyant les initiatives communautaires existantes;
4. Promouvoir la justice sensible à la spécificité des sexes dans l'Église et la société, du fait de ses nombreux liens avec les questions écologiques;
5. Encourager la jeunesse à jouer un rôle moteur dans l'Église et la société au nom de l'avenir qui lui appartient;
6. Intégrer les réflexions éco-théologiques à tous les niveaux d'éducation;
7. Cultiver les vertus écologiques et encourager des modes de vie durables dans les foyers et les communautés;
8. Outiller les personnes laïques afin qu'elles poursuivent leur vocation et exercent leur responsabilité écologique où qu'elles vivent, travaillent et prient;

9. Prendre part au dialogue multidisciplinaire qui peut rassembler et rendre justice aux données émanant des sciences, traditions et sagesses autochtones et diverses théologies;

10. Plaider pour des alliances, réseaux et partenariats interdisciplinaires avec tous les niveaux gouvernementaux, commerciaux et industriels, la société civile, les réseaux écologiques multiconfessionnels, les autres fois vivantes, et toute personne qui partage l'engagement à trouver des alternatives durables aux formes dominantes de production et de consommation.

En amont de la Onzième Assemblée du Conseil œcuménique des Églises en 2021, nous recommandons particulièrement au COE de proclamer une «Décennie de la guérison de la création» assortie des objectifs suivants:

– Mobiliser les Églises membres à réorienter leurs priorités en faveur des engagements énoncés dans l'appel de Wuppertal;

– Prendre part au programme des Objectifs de développement durable (ODD) des Nations Unies au travers de diverses alliances et différents réseaux et partenariats, et aller au-delà du programme des ODD afin de redéfinir les notions de croissance, de richesse et de bien-être qui ne sont toujours pas suffisamment explicitées au sujet des frontières planétaires actuelles;

– Plaider auprès des décideurs mondiaux la fin de l'augmentation des émissions des gaz à effet de serre à l'échelle planétaire et leur réduction draconienne dès que possible afin d'atteindre des émissions neutres en carbone et maintenir le réchauffement climatique en deçà de 1,5 degré Celsius;

– Promouvoir les processus des Nations Unies visant à doter la «Charte universelle des droits de la Terre mère» (Cochabamba, 2010) d'un cadre juridiquement contraignante, instaurer un système de jurisprudence internationale pour la Terre, et étudier les possibilités de reconnaître l'écocide comme un délit pénal au Tribunal pénal international.

Ces engagements font suite à la prise de conscience que nous nous trouvons à un kairos de l'histoire. La tâche qui nous attend est immense et nous demande de nous y dédier pendant des décennies. L'urgence de la situation exige une réponse globale qui ne peut être retardée. La prochaine décennie sera décisive pour que la Terre puisse se reposer. Les principes bibliques du sabbat et du jubilé offrent une source unique d'espérance et d'inspiration, une interruption du cycle d'exploitation et de violence, exprimés dans la vision qu'il y aura «une année sabbatique pour la terre» (Lv 25,5).

Viens, Esprit Saint, renouvelle toute ta création!

The Wuppertal Call in Spanish:

Kairós para la Creación – Confesión de esperanza para la tierra
La Declaración de Wuppertal

"Si se humilla mi pueblo sobre el cual es invocado mi nombre, si oran y buscan mi rostro y se vuelven de sus malos caminos, entonces yo oiré desde los cielos, perdonaré sus pecados y sanaré su tierra", 2 Cr. 7:14.

"De modo que si alguno está en Cristo, nueva criatura es; las cosas viejas pasaron; he aquí todas son hechas nuevas. Y todo esto proviene de Dios, quien nos reconcilió consigo mismo por medio de Cristo y nos ha dado el ministerio de la reconciliación", 2 Cor. 5:17-18

Preámbulo
Del 16 al 19 de junio de 2019 se encontraron en la ciudad de Wuppertal (Alemania) 52 participantes de 22 países y diferentes tradiciones confesionales y de fe para participar en una conferencia titulada "Juntos por la ecoteología, la ética de la sostenibilidad y las iglesias respetuosas con el medio ambiente"[1]. En Wuppertal hemos conmemorado la valiente confesión que fue formulada en la *Declaración Teológica de Barmen* (1934) contra la ideología totalitaria, inhumana y racista de aquella época. Barmen nos anima también hoy a una "alegre liberación de las impías ataduras de este mundo a un servicio libre y agradecido a sus criaturas" (Barmen 2).

Hemos compartido historias de África, Asia, Europa, América Latina, Norteamérica y Oceanía. En ellas hemos escuchado el clamor de la tierra y el clamor de los seres humanos que son afectados más dolorosamente por las consecuencias del cambio climático. Ellos son especialmente niños y personas mayores. Hemos escuchado el clamor de los jóvenes que reclaman por una justicia intergeneracional y percibido las preocupaciones de los expertos en la materia sobre las actuales tendencias del clima.

Reconocemos la urgencia de los años que se encuentran ante nosotros, y sin embargo, en esa situación, queremos tener coraje para la esperanza. Nos sentimos obligados a convocar al movimiento ecuménico global a una transformación ecológica integral de la sociedad.

Kairós: un cambio decisivo en el peregrinaje por la justicia y la paz
Ya hace mucho que el movimiento ecuménico se ha manifestado en favor de un peregrinaje por la justicia, paz e integridad de la creación. Esas metas demandan con urgencia nuevos pasos en el camino de la justicia ecológica que está ante nosotros. La urgencia de las crisis nos reclama leer los signos de los tiempos, escuchar el llamado de Dios, seguir el camino de Cristo, aprender a reconocer el movimiento del Espíritu Santo y reconocer las iniciativas positivas de las iglesias a lo largo del mundo que ya responden decididamente a ello.

---

1   La organización de la conferencia fue responsabilidad de la Obra Misionera Evangélica (Evangelischen Missionswerk [EMW], la Iglesia Evangélica en Alemania (Evangelischen Kirche in Deutschland [EKD]), la Misión Evangélica Unida (Vereinten Evangelischen Mission [UEM]), Pan para el Mundo (Brot für die Welt) y el Consejo Mundial de Iglesias (Weltkirchenrat).

Los síntomas de la crisis afectan todos los ámbitos y estructuras elementales de la vida y son reconocibles para todos:

- El agua potable está contaminada; los glaciares se derriten; los océanos están abarrotados de plástico y el blanqueamiento de los corales y la acidificación amenazan los mares (el elemento agua);
- La tierra es destruida por una agricultura no sostenible y costumbres alimentarias insanas, economías extractivas de las que se benefician compañías globales; el desmonte, la desertificación y la erosión del suelo amenazan la tierra; gimen los animales y las criaturas son modificadas genéticamente; las poblaciones de peces son aniquiladas y la destrucción de los hábitats naturales lleva a una pérdida de biodiversidad sin precedentes. La tierra y la salud de las personas son amenazadas por formas de basura industrial, agraria, urbana y nuclear y por pesticidas y químicos. Cada vez más seres humanos son obligados por esas destrucciones de la tierra a emigrar y devienen refugiados climáticos (el elemento tierra);
- Las emisiones globales de carbono continúan aumentando, los gases de efecto invernadero se concentran en la atmósfera y el clima es perturbado (el elemento aire);
- El uso de energía de combustibles fósiles impulsa esas modificaciones (el elemento fuego).

En el antropoceno el delicado sistema de la creación ha sido perturbado en una dimensión sin precedentes. Hemos traspasado los límites planetarios. La tierra no parece seguir siendo capaz de sanarse a sí misma. Toda la creación suspira (Ro.8,22). No hemos sido capaces de dedicar atención a nuestras preocupaciones ecuménicas fundamentales: la preocupación por la justicia en medio de la pobreza, desocupación e inequidad, la preocupación por una sociedad participativa en medio de conflictos violentos y la preocupación por sustentabilidad en medio de la destrucción ecológica.

Si bien los eres humano en el mundo no han contribuido en la misma medida a ocasionar la crisis climática, nos reunimos como cristian*s y confesamos nuestra culpa común y nuestra cautividad en el pecado:

- Hemos sido arrogantes al suponer que toda la tierra gira en torno a nosotros, los seres humanos, y nuestras necesidades (el pecado de la soberbia);
- Nos hemos dejado aprisionar por nuestro catastrófico deseo por un crecimiento material ilimitado y hemos sido impulsados por una omnipresente cultura consumista (el pecado de la codicia);
- Hemos abusado de los obsequios de Dios, nos hemos dejado enredar ejerciendo violencia hacia las criaturas de Dios y hemos lesionado la dignidad de los seres humanos (el pecado de la violencia);
- Nos hemos alejado de la tierra de nuestros antepasados y de las tradiciones de conocimiento indígena y hemos perdido el vínculo con los animales como co-criaturas y con la tierra como nuestra patria dada por Dios (el pecado como omisión del bien);
- Hemos sido dominados por la necedad, injusticia, negación y codicia (el pecado de libertinaje);
- Hemos sido demasiado lentos para reconocer nuestra responsabilidad por tematizar la crisis decisiva de nuestra época (el pecado de la pereza).

La autenticidad del testimonio ecuménico es minado por distorsiones del Evangelio, por narrativas y teologías tóxicas que legitiman una lógica totalitaria de muerte y destrucción. Esas son teologías que legitiman la dominación y especialmente el patriarcado bajo los pretextos de "raza", género, clase o especie; en esas falsas perspectivas cielo y tierra, alma y cuerpo, espíritu y materia son relacionados entre sí en términos dualistas y reduccionistas. Tales narrativas o teologías niegan conocimientos científicos reconocidos o los ridiculizan con el objetivo de sostener el orden vigente. Ellas repiten el mito del crecimiento infinito o confían únicamente en soluciones técnicas para los problemas ecológicos en lugar de apostar por soluciones culturales, morales o espirituales más amplias. Tales narrativas o teologías se expresan mediante formas de un pseudo-evangelio, en las cuales la mera acumulación de riqueza aparece como valor fundamental o también en el intento de exonerarse a sí mismo mediante el permanente desplazamiento de la responsabilidad a otros o incluso a través de intentos de interpretación escéptica de las víctimas de la injusticia climática.

Esperanza: coraje en tiempos de miedo y desesperanza

En medio de una desesperanza que, frente a la crisis climática, se extiende rápidamente, de forma hasta ahora desconocida, anunciamos – en medio de una creación suspirante – la esperanza en el Dios trino, "porque en esperanza fuimos salvos" (Ro.8,24). ¡Dios no ha abandonado la tierra! Adherimos a la promesa de Dios en la alianza realizada con Noé y con toda la creación, que él ha establecido con la humanidad "y todo ser viviente" (Ge.9,12). Creemos en la cercanía de Dios, así como él nos la ha revelado en Jesucristo en medio de toda la miseria ocasionada por los seres humanos. Somos consolados por la fuerza del Espíritu Santo que "renueva la faz de la tierra" (Sal. 104,30).

En vistas de narrativas económicas y políticas que distorsionan nuestra comprensión de las relaciones bienhechoras entre los seres humanos, la creación y el Creador, aunque esa esperanza pudiese parecer contrafáctica y absurda. Pero la esperanza que anunciamos no solo tiene una función crítica, en la medida en que son desafiados los sistemas opresores y patriarcales, sino también una función alentadora, al inspirarnos a tomar parte activamente de la sanación de la tierra (2 Cr. 7,14). Esperanza no es lo mismo que un optimismo ciego que solo apuesta a la actualización de las tendencias actuales. La esperanza cristiana no es barata; ella cuesta algo, es una esperanza cara. Ella persiste a pesar de una abrumadora evidencia opuesta a partir de los signos del creciente cambio climático pues ella tiene su fundamento en el Dios trino y surge desde él mismo. Es una esperanza tal que nos alienta y nos demanda una transformación ecológica integral de nuestra sociedad.

Un llamado al movimiento ecuménico mundial

En el corazón de la transformación ecológica está la necesidad de una conversión ecológica (*metanoia*), de un cambio profundo en los corazones, mentes, actitudes, costumbres y en el actuar (Ro. 12,1-2). Ese cambio tiene consecuencias sobre todos los aspectos de la vida cristiana: sobre liturgia y adoración, sobre la lectura de la Biblia, sobre la proclamación y sobre los sacramentos, sobre las comunidades y su vida de fe, sobre el orar, el ayunar, la espiritualidad, la doctrina, la ética, la formación, el arte, la música, los ministerios y los proyectos misioneros. A esa reforma ecológica de todo el cristianismo fuimos y somos alentados por nuestros padres y madres en la fe cristiana, mediante ejemplos de nuestros hermanos en la fe a lo largo de mundo y por dirigentes eclesiales de toda la ecúmene, como por ejemplo el Patriarca Ecuménico Bartolomé, el Papa Francisco y el fallecido Arzobispo Desmond Tutu, entre muchos otros.

Nosotros llamamos al movimiento ecuménico global, a las asociaciones mundiales cristianas y a todas las otras iglesias a planificar una *Década del Aprender, Confesar y Actuar Ecológico contra el Cambio Climático* a lo largo de 10 años, para establecer como prioridades de las iglesias a nivel mundial los siguientes puntos:

1. A tomar conciencia y a renovar toda la variedad de formas litúrgicas y espirituales y de tradiciones de la Iglesia Antigua con relación a la creación a la luz del actual *kairós* ecológico;
2. A volver a leer y a interpretar los textos bíblicos bajo el aspecto de la sensibilidad ecológica;
3. A establecer programas-marco para fortalecer la conciencia climática en las comunidades eclesiales ofreciéndoles el personal, el *know-how* y los recursos financieros necesarios para ello y apoyar las iniciativas de base ya existentes;
4. A promover la justicia de género en las iglesias y en la sociedad, dado que ella se halla vinculada con el cambio climático en diversos niveles;
5. A animar a los jóvenes a asumir roles de liderazgo en las iglesias y las sociedades y a allí comprometerse con su futuro;
6. A establecer reflexiones sobre la teología de la creación, y relativas a la problemática de la sustentabilidad en todos los niveles de formación;
7. A cultivar valores ecológicos y a promover estilos de vida sustentables en el hogar y en las comunidades;
8. A capacitar a los laicos en vistas de su llamado de forma tal que ellos puedan asumir responsabilidad ecológica, sea donde fuera que vivan, trabajen y oren;
9. A comprometerse en diálogos multidisciplinarios que puedan vincular los conocimientos de las ciencias naturales, de las tradiciones indígenas y de las diversas teologías, y a tomarlos en consideración;
10. A establecer asociaciones, redes y colaboraciones interdisciplinarias con todas las áreas del gobierno, con la economía y la industria, con la sociedad civil, con redes ecológicas interreligiosas, con otras comunidades de fe y con todos aquellos seres humanos que comparten con nosotros la obligación de encontrar alternativas sustentables a las formas de producción y consumo actualmente dominantes.

En vistas de la próxima 11va. Asamblea General del Consejo Mundial de Iglesias (CMI) en el año 2021, le recomendamos al CMI especialmente que declare una *Década del Obrar Ecológico por la Creación/Década de Preocupación por la Creación*, con las siguientes metas:

- Movilizar a las iglesias-miembro para que orienten sus prioridades en virtud de los compromisos de esta *Declaración de Wuppertal*;
- Apoyar la Agenda de las Metas de Desarrollo Sostenible (SDGs) de las Naciones Unidas mediante diferentes alianzas, redes y asociaciones y simultáneamente a ir más allá de la agenda SDGs para determinar de forma sostenible con respecto a los límites planetarios las definiciones de crecimiento, riqueza y bienestar que en la agenda SDGs aún no han sido suficientemente clarificados.
- A convencer a l*s dirigentes globales de que el aumento de las emisiones globales de gas de efecto invernadero deben ser drásticamente reducidas y detenidas tan pronto como sea posible para poder alcanzar aún la libertad de emisión neta y la meta de 1,5 grados.
- A apoyar el proceso de las Naciones Unidas tendiente a crear el marco de una "Carta Universal de los Derechos de la Tierra" jurídicamente vinculante ("*Universal Charter of the Rights of Mother Earth*" (Cochabamba 2010)), fijar un sistema internacional de derecho para los derechos del medioambiente ("*Earth Jurisprudence*") y explorar la posibilidad de establecer un "Consejo por los Derechos de la Naturaleza" ("*UN Council for the Rights of Nature*") y del

reconocimiento de "ecocidio" como delito ante la Tribunal Penal Internacional.

Esas obligaciones propias surgen de la comprensión del momento de *kairós* en la historia en el que nos encontramos actualmente. La tarea que tenemos ante nosotros es inmensa y demandará décadas del mayor compromiso. La urgencia de la situación no permite una respuesta demorada a esos amplios desafíos. La próxima década será decisiva para posibilitar a la tierra un tiempo de rehabilitación. Los motivos bíblicos del Sabbat y del año de jubileo ofrecen una fuente única de esperanza e inspiración para trabajar en dirección a la interrupción del circuito de explotación y violencia, expresada en la visión de que deba haber un año de descanso sabático para la tierra" (Lev. 25,5)

¡Ven, Espíritu Santo, renueva la entera creación!

The Wuppertal Call in Greek:

ΚΑΙΡΟΣ για τη Δημιουργία – Ομολογώντας την Ελπίδα για τη Γη: Η έκκληση του Βούπερταλ

«Και εάν ο λαός μου, επάνω στον οποίο ονομάστηκε το όνομά μου, ταπεινώσουν τον εαυτό τους, και προσευχηθούν, και εκζητήσουν το πρόσωπό μου, και επιστρέψουν από τους δρόμους τους, τους πονηρούς, τότε εγώ θα εισακούσω από τον ουρανό, και θα συγχωρέσω την αμαρτία τους, και θα θεραπεύσω τη γη τους» — Χρονικών Β 7:14.

«Γι' αυτό, αν κάποιος είναι εν Χριστώ, είναι ένα καινούργιο κτίσμα· τα παλιά πέρασαν, δέστε, τα πάντα έγιναν καινούργια! Τα πάντα, όμως, είναι από τον Θεό, που μας συμφιλίωσε με τον εαυτό του, διαμέσου του Ιησού Χριστού και έδωσε σε μας τη διακονία της συμφιλίωσης» – Κορινθ. Β 5:17-18

Προοίμιο
Από τις 16 έως τις 19 Ιουνίου 2019, 52 συμμετέχοντες από 22 χώρες προερχόμενοι από διαφορετικές ομολογίες και παραδόσεις πίστεως συγκεντρώθηκαν στο Βούπερταλ (Wuppertal) της Γερμανίας για ένα συνέδριο με τίτλο «Από κοινού για την οικολογική θεολογία, την ηθική της βιωσιμότητας και τις φιλικές προς το περιβάλλον εκκλησίες».[1] Στο Βούπερταλ θυμηθήκαμε τη θαρραλέα ομολογία της πίστεως που διατυπώθηκε στη Διακήρυξη του Μπάρμεν (Barmen) (1934) κατά της ολοκληρωτικής, απάνθρωπης και ρατσιστικής ιδεολογίας της εποχής. Η Διακήρυξη του Μπάρμεν συνεχίζει να μας παρακινεί σήμερα για «μια χαρούμενη απελευθέρωση από τα αντίθεα δεσμά του κόσμου τούτου για ελεύθερη και ευγνώμονα διακονία της θεϊκής δημιουργίας» (Barmen 2).
Μοιραστήκαμε ιστορίες από την Αφρική, την Ασία, την Ευρώπη, τη Λατινική Αμερική, τη Βόρεια Αμερική και την Ωκεανία. Ακούσαμε τις κραυγές της γης, τις κραυγές των ανθρώπων που είναι ευάλωτοι στις επιπτώσεις της κλιματικής αλλαγής, ιδιαίτερα των παιδιών και των ηλικιωμένων, τις κραυγές των νέων που απαιτούν δικαιοσύνη μεταξύ των γενεών και τις ανησυχίες των ειδικών για τις τρέχουσες τάσεις.
Αναγνωρίζουμε την επείγουσα ανάγκη που προβλέπεται κατά τα προσεχή έτη, εκφράζουμε όμως το θάρρος να ελπίζουμε και είμαστε υποχρεωμένοι να κάνουμε έκκληση προς το παγκόσμιο οικουμενικό κίνημα για έναν ολοκληρωμένο οικολογικό μετασχηματισμό της κοινωνίας.

ΚΑΙΡΟΣ: Για μια αποφασιστική στροφή στην ιερά πορεία μας για δικαιοσύνη και ειρήνη
Το οικουμενικό κίνημα έχει επί μακρόν δεσμευτεί προς μια ιερά πορεία για δικαιοσύνη, ειρήνη και ακεραιότητα της δημιουργίας. Αυτοί οι στόχοι θα απαιτήσουν επείγουσες ενέργειες στο άμεσο μέλλον. Ο επείγων χαρακτήρας της κρίσης μάς καλεί να διαβάσουμε τα σημάδια των καιρών, να ακούσουμε το κάλεσμα του Θεού, να ακολουθήσουμε τον δρόμο του Χριστού, να διακρίνουμε

---

[1] Το συνέδριο σχεδιάστηκε και οργανώθηκε από την Προτεσταντική Ένωση Εκκλησιών και Αποστολών (EMW), την Ευαγγελική Εκκλησία της Γερμανίας (EKD), την Ηνωμένη Ευαγγελική Αποστολή (UEM), την οργάνωση Ψωμί για τον Κόσμο (Bread for the World) και το Παγκόσμιο Συμβούλιο Εκκλησιών.

την πνοή του Αγίου Πνεύματος και, ως απάντηση, να αναγνωρίσουμε τις θετικές πρωτοβουλίες των εκκλησιών σε όλο τον κόσμο.

Τα συμπτώματα της κρίσης αγγίζουν όλα τα δομικά στοιχεία της ζωής και είναι ορατά σε όλους:

- Το πόσιμο νερό είναι μολυσμένο, οι παγετώνες λιώνουν, οι ωκεανοί μολύνονται με πλαστικά και καθίστανται όξινοι, με αποτέλεσμα οι κοραλλιογενείς ύφαλοι να υφίστανται λεύκανση (νερό).

- Το έδαφος υποβαθμίζεται μέσω της μη βιώσιμης γεωργίας και των ανθυγιεινών διατροφικών συνηθειών, των εξορυκτικών οικονομιών που κυριαρχούνται από τις παγκόσμιες οικονομικές δυνάμεις, την αποψίλωση των δασών, την απερήμωση και τη διάβρωση του εδάφους· το ζωικό βασίλειο στενάζει και τα πλάσματα τροποποιούνται γενετικά· οι πληθυσμοί ιχθύων εξαντλούνται· η απώλεια οικοτόπων οδηγεί στην άνευ προηγουμένου απώλεια της βιοποικιλότητας (γη). Τόσο η γη όσο και η υγεία των ανθρώπων δηλητηριάζονται από βιομηχανικές, γεωργικές, δημοτικές και πυρηνικές μορφές αποβλήτων και από φυτοφάρμακα και χημικά. Ένας αυξανόμενος αριθμός ατόμων αναγκάζεται να μεταναστεύσει και να γίνει κλιματικός πρόσφυγας.

- Οι παγκόσμιες εκπομπές διοξειδίου του άνθρακα εξακολουθούν να αυξάνονται, τα αέρια του θερμοκηπίου συσσωρεύονται στην ατμόσφαιρα και τα κλίματα διαταράσσονται (αέρας).

- Η συνεχώς αυξανόμενη χρήση ενέργειας από ορυκτά καύσιμα οδηγεί σε τέτοιες αλλαγές (πυρκαγιές).

Τα ευαίσθητα συστήματα ισορροπίας της κτίσης διαταράχθηκαν σε πρωτοφανή έκταση κατά την Ανθρωπόκαινο εποχή. Έχουμε υπερβεί τις αντοχές του πλανήτη. Η γη φαίνεται πλέον ανίκανη να θεραπεύσει τον εαυτό της. «Η κτίσις συστενάζει καὶ συνωδίνει» (Ρωμ. 8:22). Δεν μπορέσαμε να συντονίσουμε τις οικουμενικές ανησυχίες για τη δικαιοσύνη εν μέσω της φτώχειας, της ανεργίας και της ανισότητας, για μια συμμετοχική κοινωνία εν μέσω διαφόρων μορφών βίαιων συγκρούσεων και για τη βιωσιμότητα εν μέσω της οικολογικής καταστροφής.

Παρόλο που οι άνθρωποι δεν συνέβαλαν εξίσου στις βαθύτερες αιτίες αυτής της κρίσης, ως χριστιανοί, καλούμαστε για να ομολογήσουμε τη συνενοχή μας και τη δουλεία μας στην αμαρτία:

- Υπήρξαμε αλαζόνες υποθέτοντας ότι ολόκληρη η γη έχει ως επίκεντρο εμάς τους ανθρώπους και τις ανάγκες μας (υπερηφάνεια).

- Παγιδευτήκαμε σε μια απύθμενη επιθυμία για απεριόριστη υλική ανάπτυξη, οδηγούμενη από μια διάχυτη κουλτούρα καταναλωτισμού (απληστία).

- Εκμεταλλευτήκαμε τα δώρα του Θεού, καταφύγαμε στη βία κατά των πλασμάτων Του και παραβιάσαμε την ανθρώπινη αξιοπρέπεια (βία).

- Αποξενωθήκαμε από την προγονική γη και την παραδοσιακή σοφία, από τα ζώα ως συν-δημιουργήματα και από τη Γη ως το δοσμένο από το Θεό σπίτι μας (ιδιωτικοποίηση του καλού).

- Κυριευτήκαμε από την τρέλα, την αδικία, την άρνηση και την απληστία (αμαρτία).

- Αργήσαμε να ανταποκριθούμε στην ευθύνη μας προκειμένου να αντιμετωπίσουμε την καθοριστική κρίση της εποχής μας (οκνηρία).

Ακόμη χειρότερα, η αυθεντικότητα της οικουμενικής μαρτυρίας υπονομεύεται από μια σειρά στρεβλώσεων του ευαγγελίου, τοξικών αφηγημάτων και θεολογιών που νομιμοποιούν μια ολοκληρωτική λογική θανάτου και καταστροφής. Σε αυτά περιλαμβάνονται οι θεολογίες της κυριαρχίας στο όνομα των διαφορών ως προς τη φυλή, το φύλο, την κοινωνική τάξη και τα έμβια είδη, η θεολογική νομιμοποίηση της πατριαρχικής κυριαρχίας, οι δυαλιστικοί και αναγωγικοί τρόποι συσχετισμού ουρανού και γης, ψυχής και σώματος, πνεύματος και ύλης. Και φυσικά η άρνηση και γελοιοποίηση της επιστημονικής εμπειρογνωμοσύνης και γνώσης με σκοπό τη διατήρηση της τρέχουσας τάξης πραγμάτων, η παράταση των μύθων απεριόριστης προόδου, η αποκλειστική εμπιστοσύνη στις τεχνολογικές λύσεις στα οικολογικά προβλήματα αντί της συνειδητοποίησης της πολιτιστικής, ηθικής και πνευματικής τους φύσης. Το ψευδο-ευαγγέλιο που δίνει έμφαση στη συσσώρευση πλούτου και ευημερίας προς ίδιον όφελος κατηγορώντας πάντα τους άλλους για τα προβλήματα και οι τρόποι αποφυγής της αντιμετώπισης των θυμάτων της οικολογικής αδικίας.

Ελπίδα: Το θάρρος σε μια εποχή άγχους και απόγνωσης

Εν μέσω πρωτοφανούς απελπισίας, που συνδέεται με μια αφόρητη οικολογική κρίση, διακηρύσσουμε μια ελπίδα στον Τριαδικό Θεό, μαζί με την ωδίνουσα δημιουργία του, αφού «τῇ γὰρ ἐλπίδι ἐσώθημεν» (Ρωμ. 8:24). Ο Θεός δεν έχει εγκαταλείψει τη γη. Δεχόμαστε τις υποσχέσεις του Θεού που συμβολίζονται στη διαθήκη η οποία συνάπτεται «μεταξύ κάθε έμψυχου ζώου, σε αιώνιες γενεές» (Γένεση 9:12). Πιστεύουμε στην παρουσία του Θεού όπως αποκαλύφθηκε στον Ιησού Χριστό εντός του χάους που μας περιβάλλει. Μας παρηγορεί η δύναμη του Αγίου Πνεύματος που «ανανεώνει το πρόσωπο της γης» (Ψαλ. 104:30).

Μπροστά σε τέτοια οικονομικά και πολιτικά αφηγήματα που αλλοιώνουν την κατανόηση των σωστών σχέσεων μεταξύ ανθρώπων, δημιουργίας και Δημιουργού, μια τέτοια ελπίδα μπορεί να φαίνεται αντίθετη με τη διαίσθηση της κοινής λογικής. Η ελπίδα που διακηρύττουμε δεν ασκεί μόνο κριτική προς τα καταπιεστικά και πατριαρχικά συστήματα κυριαρχίας, αλλά μας εμπνέει να συμμετάσχουμε στη θεραπεία της κτίσης (2 Χρον. 7:14). Η ελπίδα δεν είναι ταυτόσημη με την τυφλή αισιοδοξία που εμπιστεύεται την απλή διαιώνιση της σημερινής κατάστασης. Μια τέτοια ελπίδα δεν είναι φθηνή, έχει κόστος. Πηγάζει παρά τις συντριπτικές αποδείξεις για το αντίθετο, επειδή στηρίζεται στον Τριαδικό Θεό. Είναι μια τέτοια ελπίδα που μας ενθαρρύνει και μας ωθεί προς μια ολοκληρωμένη οικολογική μεταμόρφωση της κοινωνίας.

Μια έκκληση προς το παγκόσμιο οικουμενικό κίνημα

Στην καρδιά του απαιτούμενου μετασχηματισμού υπάρχει η ανάγκη για οικολογική μεταστροφή (μετάνοια), μια αλλαγή της καρδιάς, του νου, των συμπεριφορών, των καθημερινών συνηθειών και των μορφών πρακτικής (Ρωμ. 12:1-2). Αυτό έχει συνέπειες σε όλες τις πτυχές της χριστιανικής ζωής: για τη λειτουργία και τη λατρεία, τα βιβλικά αναγνώσματα, το κήρυγμα, τα μυστήρια, την κοινωνία και πρακτική των ενοριών, την προσευχή, τη νηστεία, την πνευματικότητα, το δόγμα, το ήθος, την εκπαίδευση, την τέχνη, τη μουσική, τον κλήρο και τις ιεραποστολές. Αυτή η οικολογική μεταμόρφωση ολόκληρου του χριστιανισμού έχει ενθαρρυνθεί από τους Πατέρες και τις Μητέρες της χριστιανικής παράδοσης, από τα παραδείγματα αδελφών μας, ανδρών και γυναικών, σε όλο τον κόσμο και από οικουμενικούς ηγέτες όπως ο Οικουμενικός Πατριάρχης Βαρθολομαίος, ο Πάπας Φραγκίσκος, ο αρχιεπίσκοπος Desmond Tutu και πολλές άλλες ηγετικές προσωπικότητες.

Καλούμε το παγκόσμιο οικουμενικό κίνημα, τις χριστιανικές παγκόσμιες κοινωνίες και όλες τις άλλες εκκλησίες να σχεδιάσουν μια δεκαετία οικολογικής μάθησης, εξομολόγησης και συνολικής δράσης για να αναπροσανατολίσουν τις προτεραιότητες των εκκλησιών στις ακόλουθες δεσμεύσεις:

1. Να ανανεώσουν το πλήρες φάσμα των λειτουργικών και πνευματικών πρακτικών και των αρχαίων παραδόσεων των εκκλησιών προσανατολισμένων στη δημιουργία υπό το φως του σημερινού καιρού·

2. Να μελετήσουν εκ νέου τα βιβλικά κείμενα με οδηγό τις οικολογικές ευαισθησίες·

3. Να δημιουργήσουν πλαίσια για την καλλιέργεια οικολογικών ενοριών, παρέχοντας το απαραίτητο προσωπικό και οικονομικούς πόρους και υποστηρίζοντας υφιστάμενες πρωτοβουλίες σε επίπεδο βάσης·

4. Να προωθήσουν τη δικαιοσύνη μεταξύ των φύλων στην εκκλησία και την κοινωνία, δεδομένης της πολλαπλής σύνδεσης με οικολογικούς προβληματισμούς.
5. Να ενθαρρύνουν τη νεολαία να αναλαμβάνει ηγετικές πρωτοβουλίες στην εκκλησία και την κοινωνία για χάρη ενός μέλλοντος που της ανήκει·
6. Να ενσωματώσουν τον οικολογικό θεολογικό προβληματισμό σε όλα τα επίπεδα εκπαίδευσης·
7. Να καλλιεργήσουν οικολογικές αρετές και βιώσιμο τρόπο ζωής σε νοικοκυριά και κοινότητες·
8. Να εξοπλίσουν τους λαϊκούς για τα επαγγέλματα τους, προκειμένου να ασκήσουν οικολογική ευθύνη όπου και αν ζουν, εργάζονται και ασκούν τη λατρεία τους·
9. Να συμμετάσχουν σε ένα διεπιστημονικό διάλογο που μπορεί να συνδυάσει και να κρίνει δίκαια τις ιδέες από τις επιστήμες, τις γηγενείς παραδόσεις σοφίας και τις ποικίλες θεολογίες·
10. Να υποστηρίξουν διακλαδικές συμμαχίες, δίκτυα και συνεργασίες με όλα τα επίπεδα διακυβέρνησης, με τις επιχειρήσεις και τη βιομηχανία, με την κοινωνία των πολιτών, με πολύτιμα οικολογικά δίκτυα, με άλλες ζωντανές θρησκείες και με όλους τους ανθρώπους καλής θελήσεως για εξεύρεση βιώσιμων εναλλακτικών λύσεων απέναντι στις κυρίαρχες μορφές παραγωγής και κατανάλωσης.

Εν όψει της επικείμενης 11ης συνέλευσης του Παγκοσμίου Συμβουλίου Εκκλησιών το 2021 συνιστούμε στο ΠΣΕ, ειδικότερα, να διακηρύξει μια «Δεκαετία για τη θεραπεία της Δημιουργίας» με τους εξής στόχους:
- Να κινητοποιήσει τις εκκλησίες-μέλη να αναπροσανατολίσουν τις προτεραιότητές τους στις δεσμεύσεις που αναφέρονται στην Έκκληση του Βούπερταλ.
- Να συμμετάσχει στην ατζέντα των στόχων για τη Βιώσιμη Ανάπτυξη των Ηνωμένων Εθνών μέσω διαφόρων συμμαχιών, δικτύων και εταιρικών σχέσεων και να προχωρήσει πέρα από τους Στόχους Βιώσιμης Ανάπτυξης (SDG των 190 ηγετών) προκειμένου να επαναπροσδιορίσει τις έννοιες της ανάπτυξης, του πλούτου και της ευημερίας , οι οποίες δεν έχουν διευκρινιστεί επαρκώς όσον αφορά τα υφιστάμενα όρια αντοχής του πλανήτη.
- Να υποστηρίξει στους παγκόσμιους φορείς λήψης αποφάσεων ότι η αύξηση των παγκόσμιων εκπομπών αερίων του θερμοκηπίου θα πρέπει να σταματήσει και να μειωθεί δραστικά το συντομότερο δυνατόν, προκειμένου να επιτευχθούν μηδενικές εκπομπές διοξειδίου του άνθρακα και να διατηρηθεί η αύξηση της θερμοκρασίας του πλανήτη κάτω από 1,5 βαθμούς Κελσίου.
- Να προωθήσει τις διαδικασίες των Ηνωμένων Εθνών για τη δημιουργία ενός νομικού πλαισίου για έναν δεσμευτικό «καθολικό χάρτη δικαιωμάτων της Μητέρας Γης» (Cochabamba 2010), ένα σύστημα διεθνούς νομολογίας της Γης, και να διερευνήσει τις δυνατότητες ενός Συμβουλίου των Ηνωμένων Εθνών για τα Δικαιώματα της Φύσης και να διερευνήσει την αναγνώριση της οικοκτονίας ως ποινικού αδικήματος στο Διεθνές Δικαστήριο.

Αυτές οι δεσμεύσεις απορρέουν από την κατανόηση της ιστορικής συγκυρίας του καιρού στην ιστορία οποία βρισκόμαστε. Το έργο μπροστά είναι τεράστιο και θα απαιτήσει δεκαετίες αφοσίωσης. Ο επείγων χαρακτήρας της κατάστασης συνεπάγεται ότι δεν μπορεί να καθυστερήσει μια ολοκληρωμένη απάντηση. Η επόμενη δεκαετία θα είναι αποφασιστική για να χαρίσει στη Γη χρόνο ανάπαυσης. Τα βιβλικά μοτίβα του Σαββάτου και του Ιωβηλαίου Έτους παρέχουν μια μοναδική πηγή ελπίδας και έμπνευσης, μια διακοπή στον κύκλο εκμετάλλευσης και βίας, που εκφράζεται στο όραμα ότι θα υπάρξει «ένα έτος πλήρους ανάπαυσης για τη γη» (Λευ. 25:5).

Ελθέ, Πνεύμα Άγιον, ανακαίνισον πάσαν την Κτίσιν!

The Wuppertal Call in Indonesian:

Kairos for Creation – Confessing Hope for the Earth
The Wuppertal Call

"dan umat-Ku, yang atasnya nama-Ku disebut, merendahkan diri, berdoa dan mencari wajah-Ku, lalu berbalik dari jalan-jalannya yang jahat, maka Aku akan mendengar dari sorga dan mengampuni dosa mereka, serta memulihkan negeri mereka." – 2 Tawarikh 7:14

"Jadi siapa yang ada di dalam Kristus, ia adalah ciptaan baru; yang lama sudah berlalu, sesungguhnya yang baru sudah datang. Dan semuanya ini dari Allah, yang dengan peran-taraan Kristus telah mendamaikan kita dengan diri-Nya dan yang telah mempercayakan pelayanan pendamaian itu kepada kami." – 2 Korintus 5:17-18

Pembukaan

Dari tanggal 16 hingga 19 Juni 2019, 52 peserta dari 22 negara dan dari berbagai denominasi serta tradisi iman berkumpul di Wuppertal, Jerman untuk menghadiri konferensi bertema "Bersama menuju ekoteologi, etika kelestarian, dan gereja yang ramah lingkungan".[1] Di Wuppertal kami diingatkan akan sebuah pengakuan iman yang berani, Deklarasi Barmen (1934) yang menen-tang ideologi totaliter, hilangnya perikemanusiaan dan rasisme pada saat itu. Deklarasi Barmen terus memanggil kita hingga hari ini untuk memperjuangkan "pembebasan yang penuh sukacita dari ikatan-ikatan duniawi yang tak bertuhan untuk pelayanan yang penuh rasa syukur terhadap makhluk ciptaan-Nya" (Barmen 2).

Kami mendengar kisah-kisah dari Afrika, Asia, Eropa, Amerika Latin, Amerika Utara, dan Oseania. Kami mendengar ratapan bumi, tangisan orang-orang yang menjadi korban dari dam-pak perubahan iklim, khususnya anak-anak dan orang tua, tangisan kaum muda yang menuntut keadilan lintas generasi dan kecemasan para cendekiawan atas gaya hidup yang terjadi saat ini. Kami menyadari adanya tantangan mendesak di tahun-tahun mendatang, namun kami tetap menyatakan keberanian untuk memiliki pengharapan serta mendorong adanya seruan gerakan ekumenis global menuju sebuah transformasi ekologis yang utuh di tengah masyarakat.

Kairos: Perubahan yang menentukan dalam peziarahan keadilan dan perdamaian

Gerakan ekumenis telah lama menaruh perhatian terhadap peziarahan menuju keadilan, perda-maian, dan keutuhan ciptaan. Tujuan-tujuan ini membutuhkan langkah-langkah yang mendesak di perjalanan berikutnya. Kondisi krisis ini memaksa kita untuk membaca tanda-tanda zaman, untuk mendengar panggilan Tuhan, untuk mengikuti jalan Kristus, untuk memperhatikan gerakan Roh Kudus dan, sebagai respons, untuk mengenali berbagai inisiatif positif gereja di seluruh dunia.

Gejala-gejala krisis ini menyerang semua aspek kehidupan dan terpampang nyata terlihat oleh semua:

---

1 Konferensi ini dirancang dan diorganisir oleh *Protestant Association of Churches and Mission* (EMW), *Evan-gelical Church in Germany* (EKD), *United Evangelical Mission* (UEM), *Bread for the World*, World Council of Churches.

- Air tawar yang terkontaminasi; gletser yang terus mencair; lautan yang tercemar oleh sampah plastik dan menjadi asam sehingga terumbu karang memutih (air).
- Tanah yang terdegradasi melalui proses pertanian yang tidak berkelanjutan dan kebiasaan makan yang tidak sehat, kerakusan ekonomi yang didominasi oleh kekuatan-kekuatan keuangan global, penggundulan hutan, penggurunan dan erosi tanah; hewan-hewan mengerang dan makhluk hidup yang sedang dimodifikasi secara genetis; populasi ikan semakin berkurang; punahnya habitat yang menyebabkan hilangnya keanekaragaman hayati (tanah) yang belum pernah terjadi sebelumnya. Baik tanah dan kesehatan manusia teracuni oleh limbah-limbah industri, pertanian, kota dan nuklir dan oleh zat-zat pestisida serta bahan kimia. Terjadi peningkatan populasi manusia yang dipaksa untuk bermigrasi dan menjadi pengungsi akibat perubahan iklim.
- Emisi-emisi karbon secara global masih mengalami peningkatan; gas rumah kaca sedang terakumulasi di atmosfer dan iklim menjadi terganggu (udara).
- Peningkatan penggunaan energi dari bahan bakar fosil inilah yang mendorong terjadinya perubahan (kebakaran) tersebut.

Sistem keseimbangan dalam penciptaan telah terganggu hingga ke titik mengkhawatirkan yang belum pernah terjadi sebelumnya di dalam sejarah kemanusiaan. Kita telah melampaui ambang batas ketahanan planet itu sendiri. Bumi nampaknya tidak mampu lagi menyembuhkan dirinya sendiri. Seluruh ciptaan mengerang kesedihan (Roma 8:22). Kita telah gagal menyatukan keprihatinan-keprihatinan ekumenis bagi keadilan di tengah kemiskinan, pengangguran, dan ketidaksetaraan, terhadap partisipasi masyarakat di tengah berbagai bentuk konflik kekerasan dan kelestarian akibat kerusakan ekologis.

Meskipun umat manusia belum memberikan kontribusi bersama terhadap akar penyebab krisis ini, sebagai orang Kristen kita bersama-sama mengakui keterlibatan dan keterikatan kita terhadap dosa:
- Kita terlanjur sombong karena menganggap bahwa seluruh bumi berpusat di dalam diri manusia dan kebutuhan kita (keangkuhan).
- Kita telah terperangkap dalam keinginan busuk akan pertumbuhan materi yang tidak terbatas, didorong oleh budaya konsumerisme yang meluas (keserakahan).
- Kita telah mengeksploitasi karunia Tuhan, menggunakan kekerasan terhadap makhluk ciptaan Tuhan dan menciderai martabat kemanusiaan (kekerasan).
- Kita menjadi terasing dari tanah leluhur dan kearifan lokal, dari binatang sebagai sesama makhluk hidup dan dari Bumi sebagai rumah yang diberikan Tuhan kepada kita (hak milik untuk selamanya).
- Kita telah dikalahkan oleh kebodohan, ketidakadilan, penolakan, dan keserakahan (kesalahan).
- Kita sangat lamban menyepakati tanggung jawab kita bersama dalam mengatasi krisis di zaman ini (kemalasan).

Hal-hal di atas diperburuk, ketika otentisitas kesaksian oikumenis dirusak oleh distorsi Injil yang sangat mengkhawatirkan, cerita-cerita yang meracuni dan teologi-teologi yang melegitimasi pemikiran totalitarian tentang kematian dan kehancuran. Hal ini meliputi teologi-teologi dominasi atas nama perbedaan ras, jender, klasifikasi dan spesies, legitimasi teologi atas dominasi patriarkal; dualisme dan metode-metode dalam menyederhanakan hubungan surga dan bumi, jiwa dan tubuh, roh dan materi; penyangkalan dan penghinaan akan nilai-nilai keilmuan serta wawasan untuk mempertahankan aturan yang ada, penyebarluasan mitos tentang kemajuan yang tidak berbatas, menaruh kepercayaan hanya kepada solusi teknologi terhadap masalah-masalah ekologi daripada menyadari nilai-nilai budaya, moral dan spiritual; Injil palsu (Pseudo Gospel) yang menekankan akumulasi kemakmuran dan kesejahteraan, cara-cara pribadi yang meletakkan kesalahan kepada orang lain; dan cara-cara melarikan diri dari tanggung jawab atas ketidakadilan ekologi yang terjadi.

Pengharapan: Keberanian pada masa kegelisahan dan keputusasaan

Di tengah keputusasaan yang belum pernah terjadi sebelumnya akibat krisis ekologi yang luar biasa ini, kita menyatakan harapan kepada Allah Tritunggal di tengah-tengah ciptaan yang mengerang, "Sebab kita diselamatkan dalam pengharapan" (Roma 8:24). Allah tidak pernah meninggalkan bumi ini. Kita berpegang pada janji-janji Allah yang dilambangkan di dalam perjanjian yang dibuat „...serta segala makhluk yang hidup, yang bersama-sama dengan kamu, turun temurun, untuk selama-lamanya" (Kejadian 9:12). Kita percaya pada kehadiran Allah yang dinyatakan di dalam Yesus Kristus di tengah-tengah kekacauan di sekitar kita. Kita dihibur oleh kuasa Roh untuk "membaharui muka bumi" (Mazmur 104: 30).

Di hadapan narasi-narasi ekonomi dan politik yang merusak pemahaman kita tentang hubungan yang layak antara manusia, ciptaan, dan Sang Pencipta, harapan semacam ini mungkin terlihat berlawanan dengan bisikan hati. Harapan bahwa kita bukan hanya mengkritik sistem penindasan dan kekuasaan patriarkal tetapi juga mengilhami kita untuk terlibat dalam kesembuhan ciptaan (2 Tawarikh 7:14). Harapan tidaklah sama dengan optimisme buta, yang percaya pada kelanjutan gaya hidup saat ini. Harapan semacam ini bukanlah murahan; ini sangat mahal. Harapan ini muncul ditengah banyaknya fakta kehidupan yang saling bertentangan karena pengharapan ini hanya bersandar pada Allah Tritunggal. Harapan seperti itulah yang menguatkan dan mendorong kita melangkah menuju transformasi ekologis yang utuh.

Seruan menuju gerakan ekumenis global

Inti dari transformasi yang diperlukan saat ini adalah kebutuhan mendesak bagi transformasi ekologis (metanoia), perubahan hati, pikiran, sikap, kebiasaan sehari-hari dan gaya hidup (Roma 12: 1-2). Hal ini berdampak bagi semua aspek kehidupan Kristen: liturgi dan penyembahan, pembacaan Alkitab, pemberitaan Firman, Sakramen-sakramen, persekutuan dan pelayanan jemaat, doa, puasa, spiritualitas, doktrin, etos kehidupan, pendidikan, seni, musik, pelayanan dan misi. Reformasi ekologis di dalam semua tubuh kekristenan ini telah didorong oleh para bapa dan ibu di dalam tradisi kekristenan kita, melalui keteladanan para saudara/i kita di seluruh dunia dan oleh para pemimpin ekumenis seperti Patriark Ekumenis Bartholomew, Paus Francis, Uskup Agung emeritus Desmond Tutu dan banyak lagi suara-suara lainnya.

Kami menyerukan sebuah gerakan ekumenis global, persekutuan umat Kristen dunia dan seluruh gereja-gereja untuk merencanakan sebuah dekade pembelajaran ekologis, pengakuan dan aksi komprehensif untuk mengarahkan kembali prioritas gereja-gereja kepada komitmen-komitmen berikut:

1. Memperbaharui ragam liturgi dan kehidupan spiritual serta tradisi-tradisi gereja kuno tentang penciptaan di dalam terang „kairos" saat ini;
2. Membaca ulang teks-teks alkitab dan mempelajarinya dengan kepekaan atas kondisi ekologis;
3. Menciptakan kerangka kerja dalam mendidik jemaat-jemaat untuk ramah lingkungan, menyediakan tenaga-tenaga kerja dan sumber-sumber keuangan yang diperlukan serta mendukung inisiatif akar rumput;

4. Mempromosikan keadilan gender di tengah gereja dan masyarakat dalam keterkaitannya dengan masalah-masalah ekologis;
5. Mendorong kaum muda menerima estafet kepemimpinan di gereja dan masyarakat bagi masa depan milik mereka;
6. Menyebarluaskan refleksi ekologis di semua aras pendidikan;
7. Menumbuh kembangkan nilai-nilai luhur ekologis dan memelihara gaya hidup berkelestarian di rumah tangga serta masyarakat;
8. Memperlengkapi kaum awam untuk menunaikan panggilan dalam mewujudkan tanggung jawab ekologis di mana mereka berada, bekerja dan beribadah;
9. Untuk terlibat di dalam dialog-dialog lintas ilmu yang dapat menyatukan pemikiran secara bersama dan menyatakan keadilan dalam rangka mencoba memahami berbagai sudut pandang ilmu pengetahuan, kearifan lokal dan keberagaman teologi;
10. Untuk membela berbagai aliansi lintas ilmu, jaringan-jaringan dan kemitraan dengan semua aras pemerintahan, pelaku bisnis dan industri, dengan masyarakat sipil, dengan jaringan ekologi lintas-agama, dengan penganut agama yang berbeda, dan dengan semua insan dalam berbagi komitmen untuk menemukan alternatif-alternatif kelestarian bagi berbagai bentuk produksi dan konsumsi yang mendominasi.

Mengingat akan diselenggarakannya sidang Dewan Gereja-gereja Sedunia (DGD) ke-11 pada tahun 2021, kami merekomendasikan kepada DGD, secara khusus, untuk mendeklarasikan "Dekade bagi Kesembuhan Ciptaan" dengan tujuan-tujuan berikut:

- Memobilisasi gereja-gereja anggota untuk mengarahkan kembali prioritas mereka kepada berbagai komitmen seperti yang ditekankan dalam Seruan Wuppertal (*Wuppertal Call*);
- Untuk terlibat dalam agenda-agenda PBB tentang Tujuan Pembangunan Berkelanjutan (TPB) melalui berbagai aliansi, jaringan, dan kemitraan bahkan melampaui agenda TPB untuk mendefinisikan kembali gagasan-gagasan mengenai pertumbuhan, kemakmuran, dan keberadaan yang belum sepenuhnya terklarifikasi berkaitan dengan ambang batas kemampuan planet ini.
- Untuk mengadvokasi para pengambil keputusan global bahwa peningkatan emisi rumah kaca harus dihentikan secara global dan dikurangi secara drastis sesegera mungkin untuk mencapai emisi karbon *net-zero* dan menjaga peningkatan suhu pemanasan global di bawah 1,5 derajat Celcius.
- Mempromosikan berbagai proses di PBB dalam menciptakan sebuah kerangka hukum "Universal Charter of the Rights of Mother Earth" (Piagam Universal Hak-Hak Bumi) yang mengikat (Cochabamba 2010), sistem yurisprudensi internasional Bumi, dan mengusahakan kemungkinan dibentuknya sebuah dewan di PBB yang menangani Hak-hak Alam serta diakuinya kejahatan ekologis sebagai tindak pidana di Pengadilan Internasional.
- Komitmen-komitmen ini lahir dari sebuah pemahaman tentang momen „Kairos" di dalam sejarah yang kita temukan sendiri. Kebutuhan mendesak dari situasi ini menuntut sebuah respons menyeluruh dan tidak mungkin ditunda lagi. Dekade berikutnya akan sangat menentukan dalam memberikan kesempatan bagi bumi kita untuk beristirahat. Motif-motif alkitabiah tentang hari Sabat dan tahun Yobel memberikan sebuah sumber pengharapan dan inspirasi yang unik, yakni sebuah masa jeda dalam siklus eksploitasi dan kekerasan atas bumi, yang dinyatakan dalam visi bahwa akan ada „tahun perhentian penuh bagi tanah itu" (Imamat 25: 5).

Datanglah Roh Kudus, perbarui seluruh ciptaanMu!

The Wuppertal Call in Chinese:

保护创造的关键时刻，宣信我们对地球的盼望

乌帕塔尔倡议

"这称为我名下的子民，若是自卑、祷告，寻求我的面，转离他们的恶行，我必从天上垂听，赦免他们的罪，医治他们的地。"——代下 7：14

"若有人在基督里，他就是新造的人，旧事已过，都变成新的了。一切都是出于神，他借着基督使我们与他和好，又将劝人与他和好的职分赐给我们。"——林后 5：17-18

序言

2019 年 6 月 16-19 日，来自 22 个国家和不同宗派与信仰传统的 52 名与会者相聚在德国乌帕塔尔，参加了名为"共同走向生态神学、可持续性伦理和生态友好教会"的会议[1]。在乌帕塔尔，我们重温了发布于 1934 年《巴门宣言》，这一勇敢的信仰告白是针对当时极权主义的、非人道的和种族主义的意识形态而发出的檄文。时至今日，《巴门宣言》仍然鼓舞着我们，"从这个世界不虔不敬的束缚中解放出来，满怀喜乐，以自由和感恩之心来服侍他所创造的生命。"（《巴门宣言》第 2 条）

我们分享了来自非洲、亚洲、欧洲、拉丁美洲、北美洲和大洋洲的故事。我们聆听地球的哭泣；我们倾听气候变化效应下无助的人们，尤其是孩子和老人们的呼求；我们听到年轻人对代际公义的呼声，我们也听到专家们对于当前趋势的担忧。

我们认识到未来几年的紧迫局势，但仍然表达出盼望的勇气，同时必须呼吁全球普世运动要向着对社会进行全面的生态性转化这一目标迈进。

关键时刻：公义与和平之旅的决定性转折

普世教会运动长期以来一直行走在追求公义、和平和受造物之完整的朝圣之旅上。要实现这些目标，前行的路上有些行动步骤已经迫在眉睫。危机的紧迫性要求我们分辨时代的征兆，聆听上帝的呼召，遵循基督的道，查验圣灵的工作，并且作出回应，去分辨和肯定世界各地教会的积极行动。

以上所述的重大危机，其症状表现涵盖生活的方方面面，因此大家都有目共睹：

---

[1] 会议由德国新教教会与宣教联合会(EMW)、德国福音教会(EKD)、联合福音宣道会(UEM)、粮惠世界和世界基督教联合会共同策划主办。

- 淡水污染；冰川融化；海洋被塑料垃圾污染且被酸化以致珊瑚礁白化（水）。
- 土地退化。其成因复杂多样，包括不可持续的农业运作、不健康的饮食习惯、由全球金融巨头操控的掠夺性经济、森林砍伐、荒漠化和土壤流失；动物在呻吟，生物基因被修改；鱼类数量耗竭；栖息地丧失导致空前的生物多样性的丧失（土地）。土地和人们的健康被工业、农业、都市废弃物以及核废料、杀虫剂和化学品所毒害。越来越多的人被迫迁移，成为气候难民。
- 全球碳排放仍在上升，温室气体在大气层累积，气候规律被打乱（空气）。
- 这些变化皆缘于不断增加的化石燃料的使用。受造物的微妙平衡体系被打乱到人类历史以来前所未有的程度。我们已经越过了地球的底线，地球似乎已经无法自愈。万物在叹息、劳苦（罗 8：22）。我们要在贫穷、失业和不平等中寻求正义、在各种形式的暴力冲突中构建参与型社会、在生态破坏中重拾可持续性发展，然而人们心有余而力不足，无法把对这些问题的普世关怀集中起来。

尽管人们不是在同等的程度上有份于危机发生的根本原因，但是作为基督徒，我们要在一起为自己成为共犯、受到罪的束缚而忏悔：
- 我们傲慢无知，认为整个地球是以人类和我们的需求为中心而存在的（骄傲）。
- 我们受到无处不在的消费主义文化驱动，陷入极度渴望物质无限增长的网罗中（贪婪）。
- 我们滥用了上帝的赏赐，对上帝的造物施以暴力，侵犯了人的尊严（暴力）。
- 我们疏离了祖先的土地、原生的智慧、与我们一同受造的动物以及上帝赐予我们的地球家园（良善的丧失）。
- 我们被愚蠢、不公、拒斥和贪婪所胜（恶习）。
- 面对这一时代的关键性危机，我们没有及时意识到自己的职分。（懒惰）

更糟的是，普世见证的真实性正在被破坏，破坏的因素包括各种对福音的歪曲和有害的阐释和神学，它们为死亡和毁灭的极权逻辑提供了合法性辩护。这些言论包括打着种族、性别、阶层和物种差异名义建立起来的统治神学、对父权性统治提供正当化的神学阐释；对天与地、灵与肉、精神与物质之间的关系采取了二元论和还原论的方法；否认和嘲笑科学的专业知识和洞见、以维护现有的秩序和延长无限进步的神话、对于生态问题只相信技术解决方案而不肯承认这些问题在文化、道德和精神方面的实质；强调财富和资产积累、自私自利、永远只会怪罪别人的伪福音；还有在因生态不公而深受其害的人面前所表现出的逃避主义行径。

盼望：焦虑和绝望时代中的勇气

在由势不可挡的生态危机所引发的空前绝望中，我们在叹息劳苦的万物中间传讲存在于三一上帝里面的盼望，"因为我们得救是在乎盼望"（罗 8：24）。上帝没有弃绝地球。我们信守上帝的应许，这应许借着约得以表明，这约是上帝与"各样活物所立的永约"（创 9：12）。我们相信上帝的临在，正如借耶稣基督在我们所处的乱世中所显明的临在。我们藉着圣灵的力量得安慰，这力量要"使地面更换为新"（诗 104：30）。

一些经济的和政治的阐释歪曲了我们对人、受造物和造物主之间关系的理解。在这种情况下，这样的盼望看起来似乎有违直觉。我们所宣扬的盼望不止是批判具有压迫性的、父权式统治体系，这盼望更启发我们参与到对受造物的医治中（代下 7：14）。盼望与盲目的乐观不同，后者相信当前趋势只能蔓延。这种盼望不是廉价的；相反，它是需要付出代价的。它不顾压倒性的反向证据而顽强增长，因为这盼望是在三位一体上帝里面的。就是这样的盼望激励着我们，迫使我们走向社会的全面生态转型。

对全球普世运动的号召

这一必要转型的核心是人们需要在生态方面进行悔改(metanoia)，这指向内心、思想、态度、日常习惯和行动形式的改变（罗 12：1-2）。这样的改变影响到基督徒生活的各个方面：礼仪和崇拜、宣讲、圣礼、会众的团契和实践、祷告、禁食、灵性、教义、理念、教育、艺术、音乐、事工和使命。基督教的全面生态改革受到了多方面的激励，这些激励来自包括基督教传统中我们的先辈们，来自我们全世界弟兄姊妹所做出的榜样，也来自如东正教普世牧首巴多罗买，教宗方济各，荣休大主教德斯蒙德·图图和很多其他提出建议的领袖们。

我们号召全球普世教会运动、世界性的基督教团体和所有其他教会来规划未来十年的生态学习、忏悔和全面行动，重新定位教会的优先事务，并投身于以下的行动：

1. 鉴于当前的关键时刻，全面更新与受造物相关的礼仪和灵修实践以及古老的教会传统；
2. 带着对生态问题的关注来重新研读《圣经》；
3. 创建有利的框架来培养具有生态意识的会众，为他们提供必要的人力和财力支持，支持现有的草根行动；
4. 在教会和社会中推动性别正义，因其与生态问题在很多层面是息息相关的；
5. 鼓励青年人在教会和社会中发挥带头作用，因为未来是他们的；
6. 让生态神学在所有的教育层面上成为主流；
7. 在家庭和社区里培养生态美德，培育可持续性的生活方式；
8. 装备平信徒，使他们领受这样的呼召，无论在哪里生活、工作和崇拜，他们都能履行生态责任；
9. 参与多学科对话，使来自科学、本土智慧传统和不同神学流派的洞见得以融会贯通，使每一种洞见都能得到正确理解。
10. 倡导与各级政府、工商行业、公民社会、多信仰生态网络、其他信仰团体、以及所有志同道合的人建立跨学科联盟、网络和伙伴关系，共同来寻找能够替代主流生产和消费形式的、具有可持续性的模式选择；

对将于 2021 年举办的、世界基督教联合会第 11 届大会，我们提出特别建议，希望世基联能开启一个"医治生态的十年计划"，使以下目标得以实现：
- 发动成员教会按照乌帕塔尔的呼吁做出承诺，来重新定位优先事务；
- 通过不同的联盟、网络和伙伴关系参与并超越联合国可持续发展目标的议程，以重新为增长、财富和福祉这三个概念做出定义——鉴于现有的地球边界，这些概念尚未被充分地澄清。
- 向全球的决策者发出倡议，应当尽快遏制并大幅削减全球温室气体排放的增长，以达到净零碳排并控制地球升温在 1.5 摄氏度以下。
- 推动联合国的进程，创建有约束力的法律框架——《地球母亲的权利宪章》（科恰班巴 2010），一个和地球相关的国际法学体系，探寻成立联合国维护大自然权利理事会的可能性，并尝试在国际法庭把"生态灭绝"认定为犯罪行为。

这份承诺来自我们对自己所处的这一关键性历史时刻的认识。任重道远，形势紧迫。全面响应已经不能拖延，下一个十年是地球是否有机会休养生息的关键时段。《圣经》中有关安息日和禧年的主题为我们寻求盼望和灵感提供了独有的资源，要打破剥削和暴力的循环，这些都通过这一远象表达了出来："这年，地要守圣安息。"（利 25：5）

求圣灵降临，更新你一切的造物！

THE BARMEN DECLARATION

An appeal to the Evangelical congregations and Christians in Germany

The Confessional Synod of the German Evangelical Church met in Barmen, May 29-31 1934. Here representatives from all the German confessional churches met with one accord in a confession of the one Lord of the one, holy, apostolic church.

In fidelity to their confession of faith, members of Lutheran, Reformed, and United churches sought a common message for the need and temptation of the church in our day. With gratitude to God they are convinced that they have been given a common word to utter.

It was not their intention to found a new church or to form a union. For nothing was farther from their minds than the abolition of the confessional status of our churches. Their intention was, rather, to withstand in faith and unanimity the destruction of the confession of faith, and thus of the Evangelical Church in Germany.

In opposition to attempts to establish the unity of the German Evangelical Church by means of false doctrine, by the use of force and by insincere practices, the Confessional Synod insists that the unity of the Evangelical Churches in Germany can come only from the Word of God in faith through the Holy Spirit. Thus alone is the church renewed.

Therefore the Confessional Synod calls upon the congregations to range themselves behind it in prayer, and steadfastly to gather around those pastors and teachers who are loyal to the confessions.

Be not deceived by loose talk, as if we meant to oppose the unity of the German nation! Do not listen to the seducers who pervert our intentions, as if we wanted to break up the unity of the German Evangelical Church or to forsake the confessions of the Fathers!

Try the spirits whether they are of God! Prove also the words of the Confessional Synod of the German Evangelical Church to see whether they agree with holy scripture and with the confessions of the Fathers.

If you find that we are speaking contrary to scripture, then do not listen to us! But if you find that we are taking our stand upon scripture, then let no fear or temptation keep you from treading with us the path of faith and obedience to the Word of God, in order that God's people be of one mind upon earth and that we in faith experience what he himself has said: "I will never leave you, nor forsake you." Therefore, "Fear not, little flock, for it is your Father's good pleasure to give you the kingdom."

Theological declaration concerning the present situation of the German Evangelical Church

According to the opening words of its constitution of July 11 1933, the German Evangelical Church is a federation of confessional churches that grew our of the Reformation and that enjoy equal rights. The theological basis for the unification of these churches is laid down in Article 1 and Article 2 (1) of the constitution of the German Evangelical Church that was recognized by the Reich government on July 14 1933:

- Article 1. The inviolable foundation of the German Evangelical Church is the gospel of Jesus Christ as it is attested for us in holy scripture and brought to light again in the confessions of the Reformation. The full powers that the church needs for its mission are hereby determined and limited.
- Article 2 (1). The German Evangelical Church is divided into member churches (Landeskirchen). We, the representatives of Lutheran, Reformed, and United churches, of free synods, church assemblies, and parish organizations united in the Confessional Synod of the German Evangelical Church, declare that we stand together on the ground of the German Evangelical Church as a federation of German confessional churches. We are bound together by the confession of the one Lord of the one, holy, catholic, and apostolic church.

We publicly declare before all evangelical churches in Germany that what they hold in common in this confession is grievously imperilled, and with it the unity of the German Evangelical Church. It is threatened by the teaching methods and actions of the ruling church party of the "German Christians" and of the church administration carried on by them. These have become more and more apparent during the first year of the existence of the German Evangelical Church. This threat consists in the fact that the theological basis on which the German Evangelical Church is united has been continually and systematically thwarted and rendered ineffective by alien principles, on the part of the leaders and spokesmen of the "German Christians" as well as on the part of the church administration. When these principles are held to be valid, then, according to all the confessions in force among us, the church ceases to be the church and the German Evangelical Church, as a federation of confessional churches, becomes intrinsically impossible.

As members of Lutheran, Reformed, and United churches we may and must speak with one voice in this matter today. Precisely because we want to be and to remain faithful to our various confessions, we may not keep silent, since we believe that we have been given a common message to utter in a time of common need and temptation. We commend to God what this may mean for the interrelations of the confessional churches.

In view of the errors of the "German Christians" of the present Reich church government which are devastating the church and also therefore breaking up the unity of the German Evangelical Church, **we confess the following evangelical truths:**

1. "I am the way, and the truth, and the life; no one comes to the Father, but by me." (Jn 14.6) "Truly, truly, I say to you, he who does not enter the sheepfold by the door, but climbs in by another way, that man is a thief and a robber... I am the door; if anyone enters by me, he will be saved." (Jn 10.1, 9)

Jesus Christ, as he is attested for us in holy scripture, is the one Word of God which we have to hear and which we have to trust and obey in life and in death.

We reject the false doctrine, as though the church could and would have to acknowledge as a source of its proclamation, apart from and besides this one Word of God, still other events and powers, figures and truths, as God's revelation.

2. "Christ Jesus, whom God has made our wisdom, our righteousness and sanctification and redemption." (1 Cor 1.30)

As Jesus Christ is God's assurance of the forgiveness of all our sins, so, in the same way and with the same seriousness he is also God's mighty claim upon our whole life. Through him befalls us a joyful deliverance from the godless fetters of this world for a free, grateful service to his creatures.

We reject the false doctrine, as though there were areas of our life in which we would not belong to Jesus Christ, but to other lords - areas in which we would not need justification and sanctification through him.

3. "Rather, speaking the truth in love, we are to grow up in every way into him who is the head, into Christ, from whom the whole body [is] joined and knit together." (Eph 4.15,16)

The Christian church is the congregation of the brethren in which Jesus Christ acts presently as the Lord in word and sacrament through the Holy Spirit. As the church of pardoned sinners, it has to testify in the midst of a sinful world, with its faith as with its obedience, with its message as with its order, that it is solely his property, and that it lives and wants to live solely from his comfort and from his direction in the expectation of his appearance.

We reject the false doctrine, as though the church were permitted to abandon the form of its message and order to its own pleasure or to changes in prevailing ideological and political convictions.

4. "You know that the rulers of the gentiles lord it over them, and their great men exercise authority over them. It shall not be so among you; but whoever would be great among you must be your servant." (Mt 20.25,26)

The various offices in the church do not establish a dominion of some over the others; on the contrary, they are for the exercise of the ministry entrusted to and enjoined upon the whole congregation.

We reject the false doctrine, as though the church, apart from this ministry, could and were permitted to give itself, or allow to be given to it, special leaders vested with ruling powers.

5. "Fear God. Honour the emperor." (1 Pet 2.17)

Scripture tells us that, in the as yet unredeemed world in which the church also exists, the state has by divine appointment the task of providing for justice and peace. [It fulfils this task] by means of the threat and exercise of force, according to the measure of human judgment and human ability. The church acknowledges the benefit of this divine appointment in gratitude and reverence before him. It calls to mind the kingdom of God, God's commandment and righteousness, and thereby the responsibility both of rulers and of the ruled. It trusts and obeys the power of the Word by which God upholds all things.

We reject the false doctrine, as though the state, over and beyond its special commission, should and could become the single and totalitarian order of human life, thus fulfilling the church's vocation as well.

We reject the false doctrine, as though the church, over and beyond its special commission, should and could appropriate the characteristics, the tasks, and the dignity of the state, thus itself becoming an organ of the state.

6. "Lo, I am with you always, to the close of the age." (Mt 28.20) "The word of God is not fettered." (2 Tim 2.9)

The church's commission, upon which its freedom is founded, consists in delivering the message of the free grace of God to all people in Christ's stead, and therefore in the ministry of his own Word and work through sermon and sacrament.

We reject the false doctrine, as though the church in human arrogance could place the word and work of the Lord in the service of any arbitrarily chosen desires, purposes, and plans.

The Confessional Synod of the German Evangelical Church declares that it sees in the acknowledgement of these truths and in the rejection of these errors the indispensable theological basis of the German Evangelical Church as a federation of confessional churches. It invites all who are able to accept its declaration to be mindful of these theological principles in their decisions in church politics. It entreats all whom it concerns to return to the unity of faith, love, and hope.

(Quoted from: https://www.ekd.de/en/The-Barmen-Declaration-303.htm, November, 2019)

"LENT TO US IS THE STAR, ON WHICH WE LIVE"

The Agenda 2030: a Challenge to the Churches

Ruth Gütter

A Discussion Paper authored by the Advisory Commission of the EKD on Sustainable Development, Hanover, 2018

The Discussion paper of the Advisory Commission of the EKD on Sustainable Development, which was authorized by the governing board of EKD, describes the agenda 2030 as a challenge for politics, civil society and the churches. The authors are warning that the boundaries of load-bearing capacity of the planet are exceeded and that a radical transformation is needed to sustain the earth for the following generations. The Agenda 2030 describes many fundamental insights that the churches proclaimed in the last 40 years. The EKD is welcoming the great challenges of the agenda 2030, which include the satisfaction of the social needs and the awareness of the ecological boundaries of the planet. The Agenda 2030 is a challenge for everybody to contribute what he can to support a sustainable development. According to four practical fields like agriculture, overcoming inequality, sustainable consumption and climate protection the paper describes what churches in Germany are already doing and what more must be done.

Structure

Chapter 1 deals with the theological basis.
Chapter 2 contains a critical and constructive acknowledgment of the agenda 2030.
Chapter 3 describes our own Christian tradition and our demands on sustainability, which are higher than the agenda 2030.
Chapter 4 formulates expectations to our government and to the churches.
Chapter 5 deals with the level for action, exemplary to four SDGs in three steps:
    1) What is the message of the SDG?
    2) What is the message of the national strategy to put the SDGs in action?
    3) Which challenge is this SDG to the churches?

What sustains us?

The EKD-text describes in chapter 1 the theological and ethical views of the EKD on the Agenda 2030. Starting with the belief in God as the creator and an attitude of gratitude for the gift of the creation, the human claim to power over the creation is clearly denied. It is also very clearly mentioned that man has failed in his responsibility to maintain the integrity of creation. Especially the behavior and the life-style of the elites in all countries are not sustainable and are highly dangerous for life on earth. "We are guilty of wrongdoing. We are not fulfilling our responsibility towards creation. We do not love our neighbors as ourselves. We are not taking good care of the gifts of creation".

The creation is a victim of exploitation and calculation. The category of prizes and of benefit is dominating all parts of life and all values. Values and prizes are different things. There are values like nature, like solidarity, like compassion which should not be part of the market nor a question of benefit.

The trust in God's love, which is bigger than the sin of men, opens a way to a life in responsibility. Facing the exceeding of the planetary boundaries, the text is urging: "The exhortation to carry on is no longer feasible. The ethics of sufficiency are becoming evident, the acceptance of boundaries is useful and healthy. The Christian faith gives us the freedom to impose limits upon ourselves. It helps us to recognize that an active levying of limits upon our own possibilities and interests is an expression of Christian liberation".

Therefore, EKD welcomes the Agenda 2030 with emphasis as an agenda of transformation. It has a relevance like the Charta of human rights of 1948. The EKD see the responsibility to put this agenda into practice.

What we appreciate

In the second chapter, the extensive demand of the Agenda 2030 as an agenda for all countries and its holistic and integrative approach is underlined. The high demand of the agenda, to secure the social needs of all people – also the people of the next generation - and to respect the ecological boundaries, is remarked as a central and essential point. This can only be possible, when the old strategies of growth and development are left behind.

What we are seeking

In the third chapter it is mentioned that the agenda 2030 includes many ideas and topics which the WCC is discussing and demanding for 40 years. Mainly the demanding of a "sustainable and responsible society" (1975 Nairobi), the "conciliar process for justice, peace and integrity of creation" (1983, Vancouver) and the "pilgrimage of justice and peace" (2013, Busan).

The EKD stands for a concept of "strong sustainability", which means that the ecological boundaries must be accepted anyway. Although the Agenda 2030 stands for a high demand the seeking of the churches is going further. The uncritical connection between wealth and growth must be questioned. It is a critical point that in the agenda 2030 the concept of sufficiency is not included. At this point, the churches are pioneers because they are demanding an ethics of sufficiency since many years. The question of the cultural processes of change which are necessary to put the agenda 2030 into practice is also not addressed strongly enough in the agenda 2030. For these processes, the role of religion and spirituality is important. The churches can push these seeking processes for a change of culture and of values. They are inspired by their visions of the coming kingdom of God where justice and peace are fulfilled.

Ruth Gütter

What we expect

In the fourth chapter it is mentioned that the main responsibility to put the agenda into practice is with the governments of the countries of the UN. The German government had committed itself to put the agenda 2030 in to practice "in, with and through Germany". That means that not only the national politics have to develop strategies to fulfill the Agenda 2030 but also the international politics like the department of development and of trade must keep in mind that the strategies of other countries to fulfill the agenda 2030 are realized.

The EKD is demanding the government to develop and update the German strategy of sustainability and to solve the conflicts between different departments to put the SDGs into practice. Also, the EKD is demanding that the civil society is more integrated in the process to develop and update the German strategy of sustainability.

The paper also has expectations of the churches. The churches should be in the role of an admonisher, mediator and facilitator to put the agenda 2030 into practice. Especially for the role as a facilitator the churches must do more. The churches in the EKD are already active in the field of sustainable finances and in programs for protection of the climate, also in the field of education, awareness and spiritual reflection about sustainability there are a lot of good initiatives. But this is not enough, more powerful and more determined action is needed to put the agenda 2030 into practice.

What we need to do

In the fifth chapter, four fields of politics are chosen in which the SDGs in Germany are not fulfilled enough and in which also the role of the churches is necessary.

These fields are
- To stop hunger, to support a sustainable agriculture (SDG 2)
- Responsible and sustainable consumption (SDG 12)
- To overcome inequality (SDG 5 and SDG 10)
- To protect the climate (SDG 13)

In these four fields, the demands of the Agenda 2030 of the German strategy and the consequences for the churches is developed.

What we intend to do in gratitude

In the last chapter it is underlined that it is high time for humankind to turn to a sustainable lifestyle. "There is not a great deal of time left. Global society resembles a tanker-ship which can change direction only slowly. Only those who initiate a change of course in good time can avoid a collision". In these times the churches have an important responsibility which they must make use of with determination. The churches should choose goals to change their own practices. To the extent that they are successful, they will also be credible in their statements and preaching.

The chapter ends with the confession: "We know that the time span in which we can change direction is short. We confess that the earth belongs to God and not to us. We know that the star on which we live has only been lent to us".

FAITH FOR EARTH: IT IS TIME FOR A BEHAVIORAL REVOLUTION TOWARDS EARTH

Iyad Abumoghli

Anthropogenic climate change is widely acknowledged as presenting the most significant threat to world peace, security and prosperity, and potentially even the very existence of humanity. Transitioning to more sustainable consumption and production practices is of paramount importance and efforts towards sustainable development must be truly global in nature. However, addressing the multitude of contributing factors to climate change, as well as dealing with its negative manifestations, requires an unprecedented degree of cooperation from all stakeholders, or a behavioral revolution towards Earth.

To facilitate this incredibly complex process, 193 countries of the United Nations adopted the Sustainable Development Goals (SDGs). Implemented started in 2015 to be achieved by 2030, these 17 Goals are designed to provide ambitious targets that are people and planet centered to achieve prosperity and peace in partnership. Agenda 2030 is a global framework for the trajectory humanity must take in the following years to mitigate against climate change, protect ecosystems and life under water and above land. The SDGs are a holistic vision of sustainable development for the whole world. Notably, the SDGs implore that all stakeholders and actors, from individuals to nation states and from grassroots NGOs to multinational corporations, participate in contributing towards their attainment.

Following a 2008 General Assembly resolution, the United Nations established the UN Inter-Agency Task Force on Engaging Faith-Based Actors for Sustainable Development in 2010 to promote interreligious, intercultural and policy dialogues. This Task Force emerged after an acknowledgement that faith-based organisations (FBOs) had long been on the peripheries of secular multinational development organisations, despite their significant potential, and actual, contributions to areas such as education, human rights and conflict prevention, resolution and mediation. With increased calls for more partnerships and participation from civil society and NGOs to achieve the Sustainable Development Goals, the important role of FBOs in this field could no longer be neglected.

It is in this context; the Faith for Earth Initiative was launched in November 2017. This initiative is a cross-cutting programme of the United Nations Environment Programme, the leading global environmental authority that sets the global environmental agenda, promotes the coherent implementation of the environmental dimension of sustainable development within the United Nations system and serves as an authoritative advocate for the global environment.

The Faith for Earth initiative foremost aims to strategically engage with faith-based organisations and partner with them to collectively contribute towards the SDGs and fulfill the objectives of the 2030 Agenda. The initiative seeks to mobilize new faith and inter-faith partnerships and utilize innovative approaches to unite around the common goal of sustainable development. The Initiative is grounded on the fact that over 80% of the global population is affiliated to one or more of the estimated 4,300 religious and spiritual communities in existence. Even when people do not have a direct affiliation, religious texts, practices and laws can have influence. The UNFPA notes that even seemingly secular organisations are "guided by values and ideologies, not always made transparent" and often originating in religious doctrine (UNFPA, 2014).

FBOs are also sustainable institutions, frequently existing for many years and cultivating deep networks in the communities they are situated in. Furthermore, FBOs are often part of wider national, transnational or even global structures that cross political boundaries. Nonetheless, whether they be deeply contextual or global figures of authority such as Pope Francis, religious leaders command respect and are viewed as reliable and trustworthy sources of guidance. For many, faith teachings are the most important and absorbable sources of information, with faith being the analytical lens through which people experience and rationalize the world around them. Thus, religious leaders are well placed to help overcome discrepancies between people's beliefs and what may appear to be abstract climate science. Achieving the SDGs necessitates changes in mindsets, behaviors and consumption patterns, with faith leaders particularly well positioned to communicate such messages in a more relatable manner; the Pope's encyclical Laudato Si being a prime example. The Laudato Si explains the linkages between injustice, exclusion and environmental degradation and argues that scientific evidence and faith teachings can enter into fruitful dialogue and be complimentary, rather than dichotomous.

Many FBOs have long been actively involved in humanitarian efforts and share intrinsic notions of moral responsibility and human rights with multilateral organisations such as the United Nations. FBOs already contributed significantly towards development, notably in the areas of health, sanitation and education and continue to do so with regards to the SDGs. In the process, FBOs have often forged sustained relations with government agencies and organisations. Indeed, many FBOs operate in areas that would otherwise be neglected or underserved by governments, thus providing crucial services to communities and enabling them to achieve on the ground results. This depth and agility of FBOs, coupled with the respect religious leaders command, can facilitate the spread of knowledge and practices concerning sustainable lifestyles to poor, remote and marginalized communities, but also rich nations with abundance. Around 250 FBOs are already actively engaged with environmentally related sustainability issues and this number is continuously growing. However, faiths tend to rely on their own teachings and knowledge, so establishing inter-faith dialogues will allow new perspectives and practices to emerge.

There are an estimated 37 million churches, 3.6 million mosques, 20,000 synagogues and countless other temples and houses of worship spread around all corners of the world. Religious organisations also collectively produce more books and publications than any other network. Furthermore, there are numerous faith owned, operated or inspired TV and radio stations. Together, these elements give faith organisations immense outreach, enabling them to teach and inspire adherents all around the world to become more environmentally conscious through fundamental changes in behavior and attitudes.

Furthermore, faith-based organizations hold enormous assets and wealth, with faith-based investment corporations and bodies considered to be the third or fourth largest investment group. Many faith-based organisations apply a "no sins" criteria to screen their investments and thus avoid investing in sectors like the arms or tobacco industries. These criteria are influenced by moral beliefs and religious laws; for example, the Society of Friends (Quakers) historically avoided any investments into the system of slavery and continues to forbid financing warfare in any way. However, despite such screenings and divestment campaigns, this wealth is also not always being optimally invested into more proactively socio-environmentally responsible and oriented investments. These are investments that seek to go beyond no-harm principles and intentionally foster measurable social and/or environmental positive impact in conjunction with financial return. FBO's have the potential to significantly accelerate the Socially Responsible Investment (SRI), Faith-Consistent Investment (FCI) and Impact Investment movements. These financial concepts are gaining traction, and the number of such investments is rising. The Faith for Earth initiative seeks to catalyze further engagement between faith-based investment vehicles and these growing innovative financial practices.

Overall, all religions contain messages of environmental care and stewardship for a planet that can provide for human flourishing. Living in harmony with nature is a common ethical behavior recommended by all major faiths and adherents of every religion will be negatively affected by the effects of climate change. Christianity teaches that the world belongs to God, the Creator, who entrusted human beings to be the stewards of his creation. Genesis 2:15 states "the Lord God took the man, and put him into the garden of Eden to dress it and to keep it". Further religious teachings relate to all areas of life and thus are particularly amendable to the holistic nature of sustainability and addressing the issues on the path to achieving it. Hence, there are clear synergies between FBOs and sustainability agendas, with religious groups and leaders able to provide an additional means of mobilizing societal engagement for environmental protection in an unprecedented manner.

In order to achieve Agenda 30 and the SDGs new stakeholders and partnerships are required, as are innovative new solutions. Therefor, climate change presents both an immense challenge, but also a great opportunity for disparate groups to rally together behind the common objective of achieving sustainability. The Faith for Earth initiative provides the ideal neutral space for productive interreligious and intercultural dialogue. By fostering inter-faith communication and collaboration, this initiative's mission is to *encourage, empower and engage with faith-based organisations as partners, at all levels, towards achieving the Sustainable Development Goals and fulfilling Agenda 30.*

The Faith for Earth strategy builds on 5 principles of People living on a healthy Planet, enjoying Prosperity and Partnerships in Peaceful societies. Any and all achievements, require the initiative to collaborate and engage with FBOs and in particular encourage FBOs to collaborate with one another. This has been, and will continue to be, facilitated by inviting FBOs to be present at environmental conventions and conferences in order to engage with policy makers on the moral, ethical and religious obligations to protect the environment. The overall outcome is for faith leaders and FBOs to "integrate the environment into their work and messages and are mobilized to achieve the SDGs". This will rely on mobilizing local communities, coordinating communications and advocacy, fostering south-south cooperation and engaging in faith-environment thematic conversations.

Attaining this outcome will be derived from achieving three goals:
1) *Strengthen faith-based organisations leadership for policy impact* – the aim is to inspire, empower and engage faith leaders and their institutions to tackle environmental issues by bringing them into public policy debates. These issues would be ones where changes in behavior can have successful outcomes (eg. pollution and food waste).
2) *Green faith-based organisations assets and investments* – the aim is to see more faith-based investments and assets integrating environmental consideration and investing in greener and more socio-environmentally sustainable investments to support the implementation of the SDGs.
3) *Science-Faith-Based evidence* – the aim is to break down faith/science boundaries and establish a knowledge platform where FBOs can access, share and integrate scientific findings into their work and communicate it with decision-makers, the public and other FBOs.

These goals are naturally interlinked; empowering and partnering with global leaders requires solid, scientifically based knowledge and networking on key thematic areas. Similarly, greening faith-based investments requires both empowered leadership for policy impact and adequate evidence of successful experiences elsewhere, North and South alike.

There are currently four outputs designed to support the achievement of these goals, and ultimately the project outcome. These are:

1) High level global "Faith for Earth" Coalition to facilitate policy dialogue on environmental issues is established.
2) Facilitation and consultations services to bring FBOs closer to finance sector for greening of investments
3) A knowledge platform for religious leaders and faith communities to share and connect their individual faith-based efforts on environment conservation has been developed and made available
4) Faith-based thematic publications have been produced, shared and disseminated with FBOs.

Significant progress has been made to date. Some of the major achievements of the initiative thus far outlined below.

1) Faith for Earth has been working on developing guidelines and publications linking environmental priorities to faith. Work on faith and each of the following: climate change, conflict over natural resources, water governance, sustainable lifestyles, and finance is undergoing. An overall policy paper was published in UN Environment ProgrammeForesight linking Environmental conservation to Faith and cultural values. Link http://wedocs.unep.org/bitstream/handle/20.500.11822/25452/Foresight_008_201805.pdf?sequence=1&isAllowed=y
2) The Faith for Earth Initiative has created a growing network with currently over 2500 Faith-Based Organizations and leaders and is sharing knowledge and resources for interfaith collaboration through a bi-weekly newsletter. An advocacy campaign has been launched with a unique hashtag #Faith4Earth A website for the initiative has also been launched highlighting resources and stories. https://www.unenvironment.org/about-un-environment/faith-earth-initiative.
3) The Faith initiative working with several partners on engaging with faith-based organizations such as the Responsible Finance and Investment Foundation (RFI), Islamic Development Bank, World Council of Churches, the Church of England and many others, held a roundtable and summit on responsible financing with a focus on Islamic Financing. The roundtable discussed faith-consistent investment criteria that integrate environmental stewardship and care for the creation.
4) Concerted efforts have been exerted to increase the number of accredited Faith-based organizations to UN Environment. Accredited FBOs have increased from 10 organizations to 45 by the end of 2018.
5) The Faith for Earth Interfaith Dialogue was held during the period 11-15 March 2019 as part of the events of the Fourth Session of the UN Environment Assembly. The Faith for Earth Dialogue was organized through 11 sessions during the five days' period involving 220 Faith leaders representing 12 faiths and congregations from all continents of the world.
6) The initiative is working on establishing a global Faith for Earth Coalition at the highest faith leaders level to attract global attention to environmental emergences and to mobilize global action.

7) Faith for Earth organized with the Vatican and in collaboration with the, Catholic Youth Network on Environmental sustainability for Africa (CYNESA) and WWF the 2nd international conference on Laudato Si 15-16 July 2019 in UNEP premises with the participation of 300 faith and young leaders representing more than 50 countries.

One of the major achievements of the Faith for Earth Initiative is integrating the engagement with faith-based organizations and faith leaders in policies and practices of intergovernmental organizations. The initiative has been working with the European Union, the African Union and the Organization of Islamic Cooperation. With the latter, and through the Islamic Scientific, Education and Culture Organization, ISESCO, a strategy was adopted by 57 ministers of environment of Islamic countries to spearhead faith and environment linkages and networking.

Given the enormous diversity of religions and practices, aligning them with the SDGs will require both deeply contextual engagement and a holistic approach to incorporate all towards achieving the same common goal; a safe and sustainable planet.

To achieve sustainability, we must move beyond technocratic language and abstract ambitions and embed the need for sustainable development in everyday life which can be achieved by tapping into the spiritual wealth of people. Thus, there is no one-size-fits-all solution to either address global warming or for engaging faith actors with the SDGs. Rather a continuous process of intercultural and interdenominational dialogue is required to harness the capacities of religious groups. This, coupled with strategic guidance and the resources of the United Nations, is what the Faith for Earth initiative aims to facilitate.

LIST OF CONTRIBUTORS

Dr. *Iyad Abumoghli,* Director of Faith for Earth Initiative, United Nations Environment Programme

Hayarpi Aghakhanyan, Syunik-Development NGO, Armenia

Dr. *Louk Aourelien Andrianos,* World Council of Churches (WCC), Consultant on the care for creation, sustainability and climate justice, Greece

Rev. Prof. *Dr. Emmanuel Kwesi Anim,* Pentecost Theological Seminary in Gomoa-Fetteh, Ghana

Rev. *Dr. Neddy Astudillo,* Greenfaith, Director for Training and LatinoAmerica, USA

Maraike Joanna Belle Bangun, Indonesia, currently PhD student at Academy of Mission at the University of Hamburg

Rev. Prof. *Dr. Daniel Carlos Beros,* Campaign against Monocultural Agrobusiness, IERP, Argentina

Dr. *Soo Nguh Theresa Carino,* Amity Foundation, China/Philippines

Dr. *Mathews George Chunakara,* General Secretary, Christian Conference of Asia, Thailand

Prof. *Dr. Meehyun Chung,* Yonsei University, Prof. of Systematic Theology, National Council of Churches Korea

Prof. *Dr. Ernst Marais Conradie,* Senior Professor, Department of Religion and Theology, University of the Western Cape, South Africa

Bishop *Geoffry Davies,* The Southern African Faith Communities' Environment Institute (SAFCEI), Cape Town, South Africa

Dr. *Kate Davies,* The Southern African Faith Communities' Environment Institute (SAFCEI), Cape Town, South Africa

Rev. Prof. *Dr. Misgana Mathewos Detago,* Director, Ethiopian Graduate School of Theology, Ethiopia

Prof. *Dr. Ingeborg Gabriel,* Roman-Catholic theological Faculty, University of Vienna, Austria

Rev. *Henrik Grape,* Coordinator of the WCC Working group on Climate change, Sweden

Rev. *Dr. Ruth Gütter,* Executive secretary for sustainability, Protestant Church in Germany (EKD), Germany

Dr. *Syafiq Hasyim,* Islamic State University, Jakarta, Indonesia

Prof. *Dr. Claudia Jahnel,* Ruhr-University Bochum, Protestant Theological Faculty, Germany

Rev. *Dr. Kambale Jean-Bosco Kahongya Bwiruka,* United Evangelical Mission (UEM), Officer for Justice, Peace and the Integrity of Creation, Democratic Republic of Congo / Tanzania

Rev. *Dr. Bernd Kappes,* General Secretary Christian Education Fund and board member of the Institute for Theological Zoology, Germany

Prof. *Dr. Guillermo Eduardo Kerber Más,* Atelier oecuménique de Théologie, Switzerland, (former Coordinator of WCC Climate Justice Prorgram)

Rev. *Dr. Jochen Motte,* United Evangelical Mission (UEM), Executive Secretary for Justice, Peace and the Integrity of Creation, Germany

Prof. *Dr. Markus Mühling,* Protestant University Wuppertal/Bethel, Germany

Dr. Karen Nazaryan, Director Armenia Round Table Foundation, Armenia

Prof. *Dr. Muriel Orevillo-Montenegro,* Silliman University, Asia and Pacific Alliance YMCAs, Philippines

Rev. *Dr. Andar Parlindungan,* United Evangelical Mission (UEM), Executive secretary for training and empowerment, Indonesia / Germany

Dr. Peter Pavlovic, Conference of European Churches (CEC) / European Christian Environmental Network, Belgium

Rev. *Dr. Chad Rimmer,* Study Secretary for Lutheran Theology and Practice, Lutheran World Federation (LWF), Switzerland

Rev. *Daniel Sinaga,* Pastor of the Toba-Batak Protestant Church (HKBP) in East Borneo, Indonesia, and Global Young Reformers Network of LWF

Prof. *Dr. Nadja Furlan Štante,* Associate Professor, Science and Research Centre Koper, Slovenia

Rev. *Dr. Victor Tinambunan,* Indonesia, Principal of STT und Professor for Practical Theology

Gloriose Umuziranenge, PIASS, Protestant University of Rwanda

Prof. *Dr. Petros Vassiliadis,* President of the Center of Ecumenical, Missiological and Environmental Studies "Metropolitan Panteleimon Papageorgiou" (CEMES), Director of the Orthodox Ecumenical Theology Post-Graduate Program of the International Hellenic University (IHU), Greece

Rev. *Anja Vollendorf,* Desk for Ecumenical Relations, Evangelical Church in the Rhineland, Germany

Rev. Prof. *Dr. Dietrich Werner,* Senior Advisor Theology, Ecumenical Education and Research, Brot für die Welt, Germany

Layout and Correction Block: *Jörg Schmidt*